CONTEMPORARY THEMES IN STRATEGIC PEOPLE MANAGEMENT

CONTEMPORARY THEMES IN STRATEGIC PEOPLE MANAGEMENT

A CASE-BASED APPROACH

DAVID HALL
Principal Lecturer, University of Portsmouth, UK

STEPHEN PILBEAM
Principal Consultant, HR2020 LTD, UK

MARJORIE CORBRIDGE
Principal Lecturer, University of Portsmouth, UK

palgrave
macmillan

First published 2013 by
PALGRAVE MACMILLAN

Palgrave Macmillan in the UK is an imprint of Macmillan Publishers Limited,
registered in England, company number 785998, of Houndmills, Basingstoke,
Hampshire RG21 6XS.

Palgrave Macmillan in the US is a division of St Martin's Press LLC,
175 Fifth Avenue, New York, NY 10010.

Palgrave Macmillan is the global academic imprint of the above companies
and has companies and representatives throughout the world.

Palgrave® and Macmillan® are registered trademarks in the United States,
the United Kingdom, Europe and other countries.

ISBN 978–0–230–30338–6

This book is printed on paper suitable for recycling and made from fully
managed and sustained forest sources. Logging, pulping and manufacturing
processes are expected to conform to the environmental regulations of the
country of origin.

A catalogue record for this book is available from the British Library.

A catalog record for this book is available from the Library of Congress.

10   9   8   7   6   5   4   3   2   1
22 21 20 19 18 17 16 15 14 13

Printed in China

Contents

Tables and Figures

Tables

Figures

Acknowledgements

The authors express their sincere gratitude to all contributors of case material who gave permission for their work to be used in the production of this book. Thank you to:

Derek Adam-Smith	Liza Howe-Walsh
Louisa Allison	Debbie Jenkins
Valerie Anderson	Bridget Juniper
Jim Atherton	Rebecca Kopecek
Julia Barton	Natalie Macaulay
Maureen Bowes	Clare Matton
Ann Brine	Roger Metcalfe
Alistair Campbell	Elizabeth Nials
Mellissa Carr	Monsurat Omotayo
Linda Carter	Juliet Osbourne
Peter Cartwright	Sandie Paice
Fiona Dent	Mark Power
Yves Emery	Gary Rees
Amanda Harcus	Donna Bohnet
Terence Hart	Stacey White
Sara Hope	Steve Williams

CHAPTER 1

The Case for Strategic People Management

David Hall

> *Experience without theory is blind but theory without experience is mere intellectual play.*

The above quotation is attributed (Anon., 1962: 11) to the German philosopher, Immanuel Kant (1724–1804), who is regarded as one of the foremost thinkers of the Enlightenment or Age of Reason, the cultural movement of the eighteenth century which proffered the power of reason as a means of reform and of the advancement of knowledge. Many versions of Kant's maxim have followed as a basis for developing arguments about theory and action in diverse areas such as politics, industrial relations and education. So, why use this quotation to introduce a book about strategic people management? This quotation embodies the beliefs of the authors of this book about the nature of management (as the practice of activities) and about the epistemological considerations (about choice of methods) for acquiring knowledge that support learning. The foundations for this book lay in the shared ethos of the authors about education in business and management and about the need to consider theory and practice together, particularly how they influence each other, to develop knowledge and understanding in order to progress in both areas, which is the essence of Kant's hypotheses. All three authors of this book worked outside higher education before becoming educationalists later in their careers after gaining management experience, and this common experience has shaped their shared views.

The catalyst for this book was the realisation that the Business School at the University of Portsmouth, UK, had produced a valuable learning resource that would benefit a wide audience. That resource is the *Human Resource Bulletin: Research and Practice*, published by the University of Portsmouth and the Chartered Institute of Personnel and Development (CIPD) Portsmouth Group, which, since being first published in 2006, has featured many excellent case studies on people management in which practice has been linked to theory. These cases written by academics, managers and postgraduate students enable learners to link theory to practice and vice versa, as a basis for critique and conceptualisation, which are essential for developing high-level learning. The cases also describe examples of management practice and the experiences of those involved. One of the aims of this book is the knowledge transfer of intellectual capital by the dissemination of the experience of researchers and practitioners, based on their work in the workplace and academia. The rest of this chapter outlines the purpose and structure of this book, who it is written for and how it can be used by different groups of readers, including learners and practitioners.

Strategic people management

Some of the best known writers on management describe the people management activities to define the role, for example, Drucker (1989), Fayol (1949) and Mintzberg (1973). Today, management continues to be defined by the tasks which individuals in roles of responsibility and authority carry out to meet the objectives of the organisations they work for. Definitions of 'strategic people management' are harder to come by in the literature, although most academics and managers would have a sense of what is meant by strategic people management. The following extract provides insight into the meaning of strategic people management from an organisational perspective; it appears on the web pages of Local Government (LG) Improvement Development, an organisation which supports improvement and innovation across local government in England:

> The national local government workforce strategy advises councils to adopt a 'strategic people management' approach to ensure that their workforce is focused on achieving the council's objectives and improving services. An effective workforce strategy, integrated with the overall corporate strategic plan, will help councils ensure that they have the right people, in the right places, with the right skills, at the right time. This is often known as a 'people strategy'. This strategic approach provides a launch pad for organisational development.

The LG website goes on to explain that a workforce strategy is also called a 'people' or 'HR' (human resources) strategy that focuses on people management interventions that impact on organisational performance. For the purpose of this book, strategic people management is defined as the coordinated planning and activity of people resources in an organisation to achieve longer-term performance outcomes. Strategic people management is also known as 'strategic human resources management' (strategic HRM), which features widely in HR literature and has several definitions. Schuler's (1992: 18) definition of strategic HRM is: 'The understanding of all those activities affecting the behaviour of individuals in their efforts to formulate and implement the strategic needs of the business'. Boxall and Purcell (2011) argue that strategic HRM is concerned with explaining how HRM influences organisational performance, and they provide a comprehensive and critical treatment of this subject. Academics at the Aston Centre for Human Resources (2008) define strategic HRM as: 'Broadly speaking, strategic HRM is about systematically linking people with organisations; more specifically it is about the integration of HRM strategies into the corporate strategies'. These various descriptions of strategic people management and strategic HRM explain the subject matter of this book: how organisations strategically manage their people resources to influence performance outcomes.

'Strategic' means taking a long-term view with regard to planning and implementation, aimed at positioning an organisation to achieve a desired future state. Strategy is concerned with the capability and readiness of an organisation-as-a-whole system ('holistic') to influence stakeholder behaviour through a range of integrated interventions to achieve performance outcomes at all levels. 'Strategic people management' was chosen to appear in the title of this book because it has been written for anyone who has an interest in how people management contributes towards delivering performance outcomes in organisations. This includes students doing HR and other management courses, and HR and line managers, many of whom are working in partnership in organisations across all sectors. The use of the book and how it can be helpful to a range of readers is explained later in this chapter.

The link with performance

Most descriptions of strategic people management, including definitions of strategic HRM, make the inextricable link between this management activity and performance. From these descriptions, it is clear that the purpose of strategic people management is to influence the achievement of desirable performance outcomes. Strategic interventions by their very nature should complement each other while coordinating employee activity (behaviour) at all levels to focus on organisational aims, that is, to 'align' individual and group behaviour with the purpose of the organisation. Research investigating the relationship between people management and performance has identified a number of key elements to create a 'performance culture', which achieves alignment by encouraging and supporting employee behaviour that is congruent with organisational purpose.

Purcell, Kinnie, Hutchinson, Rayton and Swart (2003) report that a clear mission or 'Big Idea' underpinned by values is a key ingredient for creating a culture that supports organisational direction and behaviour that positively impact on performance. Purcell et al. identified a range of HR policies and practices, which if used together (described as 'bundling') can encourage employees to make decisions about their behaviour which will result in high levels of performance. People management policies applied in this way are called high-performance work practices (HPWPs). Eleven broad areas of policy and practice were identified: job security, career opportunity, performance appraisal, training and development, recruitment and selection, pay satisfaction, work–life balance, job challenge and autonomy, teamwork, involvement and communication. These policy areas feature in 'The People and Performance model' described in the report (Purcell et al., 2003: 7) showing how the application of these influence employee motivation, job satisfaction and organisational commitment to effect decision-making about behaviour leading to high levels of performance. This model can be viewed as a strategic people management model, assuming it exists within a strategic perspective, that is, the 'Big Idea'.

The role of HR and front-line management

The importance of the role of HR management is clear as people-management policy design and implementation are important factors in creating a high-performance culture. What also becomes clear from this and other research is the crucial role played by front-line managers in the effective implementation of HR policies and practices, as the 'employee-facing' part of the organisation (Purcell and Hutchinson, 2007). Front-line managers are 'champions' of the values that are promoted in their organisations as guides to expectations of employee behaviour. How front-line managers treat (and lead) employees when implementing policy is key to maintaining trust and gaining commitment from the people who report to them. It is important that HR managers and line managers work together, as well as support employees, when implementing policy, if it is to be effective. This approach to HR and line managers coordinating their efforts to deliver organisational objectives across strategic and operational areas is described by Ulrich and Brockbank (2005) as 'business partnering'. Other researchers in this area, including Sung and Ashton (2005), have highlighted the significance of leadership in creating and shaping organisations that apply HPWPs to achieve high performance, calling these organisations 'high performance work organisations' (HPWOs). In their report Sung and Ashton identify three broad areas for 'bundling' HPWPs: human resource practices, high involvement as well as reward and commitment.

The challenge of causality

One of the most challenging and controversial aspects of research in this area is the question of causality, that is, a factor or factors that causally affect or affects others, resulting in certain outcomes. This can be particularly difficult when assessing the effect of management interventions or policy on performance. How confident can one be that the implementation of a particular intervention or policy will result in a change in performance? Consider all the various factors that may influence performance in a particular situation at a given time. The issue of attribution becomes especially problematic when considering people outcomes that have no tangible value or empirical means of measurement; for example, how do you measure creativity or cooperation? There are no easy solutions to this problem but it is an area where the concept of 'human capital' has come to the fore as an approach. Human capital is an economic concept that asserts that people are assets and have economic value like other resources in an organisation (Becker, 1993). This value is created by the expertise and experience of people who enable them to be productive. This approach is based on defining appropriate metrics that are viable and reliable and that can be used to help in attributing an employee's contribution to creating value and to the performance of the organisation. Some organisations have developed 'HR scorecards' and 'Workforce scorecards', forms of performance management systems, in an attempt to measure and manage the contribution of their people to the value of those organisations. Such methods and tools can be helpful and, some would argue, are essential for organisations to effectively strategically manage people. This approach is also fraught with difficulties, which centre on the viability and reliability of the metrics and how the data is interpreted. Finally there is always the 'human factor' to consider in any management intervention, which revolves around the perception of people towards such methods, which can lead to unintended and problematic consequences as well as to benefits for employees and employers. The emotional and behavioural response of employees to changes in the way they work and the relationship they and other groups of stakeholders have with organisations can never be underestimated. The unwritten understanding between employees and employers regarding mutual expectations, known as the 'psychological contract' (Rousseau, 1995), remains an important consideration in managing people and performance.

The 'Big Idea' behind this book

First and foremost this book is a learning resource that has been designed to develop knowledge and understanding in, what is for most people, a vocational subject, by encouraging critical examination of the link between theory and practice. Because of the applied nature of this subject area, the practical aspect of management is highly significant and plays an extremely important role in the learning process. In 1975 David Kolb and Roger Fry described a model of experiential learning where the learning process is a continuous one ('The Learning Cycle') of four sequenced stages: conceptualisation (theorising), experimentation (trying things out), experience (practice) and reflection (harvesting the learning). The learning cycle involving theory and practice continually modifies our original understanding, which is the basis for learning and development. This model offers only one theory of learning but it is a prominent one that is widely acknowledged and respected in the learning profession, and many learning interventions are developed, based on this description of the learning process. The model offers a theory of experiential learning where experience based on what an individual actually does is a vital part of the process and is not only particularly relevant to vocational or applied subjects that are taught in the classroom but also to other forms of learning which take place outside the classroom, such as work-based learning and coaching. Kolb highlighted that it does not matter where in the learning cycle an individual starts, as long as they progress through all stages of the process. Individuals will start the process at different stages based on their particular situation and experience, even if they are part of the same group of learners. Formal learning, such as attending lectures, may as a starting point, consider theories and 'set' the learning process at the conceptualisation stage for the same group of learners, but this does not have to be the starting point for all learners. Work-based learning typically often starts at the experience (practice) stage.

For employees in the workplace and in the classroom, the 'experience' stage of the learning process can be readily accessed as it is typically based on the job an individual does (or has done in the past) and on their experience of being part of the organisation they work in. The 'experience' part of the learning process can be more of a challenge for full-time undergraduate students who tend to have less 'work time' and experience of organisations. For the latter group, case studies and research articles based on organisations play a vital role in bringing the 'experience' to the learner to facilitate the learning process. This format will be familiar to anyone who has attended a course in business and management, and for many learners it is the exceptional case study or research article that often sticks in the mind for years after the course. Of course case studies and research articles can be just as important to employees in the workplace and in the classroom, but there can be different reasons for that – for example, insight into what other organisations and managers are doing – but the purpose for doing so is exactly the same, that is to learn.

The aim of this book is clear – to facilitate the learning process for different groups of learners by presenting a number of cases that provide experiential insight and, with the help of the theory presented in each chapter, to enable critical consideration of the connection between theory and practice, and vice versa. The activities and discussion that follow each case are intended to encourage readers to think 'critically', that is to consider different perspectives and points of view (arguments) based on the case content and theory, thus facilitating the learning process. Finally another aim of this book is to develop curiosity and questioning by the reader, that is, to sow the seeds of research investigation.

Who can benefit from this book

This book would be a valuable resource to learners studying people management as a module on a course at level 5 and above, which includes undergraduate and postgraduate courses at university. Degree and professional award courses, as a part of which people management and HR are taught, could include Business Administration, Business Studies, Business and Management, Human Resources Management, Organisational Development, Coaching as well as Leadership and Management, but there will be many more courses which include a people management component. Learners on full-time and part-time courses, including distance learners, will find that the cases presented in this book, which are mainly based on organisational practice, offer an extremely useful insight into applied people management and HRM. The case presented in each chapter (some chapters feature two or three cases) is preceded by an outline of the main theory and context surrounding the case topic, supported with references to a range of literature, including academic textbooks, research articles, professional and institutional publications, management journals and web-based sources. These references provide more comprehensive literature coverage and are a good starting point for researching the subject matter.

Undergraduate and postgraduate students and learners on professional management courses in business and management usually undertake a major piece of research to complete their studies, which may take the form of a dissertation, independent study or management project. These projects typically require the learner to prepare a proposal and carry out research in a particular topic or issue, which could be in the area of people management or HRM. There are two specific areas related to such research projects which this book can help with:

■ *The choice of topic or issue for the project.* Many students struggle to come up with a suitable research topic, particularly undergraduate students who have limited experience of working for organisations. The subjects covered in this book and the cases provide a valuable source of potential ideas, and perhaps even inspiration, for research projects because many of these cases are based on actual research into management practice or discuss findings from a particular area of research. The cases and activities which follow lead to other questions about the subject areas and can uncover other issues that can be explored.

■ *How to carry out research*. Many of these cases are exemplars of good research, albeit in a summarised format, and provide helpful examples of how to design, implement and report effective research. In many universities and other learning institutions, the research or management project is preceded by a module on research methods which requires the student to prepare a proposal outlining and justifying their research design. Many of the cases in this book would assist first-time researchers with their project approach.

Another group which will find this book a useful resource are practising managers involved or interested in people management. HR managers and line managers can learn from the experience of other managers and researchers into management practice. Managers may face issues similar to those described in the cases and will find it useful to learn what approach other organisations took and why. This approach supports work-based learning and 'action learning' as learning interventions in the workplace. This book aims to transfer knowledge through the dissemination of management practice for the benefit of all readers of this book.

How to use this book

The chapters and cases can be read in any order, allowing learners to simply go to any chapter they are particularly interested in. For any chapter, readers can read the 'theory' that precedes the case or go straight to the case; it depends on what the reader wishes to gain from the chapter and certain outcomes from reading this book have been discussed above, for example, a final-year undergraduate student deciding on a topic for their research project will be seeking different outcomes from reading the book compared to an HR manager who is interested in how an organisation has approached a specific policy area. This highlights the book's versatility as a learning and knowledge resource, and how the individual needs of the reader determines how the book is used.

Most chapters will cover more than one subject area but the coverage of each subject within a chapter area may vary. Some chapters span several subject areas to different degrees. The chapter titles and subject areas covered in each title are summarised in Table 1.1 at the end of this chapter. All chapters, with the exception of this introductory chapter, describe at least one case and several chapters present two or more cases that cover similar subject areas. Each chapter starts with a discussion of the main theory and context associated with the main subject area, providing academic underpinning for the case(s) which follows. The bibliography at the end of each chapter provides useful sources in the academic literature and elsewhere. The case or cases that follow the theoretical treatment provide valuable 'experiential' insight which is focused on organisational interventions and research, enabling readers to reflect on and consider the relationship between

Table 1.1 Strategic people management: chapters and subject areas

Chapter titles	Ethics and corporate responsibility	Environmental scanning	Setting standards in people management	Front-line management	Psychological contract	Employer of choice	Recruitment and selection	Talent management	Performance management	Organisational learning	Employee retention	Leadership	Employee and management development	Coaching and emotional intelligence	Technology and people management	Well-being and health and safety	Added value HR and business partnering	Managing change	International dimensions
	Introduction to Strategic People Management and how learners can use the book																		
1 The case for Strategic People Management	•								•			•							
2 Corporate governance: ensuring propriety for performance			•															•	•
3 The contribution of environmental scanning to organisational learning and strategy development		•								•									
4 The influence of Civil Society Organisations on strategic people management in the UK	•		•							•									
5 The critical role of the front-line manager in operationalising people management strategies				•			•		•				•						
6 Violation of the psychological contract in employment: causes and consequences					•	•					•								
7 Building an effective employer brand: its contribution to effective resourcing					•	•	•												
8 Psychometric assessment and personality questionnaires: survey results and case study findings							•				•								

#	Chapter																						
9	The value of competency-based interviewing in recruitment and selection decisions									•													
10	Talent management practices: their importance in the recruitment and retention of employees							•		•					•	•	•		•				
11	Performance management: encouraging champions and cheats	•			•			•																
12	The strategic value of being a learning organisation					•		•	•	•		•												
13	Knowledge management: interventions for retaining human capital						•	•	•	•	•	•						•						
14	Developing leadership: keep looking in the mirror									•	•	•												
15	Employee development: a journey towards competence						•	•	•	•	•	•												
16	Approaches to workplace learning: learning on-demand and work-based learning						•	•			•													
17	Coaching for employee and organisational performance: a strategic intervention						•	•			•													
18	Mobile technology: maximising the benefits to the management of organisations			•		•	•	•	•	•	•	•												
19	The strategic value of maximising the benefits of employee well-being	•							•				•					•						
20	Health and safety at work: looking after hearts and minds	•			•				•				•											
21	HRM adding-value: managing and measuring HR's contribution		•	•					•					•	•									
22	Managing change and the role of HRM															•	•							
23	More effective implementation of strategic change: managing the change process						•	•									•							
24	Strategic people management in an international context: the challenges of managing international assignments						•	•																•

theory and practice. The activities and discussion questions which follow each case are designed with a number of outcomes in mind:

- To develop knowledge and understanding of the theory and to make connections between different theories.
- To encourage critical thinking and expression about the connection between theory and practice.
- To facilitate learning in different ways and at different levels, including individual and group or 'social' learning, particularly by sharing experiences (experiential learning) within a learning group or set.
- To raise further questions and spark curiosity to encourage further investigation and learning.
- To bring enjoyment and fun to learning – for example, divide a class in two and ask each side to debate an issue, one 'for' and the other 'against'. A simple but stimulating exercise that involves everyone in the learning process.

The book is versatile enough to be used for different modes of teaching delivery and learning. It can be used in the classroom as a casebook to support learning in the subject areas mentioned previously. The use of cases is particularly suited to seminar teaching and assignment work. The nature of the chapter material and activities which follow are suitable to differentiate learning based on the mix of knowledge and experience that will be found in most learning groups. Similarly this book can be used outside the classroom in the workplace for learning and development. Learning groups or 'sets' are a common form of intervention for organisational learning, as is the use of 'action learning' as a learning intervention which is very closely based on the principles of the learning cycle described by Kolb (1984). The activities and discussion at the end of each chapter should be used in such a way that caters for the specific learning needs and priorities of a particular group. In this way differentiated learning can be encouraged within a group.

There is a 'Learners' Guide' which accompanies this book which is a web-based support resource for lecturers, leaders of learning groups and learners. This guide features indicative guidance or approaches to the questions and activities posed at the end of each chapter.

Acknowledgements

Finally the authors would like to express their warm gratitude to colleagues and to the organisations who gave their permission to use their cases in this book; without their cooperation this book would not have been possible.

Bibliography

Anon. (1962). *General Systems*. California: The Society for the Advancement of General Systems, p. 11.

Aston Centre for Human Resources (2008). *Strategic Human Resource Management: Building Research-based Practice*. London: CIPD.

Becker, G. S. (1993). *Human Capital: A Theoretical and Empirical Analysis, with Special Reference to Education* (3rd edn). Chicago: University of Chicago Press.

Boxall, P. and Purcell, J. (2011). *Strategy and Human Resource Management*. Basingstoke: Palgrave Macmillan.

Drucker, P. (1989). *The Practice of Management*. London: Heinemann.

Easterby-Smith, M., Burgoyne, J. and Araujo, L. (Eds.) (1999). *Organizational Learning and the Learning Organization*. London: Sage.

Fayol, H. (1949). *General and Industrial Management*. London: Pitman.

Gilmore, S. and Williams, S. (Eds.) (2009). *Human Resource Management*. Oxford: Oxford University Press.

Holbeche, L. (2008). *Aligning Human Resources and Business Strategy* (2nd edn). Oxford: Butterworth-Heinemann.

Kolb, D. A. (1984). *Experiential Learning: Experience as the Source of Learning and Development*. London: Prentice Hall.

Kolb, D. A. and Fry, R. (1975). 'Toward an applied theory of experiential learning', in C. Cooper (ed.), *Theories of Group Process*. London: Prentice Hall, p. 31.

Mintzberg, H. (1973). *The Nature of Managerial Work*. New York: Harper & Row.

Pilbeam, S. and Corbridge, M. (2010). *People Resourcing and Talent Planning: HRM in Practice* (4th edn). Harlow: Financial Times/Prentice Hall.

Purcell, J. and Hutchinson, S. (2007). 'Front-line managers as agents in the HRM-performance causal chain: theory, analysis and evidence'. *Human Resource Management Journal*, 17 (1), 3–20.

Purcell, J., Kinnie, N., Hutchinson, S., Rayton, B., and Swart, J. (2003). *Understanding the People and Performance Link: Unlocking the Black Box*. London: Chartered Institute of Personnel and Development.

Rousseau, D. M. (1995). *Psychological Contracts in Organisations: Understanding Written and Unwritten Agreements*. London: Sage Publications.

Saunders, M., Milmore, M., Lewis, P., Thornhill, A. and Morrow, T. (2007). *Strategic Human Resource Management: Contemporary Issues*. Financial Times/Prentice Hall.

Schuler, R. S. (1992). 'Strategic human resource management: linking people with the needs of the business'. *Organizational Dynamics*, 21 (1), 18–32.

Strategic People Management (2001). Retrieved on 17 October 2011, from Improvement and Development Agency for Local Government (IDeA), website: http://www.idea.gov.uk/idk/core/page.do?pageId= 5433088

Sung, J. and Ashton, D. (2005). *High Performance Work Practices: Linking Strategy and Skills to Performance Outcomes*. London: Department and Trade and Industry.

Ulrich, D. and Brockbank, W. (2005). *The HR Value Proposition*. Boston, MA: Harvard Business School Press.

CHAPTER 2

Corporate Governance
Ensuring propriety for performance

David Hall

This chapter looks at the development and role of corporate governance, which in recent years has been thrust into the limelight as a result of corporate scandals and failures in governance linked to the global financial crisis. This chapter will consider:

- The meaning and models of corporate governance and how boards operate,
- UK guidelines and requirements of boards as specified in the UK Corporate Governance Code ('the Code'),
- A case study which considers the relevance and role of HRM and people management in corporate governance.

The meaning of corporate governance

The meaning of corporate governance depends on the perspective and values associated with those who are describing it, for example, stakeholders, shareholders or management. Definitions of corporate governance are shaped by ideology and the interests of particular groups of stakeholders or 'actors'. For the purpose of this chapter corporate governance is described as the systems by which companies are directed or controlled (Charkham, 1994). Another useful definition is provided by Huse (2007: 15):

> Corporate governance is seen as the interactions between various internal and external actors, and the board members in directing a firm for value creation.

In this definition the *purpose* of corporate governance is clearly stated and *behaviour* is emphasised in the process. The distinction between internal and external actors and board members is made based on the degree of risk an individual or group has with the firm, that is, a board member may not necessarily be considered a stakeholder if they have little or no risk associated with the firm. However a broad definition of stakeholders would include all actors, including board members who may influence the decision-making of a board. Internal actors are the management and employees who make decisions and act on them.

External actors, including stakeholders and shareholders, can be viewed as those who seek to influence and control decisions. A point of contention is whether board members should be regarded as internal or external actors. Functioning (and being perceived as functioning) both with common and conflicting interests can lead to dysfunctional board behaviour and governance malfunction when incompatible interests collide. The corporate scandals at Enron, WorldCom and Tyco in the US in the 2000s, the Maxwell Group in the UK in the 1990s and, more recently, the banking failures in both countries, highlighted governance failures which resulted in revisions of corporate governance and legislation.

The board of directors

The board of directors ('the Board') is one of several mechanisms in the system of governance; others include auditors, legislation and regulations. Board members can be accountable to different stakeholder groups, which can include shareholders, management or a broader set of stakeholders, for doing what is best for the company. The role and responsibility of boards can be described in terms of the tasks that they are held accountable for and, boards are directed and guided on the tasks they undertake by stakeholders, governance guidelines and legislation. Board effectiveness is determined by a combination of process and standards and can be gauged by comparing actual (board) task performance with task expectations. Board members contribute towards governance effectiveness by exercising their expertise to facilitate decision-making that is in line with the expectations for the board, while ensuring appropriate control and compliance.

Board tasks

Board tasks can be classified in different ways and the theory or 'discipline' classification by Hung (1998) presents a typology that links board theories with board tasks, providing a useful framework for considering theory and practice. The six board tasks or roles are: linking, coordination, control, strategy, maintenance and support. According to Hung these tasks are related to several theories: resource dependence theory, stakeholder theory, agency theory, stewardship theory, institutional theory and managerial hegemony theory respectively, which are summarised in the next section.

Huse (2005) arranges the typology of board tasks, based on different focuses and perspectives, as shown in Table 2.1 below:

Table 2.1   Typology of board tasks

	External perspective (Control tasks)	**Internal perspective (Service tasks)**
External focus	Board output control tasks	Board networking tasks
Internal focus	Board internal tasks	Board advisory tasks
Decision/strategy focus	Board decision control tasks	Board collaboration and mentoring tasks

Theories about board tasks

Agency theory dominates research on corporate governance. Agency theory argues that boards should monitor the actions of agents (managers) carried out on behalf of their principals (shareholders) with a view to improving corporate performance by maximising shareholder wealth (Eisenhardt, 1989). Operationally boards do this by monitoring and evaluating company strategy and performance, and whoever is responsible for these operations, typically, the Chief Executive Officer (CEO). The aim of the board is to maximise shareholder wealth and minimise agency (transaction) cost.

Agency theory has been criticised because of the negative effects it can have on society, for example redundancies caused by relocating operations to lower cost locations, and has been cited as the reason behind several corporate scandals (Ghosal, 2005). Ghosal and other authors criticise agency theory because of its assumptions and focus, citing its negative impact on management practice as a cause of dysfunctional organisational behaviour.

Stakeholder theory is concerned with balancing and managing stakeholder interests, advocating a pluralist setting for management and organisations. This approach requires the board to identify who the most important stakeholders are and to manage their needs. In this context, a stakeholder is 'any individual or group who can affect or is affected by the achievement of the organisation's objectives' (Freeman, 1984: 46). Stakeholder theory proposes that board tasks consider the interests of a broad set of stakeholders and adhere to the principles of corporate social responsibility (CSR).

Stewardship theory assumes that managers should be trusted as good stewards (Davis, Schoorman and Donaldson, 1997) and provides an alternative model to agency theory (which assumes managerial opportunism). Stewardship theory promotes the need for active control and monitoring by boards. Trust is at the core of this approach, binding and guiding collective and cohesive management for the purpose of achieving organisational goals through openness and involvement of stakeholders, particularly employees.

Resource-dependence theory looks outside the organisation from an internal perspective, focusing on linking the organisation with its external environment to reduce the risk of dependency and uncertainty. This 'linking task' emphasises the importance of board composition in terms of how 'connected' its members are with the external business environment. Board members serve to provide information about the organisation to its business environment, thereby legitimising the organisation's actions to secure valuable resources. With this focus, important board tasks become networking, accessing, legitimising and communicating. Boards need to understand their environment to be effective at these tasks (Hillman, Cannella and Paetzold, 2000).

Managerial hegemony theory describes the board as a legal fiction, viewing it as the formal but not the genuine principal governance body of the firm. Despite the board's formal governing power over management, in reality the board is dominated by corporate management, that is the interests of these managers. This model describes a lack of independence of board members associated with the selection of outside board members (non-executives), with this process being controlled by management as they influence the board through group norms and strategising techniques (Huse, 2007).

Institutional theory describes how organisations conform to the constraints and conventions of the larger social systems within which they exist and operate. The importance of norms in guiding and moderating behaviour is emphasised (Scott, 1995). Boards have a maintenance role that acknowledges that organisations will reflect the rules and norms in their social environment (over time). Institutional theories have a 'system' focus on interaction outside the boardroom rather than a performance focus.

Behavioural-based governance

In his book *Boards, Governance and Value Creation: The Human Side of Corporate Governance*, Morten Huse (2007) considers governance from a human behaviour perspective and proposes the basis of a behaviour theory of boards and governance, suggesting that appropriate building blocks include:

- Value creation through knowledge (alternative goals related to competency and creativity rather than through control of managerial behaviour),
- Strategising (through political interactions rather than objective alignments),
- Problemistic search (decisions based on workable problem-solving rather than rational decision-making),
- Norms and learning processes (understanding human interactions and how this influences learning with a view to value creation).

Corporate governance in practice

The governance of UK-listed companies is applied through Acts of Parliament (regulation) and the UK Corporate Governance Code ('the Code') which provides guidance on best practice. The UK Corporate Governance Code (2010) issued by the Financial Reporting Council (FRC) replaced the Combined Code 2008 for accounting periods beginning on or after 29 June 2010, and applies to listed companies. In publishing 'the Code', the FRC adopted the recommendations of the Walker Report (2009) on the roles of Chairman and Non-Executive Directors (NEDs), composition of the board, commitment and responsibility for risk. It also looked at provisions for developing directors, evaluating boards and the frequency of director re-election. This report concerned governance in UK banks and other financial entities following the financial crisis in 2008.

'The Code' states:

Every company should be headed by an effective board which is collectively responsible for the success of the company. The board's role is to provide entrepreneurial leadership of the company within a framework of prudent and effective controls which enables risk to be assessed and managed. The board should set the company's strategic aims, ensure the necessary financial and human resources are in place for the company to meet its objectives and review management performance. The board should set the company's values and standards and ensure that its obligations to its shareholders and others are understood and met.

(FRC, 2010: 9)

Four main principles were introduced, addressing the following:

- the chairman's responsibility for leading the board,
- the need for directors to devote sufficient time,
- the requirements for NEDs to challenge (the board) constructively and
- the need for boards to have a balance of skills and experience.

Supporting principles expand on the main principles and provide more guidance. 'The Code's' provisions state the detailed requirements to make sure that the principles are upheld. The Listing Rules place two key requirements on companies with a premium listing:

- The annual report and accounts must contain a statement explaining how the company had applied the main principles.
- The report and accounts must state whether the company has complied with the provisions throughout the year covered by the report. If the company has not complied with all of the provisions, or if it has complied with them for only part of the year, the departures must be listed and reasons for non-compliance given.

One key change is the recommendation for the annual re-election of directors. Recommendations also include the promotion of balance and diversity in terms of board composition, particularly regarding gender. Remuneration is addressed by stating that the performance criteria for performance-related pay must go beyond purely financial outcomes, and relate to the company's longer-term interests for sustainability.

    In 2010 the Institute of Directors (IoD) published a revised version of *The Director's Handbook* (Webster, 2010) which provided guidance for best boardroom practice based on The Code 2010. The IoD and the European Confederation of Directors Associations published *Corporate Guidance and Principles for Unlisted Companies in the UK* in 2010, aimed at bridging the gap between listed and unlisted companies. The guidance focuses on establishing processes and adding value for long-term success. It can be viewed as a governance framework for unlisted family-run businesses or entrepreneurs, including the majority of UK companies and start-ups.

HRM, governance and performance

There are three important questions which must be considered when looking at governance and performance: First how does board performance relate to board effectiveness? Second what is the relationship between board effectiveness and firm performance? Finally what is the role of HRM?

Corporate governance is about value creation, but how this is defined and what criteria are applied to determine it is highly contextual and contingent. This will be specified for each board by the actors (stakeholders) involved. Board effectiveness can be defined in terms of its performance in achieving the aims and outcomes defined by the board and its stakeholders, for which the board is held accountable. The strategy defined and implemented by the board provides a medium- to long-term plan by which the firm's performance can be measured and monitored, thereby providing a link between governance and firm performance.

How to determine board effectiveness is more difficult in terms of relating this to firm performance as there are many external variables that can influence firm performance, and that are independent of board effectiveness, for example a market run on a particular product, service or currency. Methods used for determining board performance include stock market measures of company value using *event studies*, for example monitoring stock market reaction to unanticipated events that affect share price. The ambiguities of the complex causal relationships involved in determining board effectiveness and performance make this a challenging area of research. Boards are encouraged by 'the Code' to be vigilant in their self-evaluation based on the principles and provisions specified in 'the Code'.

David Guest's review of the empirical evidence linking people management and organisational performance supports the conclusions that he and other researchers make: that effective management of human resources is the key for gaining competitive advantage and creating value (Guest, 2005). The rationale for this argument is that effective management in organisations is likely to be embedded in the organisational culture and is much less easy to imitate than other strategic initiatives. In other words this is a unique and tacit asset of organisations that has intangible value (difficult to measure), yet produces tangible performance outcomes. The evidence presented by Guest indicates that the adoption of a number (and the more, the better) of progressive human resource practices is associated with superior business performance. The relationship between 'High Performance Work Practices' ('High Commitment HRM practices') employees and organisational performance is complex and researchers have identified employee competence, motivation, commitment and the opportunity to participate as key causal factors in the link (Purcell, Kinnie, Huctchinson, Rayton and Swart, 2003). These practices are promoted as underpinning effective workforce management and are linked with good governance in terms of tasks and activities of governance, and by the principles specified in 'the Code'.

Role of HRM on boards

If HRM plays an important role in the effective management of firms to create value, it is interesting to consider to what extent this influence extends to boards and governance. It is estimated that about one-fifth of FTSE 100 UK companies have an HR expert as a board member. The main principles and provisions of 'the Code' (outlined in the case below) require boards to have competency in HRM, particularly in the areas of recruitment and selection, performance management, reward management and training and development. Typically this capability is accessed by boards through the 'functional support' role provided by HRM. However the strategic mandate for governance would strongly advocate HRM's role and contribution as a 'strategic partner' as described by the 'Business Partner' model of HRM (Ulrich and Brockbank, 2005).

There is also a strong case for HRM to play a leadership role in stewarding the values and ethics of organisations. These represent the very core of organisational culture and are important in influencing the attitudes and behaviours of all employees, and in shaping the perceptions of stakeholders. Corporate governance provides an opportunity for HR professionals to 'make the case' and convince boards of the unique contribution HRM can make to create value through effective strategic people management. The following case considers the position of HRM with respect to governance and draws on recent research carried out by the Chartered Institute of Personnel and Development (CIPD) on the future of the HR profession.

UK Corporate Governance and the 'Next Generation HR' – the case of the Code

Corporate governance has been under scrutiny since the financial crash in 2007. Following the Walker Review, a new UK Code on Corporate Governance ('the Code') was published by the Financial Reporting Council in June 2010. 'The Code' is aimed at regulating board practice and presents a number of significant people management challenges. This article considers the role of HR in corporate governance in the light of CIPD's response to the Walker Review and its 'Next Generation HR' research published in February 2010.

Corporate governance

The development of corporate governance over the past 20 years has largely been influenced by company scandals from the 1990s to the current day. The first version of the UK Code was produced in 1992 in response to a number of scandals in the UK, including the collapse of the Maxwell Communications Group. The Cadbury Committee report included a 'Code of Best Practice' with guidelines for board behaviour and disclosure. The new UK Corporate Governance Code is intended to help boards make decisions and behave in a way that does not destroy company value, as the boards of Northern Rock, RBS and other banks did, which led to the financial crisis of 2007 and subsequent UK government bail-outs. For an international dimension, the Sarbanes–Oxley legislation introduced in 2002 was the US response to the Enron and WorldCom multi-billion dollar fraud scandals.

The new UK Code states that 'the purpose of corporate governance is to facilitate effective, entrepreneurial and prudent management that can deliver the long-term success of the company' (2010, Para 1) and refers to the Cadbury Report as providing the classic definition of the context of 'the code': 'Corporate governance is the system by which companies are directed and controlled. Boards of directors are responsible for the government of their companies. The responsibilities of the Board include setting the company's strategic aims, providing leadership to put them into effect, supervising the management of the business and reporting to shareholders on their stewardship' (1992, Para 2.5.) UK's current corporate system is based on a combination of legislation on company law and voluntary codes requiring companies to 'comply or explain', that is, explain why a company will not comply with 'the Code'. 'The Code' applies to all FTSE 350 companies but influences governance beyond this group and the private sector.

Convergence and performance

The global nature of business, particularly in the banking and financial sectors means that the decisions of board directors affect stakeholders across borders, as powerfully demonstrated by the widespread economic recession throughout Europe and the USA in recent years. The implications of this diffusion of forces continue to 'funnel' the convergence of corporate governance within the international business community, although regional differences still persist, for example the shareholder-led nomination committee system practised in Sweden.

Despite the growth of research in corporate governance, the evidence supporting a causal relationship between corporate governance and business performance remains ambiguous – which is hardly surprising given the complex and dynamic relationships involved. However, some surveys (Carey, Keller and Patsalos-Fox, 2010) have shown that major institutional investors are increasingly willing to pay a premium for effective corporate governance believing that it helps to create value. One research report presenting empirical evidence from different world regions describes a 'positive' influence of HRM practices on employee and corporate performance (Guest, 2005), highlighting the role that HR plays in governance.

The UK Code's principles and provisions

The five main principles of 'the Code' are summarised in Table 2.2 below. For each principle, there are supporting principles and a set of code provisions which detail the requirements for compliance to 'the Code'. There are also two schedules which set out further provisions, including Schedule A: The Design of Performance-Related Remuneration for Executive Directors.

People management

Although the detail of the new Code is beyond the scope of this article, it is clear from the principles alone that there are significant and strategic people management issues for organisations who aspire to effective corporate governance. The areas of leadership, effectiveness and remuneration present enormous challenges for boards, not just in terms of compliance but also in delivering sustainable shareholder value.

A review of 'the Code' swiftly leads to the conclusion that expertise in strategic people management is an essential 'input' to enable boards (and organisations) to function effectively. With an estimated 20 per cent of HR directors on the boards of the FTSE 100 companies, there would appear to be a significant gap in the competency profile of the many FTSE company boards. This gap presents a threat to the business of these organisations as they lack the essential expertise required to

Table 2.2   The main principles of 'the Code'

Section	Main principle
Leadership	Every company should be headed by an effective board, which is collectively responsible for the long-term success of the company
Effectiveness	The board and its committees should have the appropriate balance of skills, experience, independence and knowledge of the company to enable them to discharge their respective duties and responsibilities effectively
Accountability	The board should present a balanced and understandable assessment of the company's position and prospects
Remuneration	Levels of remuneration should be sufficient to attract, retain and motivate directors of the quality to run the company successfully, but a company should avoid paying more than is necessary for this purpose. A significant proportion of directors' remuneration should be structured to link rewards to corporate and individual performance
Relationship with shareholders	There should be a dialogue with shareholders based on the mutual understanding of objectives. The board as a whole has the responsibility for ensuring that a satisfactory dialogue with shareholders takes place

help them comply with 'the Code'. These companies are also losing out on potential business opportunities because of the constraint placed on their 'human capital' capability to create value.

In its response to the Walker review (Walker, 2009), CIPD supports the view expressed by Hector Sants, FSA Chief Executive Officer, and endorsed by the Confederation of British Industry (CBI): '...the structure of governance in financial companies does not need radical overhaul. The attitudes and competence of the individuals who conduct that governance does' (CIPD, 2009: 2). The salient point made by CIPD is that it is the culture of an organisation that influences the behaviour of all employees, including directors, and it is these behaviours that determine outcomes. Without a fundamental shift in how directors approach their roles, any changes in corporate governance and how risk is managed are likely to be ineffective.

HR can play an important role in managing risk in companies, particularly in the areas of recruitment, retention, relationships and reward management. A good example of this is the set of general principles published by CIPD in 2009 on executive pay, which is designed to act as a framework to help HR directors and Remuneration Committees when developing executive remuneration policies and practices. HR managers and directors can benefit by raising awareness of the strategic people management role that is required by the stakeholders they represent, and 'the Code' provides a useful framework to assist with this. Furthermore, HR directors should be instrumental in shaping stakeholder perception by communicating a firm grasp of the issues and leading their organisations towards solutions.

'Next Generation HR'

CIPD's 'Next Generation HR' research emphasises the importance of HR to be able to generate *organisational insight*, an essential capability for any function to make a worthwhile contribution to the business. It is more helpful to consider such insight as a prerequisite to enabling senior HR managers to recognise what their organisations require from their function at board level, which is essential if they are to operate as 'Business Partners'.

The conclusion that 'sustainable organisational performance and what drives it should sit at the heart of the HR agenda' (CIPD, 2010: 22) is helpful in 'positioning' HR relative to the boardroom agenda. HR managers need to be conversant with the meaning of organisational performance at the board level while being convincing about the contribution that the HR function makes to performance. HR professionals are familiar with the concept of 'human capital' which provides the link between people management and business performance. There is growing evidence of the influence and nature of this link to encourage HR professionals to communicate this with confidence in the boardroom.

CIPD calls for Next Generation HR leaders to be partners and provocateurs. The sentiment behind the latter is nicely captured in the quote 'We're looking for the kind of person who would have stopped Sir Fred Goodwin (at RBS)' (Martin Webster in CIPD, 2009: 7). Stewardship of corporate values is an important role for which HR is ideally placed; it creates value by underpinning ethical behaviour and 'good business' in management practice, and ensuring accountability at the highest level.

Conclusion

The new UK Code on Corporate Governance has significant strategic people management implications for the management of boards and organisations. It invites HR professionals to 'step up' and lead on governance matters at senior management level, in executive director and non-executive director roles. CIPD's response to the Walker review identifies specific business challenges where HR is ideally suited to do this. The 'Next Generation HR' research also suggests how the HR profession can position itself to meet the challenges in the current business climate. It would appear that as a consequence of corporate mismanagement, 'the Code' is about to create an opportunity for the 'Next Generation' of HR leaders to secure a permanent place on the boards of UK companies. Will this economic cloud perhaps have a 'silver lining' for aspiring HR professionals?

Activities and discussion questions

1. What 'code' or guidelines does your organisation and/or place of learning follow to ensure effective governance, and can you identify any principle of governance from 'the Code' in these guidelines?

2. Describe how the governance of your organisation and/or place of learning relates to at least two theories mentioned in this chapter?

3. Who are the members of the governing body in your organisation and/ or place of learning and whose interests do they represent, for example, do they represent different stakeholders?

4. Explain the relevance and role of HRM in the governance of your organisation and/or place of learning, and discuss how the involvement of a senior HR manager could positively influence corporate governance in this organisation.

Bibliography

Carey, D., Keller, J. J., and Patsalos-Fox, M. (2010). 'How to choose the right non-executive board leader'. *McKinsey Quarterly*, May, 1–5.

Charkham, J. (1994). *Keeping Good Company: A Study of Corporate Governance in Five Countries*. Oxford: Oxford University Press.

Chartered Institute of Personnel and Development (2009). *Response: Walker Review of Corporate Governance in Financial Services*. London: CIPD.

Chartered Institute of Personnel and Development (2010). *Next Generation HR: Time for Change – Towards a Next Generation for HR*. London: CIPD.

Clarke, T. (2004). *Theories of Corporate Governance*. London: Routledge.

Davis, J. H., Schoorman, D. F. and Donaldson, L. (1997). 'Towards a stewardship theory of management'. *Academy of Management Review*, 22, 20–47.

Eisenhardt, K. M. (1989). 'Agency theory: an assessment and review'. *Academy of Management Review*, 14, 57–74.

Financial Reporting Council (2010). *The UK Corporate Governance Code*. London: FRC.

Freeman, R. E. (1984). *Strategic Management: A Stakeholder Approach*. Boston: Pitman.

Ghosal, S. (2005). 'Bad management theories are destroying good management practices'. *Academy of Management Learning and Education*, 4, 75–91.

Guest, D. (2005). 'Human resource management and corporate performance: recent empirical evidence'. *DTI Economics Paper No.13: Papers from a Joint DTI/Kings College London Seminar*.

Hillman, A. J., Cannella A. A. Jr. and Paetzold, R. L. (2000). 'The resource dependence role of corporate directors: strategic adaptation of board composition in response to environmental change'. *Journal of Management Studies*, 29, 132–54.

Hung, H. (1998). 'A typology of the theories of the roles of governing boards'. *Corporate Governance: An Internal Review* 6, 101–11.

Huse, M. (2005). 'Accountability and creating accountability: a framework for exploring behavioural perspectives of corporate governance'. *British Journal of Management*, 16 (special issue), 65–79.

Huse, M. (2007). *Boards, Governance and Value Creation*. Cambridge: Cambridge University Press.

Mallin, C. (2009). *Corporate Governance* (3rd edn.). Oxford: Oxford University Press.

Purcell, J., Kinnie, N., Hutchinson, S., Rayton, B. and Swart, J. (2003). *Understanding the People and Performance Link: Unlocking the Black Box*. London: CIPD.

Scott, R. W. (1995). *Institutions and Organisations*. London: Sage.

Ulrich, D. and Brockbank, W. (2005). *The HR Value Proposition*. Boston, MA: Harvard Business School Press.

Walker, D. (2009). *A Review of Corporate Governance of UK Banks and Other Financial Industry Entities*. London: The Walker Review Secretariat.

Webster, M. (Ed.) (2010). *The Director's Handbook* (3rd edn.). London: Kogan Page.

CHAPTER 3

The Contribution of Environmental Scanning to Organisational Learning and Strategy Development

Stephen Pilbeam and Juliet Osbourne

Environmental scanning as a route to organisational learning

This chapter focuses on environmental scanning and provides case study evidence of environmental scanning activities, and the associated outputs. Environmental scanning is 'the managerial activity of learning about events and trends in the organisation's environment, and is the first step in the ongoing chain of perceptions and actions leading to an organisation's adaptation to its environment' (Costa, 1995: 4). Environmental scanning therefore contributes to an understanding of the impact of external forces on an organisation's capabilities and resources. As the environment becomes more complex, organisations need to embrace organisational learning because it is a central tenet of an organisation's ability to be agile and adaptable. Organisational learning occurs at multiple levels, and there is an increasing recognition that organisational learning can be achieved through environmental scanning. There is a strong link between the learning achieved through environmental scanning and an emergent approach to strategy (Choo, 2002), and organisations that fail to cultivate their potential to learn may find themselves losing ground to their competitors. The complex business environment of today presents opportunities and challenges, and these have a significant impact on an organisation's strategies and performance. An organisation's capability to adapt to external changes is dependent on knowing and interpreting such environmental influences, and therefore environmental scanning constitutes a primary mode of organisational learning, the knowledge of which assists management in planning the organisation's future.

The environment consists of factors that can be conceptualised into two layers. The outer layer of the macro-environment consists of the general political, economic, socio-cultural and technological (PEST) domains, and the inner layer of the micro-environment includes customers, competitors, suppliers, employees and other stakeholders. Both layers interact and have a distinct influence on organisational behaviours and actions. Voros (2001) and Qiu (2008) suggest that environmental scanning is undertaken through the perceptual filters of organisational members, and these filters determine managerial interpretations and the effectiveness of strategic decisions. The more complex and dynamic the environment, the greater the perceived environmental uncertainty experienced by organisational decision-makers, and the higher the level of perceived uncertainty, the more frequent, intense and wider the scope of environmental scanning practices needs to be. Managers differ in their perceptions and interpretations based on influences at the individual, group and organisational levels, which may result in different actions being taken by managers in relation to the same environmental factors. Hambrick (1982) suggested that managers experience bounded rationality in that they may be overwhelmed by the volume and variability of data and consequently their perceptual filters may limit the amount of information that can be processed with the result that much of this information gets lost, dissipated or is not used. Managers may not be able to synthesise, or fully understand, the significance of the vast array of information due to its complexity and the fast pace of change, and in reality they have limited time and capacity.

Environmental scanning modes and information sources

Environmental scanning includes both *looking at* information (viewing) and *looking for* information (searching), and organisations can engage in four modes of scanning – undirected viewing, conditioned viewing, informal search and formal search. Choo (2002) contends that in order for environmental scanning to be effective, organisations should be engaged in all four modes simultaneously.

- *Undirected viewing* – Scans a variety of sources, taking advantage of what is easily accessible, and is focused on general areas of interest; targeting is minimal and it involves serendipitous discovery and 'sensing' of information.
- *Conditioned viewing* – Scanners are able to recognise topics of interest through browsing pre-selected sources on topics of interest, targeting is higher and fewer sources are used, with the aim of increasing understanding through 'sense-making'.
- *Informal search* – Scanners are able to formulate queries and the search is targeted on an issue or event; this increases knowledge within narrow limits, with a focus on 'learning'.
- *Formal search* – Scanners are able to specify targets and engage in systematic gathering of information; this information is used for planning and action and the focus is on 'deciding'.

The CEO, functional managers and employees can conduct scanning separately or together and when all levels combine their scanning efforts, and it is conducted as a systematic and integrated process, the value and quality of scanning activity is enhanced. Multinational organisations, often faced with a plethora of environmental conditions in different countries, tend to be more

	Personal	*Non-personal*
External	Customers Competitors Business or professional associates Government officials Primary research – focus groups, interviews	Newspapers, periodicals Government publications Broadcast media Industry associations and conferences Research organisations Pressure groups, civic associations Internet or web services
Internal	Board members Managers Subordinate managers Subordinate staff Peers Shareholders	Internal memos, circulars Internal reports and studies Company library E-mails Company databases Management information systems Intranet

Figure 3.1 Typology of environmental scanning sources

aware of environmental factors and, as a consequence, can be better scanners than organisations which are national in scope.

Environmental scanning sources can be classified according to whether they are internal or external to the organisation and according to whether they are personal or non-personal sources (see Figure 3.1). It is important for sources to be reliable and valid because the quality of information obtained determines the usefulness and value of the process. Multiple sources provide a comprehensive picture of the forces driving environmental changes and inform intelligent decision-making. Although environmental scanning may provide information for the formulation of strategic options, it is not a sufficient condition for strategic decision-making, because it does not necessarily result in organisational action. There can be a stronger emphasis on short-term environmental issues, rather than on long-term concerns, and it is therefore critical for strategic decision-makers to focus on emerging events and trends that are likely to impact in the longer term in order to excavate implications for strategy development.

Scanning for business direction and strategy development

A lack of fit between an organisation's strategy and the environment may result in poor performance and therefore environmental scanning is a first step in strategy development and in aligning organisational strategy with the environment. The identification of threats and opportunities, patterns and trends is fundamental to an organisation's competitive positioning. Choo (2001: 10) maintains that organisations need to 'adopt a scanning mode that provides the required information and information gathering capabilities to pursue its desired strategy'.

Research by Hagen and Amin (1995) into the relationship between Porter's generic business strategies and scanning activities indicated that organisations employing a differentiation strategy scan mainly for opportunities for growth and customer needs, while a cost leadership strategy results primarily in scanning for threats from competitors and regulators. Organisations scan more actively in specific areas related to their strategy, for example, organisations with higher growth in sales tend to have greater interest in customer-related issues, and those with higher growth in income tend towards interest in demographic changes and competitor product offerings.

Organisations have different approaches to strategy formulation, with some taking a more deliberate, formal approach and others a more emergent, informal approach (de Wit and Meyer, 2004). But Choo (1999: 23) asserts that 'as an engine of organisational learning, scanning should be planned and managed as a strategic activity' and that the overall organisational strategy is dependent on the sophistication, scope and intensity of scanning activity. Organisations can benefit from ensuring that environmental scanning processes are integrated with the strategy-making process, whether deliberate or emergent, because environmental scanning is a powerful strategic tool that supports organisational learning by enabling organisations to 'learn about events and trends in the business environment, to establish relationships between them, and to make sense of the information to extract the main implications for decision-making and strategy development' (Teare and Bowen, 1997: 274).

Much of the literature therefore highlights that organisations need to scan the external environment to learn of changes that may potentially influence decision-making. The case study research that follows found that organisations in the Cayman Islands Financial Services Industry (CIFSI) actively scan the external environments to keep up to date with events and trends in the industry in order to maintain competitiveness in the global economy, where the Cayman Islands, despite being less than 100 square miles in area and having a population of just 55,000, features as the fifth largest Offshore Financial Centre (OFC) in the world. The Cayman Islands is one of the world's leading providers of institutionally focused, specialised financial services and a preferred destination for the structuring and domiciling of sophisticated financial services products. In 2009, the financial services industry produced US$1.5 billion in GDP or 55 per cent of the Cayman economy and was responsible for generating over 12,000 jobs, representing nearly 40 per cent of all employment in the country.

An exploration of organisational learning and strategy development in the Cayman Islands Financial Services Industry (CIFSI) through the lens of environmental scanning – a case study

This case study research focused on gaining insights into environmental scanning activities and the macro-environmental factors influencing CIFSI organisations together with the implications for strategic direction. Data were generated through 15 in-depth interviews with key decision-makers in the CIFSI, the Cayman Islands

Government and the Chamber of Commerce. It was evident that all of the case organisations proactively scan their external environments to keep up to date with events and trends in the industry, emphasising that the CIFSI is dynamic and in a state of flux. Senior managers indicated that they need to be knowledgeable about events and trends, not only to acquire new business, but also to maintain current customer relationships; as one senior manager articulated:

> Everyday is prime minister's questions from clients, as we are not just creating financial statements, we are helping people arrive at the correct decisions for everything from how money should be invested, to how shareholders should be treated, to how they can group their markets and develop their financial products and we are dealing across jurisdictions with rules that are very complex and have different cultural dynamics.

The research revealed that environmental scanning is undertaken through multiple channels, through both personal and non-personal sources (see Figure 3.1 above). As one respondent put it:

> We have a combination of ways to get information – clients and their agents are a good source of information and there is the market information that is generally available including the media, several trade publications, conferences and several associations that revolve around the industry, of which we are members, and which allows us to plug in to what's happening in the environment.

Regular internal team and management meetings to share knowledge and to discuss influences, threats and opportunities are prevalent. Although, as part of a multinational network, marketing or business intelligence units across jurisdictions are tasked with keeping abreast of trends and developments and finding new business opportunities, leaders stated that they must be continuously scanning the industry for emerging patterns and changes. In addition individual departments are also required to be aware of developments in their areas of specialisation, 'It was evident that each department keeps up with information from their perspective and so, legal, compliance, risk management and accounting all scan to maintain awareness of developments affecting the industry in their respective fields'. Information is therefore excavated and viewed by a number of persons and from different perspectives, thus increasing the probability of quality data being gathered, and reducing the potential for individual perceptions to filter out important details. The CIFSI is clearly in a constant state of uncertainty, so there is a necessity to be aware of environmental changes – the higher the level of uncertainty in the environment, the more intense the environmental scanning behaviour. One telling comment was: 'In Cayman, we look for the next bad thing that's going to happen...not many positive things are coming down the line for us, so we try and prepare as best as possible.'

Environmental scanning, organisational learning and strategy development

The findings in this research indicate that CIFSI organisations rely heavily on information gained through environmental scanning activities and utilise such information in strategic decision-making. With regard to the approach to strategy development, the consensus was that while organisations may have long-term goals and objectives, the strategy for achieving these objectives has to be flexible and adaptable because of the dynamic environment in which they operate, as is evident in the statement that:

> The industry is in a constant state of flux and I think a formal plan would, in fact, be inhibitive. We actually survive by being swifter on our feet than our competitors not only in the Cayman Islands, but also in other jurisdictions... So, we don't have any formal plans, but we have a system of responsiveness to economic, statutory and client circumstances.

CIFSI organisations proactively scan the external environments to learn of events and trends, and a strong link was asserted between the learning achieved through scanning activity and strategic development and decision-making, thus supporting Choo's (2001) assertion that environmental scanning is a primary mode of organisational learning, the knowledge from which is a critical ingredient in the development of strategy. An emergent approach to strategy development is prevalent, supporting the argument that strategies can be unplanned, developing incrementally and evolving through a process of learning in order to adapt to the changing realities in the environment. To illustrate the learning from environmental scanning, significant macro-environmental influences on business operations in the CIFSI were identified. These are presented as factors that facilitate and factors that inhibit business operations.

Macro-environmental factors that facilitate CIFSI business operations

There was consensus about the factors that facilitate business operations in the CIFSI:

- Cayman tax neutrality
- The quality of the financial organisations, the financial infrastructure and the financial talent
- Cayman legislation, the Cayman Islands Monetary Authority and being a British Overseas Territory
- High standard of living

Cayman's tax neutrality and its ability to maintain the highest quality of professional services providers, such as leading international law firms, banks and audit firms, and that it enjoys sound infrastructural facilities, positions it strongly in the global financial industry, illustrated by the comment that 'Cayman is a well-known and established tax neutral jurisdiction with a good pedigree, with good infrastructure and a fantastically good range of quality professionals, more so than in many jurisdictions... the best of the best are here'. Cayman legislation, which is based on English common law, is structured to facilitate good, flexible business governance. As one senior manager put it: 'Cayman has a healthy balance of legislation and regulations... licensing requirements, compliance and operating practices are well balanced with pragmatic laws to support the industry's flexibility.'

There was enthusiasm for the Cayman Islands Monetary Authority (CIMA), the statutory body that regulates the CIFSI, which was reported to be 'flexible and business savvy', but at the same time ensuring strict compliance with local and international regulations in order to maintain and improve Cayman's track record on issues such as tax transparency and anti-money laundering activities. This enthusiasm was evident in the statement that 'Cayman has a good regulatory environment, we have access to CIMA as they are very open and we are able to meet face-to-face quickly to discuss issues . . . they are responsive and committed to being more supportive than bureaucratic'.

Other facilitating factors were the high standard of living available in Cayman, partly attributed to the fact that there is no direct taxation; the relative strength of the local currency; the climate; and the ability to connect to major international cities easily. Whilst it is often overlooked, being a British Overseas Territory brings a level of respect to Cayman through the judicial system and the political stability it allows, together with the oversight provided by the Governor and the UK Foreign Office. These facilitating factors are critical to Cayman's competitiveness.

Macro-environmental factors that inhibit CIFSI business operations

Several factors pose significant challenges to doing business:

- the seven-year rollover immigration policy,
- the high cost of doing business,
- the changing international regulations and the surrounding misperceptions of Cayman as a tax haven, which engages in tax evasion.

The seven-year rollover immigration policy

The most commonly cited inhibiting factor was that of Cayman's seven-year rollover immigration policy – effectively expatriate workers are required to leave the islands after seven years, potentially causing a talent haemorrhage for employers. Upon its introduction in 2004, this policy prompted considerable debate about its effect on businesses being able to recruit and retain the talent needed to be successful, and it remains a critical issue facing the industry, being referred to by one respondent as the 'the 800 pound gorilla in the room'. Although there is general appreciation that the rollover policy was instigated for social and political purposes in order to provide the local Caymanian population with greater employment opportunities, and to restrict the number of expatriates who would have the right to become permanent residents, CIFSI organisations in this research took serious issue with how the policy was implemented and the resulting implications for doing business, as is illustrated by the comment that 'we recognise that the government is tied in with the interest of local people, but this is not necessarily aligned with the interest of the industry, or even the country, and therefore it may be to the disadvantage of local Caymanians in the longer term'.

It was evident that the rollover is perceived to have negatively impacted on CIFSI organisations by creating difficulties in replacing talented employees, generating employees' feelings of job insecurity and provoking some organisations to relocate to other jurisdictions. As one respondent asserted: 'The rollover has affected our business because it is hard to replace talent or people of a certain calibre and so the rollover does not make doing business here easy, and because of this we decided to move significant jobs such as fund accounting and shareholder services from Cayman to Shanghai and Singapore, who are direct competitors to Cayman.'

This inhibiting factor clearly has the potential to reduce the industry's competitiveness, with many arguing it has already done so (Seymour, 2010).

The cost of doing business

A dominant view was that the cost of doing business in Cayman is very high, and some believe it is getting unreasonably so. The Cayman Islands Government (CIG), like many other countries, ran into difficulties during the global financial crisis, and in late 2009 found itself 'operating with a US$100 million deficit and, being a British Overseas Territory, had to seek approval from the UK government to negotiate bank loans of up to US$465 million. The CIG was urged to raise additional revenues to reduce the deficit, and consequently increased a plethora of government fees, including work permit, registration and business licensing fees (Fuller, 2009). This has significantly increased the cost of doing business in the CIFSI, as is evident in the statement by one respondent that:

> The costs of doing business here are not getting any better and so as a global business we have to justify why we do certain business in Cayman when there are other locations that could offer the same service at a cheaper cost, and that's why our Cayman operation is now smaller than other locations as we have to do what's best for the group.

The cost of doing business is a potential threat to organisations growing their businesses in Cayman, particularly as international corporations are not only cost sensitive, but also have the option to relocate key business areas to less expensive jurisdictions. The Channel Islands has placed advertisements in financial magazines declaring that their fees are now less than those of the Cayman Islands, and other OFCs, such as Toronto and Dublin have also offered incentives to CIFSI organisations to relocate to their jurisdictions.

International regulations and the perception of the Cayman Islands

Despite compliance with international tax regulations, Cayman is often characterised as a tax haven that facilitates criminal and terrorist activities and the diversion of legitimate government revenue through tax evasion by individuals and corporations (The Journal, 2010). This external perception of Cayman was illustrated by one senior manager who said, 'In the global arena Cayman is part of the offshore centres and all of them are bad according to the G-20'. The CIFSI, and the CIG, brand these criticisms as unfair, stereotypical mischaracterisations. However the global financial crisis has increased the misperceptions surrounding OFCs and according to Travers (2010: 1) 'there is no doubt that as a result of the global financial meltdown the CIFSI is facing a fundamentally changed set of financial and regulatory circumstances', and especially now 'in the face of declining tax revenues, the costs of financial bailouts and an aggressive policy of social reform in the US, UK and EU the pressures on the industry are unprecedented'. Jennings (2009: 24) has outlined the most significant threats to the CIFSI as coming from:

- The US with 'The Stop Tax Haven Abuse Act' among other tax legislations against tax havens.
- The OECD and G-20 with their pledge 'to take action against tax havens'.
- The UK's HM Revenue and Customs Code of Conduct for UK banks which includes issues on tax legislation.
- The European Commission proposal for an EU Directive to limit the marketing of non-EU funds, like those established in Cayman, to EU member states, thus potentially reducing the market for funds domiciled in Cayman.

There was a strong reaction to continuing criticisms of OFCs, and the CIFSI in particular, as many felt that Cayman has been used as a banner to support the misconceptions around the so-called tax havens: One reaction was:

> Whenever there are difficulties and problems in the financial industry that has some nexus to Cayman, very quickly Cayman is used as a scapegoat for what went wrong. It is unfair and it is an uneducated view of the offshore business generally, because what we do and how we do it is not well understood by the big economies of the world, politicians, law makers and regulators.

> Added to this, the expression 'tax evasion' is often used synonymously with 'tax haven' and with 'tax avoidance', but whereas tax evasion is illegal, tax avoidance is not. However, even lawful tax avoidance has now taken on a pejorative connotation as it implies cheating on one's taxes (Mitchell, 2009). Cayman's reputation as a tax haven is considered to be 'unfair labelling' as it implies a high degree of secrecy and improper dealings. In reality Cayman's confidentiality statute provides a clear gateway to ensure tax transparency, and tax exchange agreements are in place to legally share information with international governments and regulatory bodies. Nonetheless these emotive and controversial labels are often used by onshore politicians and journalists, who either through a lack of understanding or for political reasons, perpetuate the misconceptions of Cayman as a money-laundering tax haven. The implications are that clients are already leaving Cayman because of the negative portrayals and are moving business to other less maligned OFCs or to onshore centres.

Conclusions

As the examples above illustrate CIFSI organisations proactively scan the external environment and the opportunities and threats identified through this learning process contribute to strategy formulation, demonstrating that environmental scanning is a primary mode of organisational learning. The research also shows that case organisations favour an emergent, incremental approach to strategy development, allowing for creativity and flexibility in adapting to unpredictable environmental conditions. The pressure from uncertainty in the macro-environment encourages the orientation towards incrementalism; however, Choo (1999: 22) maintains that to be effective 'environmental scanning has to balance the tensions between control and creativity, focus and exploration, provide a long-range perspective for growth and should be integrated with strategy to drive performance'.

Activities and discussion questions

1. Why is environmental scanning important for organisational learning and strategy development?

2. Who should do environmental scanning, how can it be done and what should be done with the information collected?

3. Undertake environmental scanning for your organisation using a PESTLE framework and identify three significant facilitating factors and three significant inhibiting factors to successful business operations.

4. Using the significant facilitating and inhibiting factors you have identified, comment on what organisational learning accrues from this and how it should influence strategy development.

5. Prepare and deliver a presentation in which you analyse the macro-environmental factors that facilitate and inhibit CIFSI business operations. Repeat the process for your own organisation.

Bibliography

Choo, C. W. (1999). 'The art of scanning the environment'. *Bulletin of the American Society for Information Science*, 25 (3), 13–19.

Choo, C. W. (2001). 'Environmental scanning as information seeking and organizational learning'. *Information Research*, 7 (1), 1–25, 10.

Choo, C. W. (2002). 'Environmental Scanning as Information Seeking and Organizational Knowing'. PrimaVera Working Paper Series. Universiteit van Amsterdam.

Costa, J. (1995). 'An empirically-based review of the concept of environmental scanning'. *International Journal of Contemporary Hospitality Management*, 7 (7), 4–9.

de Wit B. and Meyer, R. (2004). *Strategy: Process, Content, Context. An International Perspective* (3rd edn). London: Thomson Learning.

Ebrahimi, B. P. (2000). 'Perceived strategic uncertainty and environmental scanning behavior of Hong Kong Chinese executives'. *Journal of Business Research*, 49, 67–77.

Fuller, B. (2009). 'Fees jacked up in budget'. *Cayman Compass*. http://www.caycompass.com/cgi-bin/CFPnews.cgi?ID=10385998, accessed 27 April 2012.

Hagen, A. F. and Amin, S. G. (1995). 'Corporate executives and environmental scanning activities: an empirical investigation'. *SAM Advanced Management Journal*, 60 (2), 41–8.

Hambrick, D. C. (1982). 'Environmental scanning and organizational strategy'. *Strategic Management Journal*, 3, 159–74.

Jennings, C. (2009). 'Clouds on the horizon: a snapshot of challenges facing Cayman's Financial industry'. *Cayman Financial Review*, Qtr 3 (16), 24–7.

The Journal (2010). 'Setting the financial industry record straight'. *The Cayman Islands Business Journal*, July, 14.

Markoff, A. (2010). 'The Cayman Islands: From obscurity to offshore giant. Part 5 – the bloom and gloom decade of the 2000s'. *Cayman Financial Review*, Qtr 1 (18), 10–13.

Marshall, J., Smith, S. and Buxton, S. (2009). 'Learning organisations and organisational learning: What have we learned?'. *International Journal of Knowledge, Culture and Change Management*, 8 (5), 61–72.

Matsuo, M. and Easterby-Smith, M. (2008). 'Beyond the knowledge sharing dilemma: the role of customization'. *Journal of Knowledge Management*, 12 (4), 30–43.

Mitchell, D. (2009). 'The positive global role of jurisdictional competition and international financial centres'. *Cayman Financial Review*, Qtr 3 (16), 10–13.

PESTLE Analysis (2010). *CIPD Factsheet*. London: CIPD.

Powell, T. (2007). *Knowledge Based View. Encyclopedic Dictionary of Strategic Management*. tamanpowell.com/Knowledge%20Based%20View.pdf (electronic version).

Qiu, T. (2008). 'Scanning for competitive intelligence: a managerial perspective'. *European Journal of Marketing*, 42 (7/8), 814–35.

Seymour, D. (2010). 'An industry in flux'. *Cayman Financial Review*, Qtr 1 (18), 44–6.

Shahani, A. (2009). *Knowledge Based Business – Know What and Know How*. http://ezine articles.com/?Knowledge-BasedBusiness—Know-What-and-Know-How&id=1330193 (electronic version).

Teare, R. and Bowen, J. (1997). 'Assessing information needs and external change'. *International Journal of Contemporary Hospitality Management*, 9 (7), 274–84.

Travers, A. (2010). *Cayman Finance Summit Presentation*. Caymanfinancesummit.ky/presentations/Travers.pdf (electronic version), accessed 27 April 2012.

Voros, J. (2001). 'Reframing environmental scanning: an integral approach'. *Foresight*, 3 (6), 533–51.

Wang, S. and Noe, R. A. (2010). 'Knowledge sharing: a review and directions for future research'. *Human Resource Management Review*, 20 (2), 115–31.

CHAPTER 4

The Influence of Civil Society Organisations on Strategic People Management in the UK
Standard-setting and behavioural compliance

Stephen Pilbeam and Steve Williams

The concept of 'civil society' is relevant in contemporary discussions and concerns the relationship between democracy and governance. In addition to emergent active citizenry, civil society is composed of the totality of voluntary civic and social organisations and institutions that form the basis of a functioning democratic society, in contrast to market-based commercial institutions and the force-backed structures of the state. Therefore together the state, the market and civil society constitute the entirety of a society, and the relations between these three determine the structure and the character of a society. The Centre for Civil Society at the London School of Economics and Political Science (UK) definition provides insights:

> Civil society refers to the arena of uncoerced collective action around shared interests, purposes and values. In theory, its institutional forms are distinct from those of the state, and market, though in practice, the boundaries between state, civil society, and market are often complex, blurred and negotiated.

A flourishing civil society depends on the freedom and commitment of individuals pursuing their own chosen ends, whether personal or communal.

In addition to emergent active citizenry, for example through demonstrations and protest activity in pursuit of democratic accountability, civil society is enacted by Civil Society Organisations (CSOs). Whilst the term Civil Society Organisation may be unfamiliar to many, we all know what they are. CSOs are multi-various, but normally have a matter of collective interest which, through some form of organisation, which will range from tight to loose, enables a group of interested parties to seek to achieve objectives which are desirable to its members. Collective effort and solidarity are therefore key elements of CSO activity. CSOs embrace a diversity of foci, actors and institutional forms, varying in their degree of formality, autonomy and power, and include organisations such as registered charities, non-governmental organisations, community groups, women's organisations, faith-based organisations, professional associations, trade unions, self-help groups, social movements, business associations, coalitions and advocacy groups. CSOs seek to use evidence generated in their particular zone of interest to influence agenda-setting and bring about change, whilst promoting the interests of the particular CSO membership. In the employment arena CSO objectives are therefore focused on influencing the formulation and implementation of policy regarding people management, and also the monitoring and evaluation of policy effectiveness, whether it is at organisation or national government or supranational level. Therefore CSOs are a form of civil regulation of the employment relationship.

The influence of civil society occurs not only at the national and supranational governmental levels, as evidenced by the 'Arab Spring' and the associated civil pressure being exerted on leaders and government, but is also being exerted by CSOs in the management of the employment relationship, with consequent implications for strategic people management. It is evident that senior managers and HR practitioners will benefit from having an understanding of the role of CSOs in standard-setting and in seeking behavioural compliance with their particular objectives. Whilst the focus of this chapter is on the management of people, it is also important to recognise CSO influence on the Corporate Social Responsibility (CSR) agenda and consequently the discussion questions at the end of this chapter include one activity in relation to contemporary issues in CSR.

Greenpeace is one example of a CSO and is well known for pursuing an environmental agenda and seeking to hold governments and businesses to account. Fathers for Justice is another well-known CSO example, as are Age Concern, Macmillan Cancer Relief, the Fawcett Society, the Citizens Advice Bureau, NSPCC and Amnesty International. CSOs are not typically associated with worker representation activities and therefore have received little academic attention, a lacuna that the research conducted by Steve Williams, Brian Abbott and Edmund Heery (2010a, 2010b) sought to rectify. Examples of CSOs and civil regulation in the employment arena are evident in the research report that follows.

Civil regulation and employment relations: the implications for employers – evidence from case-based research

Civil regulation and employment relations

While the study of employment relations has long been dominated by a concern with understanding the activities of employers, trade unions and governments, scholars have increasingly been turning their attention to the influence of new and emerging actors, such as community organisations, consumer activists and temporary employment agencies (Heery and Frege, 2006). In this article we report on some key findings from our study of one of these new actors – civil society organisations – and particularly of the role that they play in influencing the behaviour of employers through the process of civil regulation. For a longer version see Williams et al. (2010a).

We use the term CSO as a convenient label to encompass the variety of bodies that inhabit civil society, those that are not part of the state or the market (i.e. firms). CSOs include charities, faith groups, voluntary associations, advocacy bodies, social movement organisations, campaigning groups, community bodies and other non-governmental organisations (NGOs). Of course under this approach trade unions and professional associations may also be viewed as CSOs; however our study was not concerned with these already well-researched bodies. The research findings reported here come from interviews conducted in 2008 with 51 key informants (e.g. chief executives and policy officers) across 34 different CSOs, which operate at a national level within the UK. Among the CSOs from which we collected data were Age Concern (now Age UK), the gay and lesbian rights body Stonewall, the Migrant Rights Network, Carers UK, Working Families, Macmillan Cancer Support, Refugee Action and the Daycare Trust.

In designing the research we were concerned with investigating how these CSOs attempt to influence the policies and practices of employers, thus contributing to the regulation of employment relationships. There is an emerging business and management literature which is concerned with the topic of civil regulation. Essentially the term civil regulation is applied to governance arrangements that enable civil society and the organisations that comprise it to exercise oversight over, and thus influence, business activity, putting pressure on corporations to deliver improvements in social and environmental standards (Zadek, 2007). Generally civil regulation is portrayed as a form of private regulation, marked by the absence of any role for the state in the governance of business activities. Rather corporations themselves, in association with other non-state actors such as CSOs, determine the regulatory framework within which business operates, setting standards in areas such as environmental management for example, particularly on an international basis (Hutter and O'Mahony, 2004a, 2004b; Moon and Vogel, 2008).

How does civil regulation operate?

We were keen to use our research to investigate in more detail how civil regulation operates in the area of work and employment relations. Our data show that civil regulation encompasses three key elements: efforts to set employment standards, the processing of information and methods of influencing employers' behaviour.

Standard-setting

The first component of civil regulation concerns the efforts of CSOs to set employment standards. This is often done on an indirect basis, as CSOs lobby the government for changes in the law that would influence the policies and practices of employers. The enactment of whistle-blowing legislation, the widening of the scope of anti-discrimination legislation to cover age and sexual orientation as well as the extension of the right to request flexible working hours to cover carers of adults are all policy interventions that were influenced by CSO lobbying. Yet CSOs also attempt to affect standard-setting by engaging directly with employers. Three main interventions are used by CSOs to influence standards in this way: award schemes that promote and recognise good practice by employers, benchmarking services which regularly measure the performance of employers against a set of specific criteria and standards of good management practice which employers are encouraged to adopt. Working Families, for example, offers employers the opportunity to benchmark their work–life balance and flexible working policies 'against the best'. Perhaps the most well-known initiative of this kind is Stonewall's Diversity Champions scheme which has a membership of over 500 employers. Member organisations are required to commit themselves to achieving best practice in the management of gay, lesbian and bisexual employees, going beyond straightforward compliance with the relevant anti-discrimination legislation.

Information processing

A second key element of civil regulation concerns the processing of information. CSOs try to use their knowledge and expertise, often garnered through appropriate research, to influence the policies and practices of employers, thus helping to inform their standard-setting efforts. For example recognising that there was scope for improving organisational practice, Tommy's the Baby Charity became concerned with advising employers on how to support pregnant workers more effectively. Providing employers with relevant information is seen by many CSOs as a key way in which they can help to improve how people are managed at work. Health and well-being charities, for example, are particularly concerned with making sure that line managers are sufficiently well informed about how to handle employees with specific health conditions. We interviewed the head of a mental health charity who said that 'one of the big needs I think we've identified is line management understanding of mental health issues'.

This aspect of CSO activity is often marked by a concern with raising wider awareness among employers of the issues with which they are concerned: the benefits of instituting more flexible working arrangements, for example, or how to handle workers with specific conditions that affect their health and well-being. CSOs frequently use research findings to validate the need for desired courses of action, often drawing on the experiences of their clients. They try to act as a source of expertise, which governments, employers and others can draw upon to inform their policies and practices. The chief executive of a body which tries to improve age diversity outlined this aspect of its role: 'what we try to do is to observe the good practice that is there and draw on best practice in this country and abroad and be a repository of knowledge in relation to age management'.

Influencing behaviour

The third element of civil regulation concerns the type of approach used by CSOs to influence the behaviour of employers. A distinction can be made between a deterrence approach, where CSOs rely upon the credible threat of sanctions to effect changes in employers' behaviour, and a compliance approach, based on the use by

CSOs of non-coercive measures to encourage change. Our research indicates that the compliance approach to altering the behaviour of employers is markedly more popular among CSOs than the deterrence approach. We found little use for, or interest in, boycotts of employers, for example, or for efforts to expose employers' malpractice, although there was sometimes a preparedness to instigate legal proceedings against employers in exemplary cases. In contrast there is a notable willingness to work cooperatively with employers, based on the premise that effective people management is good for business performance.

We encountered manifold instances of how CSOs were using business case arguments to underpin their interventions with employers. The charity Macmillan Cancer Support, for example, is keen to demonstrate to employers the business benefits of retaining staff with a cancer diagnosis, something which has been a 'key driver' of its growing employment work. Perhaps surprisingly, similar business case arguments for effecting change were evident even among CSOs which might have been expected to take a more confrontational approach with employers. The representative of a community organisation which campaigns for better pay and conditions for low-paid and vulnerable workers observed that 'essentially what we are constantly trying to do is say this is actually good, not just for the individual worker, but for the business as well, and change the basic thinking'. While CSOs secure legitimacy, and their capacity to alter the behaviour of employers, on the basis of their expertise and moral authority as specialist actors in their respective fields, the emphasis on using business case arguments to promote change may, however, restrict the effectiveness of their interventions since there is little capacity or interest in imposing sanctions on employers.

Implications for strategic people management

The rise of civil regulation poses four main implications. First organisations need to be aware of the extent to which CSOs are able to influence government policy in some areas, affecting policy outcomes in matters relating to discrimination and equality, for example, or occupational health, work–life balance issues and the treatment of vulnerable workers.

Second organisations may find themselves in circumstances where it is beneficial to strike a dialogue with CSOs directly. The role of CSOs is not just restricted to influencing government policy, but is also often concerned with encouraging firms to comply with their legal obligations when it comes to managing people at work, and ideally to exceed them. Employers may wish to consider whether or not to apply standards of good management practice devised by CSOs in their own organisations, for example.

Third while instances of CSOs trying to alter the policies and practices of employers through the use of a deterrence approach are relatively uncommon, employers need to be aware that poor management practice, particularly perceived non-compliance with their statutory obligations, may provoke action from CSOs keen to demonstrate how effective they are at achieving their objectives, and benefiting their clients, particularly in the area of discrimination law. For example, in exemplary cases, Stonewall is prepared to support employment tribunal cases against employers.

Fourth while the activities of CSOs may be viewed as constituting a potential challenge for employers, senior managers and HR practitioners need to be aware that they can also be a useful source of advice, information and guidance over specialist matters (e.g. age discrimination, supporting workers with specific health conditions, managing sexual orientation and operating with a migrant workforce), where specific expertise might otherwise be hard to come by. We plan to undertake further research to examine the extent to which employers make use of the services of CSOs in this manner.

For many years, the dominant regulatory approach involved the joint regulation of employment relationships, where employment standards were determined, or at least influenced, by collective bargaining between employers and trade unions. However the decline of the unions and the diminishing reach and effectiveness of collective bargaining mean that the importance of joint regulation has substantially declined. According to one interpretation, statutory regulation exercises an increasingly marked influence on how human resources are managed. Thus the decline of joint regulation has not given way simply to unilateral management control. However we also need to acknowledge the role played by civil regulation in affecting employment standards. In particular, interventions by CSOs may contribute to the regulation of employment relationships by influencing regulatory standards elaborated by other actors, notably employers and the state. Civil regulation complements or provides an alternative to the law in many instances. The key thing about civil regulation, then, is that it is part of an evolving, complex institutional environment governing HRM. While further research is needed to determine the effectiveness of civil regulation, its development nonetheless attests to the importance of the institutional dimension of HRM.

Activities and discussion questions

1. Identify a list of 10 CSOs that have or are exerting influence in relation to employment relationships and strategic people management agendas.

2. Select three from the list you have identified and research the degree and extent of influence over HR policies and practices. Report your findings either in a 2000-word assignment or in a 20-minute PowerPoint presentation, ensuring that you communicate a clear understanding of the nature and role of CSOs in a democratic society. Differentiate between influence on employers which is concerned with

   - setting standards directly with employers in the form of the provision of expert research, management practice guidance (including Codes of Practice) and making recognition awards
   - influencing employment practice indirectly through engaging with government
   - coercing behavioural modification of employers through the exercise of sanctions, which may be substantive in terms of the impact on the product or service, or through brand impact.

3. Identify three CSOs that have or are exerting influence in relation to the Corporate Social Responsibility (CSR) agenda, other than in the area of people management, and research their degree and extent of influence over corporate strategy. Report your findings either in a 2000-word assignment or a 20-minute PowerPoint presentation, ensuring that you also communicate a clear understanding of the nature and role of CSOs in a democratic society. The setting of standards for organisations, indirect influence through engagement with government and the coercion of behavioural modification can be used as a three-prong analytical framework.

Bibliography

Burchell, J. and Cook, J. (2006). 'It's good to talk? Examining attitudes towards corporate social responsibility dialogue and engagement processes'. *Business Ethics: A European Review*, 15 (2), 154–70.

Centre for Civil Society at London School of Economics and Political Science, http://www.lse.ac.uk/collections/CCS/Default.htm

Fries, R. (2003). 'The legal environment of civil society', in M. Glasius (ed.), *Global Civil Society*. London: LSE Global Governance, 221–38.

Heery, E. and Frege, C. (2006). 'New actors in industrial relations'. *British Journal of Industrial Relations*, 44 (4), 601–4.

Hutter, B. and O'Mahony, J. (2004a). 'Business regulation: reviewing the regulatory potential of civil society organisations'. *London School of Economics and Political Science – Discussion Paper No. 26*, September.

Hutter, B. and O'Mahony, J. (2004b). 'The Role of Civil Society Organisations in Regulating Business'. *ESRC Centre for Analysis of Risk and Regulation, London School of Economics and Political Science – Discussion Paper No. 26*. London, UK.

Kohler-Koch, B. and Quittkat, C. (2009). 'What is civil society and who represents civil society in the EU? Results of an online survey among civil society experts'. *Policy and Society*, 28 (1), 11–22.

Moon, J. and Vogel, D. (2008). 'Corporate social responsibility, government and civil society', in A. Crane, A. McWilliams, D. Matten, J. Moon and D. Siegel (eds), *The Oxford Handbook of Corporate Social Responsibility*. Oxford: Oxford University Press, 305–23.

Sadler, D. (2004). 'Anti-corporate campaigning and corporate "social" responsibility: towards alternative spaces of citizenship?'. *Antipode: Radical Journal of Geography*, 36 (5), 851–70, November.

Warhurst, A. (2001). 'Corporate citizenship and corporate social investment: drivers of tri-sector partnerships'. *JCC 1*, Spring, 57–73. Warwick Business School: Greenleaf Publishing.

Williams, S., Abbott, B. and Heery, E. (2010a). 'Civil regulation and human resource management: the impact of civil society organisations on the policies and practices of employers'. *Human Resource Management Journal*, 21 (1), 45–59.

Williams, S., Abbott, B. and Heery, E. (2010b). 'Non-union worker representation through civil society organisations: evidence from the UK'. *Industrial Relations Journal*, 42 (1), 69–85.

Zadek, S. (2007). *The Civil Corporation*. London: Earthscan.

CHAPTER 5

The Critical Role of the Front-Line Manager in Operationalising People Management Strategies

Competence-based selection, performance management and management development in the Police Service

Stephen Pilbeam and Jim Atherton

This chapter focuses on the role of the front-line manager (FLM) and the competencies that are required to be effective in that role. The case study research that follows is located within a Police Force and highlights issues related to the critical role of the front-line manager, competence-based recruitment and selection, performance management and management development.

The role of the front-line manager

Line managers are those to whom individual employees or teams directly report and who in turn have responsibility to more senior management for the performance of those employees or teams. The term front-line manager is more specific and refers to managers who are in the first level of the management hierarchy, where the employees who report to them do not themselves have any managerial or supervisory responsibility. In fact FLMs are not normally given this title in the organisations that employ them and, depending on the business sector, they can be known by a variety of different titles with the more common descriptions being team leader, team manager or supervisor, or in the case of the Police Service, the title is Sergeant. FLMs are often promoted from within and appointed on potential rather than on the basis of formal management education and qualifications. Like their titles, the actual roles of FLMs vary in different organisations. According to *Business Link*, UK (2011), FLM responsibilities typically include:

- day-to-day people management,
- managing operational costs,
- providing technical expertise,
- organisation of work allocation and rotas,
- monitoring work processes,
- checking quality,
- dealing with customers/clients,
- measuring operational performance.

FLMs are increasingly carrying out activities that have traditionally been the remit of HR. Occupying a key position in the organisation, FLMs are often crucial to the difference between low-performing and high-performing organisations. They are the deliverers of success as they implement strategies that focus the efforts of individuals on business goals and translate them into positive outcomes. They are therefore key players in the performance management of employees and in the operationalisation of the organisation's people management strategies.

CIPD research based on interviews with over 1,000 employees (Hutchinson and Purcell, 2003) demonstrated that FLM behaviour was a critical factor in developing organisational commitment. The higher the employees rated their FLMs in terms of the way they managed people, the more satisfied and committed they were. This in turn resulted in higher performance. Successful FLMs need self-confidence and a strong sense of their own security in the organisation. This, in turn, requires strong support and the appropriate training and development for those newly appointed in an FLM role. Organisations need to gain FLM commitment to people management activities by clarifying their responsibilities through job descriptions, performance appraisals and the communication of the importance and value of development-related activities. A vital factor influencing FLM levels of commitment to the organisation is a good working relationship with their own managers. This includes being treated with respect and a sense of job security. FLMs need time to carry out their people management role as there is a tendency for this to be subordinated to other duties, such as budgeting and operational issues. Increasingly FLMs are active at the delivery end of people management and are involved in tasks such as performance appraisal, coaching and development, involvement and communication, absence management, discipline and grievances as well as recruitment and selection. Consequently the way that HR policies and practices are interpreted and used by FLMs has become an important determinant of the success or failure of those practices. FLMs therefore need to be carefully selected with attention paid to behavioural competencies such as communication, emotional intelligence and leadership. FLMs often do similar tasks and therefore work alongside those who they supervise and often have some experience of doing the same kind of job. This not only gives them the advantage of understanding the issues that their workers face, but also creates tension when they need to assert their authority.

Competencies and competence-based selection

There are different meanings and at least two distinct concepts to which the word competence is attached. The terms 'competence', 'competences', 'competency' and 'competencies' are used almost interchangeably, leading to some confusion, not least regarding whether the term refers to an activity, a personality trait, a skill or even a task. There is a distinction, reflected in spelling, between competency (plural – competencies), which refers to the behavioural characteristics of an individual that are causally related to effective or superior performance in a job, and competence (plural – competences), which is the ability to perform activities within an occupation to a prescribed standard. These distinct concepts reflect a difference in focus: the first relates to the inputs that help achieve successful performance at work and the second to the outcomes of competence. These are often termed as 'behavioural competencies' and 'outcome-based competences'. The simplest way to describe the difference is that competencies are about the people who do the work, while competences are about the work they do and its achievement. These two approaches are sometimes identified as American and British respectively, but today they are often found in combination or hybrid forms and the terms are used interchangeably (Horton, 2009).

According to the CIPD Learning and Development Survey (2010) there is widespread evidence that large private and public organisations, particularly in the service sector, are using competency frameworks and adopting competency management. Popular competencies are communication skills, people management, team skills, customer service, results orientation and problem-solving. Examples of competencies used for FLM positions include:

- Achieve targets, and proactively identify and pursue new and stretching targets,
- Set priorities based on information about input resources and specified organisational outcomes,
- Achieve the effective performance management of subordinate staff,
- Improve organisational performance through seeking new opportunities,
- Scrutinise and revise working methods in pursuit of continuous improvement,
- Maintain a focused interest in overall business results,
- Engage in continuous professional development.

The arguments for using competency-based approaches in recruitment and selection are first that they focus on the knowledge, skills and aptitudes that are required to do a specific job, rather than on qualifications and experience; second that they permit a more objective assessment of job candidates because they are based upon a clear profile of the job; and third that they meet equity and diversity principles because the same criteria are applied in rating each candidate. In addition to developing more relevant selection criteria, and improving interviewing and assessment techniques, the competence-based approach can provide a link to post-appointment training and management development.

Performance management of employees

The performance management process consists of interventions by management to maintain or improve the performance of an employee in his or her job. It is a process that contributes to the effective management of individuals and teams in order to achieve higher levels of organisational performance and it establishes shared understanding about what is to be achieved, and how to achieve it (Armstrong and Baron, 2004). Therefore performance management is 'a systematic and strategic approach to ensuring that employee performance enables the organisation to achieve competitive advantage or public service objectives by producing the quality of products and services that generate customer and citizen satisfaction, and thereby achieve the organisation's strategy' (Pilbeam and Corbridge, 2010). Performance management is important because organisations need to compete and survive through continuously improving organisational performance, and it is the skills, knowledge and motivation of people that make the difference. The cumulative impact of individual performance influences organisational performance. Therefore performance management is a strategic management issue, with FLMs having a critical role in managing and developing employee performance and in connecting employee performance to strategic organisational objectives. Importantly performance management enables organisations to cascade organisational objectives to departments and to teams. The objectives of performance management are:

- To link employee effort and performance with organisational objectives,
- To set standards,
- To identify performance gaps,
- To support and monitor employee performance through feedback and coaching,
- To review and appraise performance,
- To identify training and development needs,
- To reward good performance,
- To facilitate dialogue with employees and clarify their role and priorities,
- To establish a shared understanding of where the organisation is heading.

The features of the performance management cycle are set out in Figure 5.1.

Setting objectives and identifying performance standards are prerequisites to the effective performance management of employees. A three-step framework can be used for identifying performance standards:

1. *Principal job purpose* – **Why** is the job being done?
2. *Key performance areas* – **What** needs to be done to achieve the principal job purpose?
3. *Performance standards for each key area* – **How** will we know if the key performance areas have been achieved? These need to be measurable, quantitatively and and/or qualitatively.

By way of example, in relation to a school teacher:

1. *The principal job purpose* – to generate student learning;
2. *Key performance areas* – classroom teaching, setting assessments and marking and measuring student progress;
3. *Performance standards for classroom teaching* – Deploying stimulating learning methods linked to learning outcomes, maintaining student attention and engagement; completing the syllabus in the allocated timescale; and achieving learning targets.

Objectives give direction to employee effort, encourage focus and the prioritisation of activities and therefore potentially promote good performance. However objectives need to be SMART if they are to be effective:

S   *Specific and stretching*
M   *Measurable*
A   *Achievable and agreed*
R   *Relevant and reinforced*
T   *Time-related and trackable*

Good and bad examples of objectives are provided in Table 5.1 – what makes these good and bad?

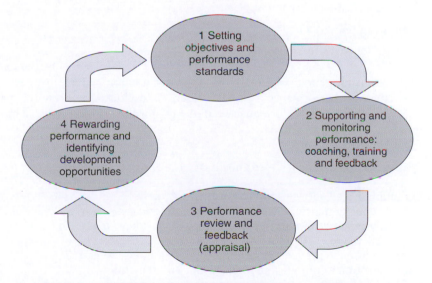

Figure 5.1   The features of the performance management cycle

Table 5.1   Good and bad examples of objectives

Bad example	Good example – SMART objectives
To get more customers to take out service agreements	To increase sales of service agreements by 15 per cent by the end of the third quarter. We will review marketing plans and sales figures together each month to monitor progress and the implementation of your negotiating-skills course
To get better at achieving deadlines	To achieve all deadlines within your control from now. Where a deadline is likely to be missed, the reasons, revised estimate and any contingency plans are to be discussed and agreed within 24 hours of it becoming known that a deadline is unlikely to be achieved
To attend a health and safety course	As a result of attending a health and safety course, to produce a risk analysis and recommendations for the department, verified by the course trainer as likely to reduce days lost due to accidents by 20 per cent within 12 months

An appraisal is 'a conversation with a purpose' and clearly an important feature of a performance management process. However it is only one part of the performance management cycle, and other parts, identified in Figure 5.1 above, are vitally important too. Appraisal should not only include reflection on the past, but also planning for the future. Common features of the appraisal process include:

- Clarifying the job,
- Self-review,
- Manager feedback,
- Performance assessment,
- Identifying training needs,
- Setting objectives and performance indicators.

Performance assessment may include an appraisal grading system in order to calibrate employee performance and may influence the allocation of rewards, particularly where there is a performance-related pay process. An indicative example of a grading system is provided in Table 5.2.

Table 5.2   An indicative example of an appraisal grading system

1. **Exceptional:** well above requirements for the job,
2. **Excellent performance:** consistently above job requirements in all key areas,
3. **Generally solid performance:** performance in most key areas within an acceptable range,
4. **Unsatisfactory:** improvement needed to meet job requirements,
5. **Poor:** performance significantly below job requirements.

There are different forms of appraisal, which can often be used in combination with a 360-degree feedback combining multiple sources:

- *Top-down:* the immediate line manager is the sole appraiser,
- *Self:* through self-reflection, the individual's views are integrated into the top-down assessment,
- *Peer:* colleagues contribute to performance assessment,
- *Upward:* the views of subordinates are taken into account,
- *360-degree feedback:* managers, colleagues, customers and other members of the employee's role set all contribute to enable self-reflection and development.

Effective performance appraisal involves a number of challenges. It is often perceived as increased bureaucracy, but the appraisal dialogue is much more important than the documentation. FLMs can see it not only as bureaucratic, but also as an imposition when they have pressing operational matters to deal with. There is also a need to reconcile potential tensions between identifying development needs (the FLM as a coach) and assessing performance (the FLM as a judge and jury). There is a huge potential for subjectivity and bias through perceptual projection, stereotypical assumptions, the recency effect, the halo/horns effect, confirmatory information seeking bias and favouritism *inter alia*. Supporting and monitoring performance through coaching, training and feedback is an essential part of the performance management process and a core FLM competence. Management development in this area is therefore a key factor in FLM effectiveness.

Management development for FLMs

FLM Management Development (MD) embraces:

- *Manager training*, which focuses on the skills managers need to perform management tasks such as team leading, performance management, planning and organising, prioritising and time management and dealing with conflict.
- *Manager development*, which focuses on enhancing the potential performance of individual managers through participation in specific developmental opportunities, and work attachments and the undertaking of management education.

According to Anderson (2010) there is a range of different approaches that may be appropriate to the development of management capability, and these include:

- Management development or management training programmes either 'in-house' or through the use of an external provider, undertaken on-site or off-site or through some form of e-learning or blended learning.

- Work-based learning methods, such as coaching, counselling, mentoring, action learning, project working and secondments.
- Organisational systems such as performance and development reviews, development centres, career planning workshops, 360-degree feedback and succession planning.
- Education and training processes, including formal courses, educational programmes, outdoor development and so on.

Mumford and Gold (2004) point out that delivering management interventions to enhance strategic capability needs a four-staged process which comprises:

1. Unplanned experiential management development – where there is the assumption that managers will 'emerge' from experience.
2. Unplanned reactive management development – where interventions occur in response to immediate pressures or problems.
3. Planned management development – where some structures, procedures and provision for management training and development are introduced.
4. Planned strategic management development – focusing on longer-term issues and identifying and developing key management capabilities or competencies.

Management development is an essential ingredient of FLM success. How effective is the management development of Police Sergeants in the case study research that follows?

Handcuffed? An investigation into the role and effectiveness of Police Sergeants within a performance management framework – case study research

The role of the Police Sergeant

This investigation is set within Hampshire Constabulary, a Home Office Police Force of around 7,000 employees – 40 per cent civilian staff and 60 per cent Police Officers. The Constabulary is organised into Operational Command Units (OCUs), and each OCU has a degree of autonomy in terms of its management, priorities and resourcing decisions, contributing to wider Force level objectives set by the Chief Constable in conjunction with the Police Authority. The role of the Sergeant as the Police Services' Front Line Manager is critical to the success of the organisation.

The Sergeant is the first line of supervision for all Police Constables, effectively an FLM responsible for managing Constable performance, and will generally supervise a team of 8–16 Constables – a front-line manager for front-line policing. An initial work placement upon promotion, or 'posting', will attempt to ensure the Officer is close to home, normally as a Targeted Patrol Team (TPT) Sergeant. These teams complete 24-hour shift patterns, responding to both emergency and non-emergency requests from the public and completing general patrol duties, essentially in a reactive, spontaneous manner. Her Majesty's Inspectorate of Constabulary (HMIC) described the

TPT Sergeants' role as 'vital to ensure the quality of service delivery' (2008: 27). Examples of a TPT Sergeant's daily work include briefing their team before they start work, managing emergency situations, focusing their team on performance objectives passed to them by senior managers, ensuring that various performance measurement systems are completed, delivering appraisals and managing team as well as individual welfare needs. The TPT Sergeant's role contains a significant proportion of those new to the rank, and therefore new to supervisory responsibility. Hampshire Constabulary has a high proportion – over 50 per cent – of Sergeants with less than 2 years' service in the rank, suggesting that relatively inexperienced Sergeants have a disproportionate influence on front-line policing delivery.

Police competencies

Competencies commonly used in the selection of Police Officers in the UK are:

- Effective Communication – Communicates needs, instructions and decisions clearly. Adapts the style of communication to meet the needs of the audience.
- Community and Customer Focus – Sees things from another's point of view and encourages others to do the same. Builds good understanding and relationships with the community that is served.
- Personal Responsibility – Takes responsibility for one's own actions and for sorting out issues or problems that arise.
- Resilience – Remains calm and confident, and responds logically and decisively in difficult situations.
- Problem-solving – Gathers information from a range of sources to understand situations, whilst ensuring the information is reliable and accurate. Identifies risks and considers alternative courses of action to make good decisions.
- Respect for Diversity – Understands other people's views and takes them into account. Treats people with dignity and respect at all times, no matter what their background, social circumstances or appearance.
- Teamwork – Works effectively as part of a team and helps build relationships

Whilst competencies commonly used in the selection of Sergeants in the UK are:

1. *Effective Communication*: Communicates ideas and information effectively, both verbally and in writing. Uses language and a style of communication that is appropriate to the situation and the people being addressed. Makes sure that others understand what is going on. Communicates all needs, instructions and decisions clearly. Adapts the style of communication to meet the needs of the audience. Checks for understanding.

2. *Maximising Potential:* Actively encourages and supports the development of people. Motivates others to achieve organisational goals. Encourages others to learn and develop, giving them clear and direct guidance and feedback on their performance. Encourages and supports staff, making sure they are motivated to achieve results.

3. *Problem-Solving:* Gathers information from a range of sources. Analyses information to identify problems and issues, and makes effective decisions. Gathers information from a range of sources to understand situations, making sure it is reliable and accurate. Analyses information to identify important issues and problems. Identifies risks and considers alternative courses of action to make good decisions.

4. *Planning and Organising:* Plans, organises and supervises activities to make sure resources are used efficiently and effectively to achieve organisational goals. Plans and carries out activities in an orderly and well-structured way. Prioritises tasks, uses time in the best possible way and works within appropriate policy and procedures.

5. *Community and Customer Focus:* Focuses on the customer and provides a high-quality service that is tailored to meet their individual needs. Understands the communities that are served and shows an active commitment to policing that reflects their needs and concerns. Sees things from the customer's point of view and encourages others to do the same. Builds a good understanding and relationship with the community that is served.

6. *Respect for Race and Diversity:* Considers and shows respect for the opinions, circumstances and feelings of colleagues and members of the public, no matter what their race, religion, position, background, circumstances, status or appearance. Understands other people's views and takes them into account. Is tactful and diplomatic when dealing with people, treating them with dignity and respect at all times. Understands and is sensitive to social, cultural and racial differences.

7. *Resilience:* Shows resilience, even in difficult circumstances. Prepared to make difficult decisions and has the confidence to see them through. Shows reliability and resilience in difficult circumstances. Remains calm and confident, and responds logically and decisively in difficult situations.

The National Police Improvement Agency (NPIA), which has a remit to improve public safety through providing critical national services, building capability across the police service and providing professional expertise to police forces and authorities, has identified an alternative set of Sergeant competencies as a Level 4 Certificate in Police First Line Management:

- Conduct intelligence-driven briefing, tasking and debriefing,
- Prepare for, monitor and maintain law-enforcement operations,
- Set objectives and provide support for team members – provide team leadership,
- Manage personal development and manage own resources,
- Supervise investigations and investigators,
- Supervise and respond to critical incidents.

Whilst performance management is implicit in both sets of Police Sergeant competencies, the critical role of the FLM in performance management perhaps warrants a higher profile, both in terms of selection for the role and also subsequent management development.

The research focus

The HMIC published a thematic inspection of the Sergeant rank and one of its conclusions was that 'the necessary capability and confidence are not being acquired, nor adequate training provided, in order for frontline sergeants to be as effective in their role as they could, and indeed should, be. There is an urgent need to re-examine processes for preparing front-line sergeants for the role, and for the significant responsibility it carries' (2008: 186). Included amongst its 27 recommendations were the following:

- Police authorities must work together with chief officers to ensure that strategic organisational objectives are effectively translated into frontline delivery activity.

- Forces should review the Personal Development Review process and ensure an appropriate balance between performance measurement and developmental activity.

- Forces need to develop a culture that enables front-line Sergeants to exercise discretion, professional judgement, risk management and intrusive supervision in support of service delivery and adherence to standards of professionalism.

In the context of these recommendations, the case study research in Hampshire Constabulary critically examined three key issues:

1. The selection process for this role,
2. The perceived organisational barriers to achieving greater performance,
3. The value of the current performance management system.

Two research methods were used. First an analysis of 12 interview records of successful Sergeant candidates and second a series of 12 semi-structured interviews with recently promoted Sergeants. The Sergeant, as the organisation's FLM, has a critical performance management function. Importantly the organisation, along with every other UK Police Force, operates a single point of entry at Police Constable rank. The organisation uses competency-based criteria to select new Officers, and appoints using Constable competencies only, which do **not** examine future managerial potential. Upon appointment, a Constable serves a 2-year probationary period before being confirmed, once all training has been completed successfully. A Constable interested in promotion is required to pass a law exam, and later a practical, scenario-based exam. The final stages in the promotion process are the completion of an application form and an interview panel, each consisting of competency-based assessment methods. The promotion interview, held internally in each Police Force, consists of a series of questions, which are aligned to a set of competencies deemed appropriate to the Sergeant's role profile. Each interview consists of up to nine questions, and the panel of three interviewers records the evidence, scores the evidence using a scale from one to five and uses a series of agreed measures to evaluate a candidate's success, or otherwise. At the competency-based interview candidates are expected to relate their past experiences and include some background understanding as well as context to the competency under examination.

The research findings

The competency-based interview appears to offer little in terms of a robust investigation of an individual's ability to manage Constable performance. Examples offered by candidates were devoid of any meaningful, sustained performance management ability. Two separate interviewer panels in this sample awarded higher scores only when extreme examples of disciplinary action were related, which may be attributed to 'fortunate' chance, rather than to a candidate's ability to effectively deal with day-to-day performance improvement.

The selection process appears to simply replace those who leave rather than use a multi-faceted succession planning approach to talent management. Such an approach would 'consider the future needs of the organisation, the strategic intent of the senior managers, and a proactive identification' of those that Guinn (2000: 392) describes as 'unexpected jewels'.

The negative impact of the initial FLM experience on interviewees was a consistent feature of this research. In many cases respondents did not feel adequately prepared for FLM responsibility. The implications of this experience are potentially twofold, a harmful alteration to the psychological contract and operational inefficiency. These implications may be a necessary part of an individual's advancement and transition into a managerial role, but there is a gap between the FLM training needs and the training delivered.

The research identified that proactive senior management support of performance management had a significantly beneficial effect on FLM confidence and competence. This support placed more pressure on the Sergeants to perform more consistently and in line with senior management's intentions. However the supported interviewees reported a much more positive experience when they were more aware of which areas of work they should be concentrating their efforts on and of how closely they were meeting their objectives. The appraisal process in the organisation was described as being separate from day-to-day performance management, and Sergeants had few options to reward superior performance.

Selection interviews did not appear to be achieving a thorough examination of a candidate's ability to manage performance, and as a result FLMs were unprepared for the demands they faced. Insufficient training and development inputs from the organisation exacerbated this. The selection process, as with the appraisal process, seemed to exist as a detached feature of the organisation's talent management process. It is clear that insufficient authority was given to the notion that performance management is a continuous and linked cycle, containing the organisational aims, the development and measurement of objectives as well as feedback and support. As it currently stands, the performance management activity within this organisation includes a number of significant 'gaps between management intentions and perceived management actions' which may be having a damaging effect on performance outcomes (Boxall and Macky, 2007: 261).

Recommendations

Selection: The competency-based interview is designed to evaluate past behaviour and its relationship to future behaviour, working on the assumption that 'behaviour patterns are consistent over time' (Pilbeam and Corbridge, 2006:

182). Consequently the selection process demands evidence of supervisory behaviour from interviewees who may have had little exposure to actual supervision. To improve the face validity and predictive validity of this method, the role of 'Acting Sergeant' should be resourced in a more controlled manner, distributing potential promotion candidates in supervisory situations where they can exercise and develop managerial potential, in preparation for an eventual interview. The Acting Sergeant role can become part of the selection process.

Performance management: The more positive interviewees indicated that they were given visible support from Senior Officers in terms of objective-setting and enforcement activity. Such support should be considered part of the organisation's performance management strategy, and suitable individuals selected and trained for this 'performance champion' role. The performance measurement regime suffers from a significant lack of credibility. The measures chosen should be established in a fair and equitable manner, be consistently applied across the whole organisation and be subject to qualitative monitoring. Some targets should be applied on a team level, rather than on an individual level. There is also a disconnection in the organisation between the appraisal, performance information and promotion opportunities. An integration programme that links performance information to the appraisal and the appraisal to promotion and development should be considered. The recommendations essentially call for a more mature performance management process.

Management development: The role of the Police Sergeant lacks investment in learning and development. The organisation should complete a training-needs analysis to ensure that future generations of FLMs are more prepared for the role that they face. Interviewees expressed preferences for a mentor scheme, a period of overlap between incoming and outgoing Sergeants and an Action Plan set by the interview panel indicating what steps they should take between the interview and placement to be more prepared for the role. The role of the Targeted Patrol Team Sergeant brings a high level of uncertainty and pressure. Other FLM positions, for example the Neighbourhood Sergeant, arguably have more structure, less uncertainty and lower levels of stress. The organisation should consider introducing FLMs into positions other than that of the TPT Sergeant, so allowing their initial training and development to be undertaken in a more controlled environment. To establish a new initial postings policy will upset the current informal hierarchy in Sergeants' roles, but will contribute to wider efforts to improve the internal perception of front-line response teams. By offering suitable pay and reward incentives allied to such a change the suggestion may bring with it significant benefits.

Activities and discussion questions

1. Identify why the FLM role is so important to the effective delivery of the Police Service and evaluate the recommendations in this case study research. How effective are Sergeants at completing the performance

management cycle based on the information in the case, and what needs to improve?

2. The Police Service has a single point of entry at Police Officer level, but the competencies required for being a Sergeant are not assessed at this stage. It would appear that whether there are enough candidates with the potential for Sergeant is down to chance. Discuss to what extent Sergeant potential and competencies should be identified at the initial recruitment stage for Police Constables as part of a talent management strategy.

3. Suggest a Management Development programme for potential Police Sergeants. What would be the features of the programme and how would effectiveness, including return on investment, be measured?

4. Some would say that it is time for the Police Service, as part of a talent management strategy, to recruit directly to the role of Police Sergeants from those with private sector managerial experience. Candidates would undertake an accelerated development programme to be appointed as Sergeant after two years. What competencies should be used in the recruitment of these accelerated trainees and what should be the structure and content of a two-year programme?

5. In terms of your own organisation, critically evaluate:

   ▪ The extent to which FLMs perform a critical organisational role,
   ▪ The competencies to be used in the selection process and how these should be assessed,
   ▪ The extent to which FLMs effectively undertake features of the performance management cycle illustrated in Figure 5.1.
   ▪ The current Management Development programme and propose an improved FLM Management Development programme incorporating both 'manager training' and 'manager development' (see Management Development section above).

Bibliography

Amanto, M. (2011). *How To Select Your Management Development Model*. http://managementdevelopment.com/management-development-model/ (electronic version).

Anderson, V. (2007). *The Value of Learning: From Return on Investment to Return on Expectation*. London: CIPD.

Anderson, V. (2010). 'Human Resource Development (Chapter 12)', in Pilbeam, S. and Corbridge, M. (eds), *People Resourcing and Talent Planning*. Harlow: Financial Times Prentice Hall.

Armstrong, M. (2006). *Handbook of Performance Management*. London: Kogan Page.

Armstrong, M. and Baron, A. (2004). *Managing Performance*. London: CIPD.

Boxall, P. and Macky, K. (2007). 'High performance work systems and organisational performance: theory and practice'. *Asia Pacific Journal of Human Resources*, 45, 261–70.

Business Link (2011). *Guide to Supporting Front Line Managers*. www.businesslink.gov.uk (electronic version).

Coaching and Mentoring. (2010). *Factsheet*. London: CIPD. http://www.cipd.co.uk/hr-resources/factsheets/coaching-mentoring.aspx

Competence and Competency Frameworks (2011). *Factsheet*. London: CIPD.

Guinn, S. L. (2000). 'Succession planning without job titles'. *Career Development International*, 5 (7), 390–3.

Hall, D. (2009). 'Performance Management', in Gilmore, S. and Williams, S. (eds), *Human Resource Management*. Oxford: OUP, Chapter 7.

Harrison, R. (2009). *Learning and Development*. London: CIPD.

Her Majesty's Inspectorate of Constabulary (2008). *Leading from the Frontline*. http://inspectorates.homeoffice.gov.uk/hmic/inspections/thematic/Frontline/ (electronic version).

Horton, S. (2009). 'Human Resource Management in the Public Sector', in Bovaird, T. and Loffler, E. (eds), *Public Management and Governance* (2nd edn.). London: Routledge.

Horton, S. (2010). 'Competencies in People Resourcing (Chapter 3)', in Pilbeam, S. and Corbridge, M. (eds), *People Resourcing and Talent Planning*. Harlow: Financial Times Prentice Hall.

Hutchinson, S. and Purcell, J. (2003). 'Bringing policies to life: the vital role of front line managers in people management'. *Executive Briefing*. London: CIPD. http://www.cipd.co.uk/Bookstore/_catalogue/CorporateAndHRStrategy/1843980533.htm

Hutchinson, S. and Purcell, J. (2007). *Line Managers in Reward, Learning and Development*. London: CIPD.

Learning and Development Survey (2010). London: CIPD. http://www.cipd.co.uk/hr-resources/survey-reports/learning-talent-development-2010.aspx

Management Development (2010). *Factsheet*. London: CIPD. http://www.cipd.co.uk/hr-resources/factsheets/management-development.aspx

Mumford, A. and Gold, J. (2004). *Management Development: Strategies for Action*. London: CIPD.

Performance Management in Action: Current Trends and Practice (2009). *Survey Report*. London: CIPD. http://www.cipd.co.uk/hr-resources/survey-reports/performance-management-trends-practice.aspx

Performance Management: An Overview (2011). *Factsheet*. London: CIPD. http://www.cipd.co.uk/hr-resources/factsheets/performance-management-overview.aspx

Pilbeam, S. and Corbridge, M. (2006). *People Resourcing: Contemporary HRM in Practice*. Harlow: Financial Times Prentice Hall.

Pilbeam, S. and Corbridge, M. (2010). *People Resourcing and Talent Planning: HRM in Practice*. Harlow: Financial Times Prentice Hall.

CHAPTER 6

Violation of the Psychological Contract in Employment

Causes and consequences

Stephen Pilbeam and Roger Metcalfe

Defining the psychological contract

The psychological contract is a term used to describe a perceived implicit and reciprocal exchange between the employer and the employee. It is a management tool that can identify complex variables and potentially forecast employee behaviour. The psychological contract concept provides employers with a means of interpreting the state of employment relations and of mapping significant changes in the individual employment relationship. According to Rousseau (1989), a prominent researcher in the field, the psychological contract refers to an individual's beliefs regarding the terms and conditions of a reciprocal exchange agreement between the focal person and another party. In relation to employment, Guest and Conway (2002) suggest that it consists of the perceptions of both parties about the reciprocal promises and obligations implied in the employment relationship. Psychological contracts in employment are therefore the belief systems of individual employees and employers regarding their mutual obligations. These obligations emerge from the promises made as employment arrangements are started and sustained, from the recruitment process through socialisation and continuing during performance management processes. McClean-Parks, Kidder and Gallagher (1998: 698) define the psychological contract between the employer and the employee in terms of 'the idiosyncratic set of reciprocal obligations held by employees concerning their obligations (i.e. what they will do for the employer) and their entitlements (i.e. what they expect in return)'. The psychological contract is important in strategic people management. It specifies how an employee 'defines the deal', whether or not the employee feels that 'the deal' has been honoured or violated and ultimately influences how well the organisation performs.

According to the CIPD Factsheet (2010) the psychological contract may have implications for strategy in a number of areas.

Process fairness: People want to know that their interests will be taken into account when important decisions are made, they would like to be treated with respect and they are more likely to be satisfied with their job if they are consulted about change.

Communications: An effective two-way dialogue between employer and employees is a necessary means of giving expression to employee 'voice'.

Management style: In many organisations managers can no longer control the business 'top down' – they have to adopt a more 'bottom up' style. Crucial information, which management needs, is known by employees through their interactions with customers and suppliers.

Managing expectations: Employers need to make clear to new recruits what they can expect from the job. Managing expectations, particularly when bad news is anticipated, will increase the chances of establishing a realistic psychological contract.

Measuring employee attitudes: Employers should monitor employee attitudes on a regular basis as a means of identifying where action may be needed in order to improve performance.

Breach of the psychological contract can seriously damage the employment relationship. It is not always possible to avoid a breach but damage is less likely if managers are open with employees about the issues that need to be addressed.

Content of the psychological contract

It can be seen from the definitions that the psychological contract is promissory, implicit, reciprocal, perceptual and consists of expectations (George, 2009). It is promissory because it can be defined in terms of promises made during the recruitment process and during employment. It is implicit because it is largely unwritten and unspoken and often only recognised when it is violated. It is reciprocal because it is embedded in beliefs about mutual expectations and obligations within the employer/employee relationship. It is perceptual because the psychological contract is formulated in the minds of the individual employees and is fundamentally psychological in nature, being based on perceived promises to which the employer has not necessarily agreed. And, it consists of series of mutual expectations and needs arising from employment. If both employer and employee live up to the psychological contract, there are potential benefits for both parties. The psychological contract is individual and dynamic, and therefore subject to change over time. It is, however, possible to check out the state of psychological contracts and aggregate the results to identify trends, particularly when a breach or violation of the contract occurs.

Guest (1998) outlines a basic theoretical model that identifies three linked categories in order to better understand the impact of the psychological contract (Figure 6.1). He cites various factors as 'causes' of the psychological contract, which include HR practices and culture, and outlines the psychological contract's

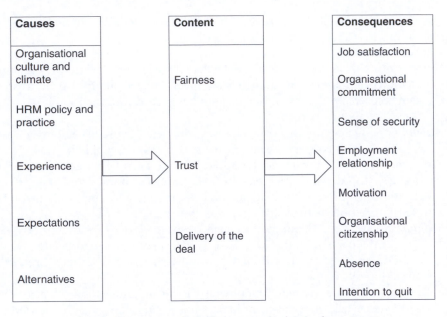

Causes	Content	Consequences
Organisational culture and climate	Fairness	Job satisfaction
		Organisational commitment
HRM policy and practice		Sense of security
		Employment relationship
Experience	Trust	
		Motivation
Expectations		Organisational citizenship
	Delivery of the deal	
		Absence
Alternatives		Intention to quit

Figure 6.1   A model of the psychological contract
Source: With the kind permission of David Guest (1998)

content as trust, fairness and delivery of the deal, with 'consequences' potentially impacting on employee behaviours, attitudes and relationships.

Types of psychological contract

Psychological contracts are often described as being either relational or transactional. Relational contracts are characterised by a high degree of social exchange and inter-dependence between employers and employees.

Relational contracts are viewed as highly mutually dependent employee–employer relationships and focus upon investment by both parties in organisation-specific skills development, long-term career planning and training. Whilst transactional contracts tend to be characterised by 'what's in it for me', and remain in place only as long as it suits the parties. Transactional contracts therefore focus more on short-term and financial-based transactions, with little emotional attachment by the employee, who can easily exit. Rousseau (1995) adds two further hybrid subsets, namely balanced and transitional relationships that appear to provide more depth to the typologies. The existence of relational or transactional psychological contracts was supported in the focus group-based research by Millward and Hopkins (1998) that devised scales to assess the psychological contract in four UK multinationals. This research suggested that employees constantly reassess their psychological contracts along the transactional to relational continuum. The relational scale was strongly correlated to permanent contracts and high commitment and the transactional was strongly correlated to temporary work arrangements and lower commitment. The psychological contract is therefore dynamic, but unlikely to be solely transactional or relational in their purest forms. Coyle-Shapiro and Kessler (2000) also suggest that employees may harbour both transactional and relational aspects within their psychological contracts and therefore a psychological contract may develop as a hybrid of relational and transactional elements.

Formation of the psychological contract

According to Rousseau (2001) there exist different phases of contract formation, depending on the stage of the employment relationship. Pre-employment perceptions generate beliefs about the organisation, and active promise exchange takes place during recruitment. The early socialisation and orientation process develops the exchange of promises, whilst later work experiences are characterised by intermittent promise exchange and the evaluation of the state of play, together with an examination of the costs and consequences of any changes generated by the internal and external environments.

Violation of the psychological contract and employee responses

Much psychological contract research has focused on employee reactions to unfulfilled promises. This is explained partly by the fact that as an influence on behaviour, the psychological contract often only becomes important when it becomes salient, that is to say broken, breached or violated in some way. A violation is therefore the failure of one party to adequately fulfil the 'promised' obligations. Perhaps training or promotion or rewards or recognition or workload adjustments or job security have been expected by the employee, but not received. This involves a mental calculation by the individual employee of what is received in relation to what was 'promised'. Violation can involve feelings of betrayal, anger, anxiety, resentment and injustice and this may provoke negative reactions to the detriment of the employment relationship. As well as emotional responses, there may be associated attitudinal changes, for example unresponsiveness to change or to requests for flexibility, and behavioural changes at work such as decreased energy or diminution in the exercise of discretionary effort, retaliation, voicing displeasure, neglect or a reduction in intention to remain with the organisation.

Insights provided by the psychological contract concept

The following case uses these dimensions to generate insights:

- Job security,
- Career development,
- Performance and reward,
- Fairness and trust,
- Loyalty,
- Work–life balance.

Job security

Herriot and Pemberton's (1995) seminal article on 'the old and new deal' placed significant emphasis on the removal of job security from employment relationships, which previously formed an exchange for ongoing employee loyalty. Global job insecurity in employees remains high due to the volatility of markets, cost pressures, competition for products and the need to provide shareholder returns. Perhaps single career jobs are dead and as a consequence employees need to manage their own careers and skill sets. Tsui, Pearce, Porter and Tripoli (1997) suggested that an employee–employer mutual investment strategy, involving a degree of employment security, engenders long-term employee commitment and stronger performance. It is acknowledged by the authors, perhaps ironically, that an 'under investment model' exists due to competitive pressures. This is a logical finding, but one that could be challenged by the new breed of employees who may be more comfortable with a lack of job security, provided other areas, such as skills development through work assignments, are available. Additionally not all employees have always enjoyed job security, which is sometimes ignored in the 'old and new deal' debate.

Career development

A common psychological contract violation involves unfulfilled development opportunities. Atkinson (2002) proved a hypothesis that failure to implement a career management strategy led to negative implications for employee motivation within the psychological contract. This qualitative research targeted a small sample, but is indicative of the need for employers to communicate changes in strategy and gain acceptance to the changes. Baruch (2001) explores the notion of 'employability' as part of a potential solution to balance the 'new employment deal', where the employer invests in the employee's development to help maintain their external marketability, whilst at the same time securing their services and discretionary effort. The design of challenging work that provides career development, recognition and skills development through stretch assignments is often crucial to the psychological contract, and achieving high levels of innovation.

Performance and reward

Observing the importance of performance to the health of the psychological contract, Stiles, Gratton, Truss, Hope-Hailey and McGovern (1997) suggest that 'performance management processes play a key role in creating the framework in which the psychological contract is determined'. They define performance management as including objective setting, performance assessment and linked reward. Their case study research concludes that top-down implementation and lack of consultation in relation to performance management processes results in negative employee reaction. The performance appraisal, reward decisions and also the recruitment and selection process are key interventions in psychological contract creation and change.

Fairness, trust and loyalty

The employee and the employer must feel that the deal is a fair exchange to achieve an effective outcome. Trust between individuals and groups in an organisation is key to long-term stability and mediates the relationship between contract breach and value-add to the organisation. Morrison and Robinson (1997) link high trust by employees in the organisation with a greater tolerance to a breach and unmet promises. As Figure 6.1 indicates, fairness and trust are viewed by Guest (1998) as a key integrative concept of the psychological contract and fundamental to its content. Guest views trust from the perspective of management looking after employees' interests and fairness with respect to mutually met promises and commitments. These findings indicate a link between high trust and fairness perceptions on the one hand, and with positive employee behaviours on the other. This is potentially beneficial to employers and employees, particularly where relational aspects of the psychological contract are part of the deal. Loyalty is a prime responsibility of the employee in exchange for security, under the 'old deal'. King (2000: 80) argues that loyalty is 'at the centre of the traditional white-collar employment relationship', and suggests a strong link between worker insecurity and lack of loyalty to the organisation. Loyalty to the organisation is viewed by many to be the first casualty of psychological contract violation. The challenge is therefore to retain sufficient employee loyalty to achieve the organisations goals.

Work–life balance

This is an area that is receiving significant attention due to the increasingly competitive business world, changing personal desires and degree of environmental change. Even back in 2001, Guest and Conway (2001: 1) had identified a growing trend of stress in the workplace and suggested that HR has a key role in managing this issue because employees continue to view a safe and healthy working environment as a key employer obligation. Research by Smithson and Lewis (2000), on the effect of job insecurity on the psychological contract of young workers, highlighted a dominant transactional psychological contract where a short-term commitment and balanced lives contract prevailed; the employee aim being that of achieving a work–life balance in exchange for reduced job security.

In summary, the psychological contract is a concept that potentially provides insights into the employment relationship and employee behaviour at work. It is a lens through which the employment relationship can be viewed and assessed, but some form of measurement is necessary. Violations of the psychological contract of front-line managers, and the implications, are explored in the case study that follows.

The violation of the psychological contract and the implications for employers – a case study in the IT sector

In addition to the economic contract (payment for work) and the legal contract (the express and implied terms and conditions of employment), it can be useful for managers to assess the state of the psychological contract to establish the health of the employment relationship and the extent to which employees are committed to exercising discretionary effort in pursuit of corporate objectives. The work of Rousseau (1989, 1995, 2001) energised the development of the concept and provided a trigger for interest in forms of the psychological contract, violations and practical applications in the workplace. The Guest and Conway (2001) definition of the psychological contract is relevant to this case study, that it is 'the perceptions of both parties to the employment relationship, the organisation and individual, of the reciprocal promises and obligations implied in that relationship'. The psychological contract therefore involves a process of giving and receiving by the individual employee and the employing organisation, but is no more than a conceptual framework for identifying the perceived, and normally unwritten, expectations and obligations that exist between employers and employees. Employee expectations of employers may include the provision of a safe working environment, reasonable job security, interesting work, rewards commensurate with contribution and being treated with respect, whilst employer expectations of the employee might include an adherence to rules, identification with corporate goals and culture, working diligently, demonstrating loyalty and working harmoniously with colleagues and customers. Clearly where there is mutuality in these expectations a healthy psychological contract can be said to exist, but where there is a difference between employee expectations and the delivery of the deal by employers the psychological contract can be perceived as being violated, and this will be detrimental to the employment relationship and to the employing organisation. The psychological contract is dynamic in nature, and also personal to the individual, but collective effects of changes on the psychological contract can occur and be measured.

The case study organisation

The organisation studied employed 1,000 highly skilled people in the UK within the IT sector. The declared HR objectives included attracting, retaining and motivating the best talent through the maintenance of the currency of skills to achieve outstanding performance and commitment, but there were several influences on the state of the psychological contract and these included:

- Many employees transferred in from another global company under a purchase agreement and the employee benefits of these 'legacy employees' had been considerably diluted.
- Cost-cutting strategies had been introduced, including a significant reduction in the training budget.
- New product markets had been entered, necessitating new ways of working.
- Investment in new business opportunities had met with limited success and compulsory redundancies had been declared for the first time.

The research and the findings

The research focused on managers' perceptions of the state of their psychological contract. A 20 per cent sample was interviewed and, with their informed consent, their frames of reference were infiltrated. The following dimensions of the psychological contract were explored:

- Job security,
- Career development opportunities,
- Performance and reward,
- Fairness, trust and loyalty,
- Work–life balance.

All was not well with the psychological contract, as is evident from the illustrative respondent quotes below. Pre-existing expectations included job security, skills and career development, market-competitive financial rewards, a high-trust work environment and work–life balance opportunities.

> I think at this point in time, the company is offering me the job security in proportion to the contracts that it can desperately find, nothing more than that. I don't feel that I've got any job security.

> The feeling of insecurity and potential vulnerability once you've been through a redundancy hit is marked. The redundancies shocked everyone, as they were simply not needed.

A violation of the deal on job security had significantly reduced the degree of loyalty to the company and its goals. In addition the employer 'promise' of providing employability through skills development had not been delivered. This resulted in a serious psychological contract consequence:

> Training is a big part of the psychological contract at recruitment but training now has a zero budget. It's a joke, I feel cheated. Actions don't match words.

> Training and development are part of the deal and good in the past, but there is less scope now as the deal is changing. I feel dropped into roles now without training, you either sink or swim.

The strong performance culture in times of downsizing had created tensions that impacted on work–life balance. There was a fear of being managed out of the business if the manager was perceived as not totally committed to performance goals or not working long hours.

> Weekend working is expected and not even appreciated, personal lives are torn apart. Volumes are killing me and my manager is not helping me. I'm grossly over worked.

The senior managers were not demonstrating the skills and competencies required to manage the psychological contract, creating further tensions and damaging negative responses.

> The psychological contract is heavily influenced by my manager. He makes or breaks it, but he doesn't understand the psychological contract or even its principles, so it's lost on him.

The negative consequences of a violated psychological contract and the implications for management action

A key finding was that perceptions of a violated psychological contract result in damaging employee behaviours which include, but are not limited to, covert job search, withdrawn creativity, a lack of confidence in recommending the company as a good employer, working to rule and a desire not to challenge the *status quo*.

> Negative impacts of the deal don't lead to a formal work to rule attitude but I just don't contribute ideas or say much. No loyalty is delivered to me now. Things have changed, I would go if a better job came along.

> Pension betrayal has meant I work less hard and aim to keep within 48 hours. As my pension has fallen, I will work more years and thus need to pace myself better.

It is evident that if analysis of the psychological contract is to be used to engender a healthy employment relationship, then high levels of management focus need to include:

1. A commitment to explore the desired future state of the psychological contract, with emphasis upon enhancing mutual trust, loyalty and commitment,
2. An assessment of managers' capabilities as leaders and coaches and action to close any skill gap,
3. A review of the total reward 'value proposition',
4. A clear articulation and dissemination of the company values and receptiveness to employee voice.

This diagnostic activity can then lead to the development of focused HR interventions and practices.

This case study research highlights the significance of a healthy psychological contract to a business that seeks to leverage its talent. The message is clear – violate the psychological contract and pay the price of reduced employee performance and a haemorrhage of your best people. However the psychological contract is only a conceptual tool – it is diagnosis and action by management that will make the difference. How healthy is the psychological contract in your organisation?

Activities and discussion questions

1. Create a psychological contract by constructing a list of things that you expect from your employer and a list of things your employer expects

from you, and discuss the extent to which the lists are similar. Using the lists created analyse the degree to which your psychological contract is balanced and healthy.

2. What advice would you give to managers about using the psychological contract to garner insights into the health of the employment relationship?

3. What violations took place in the case above and what were the implications?

4. Explore the implications and consequences of psychological contract violation for the employment relationship in organisations in general in the current economic climate.

5. Identify HR practices that can contribute to the formation, development and maintenance of a good psychological contract.

Bibliography

Atkinson, C. (2002). 'Career management and the changing psychological contract'. *Career Development International*, 7 (1), 14–23.

Baruch, Y. (2001). 'Employability: a substitute for loyalty?'. *Human Resource Development International*, 4 (4), 543–66.

Cappelli, P. (1999). 'Career jobs are dead'. *California Management Review*, 42 (1), 146–67.

Conway, N. and Briner, R. (2005). *Understanding Psychological Contracts at Work: A Critical Evaluation of Theory and Research*. Oxford: Oxford University Press.

Coyle-Shapiro, J. and Kessler, I. (2000). 'Consequences of the psychological contract for employment: a large scale survey'. *Journal of Management Studies*, 37 (7), 903–30.

Coyle-Shapiro, J. and Shore, L. M. (2007). 'The employee–organization relationship: where do we go from here?'. *Human Resource Management Review*, 17 (2), 166–79.

Cullinane, N. and Dundon, T. (2006). 'The psychological contract: a critical review'. *International Journal of Management Reviews*, 8 (2), 113–29.

George, C. (2009). *The Psychological Contract*. Maidenhead: Oxford University Press.

Guest, D. E. (1998). 'Is the psychological contract worth taking seriously?'. *Journal of Organizational Behavior*, 19, 649–64.

Guest, D. E. and Conway, N. (2001). *Employer Perceptions of the Psychological Contract*. London: Chartered Institute of Personnel and Development.

Guest, D. E. and Conway, N. (2002). 'Communicating the psychological contract: an employer perspective'. *Human Resource Management Journal*, 12 (2), 22–38.

Herriot, P., Manning, W. and Kidd, J. (1997). 'The content of the psychological contract'. *British Journal of Management*, 8, 151–62.

Herriot, P. and Pemberton, C. (1995). *New Deals: The Revolution in Management Careers*. Chichester: Wiley.

King, J. E. (2000). 'White-collar reactions to job insecurity and the role of the psychological contract: Implications for HRM'. *Human Resource Management*, 39 (1), 79–82.

Maguire, H. (2002). 'Psychological contracts: are they still relevant?'. *Career Development International*, 7 (3), 167–80.

McClean-Parks, J., Kidder, D. L. and Gallagher, D. G. (1998). 'Fitting square pegs into round holes: mapping the domain of contingent work arrangements onto the psychological contract'. *Journal of Organizational Behavior*, 19, 697–730.

Millward, L. J. and Hopkins, L. J. (1998). 'Psychological contracts, organizational and job commitment'. *Journal of Applied Social Psychology*, 28 (16), 1530–56.

Morrison, E. W. and Robinson, S. L. (1997). 'When employees feel betrayed a model of how psychological contract violation occurs'. *Academy of Management Review*, 22 (1), 226–56.

Psychological Contract Factsheet (2010). London: CIPD. http://www.cipd.co.uk/hr-resources/factsheets/psychological-contract.aspx

Roehling, M. V. (1997). 'The origins and early development of the psychological contract'. *Journal of Management History*, 3 (2), 204–17.

Rousseau, D. M. (1989). 'Psychological and implied contracts in organizations'. *Employee Rights and Responsibilities Journal*, 2 (2), 121–39.

Rousseau, D. M. (1990). 'New hire perceptions of their own and their employer's obligations – a study of psychological contracts'. *Journal of Organizational Behavior*, 11, 389–400.

Rousseau, D. M. (1995). *Psychological Contracts in Organizations, Understanding Written and Unwritten Agreements*. London: Sage.

Rousseau, D. M. (2001). 'Schema, promise and mutuality: the building blocks of the psychological contract'. *Journal of Occupational and Organizational Psychology*, 74 (14), 511–31.

Rousseau, D. M. and Greller, M. M. (1994). 'Psychological contracts and human resources practices'. *Human Resource Management*, 33 (3), 385–401.

Rousseau, D. M. and Schalk, R. (2000). *Psychological Contracts in Employment: Cross National Perspectives*. London: Sage.

Smithson, J. and Lewis, S. (2000). 'Is job insecurity changing the psychological contract?'. *Personnel Review*, 29 (6), 680–702.

Sparrow, P. R. (2000). 'New employee behaviours work design and forms of work organization. What is in store for the future of work?'. *Journal of Applied Psychology*, 15 (3), 202–18.

Stiles, P., Gratton, L., Truss, C., Hope-Hailey, V. and McGovern, P. (1997). 'Performance management and the psychological contract'. *Human Resource Management Journal*, 7 (1), 57–66.

Thompson, M. and Heron, P. (2002). *Innovation and the Psychological Contract in the Knowledge Business*. Oxford: Templeton.

Truss, C., Soane, E. and Edwards, C. (2006). *Working Life: Employee Attitudes and Engagement 2006*. Research report. London: Chartered Institute of Personnel and Development.

Tsui, A. S., Pearce, J. L., Porter, L. W. and Tripoli, A. M. (1997). 'Alternative approaches to the employee–organization relationship: does investment in employees pay off?'. *Academy of Management Journal*, 40 (5), 1089–121.

Wellin, M. (2007). *Managing the Psychological Contract: Using the Personal Deal to Increase Business Performance*. Aldershot: Gower.

CHAPTER 7

Building an Effective Employer Brand

Contributing to successful resourcing

Marjorie Corbridge and Ann Brine

Competition for high-quality, high-performing employees remains a feature of the global labour market and employers continue to strive to ensure that they develop effective strategies to get the best staff and keep them. It is no longer appropriate to rely on turning to the market when a member of the staff leaves and to expect the best person to be there ready and waiting. Employers need to be proactive in examining what they have to offer to employees and potential employees and to ensure that they deliver the promise. Moroko and Uncles (2008: 160) sum this up very clearly when stating that

> Cultivating an employer brand is one method firms have chosen to secure and retain the most sought after employees; those who will enable them to perpetuate their brand success and secure ongoing profitability. Potentially, those firms that embrace employer branding will have a competitive edge. Indeed, the motivation to employ strategies to attract and retain staff has never been more pressing as financial markets are increasingly recognizing 'human capital'– or the skills, experience and knowledge of employees – as sources of value to the firm and to shareholders.

By examining the employer brand and exploring the employer value proposition and ensuring that this message is delivered clearly to the employees and potential employees, organisations are able to build these relationships effectively and increase their chance of employing the best.

The strategic value of employer branding

The Employer Brand is described by Rosethorn and Mensink (2007: 4) as 'the deal between the organization and its employees'. Most of us, as consumers, are aware of company brands, and our expectations of the quality of what we are about to purchase are framed by this brand awareness. If the quality falls short of our expectations in any way then the company brand has been compromised. To what extent can this simple proposition be extended to encompass the concept of an employer brand? What expectations are created by organisations when it comes to employment and to what extent do employees 'live the brand'? The CIPD (2009: 1) defines employer brand as 'a set of attributes and qualities – often intangible – that makes an organisation distinctive, promises a particular kind of employment experience, and appeals to those people who will thrive and perform to their best in its culture'. This definition encapsulates the feeling of the employment experience and enables a statement to be made by the organisation about 'what it is like to work here'. According to several writers (Rosethorn and Mensink, 2007; McKinsey, 2008; CIPD, 2009) the war for talent as coined by McKinsey in 1997 and cited in Michaels, Handfield-Jones and Axelrod (2001) is still evident despite changing economic times, and the development of a strong employer brand may be the feature that enables organisations to attract and retain the talent they need. Making a strong statement and delivering on that promise enable the organisation to compete successfully in the 'war for talent', as Guthridge, Komm and Lawson (2008) contend that 'business leaders are deeply concerned [about the availability of talent]' and 'finding talented people is likely to be the single most important managerial preoccupation for the rest of this decade'. Hence organisations need to have a clear strategy to recruit and retain the best people they can if they are to continue to be successful in an ever-changing and highly competitive global market. Moroko and Uncles (2008: 161) indicate that there is 'keen awareness of the impact of employees on business effectiveness, particularly with respect to brand strategy and management. The ongoing personal contact of employees with consumers gives them a great deal of influence over the way in which consumers view the company'.

What makes a successful employer brand?

Research conducted by Moroko and Uncles (2008: 163) identifies three features that resonate with 'consumer-focused and corporate branding theory and practice'. First, 'being known and noticeable' refers to the extent to which employees, potential employees and decision-makers in placing staff have a positive view about the organisation as an employer. Commonly potential employees will be attracted by the strong employer brand and have less concern about the particular role that might be on offer. Second, 'being seen as relevant and resonant' refers to the extent to which current employees as well as future employees relate to the employer value proposition, or the package of opportunities and benefits provided by the organisation. Unless this is perceived as having value to the employee then the employer brand will not be successful. Third, 'being differentiated from direct competitors' is seen as vital to the success of the employer brand in order to win the war for talent. The research indicates that respondents were very clear that differentiation was very important; it was usually referred to with reference to unsuccessful brands. They knew who they did not want to work for! In addition to the consumer focus in identifying a successful employer brand, Moroko and Uncles (2008: 165) identify an additional theme which relates to the organisation's ability to deliver on the promise made by the employer brand. The perceptions of potential employees could be managed effectively through fulfilment of the *psychological contract*. If a healthy psychological contract is maintained, the employee is more likely to retain employer loyalty and increased engagement with the strategic aims of the business. However if the psychological contract is compromised by the employer not delivering the promise of the employer brand then disengagement may occur with a consequential impact on labour turnover.

The employment value proposition and the employer brand

The employment value proposition can be seen as another component of the employer brand. The term employment value proposition is described by Heger (2007) as 'the value that the employee derives from his or her membership of an organisation … and it is suggested that this is a determinant of employee engagement and retention, both of which are critical business outcomes'. The development of a clear employment value proposition acts as a differentiator in the market which, as we have seen, is a critical success factor in the establishment of the employer brand. Bibb (2010) describes the benefits of an employment value proposition as including the enhancement of the organisation's appeal to different markets and to 'tough to hire groups', creating a strong 'people brand' and reducing the need for premiums for hard-to-recruit areas. She cites the situation of Apple as a 'great example of a strong and credible employment value proposition who are well known for the way in which they treat their employees and who do not need to enter the war for talent as they have excellent people queuing up to join them'. However in order to develop a meaningful employment value proposition it is necessary to have a clear picture of what is important to your employees so that the organisation knows what they value and what changes have to be made to ensure that high-performing employees are retained. A meaningful employment value proposition can be developed in several ways, but a good starting point will be the information that should be already available in the organisation. This may include an employee satisfaction survey and the data from exit interviews as well as what employees say at their regular reviews. An effective employment value proposition should include reference to and synergy with the organisation's strategic objectives, current truths as well as aspirations. It needs to reflect the corporate brand as well as the employer brand and if it is put into practice effectively it should increase employee engagement, contribute to the recruitment message and inform HR strategic priorities.

Living the brand

In order to sustain the experience of the promise of the employer brand and the health of the psychological contract it is important that employees are managed in such a way as to ensure that the employees live the brand. The development of a brand is traditionally the domain of the marketing people, who focus on the behaviour of customers, with employee engagement being the focus of HR attention. This diversification of attention may lead to a lack of fit in terms of consistency of the message. This can present new challenges to those in HR and, as cited by Maxwell and Knox (2009: 895), Henkel, Tomczak, Heitman and Herrman (2007) explain that 'it is not sufficient to focus on generic measures such as friendliness or competence; employees must be motivated to personify and deliver the brand promise and to act as ambassadors for the brand'. The challenge in achieving this is to take a multidisciplinary, cross-functional approach which in practice means that HR and marketing should be, as cited by Maxwell and Knox (2009) and described by Hulberg (2006), 'more fully integrated in order to recruit, retain and develop people who are accordant with the brand'. However there is little research which looks at the employer brand from the perspective of actual employees, those who are required to 'live the brand'. Maxwell and Knox (2009: 897) seek to identify what it is that 'makes an organisation's employer brand more or less attractive to current employees, and therefore to explain what motivates employees to live the brand when interacting with external stakeholders'. Their results show that there are four important influences on the employee: 'aspects of employment', such as style of management, type of work, work environment, employee rewards, manager–workforce relations and attributes of the workforce; 'organisational success', such as current standing, past success and future success; 'products or services', such as their attributes or values (creative, fun, inspirational); and 'construed external image', such as respect, worldwide reputation and public perception. This work highlights the importance of each organisation knowing and understanding the factors that are important to the employer brand from the perspective of current employees as it is through using this knowledge that an employer brand can be developed and maintained in such a way that it continues to reflect what it is that employees find attractive about working there.

Employer branding: look inside to add value to your business – a case study

Definition of employer branding

Often managers and business owners look only at prospective customers as the key to organisational growth, and clearly it is important to encourage managers to look at customers' wants and needs, as opposed to what the organisation can produce. Astute organisations also know that their current customers offer great potential for increasing profitability. However it is the really savvy business leader who knows that the key to longer-term growth is developing a brand, from the inside outwards, and using that brand to attract and retain employees as well as customers. A marketing function creates and develops brands, identities, logos and personalities for the organisation, yet seldom do HR and Marketing come together to develop an all-encompassing stakeholder experience inside and outside the organisation. When they do, the results are clear and measurable – the business develops a strong brand identity and with it an employer brand. Interest from the HR profession in employer branding builds on the late twentieth century concepts associated with being an 'employer of choice' and being able to compete effectively in the 'war for talent'.

These concepts highlight the importance of employers becoming proactive in both attracting and retaining staff in the context of increased competition for labour. Ruch (2002) defines employer branding as 'the company's image as seen through the eyes of its associates (employees) and potential hires and is intimately linked to the employment experience of what it is like to work at a company, including tangibles such as salary and intangibles such as company culture and values'. Employers 'living the brand' is key to developing and sustaining the employer brand and therefore employing people who are already loyal to the brand is of great importance (Martin and Beaumont, 2003).

The value of employer branding

Developing a strong brand can be a lengthy and time-consuming activity and for many organisations it also requires a large budget. Although most professional HR functions acknowledge the role of the brand, many employers outside the traditional blue chip organisations often struggle with the challenges of understanding, measuring and then positioning their employer brand and aligning it with marketing practice. For a business, whether large or small, developing a strong brand can ultimately have four effects on the market in which they operate or from which they recruit. First, a *reduction in acquisition costs* – whether it is a customer or an employee the amount of money it takes to 'capture' a target is increasingly costly to a business. Advertising production costs continue to rise and call for a high level of support and creative thinking. If the need to buy staff advertising media, or the frequency with which that media is required, can be reduced, value can be added straight to the profitability of the organisation. Second, *strong brands create relationships between consumer and producer*. For example an office worker takes a late lunch and nips out to grab a sandwich. Going into the local shop – they have sold out – 'What a waste of time', he or she declares to all their work colleagues. Meanwhile a brand-loyal consumer walks into Marks and Spencer at 3 pm looking for a smoked salmon sandwich. He or she discovers that all the sandwiches have been sold. 'Ah', the person exclaims, 'I got here too late'. Brands guarantee performance, but as the sandwich example demonstrates, brand relationships also influence the perception of that performance. Brands can also identify target groups of employees; for instance many people make decisions on working for a particular employer because they relate to their products. Third, *strong brands increase loyalty*; this can lead to increased customer and employee retention. Tony O'Reilly, as chief executive of Heinz, had the simplest definition of brand loyalty. 'A consumer walks into a supermarket looking for beans. There is every brand of beans on the shelf except Heinz. She leaves without any beans.' Strong brands are not only able to attract consumers for less, they are likely to keep them loyal for longer too. New brands such as Innocent Smoothies have managed to position themselves in the hearts of customers as well as of potential employees. Their website gives the employee experience equal prominence in comparison to the goods they sell. Fourth, *strong brands demand and receive a higher premium*. The company Intel has a small army of consumer researchers stalking the malls of the US for consumers about to buy a PC with 'Intel Inside'. These consumers are then offered a machine that is identical to their choice, except it uses an equally powerful non-Intel processor chip. How much cheaper would the non-Intel machine need to be for the consumer to put down Intel PC and take the alternative? The answer is usually between 20 per cent and 30 per cent. Like most people, PC consumers expect to pay more for the brand leader and that price premium is the final icing on the cake for manufacturers of strong brands.

Leveraging the employer brand

An organisation with a strong employer brand that leverages it appropriately can also use these same four factors to impact on the increasingly costly war for talent. With a strong employer brand the costs of employee acquisition decrease markedly. Candidates will come to larger organisations because of their knowledge of the brand. Equally small businesses can also develop their own positioning in the market. Owner managers often recognise the issues of recruitment more readily than marketing directors in large organisations. Most realise that in order to beat the competition it is not simply a case of cutting prices or improving efficiency, but developing a team under a common understanding about the organisation's vision and longer-term objectives. Becoming the 'employer of choice' can contribute to ensuring that the business attracts and subsequently retains the best available talent. Following on from the advantages within the recruitment process, there is evidence to suggest that with a strong employer brand, the relationships between employees and employer can improve significantly. The average length of employee retention may extend and overall goodwill amongst the work force is increased. In some cases organisations can attract the same calibre of employees and yet not offer comparable total reward packages to their competitors with weaker employer brands. The challenge of employer branding, across any size of business, is perhaps not to train HR professionals in marketing and branding philosophies and techniques, but rather to promote a collaboration and understanding between the two professions. In many organisations these two groups remain independent of each other, often in conflict about how the 'brand' should be represented. Organisations, whether public or private sector, that can unite these adding-value functions behind the power of the brand will be able to compete more effectively in the war for talent.

The Martin and Beaumont model

Martin and Beaumont (2003) identify the stages through which an organisation needs to progress in order for both HR and Marketing to maximise the benefit for the acquisition and retention of staff. It could also be said that the development of a strong employer brand extends right through the business – employees who clearly understand and engage with the goals and objectives of the business will potentially be brand ambassadors for the organisation. It seems logical that when all areas of a business work together, this contributes to maximum success and bottom-line profit. The Martin and Beaumont model demonstrates that progressive increases in the role of the brand in business strategy and in the perceived value of HR in the branding process enable the organisation to pass through four stages of brand development and use:

Stage 1 – Where there is a low brand role in business strategy and HR value, branding is seen as little more than a logo for particular products, services or businesses, with HR professionals playing little or no role in supporting the brand.

Stage 2 – At this stage organisations may have a master brand or logo and also place more emphasis on the vision and values behind it with HR's role being to support those individual brands.

Stage 3 – Organisations capitalise on the values and vision of a strong corporate brand to facilitate organisational change, such as bringing together units through mergers with HR supporting these developments by aligning change programmes and supporting the development of the employer brand.

Stage 4 – The corporate brand is the centrepiece of the overall strategy, with HR holding a pivotal role in facilitating employees to act as 'brand ambassadors'.

This study identifies the importance of the synergy of marketing tools and HR activities and the way in which these are fundamental to the development of a successful employer brand. It also explores the ways in which a strong brand contributes to being an employer of choice in the labour market. What is your value proposition in terms of your total rewards package? How easy is it for you to identify your organisation's brand? Is that brand recognised and 'lived' by your employees?

Activities and discussion questions

1. This study suggests that organisations should look inside themselves to add value to the business through the development of a strong Employer Brand. It also highlights the importance of a multidisciplinary, cross-functional approach to this, with HR and Marketing working together. If you were to look inside your organisation what evidence would you find of this approach? What barriers to effective multidisciplinary working might you find and how could these be overcome for the benefit of the business?

2. Examine your own organisation and identify the Employer Brand? Using the Martin and Beaumont model at what stage of the model would you assess your organisation to be and what evidence do you have for that assessment?

3. What elements feature in your employer brand and what evidence can you put forward to support your findings?

4. Identify an organisation that you would like to work for. What attracts you to that organisation? Can you describe the employer brand of that organisation?

5. Examine the differences between:

   a. an employer brand
   b. an employment/employee value proposition
   c. the psychological contract.

6. Your executive team is holding an away-day to focus on the organisational strategy for the coming year. You have been asked to lead the discussion on the Employee Brand. Prepare a briefing paper for this event which sets out the areas for discussion and the areas for decisions that should be made.

7. Prepare a presentation for your management team which sets out the case for a strong employer brand and puts forward ways to achieve it.

Bibliography

Barrow, S. and Mosely R. (2006). *The Employer Brand: Bringing the Best of Brand Management to People at Work*. Chichester: John Wiley and Sons Ltd.

Bibb, S. (2010). *Employee Value Proposition Explained*. Retrieved on 18 May 2011 from www.talentsmoothie.com

CIPD (2008). *Employer Branding: A No Nonsense Approach*. London: CIPD.

CIPD (2009). *Employer Branding: Maintaining Momentum in a Recession*. London: CIPD.

CIPD (2010). *Employer Branding and Total Reward*. London: CIPD.

Corporate Leadership Council (2006). *Attracting and Retaining Critical Talent Segments: Building a Competitive Employment Value Proposition*. Washington, DC: Corporate Executive Board.

Guthridge, M., Komm, A. B. and Lawson, E. (2008). 'Making talent a strategic priority'. Retrieved on 19 May from https://www.mckinseyquarterly.com/article

Heger, B. K. (2007). 'Linking the employee value proposition to employee engagement and business outcomes: preliminary findings from a linkage research pilot study'. *Organizational Development Journal*, 25 (1), 121–32.

Henkel, S., Tomczak, M., Heitman, M. and Herrman, A. (2007). 'Managing brand consistent with employee behavior: relevance and managerial control of behavioural branding'. *Journal of Product and Brand Management*, 16 (5), 310–20.

Hulberg, J. (2006). 'Integrating corporate branding and sociological paradigms: a literature study'. *Brand Management* 14 (1–2), 60–73.

Martin, G. and Beaumont, P. (2003). 'Branding and people management: what's in a name?'. *Research Report*. London: CIPD.

Maxwell, R. and Knox, S. (2009). 'Motivating employees to "live the brand": a comparative case study of employer brand attractiveness within the firm'. *Journal of Marketing Management* 25 (9–10), 893–907.

Michaels, E., Handfield-Jones, H. and Axelrod, B. (2001). *The War for Talent*. Boston: McKinsey.

Moroko, L. and Uncles, M. D. (2008). 'Characteristics of employer brands'. *Journal of Brand Management* 16, 160–75.

Moroko, L. and Uncles, M. D. (2009). 'Employer branding and market segmentation'. *Journal of Brand Management* 17, 181–96.

Rosethorn, H. (2009). *The Employer Brand: Keeping Faith with the Deal*. Farnham: Gower.

Rosethorn, H. and Mensink, J. (2007). *Employer Branding: The Latest Fad or the Future for HR*. London: CIPD.

Ruch, W. (2002). *Employer Brand Evolution: A Guide to Building Loyalty in Your Organization*. Milwaukee: Versant Solutions.

The Telegraph (2010). *Top Employers Need Top Employer Branding*, 23 March 2010.

Tsui, A. S. and Wu, J. B. (2005). 'The new employment relationship versus the mutual investment approach: implications for human resource management'. *Human Resource Management* 44 (2), 115–21.

Turban, D. B., Forret, M. L. and Hendrickson, C. L. (1998). 'Applicant attraction to firms: influences of organization reputation, job and organizational attributes, and recruiter behaviors'. *Journal of Vocational Behavior* 52 (1), 24–44.

Van Mossevelde, C. (2010). *Employer Branding: Five Reasons Why It Matters and Five Steps to Action*. Retrieved on 5 May from http://www.employerbrandingtoday.com/uk/2010/03/25/employer-branding-five-reasons-why-it-matters-five-steps-to-action/

CHAPTER 8

Psychometric Assessment and Personality Questionnaires
Survey results and case study findings

Stephen Pilbeam, Louisa Allison and Stacey White

Psychometrics is a term which encompasses all forms of psychological assessment – 'psycho' relates to the mind and 'metric' implies measurement, so 'psychometric' is the measurement of the mind – an ambitious task! In an occupational setting psychometric assessment consists of tests and questionnaires designed to measure individual differences. These psychometric 'instruments' are capable of being systematically scored and are supported by evidence and statistical data which seek to demonstrate their validity in contributing to decisions about suitability for particular types of work or specific positions within an organisation to achieve the strategic people management aim of having the right people in the right place at the right time, with the right abilities, competencies and motivation. Psychometric instruments seek to measure Attainment, General Intelligence, Cognitive Ability, Trainability and Personality. In the case of properly validated attainment, general intelligence, cognitive ability and trainability tests, measurement outputs can be related to specific jobs and, appropriately chosen and used, there is little contention that they are able to provide useful information for selection decisions. The assessment of personality, the focus of this chapter, provides a more challenging arena because it aims to infer relatively enduring individual characteristics and traits as a basis for predicting behaviour at work.

Personality 'tests' do not generate 'right' or 'wrong' answers; they are designed to present a profile of an individual. Arguably 'testing' is a misnomer because it implies that a personality test can be failed, and it is self-evident that every individual has a personality. Personality assessment therefore seeks to describe an individual's personality using a particular personality 'construct'; it does not establish whether an individual has a personality or not. As human beings, existing in a social world, we all make judgements about the personality and behavioural dispositions of others and we use personal constructs to do this, but we need to recognise that these personal constructs are subjective, unreliable and have no proven validity. This will not stop our making judgements about others, but there is a need for professional caution about assuming behavioural traits based on our incomplete and unverified construction of personality profiles. For example a 'bubbly personality' may be attractive to some, but to others this putative effervescence may be an anathema. And in any case where is the evidence that 'bubbly' translates into effective work performance? You might say – 'well, in a sales environment of course' – but the evidence suggests that the best sales people are the ones who are the most effective listeners, so we would need to know to what extent the bubbly person could listen, as well as effervesce. This is merely used as an example to demonstrate that we cannot trust our instincts on 'personality' in an occupational setting. In any case personality characteristics are often most observable when they are in the extreme and, as personality characteristics often demonstrate a normal distribution, the extremes are confined to a small minority.

Most personality assessment instruments are designed and developed by occupational psychologists and instrument providers supply the data to establish the reliability of the instrument and the normative information against which results may be compared. Administering instruments and analysing the results is a task that requires much skill. Scoring is often complex and how it is done will depend on what the instrument is purporting to measure. Personality questionnaires produce either a profile or a descriptive narrative of an individual. This raises the question of which profile or description is the 'best type' for the job. It is the identification of this 'best type' that is elusive. The individual personality information is compared with the profile of a representative sample of an appropriate population, either produced by the questionnaire supplier or generated by the user on the basis of the personality characteristics of successful and less successful organisational performers.

By way of illustration of different constructions of personality, the Five-Factor Model (FFM) is a widely recognised taxonomy of personality traits, with the five factors being neuroticism, extraversion, openness to experience, agreeableness and conscientiousness; whilst popular examples of personality assessment include:

The Myers–Briggs Type Indicator (MBTI) identifies four preference dimensions: extroversion/introversion, sensing/intuition, thinking/feeling and judgement/perception. Combining the four produces a personality type, such as ESTJ (Extraversion, Sensing, Thinking, Judgment). Each personality type has identified characteristics and the MBTI is useful for developing interpersonal skills, enhancing self-awareness, career counselling and team building.

Cattells 16 PF (Personality Factors) profiles relatively enduring personality characteristics, with each characteristic measured on a scale. The factors are grouped into the themes of extroversion, anxiety, will, self-control and independence.

The Occupational Personality Questionnaire (OPQ) generates insights in relation to three dimensions: people relationships, thinking styles and emotions. OPQ provides insights into behavioural predisposition at work.

Belbin's team roles identify patterns of behaviour that may characterise individual contributions to a team. The team roles are grouped into action-oriented, people-orientated and cerebral, and the potential for self-awareness facilitates greater flexibility in the adoption of different roles by individual team members. It also provides insights into team make-up and team building.

Fundamental Interpersonal Relations Orientation-Behaviour (FIRO-B) assesses interpersonal needs and the impact on the individual's behaviour towards others. The dimensions include: giving and receiving; desire to form new relationships; control, influence and structure; need for dominance and/or power; and emotionality and warmth. It can identify team member similarities and potential for conflict.

Personality assessment which seeks to identify 'the one best personality type' can be charged with being 'Tayloristic' by not fully taking into account contingency factors and also being at odds with concepts of promoting and managing diversity. It also raises the question of whether selection on the basis of personality profiling is an ethically acceptable form of social engineering in pursuit of corporate conformity. There are also issues about the acceptability of the intrusive nature of some of the instruments used to assess personality. These arguments are similar to those being used to debate the acceptability of using genetic profiling in employment decisions. It is important to recognise that personality assessment tends to measure stated preferences rather than behaviour, and although preferences shape individual behaviour, the correlation between these two factors is not necessarily strong and will be moderated by other variables in the workplace. The increased availability and use of psychometric instruments give rise to concerns about the huge potential for poor instrument design, indiscriminate use and inappropriate interpretation of outcomes. According to Pilbeam and Corbridge (2010):

> the dangers to potential users lie in two beguiling features. First, the 'scientific' nature of psychometric devices can create an exaggerated impression of their value and accuracy. Second, design features in the instrument may generate information which effectively takes responsibility for a selection decision by indicating a pass or fail outcome, satisfying the risk aversion needs of the selector.

Despite the challenges, a potentially useful selection device need not be discarded because it has potential to enable managers to develop more informed perceptions about the ability and potential of individuals. The arguments in favour of personality assessment are threefold:

1. Personality assessment, used appropriately, can have predictive validity.
2. Factors which enhance the potential contribution of personality assessment include:

- using only properly validated instruments,
- the appropriate training of administrators of the instruments and the interpreters of the information generated,
- administering in standard conditions,
- confidentiality and sensitivity in giving feedback on the results,
- validating the match between individual personality characteristics and job requirements and performance.

3. Personality assessment should be restricted to providing additional information for the selection process and should not constitute the sole method or principal basis for decision-making.

As can be seen by the survey that follows, there remains scope to improve the use of personality assessment in practice, whilst the case study suggests that constructive use is possible and beneficial.

The application of personality assessments to selection procedures, and the need for more reflective practice – case-based survey results

The use of personality assessment in the recruitment phase of employment has become increasingly popular (Morgeson et al., 2007). One of the reasons behind this increase has been the factors in the external environment, and in particular factors such as an ageing workforce and shrinking talent pools, which combine to make recruitment an intensely competitive process. Even in these recessionary times the competition for talent is intense as organisations seek the best people (CIPD, 2009). As one corporate HR leader put it:

> Talent management initiatives are robust and believed to add value to the organisation. We therefore believe that the attraction and retention of talent is even more important in the current economic environment than it has been at any time in the past.

In order to establish the extent to which personality assessments are used, and to examine how they were administered and interpreted, their perceived validity and their impact on HR practice, interviews were conducted with 14 senior HR professionals across a broad selection of industries. These represented both public and private sector employers, ranging from 160 to 38,000 employees. Of these, four were using personality assessments for selection purposes for all posts and 10 were using personality assessments for selected posts. What emerged from the research is that the use of personality assessments is both time- and resource-intensive, which has a direct impact upon effective practice in this area.

Key survey findings

First almost half of surveyed organisations had no articulated objectives for psychometric testing and any perceived gains such as 'better employee fit' were not measured against pre-determined objectives. Second it was evident that once an instrument was selected it was often used regardless of its applicability for the chosen task and respondents were unable to report that assessment instruments were validated. These two findings are in stark contrast to advice from the British Psychological Society (BPS), which stresses that the success of personality assessments is dependent on the clarity of what is to be measured in order to ensure an appropriate instrument is selected, because a test validated for one application might be completely irrelevant for another. None of the organisations had a written policy on testing and there was nothing formal in place to shape and guide behaviour or to ensure consistency in approach. The monitoring or benchmarking of staff involved in administering, scoring and interpreting assessment outputs was not evident, suggesting that the training process is akin to learning to drive in that once a learner has passed the test and been allowed out on the road, there is no follow-up to ensure driving competency and to minimise the development of bad habits. Only one organisation had developed a business case for the use of testing, suggesting that organisations are willing to spend considerable sums of money despite having no real understanding of what benefits are potentially realised.

Whilst the issue of applicant 'faking' on personality assessments is a potential weakness of personality assessment, the employers in this survey took a philosophical approach to this phenomenon. There was reliance on the instruments' 'lie scales' or 'consistency scores' to highlight faking behaviour and it did not generate significant concern. The predictive validity of the assessment instrument was generally taken at face value. Respondents indicated that they did not have the expertise to measure the validity of the instruments and therefore validity was a question of faith in the supplier. Two-thirds of those interviewed utilised online personality testing, but there was little evidence of ensuring control over the testing environment and sometimes no guarantee that the persons taking the assessment were not being coached, using materials that were not permitted or employing someone else to compete the assessment for them. Three online testing variations are available:

1. *Uncontrolled and unsupervised:* the applicant takes the test on the open Internet.
2. *Controlled but unsupervised:* the organisation making use of the test registers the applicant and ensures their identity, but takes no other action to supervise the timing of the test or the test environment.
3. *Controlled and supervised:* a qualified test user is required to log in the applicant and ensure that timing and other test requirements are met.

On-line testing issues therefore include security, identity, confidentiality, technical issues of equivalence, equality of access and fairness. Ensuring candidate fidelity and on-line test reliability are therefore major challenges.

Conclusions and recommendations

The lack of articulated objectives made it difficult to establish why personality assessment is being used and the validity of personality assessment is not evidenced because no evaluation takes place to ensure the results are contributing to effective selection decisions. There were no policies in place to ensure consistency of approach or adherence to regulatory guidelines recommended by the BPS. This calls into question the results, with the consequent risk of less-than-optimum selection decisions. If invalid or spurious results are to be avoided, it is imperative to have a clear understanding of what is to be measured to ensure an appropriate assessment instrument is deployed. The purpose of this research was to encourage more reflective practice within the HR community in relation to personality assessments. The evidence illustrates that the use of personality assessment is a complex and resource-intensive process and this impacts on HR practice and on the predictive validity of selection processes. The following recommendations are intended to encourage more reflective practice in the area of personality assessment and provide the basis for continuous improvement in the application of personality profiling to the selection of employees:

1. **Clarify the objectives** – Be clear about what is to be measured and why. If the objective is to improve employee 'fit' for example, then the process must begin with a detailed analysis of the role. This means writing an appropriate job description and person specification to enable the identification of the key behaviours to be measured, which in turn will facilitate the selection of an appropriate psychometric instrument.

2. **Develop a written policy on personality assessment** – Set standards and guide the behaviour of those who administer, score and interpret the assessment results. Cultural and gender bias also need to be addressed in the selection and use of the assessment instruments. The written policy should include an effectiveness review process.

3. **Evaluate the process** – Is it producing the desired results? If so, these data can be used to make a business case to justify continuing use or to expand use in the organisation. If not, then seek something more appropriate.

4. **Develop in-house expertise in assessments** – This will enable the organisation to maximise the potential of personality assessment, to identify opportunities for further use and to take advantage of new technologies.

Psychometric Assessment: not just a recruitment and selection tool at Hillcrest Care – a case study

Established in 1994, Hillcrest Care is a privately owned care company providing services to a range of people of all ages. The services provided by Hillcrest include: 10 specialist children's homes across England and Wales, providing residential care and education for children up to the age of 17 with emotional and behavioural difficulties; nationwide fostering services; learning disability services, including residential homes and supported living services for adults with learning disabilities, and a specialist home for children with severe learning disabilities. The services provided are highly regulated by local authorities and regulatory bodies, such as OFSTED and the Care Quality Commission, so high standards are paramount to the continued success of the organisation. Hillcrest Care employs around 600 staff in a range of positions to provide quality care to its service users. Effective recruitment and selection, combined with an effective management team are essential in order to ensure that care standards remain high.

How Hillcrest used psychometric assessment, and why

Hillcrest Care implemented psychometric testing within its recruitment process for senior positions, using tools provided by Thomas International. The use of psychometric instruments, one of the recommendations of the regulatory bodies, was intended to promote more robust methods of recruitment and selection of care staff. The Personality Profile Analysis (PPA) provided by Thomas International used a series of 24 forced-choice questions. The individual taking the PPA selects one adjective most like them and one adjective least like them, whilst considering themselves in the work environment. Examples of the type of adjectives used were *Dutiful, Stubborn, Attractive and Pleasant*. The results provide some understanding of how a person prefers to behave at work and the characteristics they have a predisposition to exhibit. Examples of these include 'The objectives and requirements of the job must be clearly communicated and then the individual should be given the authority and responsibility to go out and achieve the results'; 'Likes to see a task through to its conclusion before moving on to the next'; and 'needs to be able to identify with the organisation and has an inherent need to feel secure'. The results are presented in a report which describes the individual's strengths, weaknesses and motivators, and shows the individual's preferred working style and the behaviours they are likely to demonstrate whilst under pressure. An 'ideal' profile is obtained for each job by entering details from the job description into the online system and candidates are measured against this profile, alongside a variety of other selection activities, such as a formal interview, written exercises, presentations and budgeting exercises, to assist recruiting managers in making the right selection decisions. During the recruitment process the individual is given feedback from the PPA report, and the outcome is discussed in relation to work situations and also with respect to what the individual would expect from their line manager.

Although the use of psychometric assessments appears to be most popular during the selection process, Thomas International also markets its products towards team building and management development. Following discussions with the supplier, Hillcrest Care identified that the PPA report could also be utilised to improve the working relationships between managers at different levels within the organisation. The relative effectiveness of different management styles has long been debated within professional literature, and one element in this debate is the importance of the ability to adapt management styles to differing situations. The use of the PPA feedback has enabled Hillcrest Care to take this a step further and help managers to adapt their management style not only to situations but also to individuals. Hillcrest Care arranged for a selection of managers to attend a training workshop titled 'Self Awareness and Modifying Behaviour'. The managers who attended were at various levels and were asked to complete a PPA assessment prior to the workshop. During the workshop the participants carefully considered both their personal profiles and their individual working styles, in order to identify how these could impact on the people they manage. The workshop then encouraged the managers to identify ways in which they could modify their behaviour in order to become more effective managers.

The Head of HR develops a comprehensive annual training calendar for the year ahead. The 'Self Awareness and Modifying Behaviour' workshop was included within the training calendar and was run at the Head Office Site by a supplier representative. The course objectives were extensive and included:

- to understand why we need to know ourselves and appreciate our own personal strengths and limitations in the current work role;
- to recognise the strengths, limitations, fears, motivators and values of the organisation and/or team of people with different work styles;
- to learn how to successfully motivate different people;
- to now the value of supporting and managing personal limitations;
- to spot observable behaviours in others;
- to appreciate how and where to modify personal work style and behaviour to achieve the desired outcome;
- to develop a personal action plan to develop and use the skills outlined above.

The course was popular with the managers who attended and the feedback received was positive, with managers considering the learning to be wholly relevant to their roles. When asked what aspects of the programme were most useful the comments included: 'understanding my management style and how to improve upon it to get the best from my team'; 'better understanding of the needs of other profiles'; and, 'learning how different personality traits influence each other'. The managers attending were also asked what specific actions they were planning to take in their work setting as a result of the training. Responses included: 'undertake an assessment of my colleagues and how I can support them in different ways'; 'look at how I can adapt my management style to improve team performance'; and 'consider how to adapt my behaviour when dealing with different people'. Following the success of the training course Hillcrest has extended the use of psychometric assessment by utilising the information gathered in the recruitment process. On recruitment to a position the line manager is given an overview of the person's working style so they have a greater understanding of their new employee from the start. This information is provided by a certified PPA practitioner, who can discuss the profile of the individual's preferred working style and compare it with the working style of the manager. This enables the manager to recognise how they can adapt their management style to get the best from the new employee.

The impact, the benefits and the challenges

The impact of the training provided has been positive, and Hillcrest has looked at a variety of ways to measure this, including specific examples of where relationships have improved, where staff turnover and disciplinary issues have decreased and where business performance has improved. At one of the sites staff turnover decreased from 33 per cent to only 12 per cent in a year and in another there was a similar story, with turnover decreasing from 36 per cent to just 9 per cent. Hillcrest

Care is aware that labour market conditions may also have had an impact on this, with people being more likely to seek job security in difficult economic times. One example of how the training worked to improve working relationships was identified between an Operations Manager and a recently recruited Service Manager who reported to him. The Service Manager had been recruited to take over the running of a newly created supported living service, and the feedback from the Operations Manager was that the Service Manager was not performing particularly well and that she was generally ignoring any advice. Both managers attended the course and by discussing their own profiles began to see where the professional relationship between them had potential for improvement. The profile of the Operations Manager showed him to be highly influential, persuasive and talkative; he would move very quickly from one subject to the next and as a result did not stop to clearly explain what he was looking for. The profile of the Service Manager showed her to be systematic, precise and logical, needing clear direction and understanding of what was required within the role. As a result of undertaking the training, they were both able to see how their working styles were impacting on performance. The Operations Manager was able to adapt his working style for the Service Manager by taking more time to explain what was required, and the Service Manager had a greater understanding of what was required. As a result the relationship between them improved significantly and had a positive impact on the business performance of the service.

A challenge to implementing psychometric assessment has been the cost and the time involved. At £2500 per person, plus travel and accommodation, the initial supplier training course was costly. Completing the PPA takes around eight minutes; however preparing and giving feedback to the employee generally takes around an hour for preparation and an hour for the feedback. Following this, preparation for the discussion with the relevant manager requires about another hour for each. In addition there is the cost of the PPA and, due to the multiple locations of Hillcrest Care services, there are the time and the costs of travel to take into account. Hillcrest Care has, however, identified the benefits of carrying out this process. The managers who have undertaken the PPA and received the feedback tend to have lower numbers of employee relations issues occurring within their services; the staff turnover rates for those services have been lower; and inspection reports from Office for Standards in Education (OFSTED) and Care Quality Commission (CQC) are of a higher standard. This has had a positive impact on the reputation and the overall performance of the business. The use of PPAs has a positive reputation throughout the company, and employees are eager to undertake an assessment in order to learn more about themselves, the way they work and how this influences others. In addition Hillcrest Care continues to receive requests from managers for PPAs of their teams with the aim of improving how they work together.

Activities and discussion questions

1. First, comment on the extent to which personality assessment is being used effectively in the case-based survey organisations above. Second, evaluate the appropriateness and viability of the recommendations.

2. Using the case study examine the benefits that are accruing to Hillcrest through the use of the psychometric assessment. What factors have enabled Hillcrest to maximise these benefits?

3. Discuss the extent to which personality traits are a determinant of behaviour or whether they merely create a predisposition to behave in a particular way. In addition identify which moderating variables might impact on a causal link between personality traits and behaviours in a work situation.

4. Discuss the extent to which, and how, the predictive validity of personality can be measured?

5. Go online and seek out personality assessment instrument examples and prepare a 15-minute presentation which, for an instrument of your choice:

   ▪ identifies the personality dimensions being used (the construct),
   ▪ how these dimensions are assessed,
   ▪ the predictive validity of the instrument.

Bibliography

Barak, A. (2003). 'Ethical and professional issues in career assessment on the Internet'. *Journal of Career Assessment* 11 (1), 3–21.

Carless, S. A. (2009). 'Psychological testing for selection purposes: a guide to evidence-based practice for human resource professionals'. *The International Journal of Human Resource Management* 20 (12), 251732.

CIPD (2009). *The War on Talent? Talent Management under Threat in Uncertain Times*. Hot topics. London: CIPD.

Damon, N. (2009). *Using Psychometric Tests for Learning and Development*, 1 March. (Electronic version), www.training&coachingtoday.com

Hausdorf, P. A. and Risavy, S. D. (2010). 'Decision making using personality assessment: implications for adverse impact and hiring rates'. *Applied H.R.M. Research: University of Guelph* 12 (1), 100–120. (Electronic version), www.xavier.edu/appliedhrmresearch/2010-Winter/Article_7_Hausdorf_Decision%20Making%20Using%20Personality%20Assessment.pdf

IRS (2003). 'Psyching out tests'. *Employment Review* 787, 43–8.

Landers, R. N., Sackett, P. R. and Tuzinski, K. A. (2011). 'Retesting after initial failure, coaching rumors, and warnings against faking in online personality measures for selection'. *Journal of Applied Psychology* 96 (1), 202–10.

Morgeson, F. P., Campion, M. A., Dipboye, R. L., Hollenbeck, J. R., Murphy, K. and Schmitt, N. (2007). 'Reconsidering the use of personality tests in personnel selection contexts'. *Personnel Psychology* 60 (3), 683–729.

Paton, N. (2007). 'Investors in leaders'. *Personnel Today*, 16 January.

Pilbeam, S. and Corbridge, M. (2010). *People Resourcing and Talent Planning: HRM in Practice*. Harlow: Financial Times Prentice Hall.

Redford, K. (2007). *Psychometric Profiling and Training Grows Online*, 1 July. (Electronic version), www.training&coachingtoday.com

Robertson, I. T. and Smith, M. (2001). 'Personnel selection'. *Journal of Occupational and Organizational Psychology* 74 (4), 441–72.

Suff, P. (2003). 'Testing times for selectors'. *IRS Employment Review* 769 (February), 32–38.

Woodhouse, M. and Thorne, K. (2003). 'Talent management: how to manage talent'. (Electronic version), *One Stop Guide*, 1 March. www.xperthr.co.uk
www.excellerate.co.nz/free_psychometric_tests.html
www.markparkinson.co.uk/psychometric_links.htm
www.prospects.ac.uk/psychometric_tests.htm
www.psychometric-success.com/
www.shldirect.com/

CHAPTER 9

The Value of Competency-Based Interviewing in Recruitment and Selection Decisions

The right people, in the right place, at the right time, with the right competencies

Stephen Pilbeam, Debbie Jenkins and Derek Adam-Smith

The recruitment and selection system

Clearly effective recruitment and selection of employees is a key strategic people management issue because having the right people, in the right place, at the right time, with the right competencies is critical to organisational success. There are also severe consequences for getting it wrong with much wasted time and effort, distress for managers, and of course the badly selected employees, and potential damage to the business through reduced quality and service to customers and clients. It is important to recognise that recruitment and selection processes consist of sequential stages within a system, each stage interconnected and chronologically dependent on the others, and the aim of the recruitment and selection system is for it to be functioning in harmony in order to produce the best possible results for the organisation in terms of the talent it produces. Of course fairness and legal compliance with discrimination law are important factors but the primary goal of recruitment and selection is to secure good talent – this is expressed as the predictive validity of the recruitment and selection system; in other words how effective is the recruitment and selection system in producing employees who perform effectively in the jobs for which they have been recruited? The aim of course is high predictive validity.

As the case study that follows illustrates, employers can use competencies as the basis for recruitment and selection of employees in order to improve predictive validity.

The sequential stages in recruitment and selection are Attraction, Reduction, Selection and Transition (Pilbeam and Corbridge, 2010). Each stage requires attention in order to achieve the desired outcomes. For example great advertising to attract talented candidates may be squandered by poor interviewing techniques, and great results from an assessment centre of selection activities may be squandered by poor transition from great candidate to non-performing employee. Each of the four stages needs skilled attention and whilst the case study focuses on the selection stage, the activities and discussion topics which follow provide scope for competencies to be deployed in each of the four stages of Attraction, Reduction, Selection and Transition. The elements within each of the four stages of the recruitment and selection process are as follows:

1. *Attraction*: labour market analysis and job analysis leading to a person specification and job description and the use of recruitment methods to attract applicants,
2. *Reduction*: Filtering, screening and shortlisting against the criteria in the person specification,
3. *Selection*: Use of selection methods and techniques,
4. *Transition*: Pre-engagement process, orientation, induction, training needs analysis, training and feedback, appraisal, performance management and rewards.

What are competencies?

Competencies emerged during the 1980s as a response to demands for organisational flexibility and responsiveness in competitive markets and have become an accepted part of strategic people management. Competencies define the behaviours and technical abilities that are necessary to do the job. Competency frameworks originally consisted mainly of behavioural elements, an expression of the softer skills involved in effective performance, and it is common for these to be expressed within a single organisational framework, termed a competency map. A competency map, as the terms suggests, maps out individual competencies required by employees to be effective performers in their role. In the past, HR professionals have tended to draw a distinction between 'competences' and 'competencies' and the theoretical differences between competencies, competences and competency are discussed in the chapter relating to the role of the front-line manager (FLM). However effective performance requires a mix of behaviours, technical skills, attitudes and actions and consequently the terms are now used interchangeably. It is rather like the debate about whether there is a difference between HRM and personnel management; it is largely sterile because it is not what label is put on competencies or competences or competency, but how they are articulated and deployed in achieving

Table 9.1   Examples of competencies

Generic competencies	Leadership competencies
Team working	Decision-making
Customer service	Planning and evaluation
Influencing	Conflict management
Decision-making	Self-management
Innovation	Self-esteem
Communicating and influencing	Oral communication
Adaptability	Analytic, strategic and creative thinking
Making informed decisions	Emotional intelligence
Creativity and innovation	Managing people

strategic people management outcomes. In this chapter we will use competencies and competency as inclusive terms. Effectively competency represents the language of performance in an organisation. Typical competencies (CIPD, 2011) include communication skills, people management, team skills, customer service skills, results-orientation and problem-solving – further examples are provided in Table 9.1.

Each competency requires detailed explanation and some form of metrics, examples, definitions and behavioural indicators, and assessment mechanisms need to be developed for each competency. Competency frameworks can be imported as an off-the-shelf package or by drawing on the external competency structures produced for occupational standards, such as National Vocational Qualifications (NVQs). Alternatively competency maps can be developed internally through job analysis, or a hybrid model, which combines external frameworks, but ensures relevance through tailoring the competencies to organisational circumstances, can be adopted. Competencies can be identified and articulated through the process of job analysis so that they can be used not only in recruitment and selection, but also for training needs analysis, performance management, reward decisions, promotion and career development, and for linking with the corporate strategy. In other words, competencies are the glue that binds people management activities together in a strategic way. When used in the recruitment and selection of employees, competencies need to be articulated as part of the person specification in order to provide the foundation for the recruitment and selection activity that follows.

Job analysis

Job analysis provides the opportunity for assessing whether a job has changed and for reviewing the knowledge, skills and competencies required; for a newly created position the job analysis is a predictive activity. It is the systematic process of collecting information about the tasks, responsibilities, competencies and contexts of a job. The job analysis process generates information which is converted into the tangible outputs of a job description and a person specification, and it is important to distinguish between these two outputs. A job description specifies the purpose, the task and the scope of the job, and the person specification profiles the competencies and people characteristics required to do the job effectively – the job description is the 'what' (has to be done) and the person specification is the 'who' (does it).

Job analysis is an information-gathering process and decisions need to be made about who does the job analysis, what information-collection methods are appropriate and which sources of information are the most useful. Job analysis can be undertaken solely or jointly by the line manager or the HR specialist, depending on the techniques being used, the expertise of the analyst and the complexity of the job. The sources of information include the line manager, the supervisor, the existing job holder and other members of the team. A triangulation of these sources will generate the most balanced data, as different perspectives will be provided by each of the contributors. Informal and formal job analysis methods are available and include questionnaires, interviews, observation, critical incident techniques, the use of standard checklists and the keeping of work logs and diaries. The information to be collected includes data which identifies the job and locates it within the organisational structure, job objectives and performance measures, accountabilities, responsibilities and organisational relationships, job duties and content, terms of employment and work conditions and any other distinctive job characteristics. From this information it becomes possible to identify the competencies required and how they might be measured.

The assessment of competencies

An example of a question relating to an easily recognisable competency is: 'Describe how you provided leadership for a team and how you set about achieving the team's objectives', and as part of the activities at the end of this chapter there is the opportunity to design competency-based questions in relation to a specified job. Further examples of questions are provided in Table 9.2.

However it is important not to rely entirely on interviews and interview questions as the only source of competence assessment because other selection techniques lend themselves to assessing competencies. The end-of-chapter activities and discussion topics are designed to explore the questioning aspects

	Scheduling exercise	Oral presentation	Group exercise	Interview questions	Work simulation	Fact find exercise
Team working			x			
Customer focus		x		x	x	x
Communicating and influencing		x		x		x
Adaptability	x					
Making informed decisions	x				x	x
Creativity and innovation		x		x	x	

Figure 9.1 Examples of competencies mapped against assessment activities

Table 9.2   Examples of competency-based questions

Team working

Tell me about the last time you worked as part of a team.

- What was your role in the team?
- How did you encourage other team members to co-operate?

Give me an example of when you helped improve the performance of your team.

- What improvement did you identify?
- How did this improve team performance?

Give me an example of how you have used your leadership skills to manage and improve team performance.

- How did you get team buy-in?
- How did you handle any difficult situations that arose amongst the team?
- What, if anything, would you do differently next time?

Customer focus and service

Describe a time when you exceeded a customer's expectations.

- How did you know you had exceeded?
- What did your actions achieve?

Describe a situation where you had to deal with a dissatisfied customer.

- How did the customer respond to the actions you took?
- What did you do to ensure that the situation did not occur again with other customers?

Give us an example of when and how you initiated the development of working relationships with external partners to develop strategies to enhance your service delivery.

- What strategies did you develop?
- How did your organisation benefit?
- How did you monitor the impact of these strategies on service delivery?

of competency assessment, but the range of assessment techniques includes psychometric instruments, job sampling and work simulation, group activities, individual performances, role plays or presentations and assessment centres which combine assessment techniques *inter alia*. Figure 9.1 provides an example of competencies being mapped against assessment activities.

In summary the arguments for using competency-based approaches in recruitment and selection are first that it focuses on the knowledge, skills and aptitudes that are required to do a specific job, rather than on qualifications and experience; second that it permits a more objective assessment of job candidates because it is based on a clear profile of the job; and third that it meets equity and diversity principles because the same criteria are applied in rating each candidate. In addition to developing more relevant selection criteria, and improving interviewing and assessment techniques, the competence-based approach can provide a link to post-appointment training and development and performance management.

Competent but not perfect: the value of competency-based interviewing in the selection decision at Thomas Eggar LLP – a case study

In common with all other organisations, Thomas Eggar LLP, a regional law organisation, seeks to ensure that the staff it recruits are the best candidates from those who apply for their vacancies. Broadly it employs two types of staff: those with legal qualifications who provide direct service to clients and those who provide administrative and clerical support. In both cases any selection method that can assist in 'getting the right person for the job' will be of significant benefit. Considerable attention has been paid in recent years to the validity of selection methods in an attempt to find means to assist in the effective staff resourcing of organisations and the retention of those recruited. One of these techniques is competency-based interviewing (CBI). While there is debate over whether there should be a focus on the outputs of the job (competences) or the traits needed by an individual to be effective (competencies), many organisations have been attracted to the 'competence' movement, particularly as an aid to effective recruitment (CIPD, 2011). In essence CBI requires the identification of the skills and behaviours needed by employees to be effective performers. Once these are determined, the purpose of the interview is to seek evidence that the applicant possesses these attributes. CBI is based on the assumption that if someone has behaved in a certain way in a past situation, they are likely to behave in a similar way should the same situation arise in the future. Thus selection interview questions are designed to probe candidates' descriptions of past behaviours relevant to the particular competence being explored, rather than for providing hypothetical situations and asking candidates how they would behave.

In order to examine the use of CBI, interviews were conducted with those responsible for recruitment in 15 law organisations (or organisations that had a connection with the legal profession). Of these, 12 were using CBI and the remainder were considering its use. This provided relevant evidence of the experience of CBI, its perceived and actual benefits and also the possible limitations as a selection device. What emerged from this research was not only that CBI provided important benefits, but that it also possessed some drawbacks and limitations. Each of these is summarised below.

The 'Upsides'

In all cases, organisations were seeking nothing different through the use of CBIs than was sought through other selection methods: the successful filling of vacancies with the best person from applications received. All claimed, however, that CBI offered an improved chance of success. In this respect CBI offers a number of key benefits. First it focuses the interviewer(s) on the key factors of the position and the candidates' relative abilities in each aspect of the work they are required to do. Second, and relatedly, it requires candidates to explain their skills in the context of their own, real experience rather than in relation to hypothetical situations. Third probing candidates becomes a more robust process since it is more difficult for candidates to fake evidence. Thus interviewers have greater certainty that the interview will show how a potential employee will behave in the workplace, and the ranking of candidates against expected behaviours becomes an easier process. Fourth CBI can be considered as a transparent process which more closely accords with current definitions of equal opportunities since each candidate will undergo an experience similar to that of others through the discussion of specific job competencies. Fifth, those using CBI explained that giving feedback to unsuccessful candidates was an easier task since this could be provided against each of the competencies required, and specific weaknesses explained. Finally from the candidates' perspective, it provides them with a much clearer picture of the job, allowing a more informed choice to be made as to whether they wish to accept the job offer should it be made.

Interestingly many of the respondents reported that some candidates had observed that the use of CBI provided a more 'professional and business-like' approach, rather than just a 'romp' through the *curriculum vitae*. This reflected well on the organisation, in general. It tended to mean that even unsuccessful applicants retained a positive image of the business, while for some successful candidates it was a factor in deciding to accept the job offer.

The 'Downsides'

It was evident from the research that CBI was most successful in those organisations that had thoroughly prepared for its use. Some organisations had invested heavily in a detailed study of job competencies and had produced a competency framework for use across the whole organisation. In one case a tailor-made framework was developed after interviews with clients to determine what was wanted from the organisation and what made it different from its competitors; discussions with the partners of the organisation; and workshops with current staff. Although providing benefits beyond recruitment and selection, for example, for performance management purposes, it was clear that developing an appropriate framework could be a time-consuming exercise, perhaps taking over a year to determine. Where sophisticated frameworks had been established and applied with some zeal, it was noted that there could be unintended consequences. In one case, the framework identified 'key words' which should be looked for during the interview and in application forms. There was a concern that an otherwise good candidate was not selected or even called for an interview because of the absence of these words. In another, scores were awarded to candidates' answers to questions on specific competencies and the person with the highest score was offered the post. No room was provided to explore motivation for the application or future career development, which might have an influence on how the candidate was judged.

At a more practical level, two further problems with the use of CBI were noted. First there was some evidence that candidates were becoming 'interview-savvy'. While this may mean better prepared candidates and a more effective selection process, it can also allow applicants to 'create' experiences to illustrate their skills. If so, this could undermine CBI's claimed benefit of focusing on real experience. Second, respondents expressed some concern that those with little or no work experience would be at a disadvantage. While candidates can be encouraged to relate the questions to non-employment activities such as voluntary work, such answers may not have (or may be treated by interviewers as not having) the same credibility as those related to paid work.

The limitations

Judging the overall success of CBI was difficult. A number of organisations identified typical measures such as satisfactory completion of the probationary period, annual appraisal outcomes as well as financial measures. All of these can, and often are, equally applied to other selection methods. Thus assessing the value of CBI in comparison with other selection methods was difficult. However, the major limitation of CBI came in the form of the non-competency-based issues of concern in the selection process. This was variously described as a 'ticking all the boxes', offering 'a bit of oomph', 'sparkle' and 'pizzaz'. It was clear that, although impossible to define, these 'I know it when I see it' characteristics of candidates were of significant influence in the decision-making process. The elusive search for this 'good fit' related to a number of aspects. A personality that will fit the culture or dynamics of the organisation and/or the team seemed uppermost in the minds of those who expressed this view. Often however the respondents were at pain to point out that this was not a search for a 'clone'. This probably expresses well the tension inherent in advocating a CBI approach while still searching for this something else. Seeking a 'good fit', but not a 'clone' suggests a potentially contradictory stance.

Thus competency-based interviews offer those responsible for selecting staff an additional instrument in the toolkit. Its unequivocal focus on the attributes needed to successfully perform a job can assist in helping to choose the best candidate. It requires a clear identification of the competencies needed and the choice of questions that allow candidates to draw on their experience to answer them. However, like all methods, it has its own limitations and it is not 'the be all and end all' answer to the selection question.

Activities and discussion questions

1. Critically evaluate competency-based interviewing (CBI) and identify three advantages and three disadvantages of this approach in getting the right people, in the right place, at the right time. Write this up as an executive briefing for the senior management team in your organisation. In your briefing include a description together with examples of competencies and CBI questions.

2. Select a position in your organisation, or one with which you are familiar, and use job analysis techniques to identify the competencies that are necessary to do the job. Justify your choices of competencies by providing a brief supporting argument for each.

3. Using the competencies identified in (2) above:

- Prepare a competency-based person specification
- Prepare a list of questions that can be asked at interview which will excavate information about the extent to which the candidate being interviewed has each competency.
- Design and practice at least two other competency assessment techniques that can be used to evaluate competency. You could use assessment techniques such as work sampling, job simulation, group activities, presentations, in-tray exercises, psychometrics, assessment centre activities *inter alia*.

4. Research the concept of predictive validity in recruitment and selection and consider how predictive validity of CBI and the other competency assessment techniques you designed and practiced in (3) above can be measured.

5. Consider how the competencies that you identified in (2) above can be used not only in the *Selection* stage of the recruitment and selection process, but also in:

- *Attraction* and advertising: using the competencies, design an advert or a vacancy board insertion or brief for an advertising agency.
- *Reduction* and shortlisting: using the competencies design a shortlisting grid which enables the assessment of competencies based on the application information, with a scoring system and descriptors for the competencies.
- *Transition*: consider how the competencies can be used in orientation, induction, in training needs analysis and performance management and rewards, and produce a two-page briefing paper for line managers.

Bibliography

ACAS (2011). 'Recruitment and induction'. *Advisory Booklet*. London: ACAS. http://www. acas.org.uk/media/pdf/5/e/Recruitment_and_induction_(OCTOBER_2010).pdf

Bourne, A. (2009). 'Screening: best practice'. *HR Director*, 55 (February), 28–30.

Boyatzis, R. E. (1982). *The Competent Manager: A Model for Effective Performance*. London: Wiley.

CIPD Factsheet (2011). *Competency and Competency Frameworks*. London: CIPD.

Clardy, A. (2008). 'The strategic role of human resource development in managing core competencies'. *Human Resource Development International*, 11 (2), 183–97.

Clifford, B. (2008). 'How to evaluate your selection process'. *People Management*, 14 (1), 2–43 (10 January).

Crisman, D. W. (2008). 'Using competencies to drive talent management'. *Workspan*, 51 (9), 70–75.

Furnham, A. (2008). 'HR professionals' beliefs about, and knowledge of, assessment techniques and psychometric tests'. *International Journal of Selection and Assessment*, 16 (3), 300–5.

Incomes Data Services (2008a). *Assessment Centres – HR Study 876*. London: IDS.

Incomes Data Services (2008b). *Competency Frameworks – HR Study 865*. London: IDS.

Landon, T. E. and Arvey, R. D. (2007). 'Ratings of test fairness by human resource professionals. International'. *Journal of Selection and Assessment*, 15 (2), 185–96.

Murphy, N. (2008). 'Trends in recruitment methods in 2006 and 2007 – 3 Selection'. *IRS Employment Review 893*, 20 March. http://www.xperthr.co.uk/article/83675/trends-in-recruitment-methods-in-2006-and-2007-(1)--attraction.aspx (electronic version).

Miller, L., Rankin, N. and Neathy, F. (2001). *Competency Frameworks in UK Organisations: Key Issues in Employers' Use of Competencies*. London: CIPD.

Milsom, J. (2009). 'Key trends and issues in employers' use of behavioural competencies'. *IRS Employment Review 918*, 30 March. http://www.xperthr.co.uk/article/92496/key-trends-and-issues-in-employers-use-of-behavioural-competencies.aspx (electronic version).

Pilbeam, S. and Corbridge, M. (2010). *People Resourcing and Talent Planning: HRM in Practice*. Harlow: Prentice Hall.

Spence, B. (2009). 'How to filter job applications'. *People Management*, 12 March, 45–6.

Suff, R. (2010a). 'Benchmarking competencies: the 2010 survey'. *IRS Employment Review*, 23 August. XpertHR. http://www.xperthr.co.uk/article/104210/benchmarking-competencies--the-2010-irs-survey.aspx (electronic version).

Suff, R. (2010b). 'Using competencies in HR practices: the 2010 IRS survey'. *IRS Employment Review*, 23 August. http://www.xperthr.co.uk/article/104209/using-competencies-in-HR-practices-the-2010-irs-survey.aspx (electronic version).

Trickey, G. (2007). 'Competency metrics'. *Selection and Development Review*, 23 (1), 3–6.

Ulrich, D., Brockbank, W. and Johnson, D. (2008). *HR Competencies: Mastery at the Intersection of People and Business*. Alexandria, VA: Society for Human Resource Management.

Whiddett, S. and Hollyforde, S. (2003). *A Practical Guide to Competencies: How to Enhance Individual and Organisational Performance*. London: CIPD.

CHAPTER 10

Talent Management Practices
Recruiting and retaining employees

Marjorie Corbridge and Monsurat Omotayo

Talent management and its strategic value in modern organisations

A recent survey by the McKinsey Quarterly revealed that 'finding talented people was the single biggest managerial preoccupation of this decade ... nearly half of respondents expect intensifying competition for talent – and the increasingly global nature of that competition – to have a major effect on their companies in the next five years. No other trend was considered nearly as significant' (Guthridge, Komm and Lawson, 2008: 49).

Guthridge et al. (2008: 50) go on to explore some of the factors that are challenging effective talent management. First the *demographic changes* and in particular the differences between established economies, which are facing an ageing working population and increasing retirement ages, together with falling birth rates, and the emerging economies, which are seen to have a surplus of talent with 'twice as many university educated professionals as the developed world'. An additional aspect of this are the features associated with Generation Y, those born after 1980, whose attitudes to and expectations from work are seen to be different. Generation Y employees are seen to envision their employment as a series of short-term 'chapters' and are willing to change jobs if their expectations are not met. This places organisations under threat of high levels of attrition and a leaching of talent from the organisation if they fail to meet these expectations. Second the *increasing globalisation of business* as organisations move into the emerging markets. In order to succeed in this competitive environment, organisations need talent that is mobile and prepared to work abroad. Third the *rise of the knowledge worker* is a key challenge as these workers are seen to 'create more profit than other employees do – up to three times more according to this research' (Guthridge et al., 2008: 51). However this does not always feed through into the bottom-line performance of this type of organisation, with some organisations outperforming others by a significant degree. It would appear from this that some organisations are not maximising the value to be obtained from these knowledge workers. These external challenges can also be combined with internal difficulties, which can place organisational talent management strategies under considerable pressure. One factor which features (Guthridge and Lawson, 2008; Guthridge et al., 2008; CIPD, 2007b) is a business focus on short-term performance that can drive out the strategic planning needed for the acquisition and retention of talent. However a failure to plan strategically and to invest in the development of talent can become a downward spiral as the 'so-called' talent management initiatives, starved of investment, are perceived by the organisation as not delivering the performance expected. This can lead to falling profits, which generates even less engagement with and investment in the talent management pipeline. But how can organisations deliver on this investment? In order to address these negative perceptions it is important that the organisation makes an assessment as to its current position with regard to managing talent in order to ensure that its approach has a chance of success. Research undertaken by CIPD (2007b: 6) found that about three-quarters of the respondents did not have 'a well developed plan for talent management' but they did find that 'three quarters of organisations employing over 500 staff [were] doing some form of talent management'. From this research, evidence of a continuum of strategic engagement was identified, indicating different levels of maturity of organisational talent management. This continuum has five levels of maturity:

Level 1 – No talent management strategies, policies or formally developed practices. However, there may be management of talent be it informally or incidentally.

Level 2 – Isolated, tactical or local pockets of talent management activities but with no overall strategy or plans for talent management.

Level 3 – Integrated and co-ordinated talent management activities for a segment of the organisation.

Level 4 – Talent management strategy defined to deliver corporate and HR management strategies. Formal talent management initiatives linked horizontally to HR management and vertically to corporate strategy-making processes.

Level 5 – Talent management strategy informs and is informed by corporate strategy. Individual pooled talent is understood and is taken into consideration in the strategic process. Analysing the organisation in this way will enable an assessment to be made and a strategy developed which acknowledges the starting point.

An examination of what we mean by Talent Management

The concept of talent management has, in recent years, evolved into a common and essential management practice and, what was once solely associated with recruitment now covers a multitude of areas including organisational capability, individual development, performance enhancement, workforce planning and succession planning.

(McCartney and Garrow, 2006)

The War for Talent (1998) emphasised the acquisition and retention of those in key posts or the 'A list employees'. However this has now broadened to a more inclusive model which seeks to bring in the B-list employees who are those who make a positive contribution and who the organisation would not want to lose. It is perhaps seen to be increasingly important to consider the talent of employees at all levels of the business. Definitions of talent are difficult to pin down. According to Tansley, Turner, Foster, Harris, Sempik, Stewart and Williams (2007) 'talent definitions [are] organisationally specific and influenced by the type of industry and the nature of its work dynamic'. The organisational strategy developed needs to support the *definition* of talent appropriate to the business, whether it is to be an exclusive, inclusive or a hybrid model. The definition also helps to identify the talent pools created or needed.

An exclusive, an inclusive or a hybrid model

An exclusive approach to talent planning and talent management focuses on the high performers and the key positions for succession planning, and these are usually located in a single talent pool. An inclusive approach recognises that there are many employees at all levels of the organisation who have talent which is useful for the organisation and that making use of all talent will maximise the benefits to the business; this approach will normally be characterised by multiple talent pools. Tansley et al. (2007: 21) identify the pros and cons of these two approaches and also go on to say that 'the research suggests that most organisations have hybrid view of talent that bring together aspects of both. In reality these approaches may be opposite ends of a continuum with practice in organisations lying somewhere along that line as appropriate to the needs of that organisation'. This research (Tansley et al., 2007: 22) goes on to identify the benefits of an exclusive approach, including the ability to focus on succession planning for the future and ensure a supply of future leaders of the organisation, target resources and also enable effective monitoring of return on investment and promote the individual development of the members of the talent pool. However there are disadvantages which include the disengagement of those staff who are not members of the talent pool with consequential potential for attrition from this group, a reduction in development resources for those excluded from the talent pool and the diversion of attention from a diverse range of talent. Looking at the inclusive model, Tansley et al. (2007: 22) also identifies the benefits of this approach, which include increased employee engagement where there is the possibility of all members of the organisation having access to the talent pool; planning to fill all key roles, not only senior management roles; increasing diversity; and the opportunity to access the talent of all the employees. In practice an organisation might have a major focus on the 'A team', with an exclusive approach to this, whilst also creating a talent pool of other key post-holders – perhaps those highly skilled technical people who are seen to be critical to business.

Global talent management

As identified by Guthridge et al. (2008: 50) increased globalisation challenges many organisations and in particular the multinational business facing intense competition for talent within the global labour market. A research project entitled 'Creating People Advantage' undertaken by the CIPD (2010) looked at, among other things, the talent management and human capital challenges facing the BRIC countries. However these economies are much different from each other in composition in terms of both their industries and their consumer behaviours. In order to be able to compete successfully with organisations in the global market and to 'assess the global talent challenge [we are facing] we need to understand the drivers of learning and talent development in all of the countries we seek to operate in and from' (CIPD, 2010: 1). This is potentially a complex process but the use of tools such as PESTLE will enable organisations to examine the context of the countries they are competing with and better understand the issues they face. The research (CIPD, 2010: 5) identified three 'action categories' which could be applied to each issue identified and the appropriate talent management initiatives developed. The three action categories are first a 'strong need to act' when the organisation sees the issue as 'a near term critical priority where there is insufficient capability and associated business risks are perceived as high'. Second 'a medium need to act where the issue is seen as one in which current capability is satisfactory but needs to be developed and maintained'. Third 'a low need to act where the issue is seen as one in which capability is well developed and the associated business risks are perceived as low'. Careful analysis will enable targeted talent management activity to impact positively on talent management outcomes. A deep understanding of the issues in emerging economies and the cultural differences that prevail should facilitate more successful development of talent management strategies and more appropriate implementation of talent management initiatives. An interesting observation by Hofstede and Hofstede (2004) cited by CIPD (2010: 18) sums this up nicely: 'People tend to have a human instinct that "deep inside" all people are the same – but they are not. Therefore if we go into another country and make decisions based in how we operate in our own home country the chances are we will make some very bad decisions.'

The research study which follows examines the talent management practices within BAT Nigeria and the impact on talent mobility and retention. The findings seem to concur with Hofstedes' view that the national context is an important issue that should not be ignored.

Talent Management practice in British American Tobacco, Nigeria – a case study

Nigeria is among 54 developing countries considered by the International Finance Corporation to be 'emerging economies'. A democracy since 1999, the country is experiencing growing political stability, combined with Foreign Direct Investment. Nigeria's transition to democracy, its relative political stability and pro-market economy policies have rekindled foreign interest (Anakwe, 2002). Ranking as the world's sixth largest exporter of oil, Nigeria produces an estimated 3 per cent of the global output of petroleum and supplies 8 per cent of US imports (Rotberg, 2004: 1, 2007: 3), thus adding to its world significance. Nigeria has potential beyond oil and is one of the fastest growing telecom markets in the world. With a thriving stock market, it is home to over 200 multinational companies. These current prevailing economic conditions are raising the importance of ensuring the effective strategic management of the country's workforce.

British American Tobacco Plc

Talent Management (TM) is a contemporary HRM issue but there is limited research into TM in developing countries and emerging markets. This research explored TM practice in a multinational company operating in Nigeria. British American Tobacco (BAT) plc operates in 180 markets, has a global market share of 17 per cent and employs 75,000 people. BAT Nigeria is a 'Top 10' contributor to the global target and therefore has a significant role to play in enabling BAT plc to achieve its leadership vision of being the world's leader in the tobacco industry. BAT Nigeria recruits 95 per cent of employees locally, with expatriates occupying just 5 per cent of all positions. Although specified at a global level, employment principles are applied with due regard for local legislative, practical and cultural frameworks. With staff turnover rising by 50 per cent in 2008 talent retention is a strategic issue in BAT. There are also issues relating to succession planning and the leadership pipeline, with few ready replacements being available when senior managers leave.

Talent management

'If great talent is hard to find, it's even harder to keep. In today's world you need the best and the brightest on your team in order to stay competitive' (Cappelli, 2008). Growing skills shortages, the changing demographics of the labour market, an increasingly ageing workforce, a shift in the nature of work from manufacturing to service, a globalised world, advanced internet technology and virtual work environments (CIPD, 2006, 2007a; Pilbeam and Corbridge, 2006) have brought about increased competition amongst organisations, both nationally and internationally.

This has contributed to the 'war for talent' (Chambers, Foulon, Handfield-Jones, Hankin, and Michael III, 1998) resulting in an increasing need to hire the best talent as a source of competitive advantage. Barney (2001) argued that an organisation's human resources that are 'valuable, rare and inimitable' generate greater organisational performance, which cannot be easily duplicated by competitors. Therefore, to stay competitive, organisations are adopting HR practices that enhance their ability to attract, develop, engage and retain talent for high business performance and growth. Retaining talent has emerged as a key issue, cutting across global boundaries, with globalisation, e-commerce, changing technology, generational and demographic change observed as key drivers influencing the struggle for talent.

The Nigerian context

Nigeria experiences skills shortages created by the low quality of education, 'brain drain' and migration. In emerging markets such as Asia, studies highlight serious competition amongst organisations to attract and retain the best talent. These markets, led by China and India, expanded by an estimated 6 per cent in 2007, which explains the rising need for talented individuals within such countries. Conceptually HRM practice in Nigeria has exhibited a dual system, which seeks to integrate foreign and traditional practices. However in multinationals which include banks, oil firms, telecom and FMCGs, foreign practices are seen as being dominant. A study conducted by Okpara and Wynn (2008) showed that Nigerian organisations exhibit HRM practices such as recruitment, selection and performance appraisal, but are faced with larger issues relating to the external environment, such as corruption, poaching, brain drain and low skills. Lack of skilled labour has been identified as a major challenge faced by Nigerian organisations. The literature reveals few studies conducted on the effectiveness of HRM practices outside Western economies. Little research has been undertaken on HRM practice in Nigeria and none on talent management and retention. Indeed it can be argued that the Nigerian terrain has been neglected by management researchers, thus creating a gap in the understanding of HRM and TM in Nigeria.

Research results

Primary data were collected by using a mixed-method approach in order to gain an in-depth understanding of the BAT talent retention issues. The three perspectives were obtained from five interviews with the HR talent management team, 41 employee questionnaires and five telephone interviews with employees who had recently left.

Three research areas were addressed:

1. *The strategic importance and challenges of TM and retention practices at BAT, Nigeria*
   Talent management practice exists in BAT and it is aligned to the overall strategy of the organisation. Using the CIPD (2007b: 6) levels of talent management BAT sits high up, on the fourth level – 'TM strategy designed to deliver corporate and HRM strategies' and 'Formal talent management initiatives linked horizontally to HRM and vertically to corporate strategy-making processes'. However the talent management strategy does not yet fully address talent retention issues. To achieve leadership of the tobacco industry, BAT needs to make sure talent loss is reduced and aim to move to the fifth TM level – 'TM strategy informs and is informed by corporate strategy' and 'Individual and pooled talent understood and taken into consideration in the strategic process'. BAT may also need to focus on further developing as a learning organisation where knowledge sharing becomes an even higher strategic priority. A primary area of focus needs to be on scanning the dynamic external environment, because this will continue to generate challenges in relation to new market entrants, low-skill levels, talent shortages and the poaching and head-hunting of talented employees.

2. *The key drivers of talent mobility at BAT, Nigeria*
   This second research question was aimed at identifying the key factors that are driving talent mobility at BAT. Some concerns were evident in relation to career advancement and self-development opportunities, and this was also evident

amongst ex-employees as a contributory reason for their exit, together with some concerns about achieving a work–life balance. This was in line with the challenges identified in interviews with the TM team.

3. ***The extent to which the mobility drivers are influenced by the Nigerian context***
   The Nigerian external environment has impacted on talent retention at BAT. This is largely due to increased competition arising from influx of new Foreign Direct investment and the growth of indigenous companies, as well as low skills causing talent shortages. Issues affecting the Nigerian economy such as the standard of living, poor infrastructure and poor health care facilities make pay and benefits more significant as a point of attraction when compared with the work–life balance concerns, which are more evident in developed countries. As Reiche (2008: 677) contends, 'the home-country context has a significant impact on the way multinational companies behave abroad'. He argues that economic activities such as labour market trends and market structure vary from country to country; as such retention practices are likely to vary across different national origins. This follows Anakwe's (2002: 1043) argument that HRM practices are more effective in a country's context and that organisations should seek to recognise specific factors relating to the country of operation.

Conclusions

BAT is clearly viewed as a good employer and offers many attractions for the retention of talented employees. This research highlights areas of potential development in talent management practices in order to further strengthen the brand and competitive advantage. Although the global recession of 2009 has focused attention on corporate survival, attracting and retaining talented employees remains a significant issue for multinational organisations. Organisations will benefit from assessing their ability to attract and retain talent as the global economy emerges from recession and the war for talent resumes in earnest.

Activities and discussion questions

1. Examine your organisation (or an organisation that you are familiar with) and address the following questions:

   a. Does the organisation have a formal Talent Management strategy?
   b. How is talent defined in that strategy?
   c. What talent management practices are in place to support the strategy? What talent management pipeline exists?
   d. What evidence can you see that the strategy is working?

2. Using the case of BAT Nigeria and the analysis of the challenges faced in competing for talent in an international labour market, what Talent Management practices should be the focus of attention for BAT?

3. Using the framework in the case study, and applying it to your organisation, examine:

   a. The strategic importance and challenges of Talent Management and retention strategies,
   b. The key drivers of talent mobility,
   c. The extent to which the mobility drivers are influenced by the external context.

4. Examine the inclusive and exclusive definitions of Talent Management and prepare a paper for the senior management team of a multinational organisation suggesting ways in which these could be used to develop a suitable talent management strategy.

Bibliography

Anakwe, U. P. (2002). 'Human resources management practices in Nigeria: challenges and insights'. *The International Journal of Human Resources Management*, 13(7), 1042–59.

Barney, J. B. (2001). 'Resource-based theories of competitive advantage: a ten-year retrospective on the resource-based view'. *Journal of Management*, 27(6), 643–50.

Caplan, J. (2011). *The Value of Talent: Promoting Talent Management across the Organization*. London: Kogan Page.

Cappelli, P. (2008). 'Talent management for the twenty-first century'. *Harvard Business Review*, 86 (3), 76–81.

Chambers, E. G., Foulon, M., Handfield-Jones, H., Hankin, S. M., and Michael III, E. G. (1998). 'The war for talent' (Electronic version). *McKinsey Quarterly*, 3, 44–57.

CIPD (2007a). *Talent Management*. (Electronic version), http://www.cipd.co.uk/binaries/talentmanage.pdf

CIPD (2007b). *Talent Management: Understanding the Dimensions*. (Electronic version), http://www.cipd.co.uk/binaries/3832%20Talent%20management.pdf

CIPD (2010). *Talent Development in the BRIC Countries*. London: CIPD.

CIPD (2011). *Talent Management: An Overview*. London: CIPD.

Davenport, T. H., Harris, J. and Shapiro, J. (2010). 'Competing on talent analytics'. *Harvard Business Review*, 88 (10), 52–8.

Guthridge, M., Komm, A. B. and Lawson, E. (2008). 'Making talent a strategic priority'. *The McKinsey Quarterly*, 1, 49–59.

Guthridge, M. and Lawson, E. (2008). 'Divide and survive'. *People Management*, September, 40–4.

Hatum, A. (2010). *Next Generation Talent Management: Talent Management to Survive Turmoil*. Basingstoke: Palgrave Macmillan.

Hofstede, G. and Hofstede, G. L. (2004). *Cultures and Organizations: Software of the Mind*. New York: McGraw-Hill.

Incomes Data Services (2010). *Talent Management*. HR studies, No. 918. London: IDS.

McCartney, C. and Garrow, V. (2006). *The Talent Management Journey*. Research reports. Horsham: Roffey Park Institute.

Okpara, J. O., and Wynn, P. (2008). 'Human resources management practice in a transition economy: challenges and prospects'. *Management Research News*, 31 (1), 57–76.

Parry, E. and Urwin, P. (2009). *Tapping into Talent: The Age Factor and Generation Issues. Research into Practice*. London: Chartered Institute of Personnel and Development.

Peiker, S. (2011). 'Best practices for optimizing the global talent pool'. *Workspan*, 54 (4), 42–7.

Pilbeam, S. and Corbridge, M. (2006). *People Resourcing: Contemporary HRM in Practice*. Harlow: FT Prentice Hall.

Reiche, B. S. (2008). 'The configuration of employee retention practices in multinational corporations' foreign subsidiaries'. *International Business Review*, 17, 676–87.

Rotberg, R. I. (2004). *Crafting the New Nigeria: Confronting the Challenges*. London: Rienner.

Rotberg, R. I. (2007). *Nigeria: Elections and Continuing Challenges (Council Special Report)*. New York: Council on Foreign Relations.

Sinclair, A., Robertson-Smith, G. and McCartney, C. (2008). *Managing Teams across Cultures: How to Manage across Borders, Time Zones and Cultures*. Research report. Horsham: Roffey Park Institute.

Sirkin, H., Hemerling, J. W. and Bhattacharya, A. K. (2008). *Globality: Competing Everywhere with Everyone for Everything*. London: Headline.

Strack, R. and Caye, J-M. (2009). *Creating People Advantage: How to Tackle the Major HR Challenges during the Crisis and Beyond*. Boston, MA: Boston Consulting Group/European Association for People Management.

Strack, R., Dyer, A. and Caye, J-M. (2008). *Creating People Advantage: How to Address HR Challenges Worldwide through 2015*. Boston, MA: Boston Consulting.

Tansley, C., Turner, P., Foster, C., Harris, L., Sempik, A., Stewart, J. and Williams, H. (2007). *Talent: Strategy, Management and Measurement*. London: CIPD.

CHAPTER 11

Performance Management

Encouraging champions and cheats

David Hall

This chapter examines the proliferation of performance management at the workplace, catalysed by the development of management information systems which can store and transfer vast amounts of data which can be used to analyse performance. However as organisations ride the technology wave that provides such capability, the heart of organisational performance is a human one and its 'beat' is the behaviour of people. This chapter will look at:

- The development and activities associated with performance management
- The relationship between performance management and people behaviour based on theory and practice
- A case study which considers different perspectives and consequences of performance management, not all desirable.

Top of the agenda

Performance management has been enthusiastically embraced by managers of organisations across all sectors in the past 20 years to make it a workplace phenomenon of the twenty-first century. The 'promise' of performance management is so attractive that it is difficult for organisations to ignore it. However, like other interventions, if performance management is not well designed or implemented, there can be serious consequences for stakeholders. The case presented in this chapter looks at some examples where performance management resulted in some serious problems. The key learning point from this is to recognise the limitations and weaknesses in performance management interventions, and to try to avoid the 'unintended consequences' and damaging dysfunctional behaviour that can result.

Performance management has been near the top of many organisations' agendas for several years, in the face of unrelenting pressure to improve productivity in view of increasing competitiveness and demand from shareholders. The public sector faces extraordinary challenges to deliver better value for money for increasingly expensive services against a background of severe cost-cutting. The difficulties experienced by both sectors since the financial crash of 2007 have been exacerbated by a mixture of debt, lack of credit and funding, which have only increased the intensity of the spotlight on organisational performance.

Globalisation, digitalisation and corporate governance regulation (the latter due to failures to effectively manage performance in the financial sector) continue to combine to drive the adoption of performance management methods across industry sectors and international boundaries. These factors have encouraged rapid development of 'mechanistic' control capabilities through the use of information and management systems ('hard' systems) to support performance management. 'Organic' control methods ('soft' systems) which centre on people, particularly in the areas of involvement, creativity, learning and development, struggle to keep pace. The latter form of control is about effective people management through motivation, opportunity and behaviour and is a necessary and vital component of managing performance. The case presented in this chapter focuses on some of the key issues in this area and what can go wrong (and how to avoid this happening) when organisations focus too heavily on the harder methods of performance management and do not pay enough attention to softer aspects, such as behaviour which is at the heart of managing people and performance.

Meaning of performance management

There are several definitions of performance management (which is interchangeable with the term 'managing performance' in this chapter) that emphasise the strategic nature of this intervention and its significance to managing people.

The term 'performance management' was first used in the 1970s by Beer and Ruh (1976) but the first formal definition was provided by the Institute of Personnel Management (IPM, 1992), now the Chartered Institute of Personnel Management (CIPD) as a result of the first research carried out on performance management in the UK in 1992:

> A strategy which relates to every activity of the organisation; set in the context of its human resource policies, culture, style and communication systems. The nature of the strategy depends on the organisational context and can vary from organisation to organisation.

According to this definition, performance management *is* strategy set in the context of human resource policies, that is it is about managing people, and the contextual nature of performance management is highlighted. A definition of managing performance by Hall (2009: 142) connects employee behaviour to the (strategic) intentions of organisations:

> Managing performance is about individuals, groups and organisations achieving something that is desirable or intended as a consequence of their actions

which leads to improvement and, is invariably associated with effectiveness and efficiency. But it is also about how the outcomes are achieved and, what individuals and teams learn from experience to help improve performance in the future.

The significance of *how* outcomes are achieved is an important aspect of this definition, which will be discussed later in this chapter. A concise yet sublime definition which captures the essence of performance management is provided by Mohrman and Mohrman (1995) as simply 'managing the business', implying that performance management is an integral activity in running a business and is the responsibility of all managers.

Performance management and HRM

Performance management was influential in the development of HRM and the early HR models. Performance is, quite literally, at the centre of one of the first HRM models, the Michigan model of HRM (Fombrun, Tichy and Devanna, 1984), and makes the connection between selection, appraisal and development as people management interventions for managing performance. This first HR model claimed that performance management was part of the HR domain.

Unlike the model by Fombrun, the Harvard model of HRM (Beer, Spencer, Lawrence, Quinn Mills and Walton, 1984) acknowledges the influence of external factors on HR policy formulation, including stakeholder interests, and that the implementation of these policies has long-term consequences for organisational effectiveness.

Guest's theory of HRM, with its four HR policy goals of strategic integration, commitment, flexibility and quality, attempted to describe how HR policy implementation led to certain organisational outcomes, including job performance and other outcomes which affect organisational performance (Guest, 1989).

These HRM models identified the importance of aligning HRM policies with business strategy, and introduced the term 'strategic HRM'. The relationship between strategic HRM and performance is emphasised by Boxall and Purcell (2003) who state that strategic HRM is about how HRM influences organisational performance.

Performance management systems

A performance management system (PMS) provides a coherent and holistic framework of integrated processes which enables organisations to systematically manage strategy and performance. In doing so, a PMS 'connects' an organisation's strategic purpose with the objectives of groups and individuals. This form of intervention provides a means for aligning the actions (behaviour) of employees with the strategic aims of their employer.

Although not usually described as a PMS, Managing by Objectives (MBO) model by Drucker (1955) was the first systematic approach that attempted to align organisational goals with employee performance and development, a key feature of all performance management systems today. MBO describes a cycle of integrated management activities that communicate and cascade organisational aims to employees, providing the basis for agreeing individual objectives which can be monitored and reviewed using an appraisal process.

The key principles in the practice of MBO and performance management systems are the setting of objectives (goals), the participation of managers in agreeing to objectives and performance criteria as well as continual review and appraisal of results.

The Balanced Scorecard by Kaplan and Norton (1996) is one of the most popular forms of PMS today and is in widespread use across all sectors. In practice it has all of the elements of MBO but the unique features of the Balanced Scorecard are the specific performance perspectives or dimensions in which organisations are encouraged to manage performance: financial, customer, operational and people.

Performance management and behaviour

The principle of using objectives to manage performance is described by Locke's Goal-setting theory (Locke, 1968), which states that individuals are motivated to behave in such a way that they achieve goals that are personally desirable. The significance of goals being 'personally desirable' is paramount and the implications of this will become apparent below. The assertion behind goal-setting theory and the use of goals and targets in performance management is that clear goals will enhance an individual's ability to create the precise intention needed to facilitate behaviour which will lead to achievement of the desired goal.

Discretionary behaviour is identified by Purcell in the People–Performance model (Purcell, Kinnie, Hutchinson, Rayton and Swart, 2003) as the link in the relationship between motivated and committed employees and performance. In other words, positive performance outcomes are a consequence of individuals making choices about the behaviours they engage in, as opposed to being told to do so by a manager or supervisor.

Expectancy theory (Vroom, 1964) is an important motivational theory because it describes the relationship between goals and rewards, and how this influences behaviour. Expectancy theory argues that an individual's motivation (force of intent to act) depends on that person's perception of the probability that their effort will result in a level of performance which will be good enough to achieve an outcome that they will value and that will influence their motivation. This theory provides a rationale for designing goal-based performance management interventions which incorporate specific outcomes in the form of rewards to influence employee behaviour and performance.

Another motivation theory which is helpful in informing managers about managing performance and reward is Herzberg's Two-Factor Theory (Herzberg, 1959). This theory describes how 'motivator factors' influence workers to produce a superior performance and effort, and how 'hygiene factors' prevent people from becoming dissatisfied with work. In terms of performance management, the 'motivating factors' are a form of (intangible) 'intrinsic' rewards, for example achievement, recognition, responsibility, advancement and so on while 'hygiene factors' tend to be (tangible) 'extrinsic' rewards, for example salary, company policy and administration, supervision and so on. These two motivation theories, along with goal-setting theory, provide the theoretical grounding for the design of performance management interventions which attempt to influence employee behaviour by using goals and rewards.

Management control

Performance management is an intervention for controlling behaviour to ensure that employee efforts are focused on contributing towards the aims of the organisation. The use of incentives and rewards, both intrinsic and extrinsic, are used to encourage 'desired' and often discretionary behaviour which is deemed necessary to achieve performance standards. The use of bonus payments in sales environments is common practice and is a good example of such encouragement, where the standard of performance can readily be specified as a target (a measurable goal) in financial or volume terms.

There are working environments where it is more difficult to define performance standards and outcomes as measurable goals (targets), for example policing, teaching and health care professions, and this form of intervention is not as viable or reliable for monitoring and reviewing performance. However this has not deterred employers in these sectors from introducing a multitude of targets in an attempt to gain more effective management control and to improve performance.

The use of rewards and penalties, for example the risk of not gaining promotion, salary increase and even losing one's job, linked to goals and targets can be powerful influencers of behaviour but not always in a positive way. The expectation of reward and the fear of failure can cause unintended consequences in the form of negative or undesirable behaviour known as dysfunctional behaviour. Examples of dysfunctional behaviour would be the miss-selling of inappropriate financial products to meet quarterly targets, which would result in earning maximum bonus. Another example would be not checking a patient into an Accident and Emergency department because the shortage of medical staff on duty would result in the hospital not meeting the four-hour target. In the first example, the target will have been achieved but not in the second, illustrating that dysfunctional behaviour can occur when targets are met and also when they are not. The case study in this chapter outlines examples of dysfunctional behaviour, including the example from the NHS involving targets.

Such dysfunctional behaviour can have serious consequences for the individuals who are affected by this type of behaviour – the individuals who behaved in a dysfunctional way, those who are affected by dysfunctional behaviour and the organisations linked to such behaviour whose reputation can be seriously damaged. Potentially everyone involved in dysfunctional behaviour stands to lose out in some way.

Many organisations use 'core values' to guide and support the behaviour of employees in achieving their vision and objectives. These values are often incorporated into the appraisal process as a basis for encouraging and rewarding the desired behaviours that an organisation wishes its employees to display when performing. The incorporation of values, attitudes and behaviour (VAB) in performance management is growing in popularity because it focuses on the behaviour of employees and *how* performance levels are achieved, that is outcomes rather than the outputs. Outcomes linked with learning and development are often desirable for employers and employees because they support the personal development necessary for performance improvement.

The case below examines some of the issues outlined above, exploring some of the controversies around the use of targets which have been the subject of several headlines in recent years. Psychological concepts related to the use of performance management methods are examined by providing a link to research into the people–performance relationship.

How 'smart' are targets? – the case of the bad press

One can say with some confidence that one of the outstanding achievements of targets in recent years has been the ability to attract very bad press. In March 2009, the national news headlines were all about the Healthcare Commissions report on Mid-Staffordshire Hospitals. On 18 March 2009, *The Daily Telegraph* ran the front page headline 'Targets blamed for 1,200 deaths at hospital' (Smith, 2009: 1). The BBC televised news programmes opened with the same story that day. There has not been a more damning headline implicating targets in organisational failure with such catastrophic consequences.

The Mid-Staffordshire Hospitals case is only one of many stories about dysfunctional behaviour which has targets at its roots (Healthcare Commission, March 2009.) In October 2008, the press (Irvine, 2008) reported that BT had been fined £1.3 m after it was discovered that staff had been calling each other to meet call-answering targets, which were part of BT's contract to service the Armed Forces telephone system. Recent headlines about payment of excessive bonuses linked to targets in the banking sector continue to harden public perception and damage reputations.

Deserved criticism?

Based on these examples, we know that objective setting, and particularly the use of targets, can lead to unintended consequences, causing serious problems for organisations, employees and other stakeholders. But there is another side to the stories. The 2005 CIPD Performance Management survey indicated that the majority of organisations, across all sectors, used some form of objective- or target-setting as a performance management technique, and this practice is unlikely to change (CIPD, 2005). The same survey also suggests that managers get it right most of the time, as objective-setting is regarded as being effective by the vast majority of organisations using it as an intervention. So where does it all go wrong? Understanding the theory is a good place to start.

The theory behind the practice

Starting with the individual perspective, a good place to start is goal-setting theory, developed by Edwin Locke (Locke, 1968). Locke said that goals, when translated into personal objectives, positively affect individual effort, persistence and direction of behaviour, and result in enhanced performance. The motivational effect of goals on work motivation is one of the key findings in organisational behaviour and has played a major role in shaping performance management methods, from Drucker's 'Management by Objectives' (the 'original' performance management system) to Kaplan and Norton's prolific 'Balanced Scorecard'.

Goal-setting theory states that for goals to be effective, managers should consider several factors when designing and implementing goals: goal difficulty, goal specificity, goal commitment, participation in setting goals and feedback. Managers also need to take into account the perceived value of goals to individual employees as this will influence motivation and behaviour, and it will differ from one person to another.

Expectancy theory provides a major contribution to our understanding of people behaviour that is linked to objectives. Vroom describes a process based on the individual's perception of the amount of effort needed to achieve specified performance levels and the value of reward. The important point is that, as in the case of goal theory, the outcome manifests itself in behaviour and the variables provide a means for intervention that can influence and even predict behaviour. This is one of the key theories that have shaped performance and reward practice as we know it today.

Job enrichment is often cited as an important factor in improving motivation, satisfaction and performance. Hackman and Oldham (1980) developed a comprehensive model of job enrichment featuring five core job dimensions: skill variety, task identity, task significance, autonomy and feedback. These, in turn, lead to three psychological states:

- Experienced meaningfulness of the work,
- Experienced responsibility for the outcomes of the work and
- Knowledge of the actual results of the work activities.

Hackman and Oldham's work on job enrichment was developed into a Job Diagnostic Survey and is the basis for many employee job satisfaction surveys that are around today.

Policy and performance

Johnny Sung and David Ashton wrote a research report *High Performance Work Practices: linking strategy and skills to performance outcomes* (Ashton and Sung, 2005) describing how 'High Performing Organisations' (HPOs) apply 'High Performance Work Practices' (HPWPs) (Ashton and Sung, 2005) to drive performance. The report presents several case studies of organisations using targets to improve performance, including the Scotland-based garment manufacturer, W L Gore, where team members determine their own objectives.

HPOs are described as organisations that design work and people management practices that systematically link the achievement of organisational objectives and performance. This and other research which has investigated the link between managing people and performance describes the application of integrated people management policy and practices, which is termed 'bundling'. Sung and Ashton call these policies and practices 'High Performance Work Practices' (HPWPs) and categorise them under three broad headings: high involvement, human resource practices, and reward and commitment.

In another report, Professor David Guest, drawing on data from the UK, Australia and New Zealand, categorises the 18 HPWPs he identifies into four dimensions (Guest, 2005):

- Employee autonomy and involvement in decision-making,
- Training, development and support for employee performance,
- Rewards for performance,
- Sharing information and knowledge.

To understand how management practices influence employee performance, Professor John Purcell and his group at Bath University produced a research report *Understanding the People and Performance Link: Unlocking the Black Box* (Purcell et al., 2003) and in it described performance as a function of ability, motivation and opportunity.

Based on his findings, Purcell proposed in his model that the application of integrated HR policies or practices positively influences commitment and job satisfaction. This in turn encourages positive employee behaviour based on free will, that is, 'discretionary behaviour', which produces improved performance, as depicted in Figure 11.1 below. One of the 11 policy areas that Purcell identified as driving this model in practice is appraising individual performance and development, and setting objectives and targets that will play a role in this for many employees.

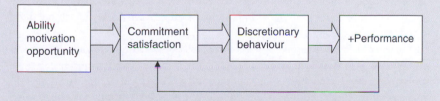

Figure 11.1   People–performance model

The principle of applying integrated people management policies and practices is key, because the use of objectives alone, particularly narrowly defined targets, tends not to be enough to positively influence employee engagement, commitment and satisfaction which were found to be antecedent to improved performance. Badly designed and badly applied targets can actually encourage undesirable or 'dysfunctional' behaviour. 'Gaming' is one such form of this behaviour, where employees attempt to beat the system to achieve the target. Dysfunctional behaviour can lead to 'unintended consequences' and it can happen at an individual level or be systemic, as in the case of the BT call centre.

When targets are linked to powerful motivators such as fear and reward, this can have a strong effect. Managers need to be conscious of the directional nature of motivation in terms of how this can lead to undesirable behaviour. Many organisations use performance management methods based on appraising attitudes and values to 'guide' employee behaviour in achieving good outcomes for the individual, organisation and other stakeholders.

Conclusions and lessons

Focusing organisation and individual activity on what matters, through the use of targets linked to strategic aims can be a powerful management 'tool' but careful consideration needs to be given to what is targeted, how targets are applied and to whom targets are applied.

Targets can also be viewed as an extreme form of management control which not all employees will feel are appropriate or be comfortable and may not respond well to. Individual differences in attitude, motivation and personality will mean that different individuals are likely to respond differently to targets and objectives, some more positively than others, for example individuals will have a strong sense of what influence they can bring to a situation to achieve a target and therefore of how fair the target is.

Research has identified autonomy, the meaning of work and feedback as being key to encouraging employee engagement, commitment and satisfaction, which are antecedent to performance. Good people management, enabled by integrated HR policies and effective line management, is essential for maintaining positive employment relationships and improving performance.

Objectives and target-setting may play a part in improving performance but only a part, and this technique should only be used as part of an overall strategy aimed at developing those conditions which influence behaviour and performance. The next time you are involved in setting and agreeing targets, ask yourself how the target will encourage employee engagement, commitment and satisfaction, and what the outcome is likely to be in terms of behaviour. In other words, ask yourself just how 'smart' the target really is.

The use of too many targets will have a cost, a human cost as well as a cost to the bottom line, as professional judgement and leadership are eroded by increasing pressures to 'manage by numbers'. This phenomenon has been widely reported in several areas of public service such as health, police and teaching, as professional practice is compromised by over-bearing compliance regimes which demand that targets are shown to have been met.

There is a danger that as governments and organisations attempt to drive performance using a plethora of targets, the total cost of managing such grandiose interventions undermines the very reason why they were introduced in the first place. When the 'tail begins to wag the dog', you know there is a problem!

Activities and discussion questions

1. Consider what motivates you in work and how your manager and the organisation having that information could effectively support you in your job.

2. Based on your experiences and/or observations of performance management in organisations, for example appraisal, can you relate the theory presented in this chapter to practice? What specific knowledge of theory do you think would help managers to more effectively manage people and performance and why?

3. Imagine working for an organisation that did not have a formal approach to performance management. How would you imagine this organisation functioning and what would you suggest would need to happen to make it work?

4. Based on what you have read or seen on TV or the www, can you think of an example of organisational or individual employee 'dysfunctional behaviour?' What did it mean for those involved? You may want to consider the banking crisis of 2007 and/or the BP Gulf of Mexico drilling incident in 2010. There is information on the www reporting the situation at NHS Mid-Staffordshire Hospitals before the headlines in 2009.

5. Consider what could lead to dysfunctional behaviour in individuals and groups in the workplace (consider your answer to Q4) and what is the theoretical basis for this?

Bibliography

Ashton, D. and Sung, J. (2005). *High Performance Work Practices: Linking Strategy and Skills to Performance Outcomes*. London: DTi/CIPD.

Austin, R. D. (1996). *Measuring and Managing Performance in Organizations*. New York: Dorset House publishing.

Beer, M. and Ruh, R. A. (1976). 'Employee growth through performance management'. *Harvard Business Review*, July–August, 59–66.

Beer, M., Spencer, P. R., Lawrence, Quinn Mills, D. and Walton, R. E. (1984). *Managing Human Assets*. New York: The Free Press.

Boxall, P. and Purcell, J. (2003). *Strategy and Human Resource Management*. Basingstoke: Palgrave Macmillan.

CIPD (2005). *Survey Report September 2005: Performance Management*. London: CIPD.

Drucker, P. F. (1955). *The Practice of Management*. London: Heinemann.

Fombrun, C. J., Tichy, N. M. and Devanna, M. A. (1984). *Strategic Human Resource Management*. New York: Wiley.

Guest, D. (1989). 'Personnel and HRM: can you tell the difference?' *Personnel Management*, January, 49.

Guest, D. (2005). *Conference Session 5 Human resource Management and Corporate Performance: Recent Empirical Evidence in DTI Economics Paper No.13*. Corporate Governance, Human Resource Management and Firm Performance. London: Department of Trade and Industry.

Hackman, J. R. and Oldham, G. R. (1980). *Work Redesign*. Reading, MA: Addison-Wesley.

Hall, D. (2009) 'Managing performance', in Gilmore, S. and Williams, S. (Eds), *Human Resource Management*. Oxford University Press, 142.

Healthcare Commission (2009). *Investigation into the Mid-Staffordshire NHS Foundation Trust*. London: Healthcare Commission.

Herzberg, F. (1959). *The Motivation to Work*. New York: Wiley.

Institute of Personnel Management (1992). *Performance Management in the UK: An Analysis of the Issues*. London: IPM.

Irvine, C. (30 October 2008). 'BT fined £1.3 million after staff admit phoning each other to meet targets', retrieved on 24 October 2011, from *The Daily Telegraph* website: http://www.telegraph.co.uk/news/uknews/defence/3282730/BT-fined-1.3-million-after-staff-admit-phoning-each-other-to-meet-targets.html

Jones, P. (2007). *Managing for Performance: Delivering Results through Others*. Harlow: Prentice Hall.

Kaplan, R. S and Norton, D. P. (1996). *The Balanced Scorecard – Translating Strategy into Action*. Boston, MA: Harvard Business School Press.

Locke, E. A. (1968). 'Towards a theory of task motivation and incentives'. *Organisational Behaviour and Human Performance*, 3 (2), 157–89.

Marr, B. (2010). *Managing and Delivering Performance: How Government, Public Sector and Not-for-Profit Organisations Can Measure and Manage What Really Matters*. Oxford: Butterworth-Heinemann.

Mohrman, A. M. and Mohrman, S. A. (1995). 'Performance management is "running the business" '. *Compensation and Benefits Review*, July–August, 69–75.

Mullins, L. J. (2007). *Management and Organisational Behaviour* (8th edn.). Harlow: FT/Prentice Hall.

Purcell, J., Kinnie, N. Hutchinson, S., Rayton, B. and Swart, J. (2003). *Understanding the People and Performance Link: Unlocking the Black Box*. London: CIPD.

Smith, R. (18 March 2009). *'NHS Targets "May Have Led to 1,200 Deaths" in Mid-Staffordshire'*. London: *The Daily Telegraph*, 1.

Vroom, V. H. (1964). *Work and Motivation*. New York: Wiley.

CHAPTER 12

The Strategic Value of being a Learning Organisation

Marjorie Corbridge, Elizabeth Nials, Terence Hart and Sandie Paice

Investing in employees is a key aspect of the employer brand or a determinant of being an employer of choice, but with increasing competition for organisational resources, the strategic decision facing employers is how to get the best return on investment in the employee. As Garvin, Edmondson and Gino (2008: 109) state, 'Leaders might think that getting their organizations to learn is only a matter of articulating a clear vision, giving employees the right incentives, and providing lots of training. This assumption is not merely flawed – it is risky in the face of intensifying competition, advances in technology and shifts in customer preferences. Organisations need to learn more than ever as they confront these mounting forces.' To keep pace with the changes in the global environment the organisation needs to maximise the investment in learning and development and to embed the concept of continuous learning into the culture of the organisation. Embracing the philosophy of the learning organisation is one approach that may point the way forward for the business.

The concept of the learning organisation has been around for several years and it may be that the overriding benefit from becoming a learning organisation derives from the message that it sends out within the organisation in terms of what is important. Having a focus on and indeed a 'label' for learning within the organisation can raise its profile and may also increase the investment made in the learning of members of the organisation. There have been discussions on whether *organisations* can 'learn', and it is inappropriate to rehearse that argument here, but undoubtedly investment in the learning of organisational members develops organisation knowledge, which may be deemed a critical success factor in the performance of the business.

The Learning Organisation

The definition of 'The Learning Organisation' according to Senge (1990: 3) applies to organisations 'where people continually expand their capacity to create the results they truly desire, where new and expansive patterns of thinking are nurtured, where collective aspiration is set free, and where people are continuing to see the whole together'. He goes on to argue that what distinguishes organisations that are learning organisations is the 'mastery' of basic disciplines in the approach to learning. These disciplines include systems thinking, personal mastery, mental models, building a shared vision and team thinking. These disciplines recognise that people are not just bystanders when it comes to learning but rather that they are active participants who are able to 'create' a future for their organisations. The concept of the learning organisation has been around since the 1980s and was well explored and investigated by Pedler, Boydell and Burgoyne (1989) through a project 'Developing the Learning Company', which examined the reasons why organisations invested in planned, structured and people-focused initiatives. Their findings showed that this investment was made by organisations in an effort to bring about change and increase performance in an increasingly competitive world. These ideas still resonate today. The work of Pedler, Burgoyne and Boydell (1991), as explained by Reid, Barrington and Brown (2004), led to the identification of 11 principles under five headings. The five headings are strategic, looking in, structures, looking out and learning opportunities. Each of these is examined in turn below:

Strategic includes two principles: first the feedback on strategy from learning – in other words a constant review of strategy to ensure that what is being learned and experienced by staff is feeding through to the decision-makers; second the encouragement of participation in policy making which should ensure that policy reflects the culture of the organisation and what the workforce experiences in working there. *Looking in* has four principles: first empowerment through information which involves the sharing of high-quality information across the organisation; second the examination and review of bureaucratic controls and procedures to ensure that these are 'fit for purpose' and facilitate effective working; third interdepartmental and interdisciplinary exchanges to facilitate understanding of and respect for the contribution made by everyone in the organisation; and fourth making sure to reward what is important to the organisation to facilitate creativity and innovation. *Structure* has just one underlying principle, that is the features of the organisation should be facilitative and enabling. This in practice will mean more flexible structures where knowledge and learning can be more easily shared. *Looking out* has two principles: first environmental (external) scanning, in particular by boundary workers who come into contact with clients and customers. Second inter-company learning by those employees who come into contact with other organisations and who are able to feed back their experiences and learning. *Learning opportunities* include two principles: the learning climate or culture that supports learning and finally self-development which encourages all members of staff to take responsibility for their own learning. This extensive model certainly provides the basis for a strong learning and development culture, but is it convincing in terms of being transformational? If a key aspect of the learning organisation is to bring about change, where in this are the characteristics that drive change?

Garvin et al. (2008: 110) argue that 'the ideal of the learning organization has not yet been realized' and cite three main reasons for this: first they argue that the early messages about the learning organisation were celebrations of an ideal and a better world rather than a mechanism for showing the way; as they eloquently say, 'it emphasised the forest and paid little attention to the trees' and by this they mean that the headings and principles were difficult to implement. Second the concept of the learning organisation was aimed largely at CEOs and leaders in the organisation rather than at the level of line manager, where much of the learning and development was actually done, which left the manager with little understanding of whether what was happening 'on the ground' was having any impact on overall organisational performance at all. Third there was a distinct lack of valid mechanisms for assessment, leaving organisations with little to facilitate benchmarking or even accurately assess progress. Garvin et al. (2008: 111) go on to identify three factors that they contend are 'essential for organizational learning and adaptability: a supportive learning environment, concrete learning processes and practices and leadership behavior that provides reinforcement' which they refer to as 'the building blocks of the learning organization'. Further examination of the components of these 'building blocks' can help to illuminate the characteristics of each.

Building block 1 – A supportive learning environment

A supportive learning environment requires the following:

Psychological safety – This suggests that employees need to feel 'safe' to express their ideas and their concerns. Any member of staff feeling inhibited or threatened when disagreeing with managers or colleagues will soon refuse to contribute or to engage, with the potential consequence that the leaders fail to capture key information or views. It is not always the ones with the most to say who make the incisive contribution! A culture where staff feel free to express their observations and experiences and where they feel included is likely to be in an organisation which benefits from this and which values learning. How people feel about where they work is an important feature of a learning organisation.

Appreciation of difference – This ensues when people are aware of and respect alternative views. This can motivate and initiate discussions on new ideas and prevent stagnation and disconnection.

Openness to new ideas – means that various responses to situations can be expressed and discussed. An important part of learning is to test the unknown and develop evaluation and judgement skills to know what might be suitable for the organisation. A learning organisation does not 'play safe'.

Time for reflection – It requires just that, time and space to assess what has been learned, to reflect on what is and what is not suitable for the organisation and to be very clear about why you believe that to be the case. A pressure felt by many people at work is time pressure. Denying your employees the space and the time to reflect denies them the opportunity to learn from what they are experiencing around them and this denies the organisation the chance to learn. In this situation employees may fail to develop the skills and abilities to diagnose problems, develop solutions and learn from those experiences. One of the most reinforcing aspects of an organisation is its culture and a culture that disrespects time and blames employees for mistakes will fail to learn.

Building block 2 – Concrete learning processes and practices

Concrete learning processes and practices are key components of an effective learning organisation. They do not occur without effort on the part of the drivers of the organisation. The development of effective learning processes requires the generation and analysis of 'good' information. This includes:

Experimenting with new and different ways of doing things – seeking out new products or new services can bring with them new ways of working.

Intelligence gathering – 'looking out' may identify trends in technology, trends in what competitors are doing or trends in what customers want, and this provides the opportunity for the development of concrete processes based on 'good information'.

Careful analysis and interpretation help to identify possible problems and develop workable solutions.

Education and training will ensure that the organisation will have a workforce fit for future challenges based on thorough investigation and concrete learning processes.

However to capitalise on this structured analysis, knowledge must be shared, it must travel horizontally across the organisation and vertically through the organisation. Carefully constructed de-briefs or reviews are needed to identify gaps in skills and knowledge and to put plans in place to bridge those gaps.

Building block 3 – Leadership that reinforces learning

Leaders are very influential in developing and sustaining organisational learning. If leadership teams send out signals that they value the time that staff spend on identifying problems, seeking solutions and reviewing how staff are able to do their jobs then they also signal that learning and development are important. Staff are more likely to feel not only that they are 'being watched' but that they also have a voice and can discuss openly how well they feel able to perform the tasks required of them.

These three building blocks are not mutually exclusive; they overlap and reinforce each other creating an environment in which the employees can feel that they belong to a learning organisation. But in many organisations, especially large organisations, there is often not a single culture or even a single leader. Managers need to be mindful of differences, respect those differences, share experiences and bring people with them in developing and sustaining the learning organisation. However Garvin et al. (2008: 116) provide us with insights that might help managers who strive to cultivate a learning organisation. They identify four factors that are important to managers who want to stimulate learning within their organisations. First they contend that leaders who display behaviours such as openness, consideration of different options and acceptance of others' views are likely to encourage learning but these leadership behaviours alone are insufficient. They explain that the organisational culture and the processes in place to support learning are key factors in employees' embracing of learning and transferring their learning to enhance organisational performance. Second they explain that organisations are not uniform in character. This means there will not be a standard approach to or acceptance of learning across the organisation, so a 'one size fits all' strategy may not be appropriate. Third they claim that comparative performance is the critical measure. Organisations may place a high value on education and training, or on openness to new ideas, but this may not translate into a competitive advantage; the key factor is how well your organisation is doing in comparison to competitors. Fourth they state that learning is multidimensional and that 'you can enhance learning in an organisation in various ways depending on [what ...] you emphasise'. One organisation may promote reflection while another may see an appreciation of difference as a lever of influence.

Organisational learning

The debate around definitions and differences between the concept of the 'Learning Organisation' and the idea of organisational learning has been taking place since the 1990s, with some authors (Easterby-Smith, Burgoyne and Araujo, 1999: 2) attempting to 'identify templates or ideal types' of the Learning Organisation that organisations could try to match or apply to their own organisations. Finger and Brand (1999: 136) see organisational learning as 'an activity or a process by which organisations eventually reach the ideal of the Learning Organisation'. This raises the issue as to whether these should be seen as an 'either/or' option or perhaps more helpfully as a way of using the models of Senge (1990) and Pedler et al. (1991) as tools and methods that can be applied to the process of organisational learning. Swart and Kinnie (2010: 64) examine the links between HR practices and organisational learning, which they define as 'both the refinement (exploitative learning) and the renewal (exploratory learning) of knowledge'. This is useful in its recognition of the need to both *exploit* what is known in the organisation and identify how it is able to be best used within the business, and to *explore* the need for 'new knowledge and skills' and to identify the best way to acquire these. The work of Swart and Kinnie acknowledges the importance of knowledge assets (what the employees know) and the company's ability to 'acquire, develop and integrate new knowledge to create value for the organisation'. Their work seeks to identify the strategic HR policies that support the creation of high-value human capital and also the way to ensure that the organisation achieves the maximum value from that capital. They go on to look at the work of Jaw and Liu (2003) who propose five HR practices: empowerment, benefits programmes, encouraging commitment, comprehensive training and an emphasis on performance, which [together] comprise an organisational learning-orientated HRM which is designed to stimulate organisational self-renewal.

Marshall and Smith (2009a: 36) seek to examine the influences that may affect organisational learning, including 'the learning climate and capability, the effects of different sub-cultures or communities [in the same firm] on learning and the impact, if any, of learning on organisational performance'. One recurring message about organisational learning (Ortenblad, 2002; Shipton, 2006) is the difficulty of establishing a link between organisational learning and organisational performance, which is at best tenuous, with little empirical evidence to support this link. The factors used by some researchers (Tippins and Sohi, 2003; Lopez, Peon and Ordas, 2005) to examine organisational learning and organisational performance, such as profitability, return on investment and customer growth, can clearly be applied to 'for profit' organisations but are inappropriate for public sector organisations and it is difficult to find any studies that link individual learning with organisational performance outcomes. Marshall and Smith (2009b: 16) conclude: 'While it is difficult to generalise from the ... studies, the findings (political and cultural factors, difficulties in the transfer of knowledge, a lack of clarity between learning and performance) ... led [them] to conclude that ... the prescriptive perspective is based on an idealisation of real organisational life.' But surely to acquire and retain organisational investment in learning one would think that some organisational benefit would have to be identified. One area worthy of further mention in looking at organisational learning is the link with or processes for knowledge transfer within the organisation. Organisational learning often resides within the employee. There needs to be processes in place for capturing and sharing this knowledge for the benefit of the organisation and to ensure that this is not lost when an employee leaves. However, looking at a range of literature has highlighted the complexity of structuring learning within an organisation. Working towards becoming a learning organisation enables the organisation to develop appropriate systems through consultation with staff and implement processes which might be seen by the staff to be both meaningful and achievable. However it is important not to lose sight of organisational learning and knowledge transfer, which together may be the mechanism for enhancing organisational performance.

The case study that follows takes a systematic look at the development and implementation of an extensive programme for using the learning organisation vision to engage staff and to identify what is important for their future. This fits well with the importance of culture and vision that becomes evident through the literature.

Promoting the vision of the learning organisation in the Isle of Wight Primary Care Trust – a case study

The Isle of Wight NHS Primary Care Trust (the Trust) came into being in October 2006 with the dissolution of the Primary Care and Healthcare NHS Trusts. The Isle of Wight NHS system is unique, being the only integrated health system in England, as both a commissioner and provider of a diverse range of services: district general hospital, mental health services, community services and ambulance services. It provides clarity on where the responsibility for running local health services lies. Ninety per cent of the £216 million allocation is spent on commissioning services with local providers. The PCT has approximately 3,500 employees.

The four levers of influence and the four key traits of a learning organisation

The Trust was one of four PCTs to participate in a second wave Learning Organisation Programme (LOP) pilot, sponsored by the NHS Institute for Innovation and Improvement, and delivered in conjunction with McKinsey, the international organisational development consultants. The LOP aimed to promote the vision of an 'organisation that continually expands its capacity to create its future' (Senge, Kleiner, Robert, Ross and Smith 1994), and focused on tools designed to change organisational behaviour, using four 'levers of influence'. Based upon responses to the statement 'I would change my behaviour to become a better learner if...', these levers are:

Conviction and understanding: 'I understand why continuous learning is important for our organisation and what my role is in it.'

Formal mechanism: 'The structures, process and systems reinforce continuous learning.'

Skills and capabilities: 'I am supported in continuously developing the capabilities I need.'

Role-modelling: 'I see superiors, peers and subordinates behaviour that encourages learning.'

The LOP comprised several key interventions – interviews with 50 senior managers, including the executive team and senior clinicians, experiential workshops against a structured development programme and the development of internal change agents. The themes associated with these interventions centred on four key learning organisation traits:

Alignment and engagement: Clarifying, sharing and discussing the vision and each person's role in achieving it to motivate staff to constantly learn and focus their efforts,

Continuous improvement mindset: Encouraging reflection, planning and innovation to enable high-quality execution and continuous improvement,

Focus on people development: Motivating, developing and empowering people to increase their capacity to deliver results in a changing environment,

Proactive collaboration and idea sharing: Drawing on diverse perspectives and the best ideas internally and externally to devise solutions and leverage resources more effectively.

The LOP ran over 12 weeks and provided the Trust with an opportunity to create energy, capability and motivation in a critical mass of leaders towards continuous improvement (Table 12.1).

The workshops were designed to build motivation and the basic skills needed to create a learning environment. Executive team workshops set the direction for divisional workshops. Chaired by the Director of HR and OD, a Project Board was established, whose membership included the Chief Executive, Director of Corporate Affairs, Chief Operating Officer, Assistant Director of OD (project manager) and a McKinsey project lead. A project team had representation from across the

Table 12.1   The learning organisation pilot

Weeks	1–4	5–8	9–11	12
Phase	*Building a motivational team*	*Being a learning leader*	*Learning through work*	*Spreading and embedding*
Purpose	Feedback from interviews and defining learning benefits and aspirations	Defining leadership behaviours and building coaching skills in leaders	Understanding different learning styles using MBTI and a learning cycle approach to problem-solving	Action planning and clarity about how to embed the learning from the programme

organisation and the Project Board's primary role was to ensure successful programme implementation and action planning to embed the resultant learning.

The Learning Organisation Programme outcomes

The programme has enabled the Trust to gather the views and experiences of a wide range of staff with respect to the *four key traits of a learning organisation* and their perceived application within the organisation. The feedback from the interviews with senior staff resulted in a workshop at which the executive team absorbed the themes and messages and constructed a 'story' about the organisation and its future. This was a powerful factor in understanding the extent to which behaviour and mindset shifts needed to occur. For those who participated in the programme, significant learning has taken place, and the experience has had a positive impact on their respective teams. Throughout the programme, participants learned new skills and tools which they have applied to their operational roles. For example, managers have coaching conversations with their staff and have been actively using these coaching skills to support staff development. The PCT intends to train staff to become Myers Briggs facilitators because managers now recognise the value of understanding personality preferences within their teams. This positive outcome has been influenced by the role modelling of Directors of the Trust, including the Chief Executive. The *four levers of influence* on changing behaviour form the basis for the resultant action plan. Through the implementation of this plan, the organisation aims to ensure that the learning organisation traits are applied to support the establishment of a 'continuous cycle' of organisational learning. Successful implementation of the action plan will depend on factors such as effective internal communications, the assimilation of individual knowledge into everyday work situations, a clear restatement of desired employee behaviours through the Trust's Employee Qualities Framework (EQF) and the integration of the provisions of the plan into the overall Organisational Development (OD) Plan for 2008–2010 (Figure 12.1).

	Employee quality	Competence required
Improving patient's experience	Achieves Results	Drives for and delivers results Takes responsibility for decisions Meets deadlines
	Embraces collaborative working	Actively seeks opportunities to collaborate with other PCT colleagues Seeks and shares best practice Works in partnership with external agencies
	Delivers Change	Improves continuously Challenges norms and innovates Is flexible and adaptable
	Displays great interpersonal skills	Treats others with respect Recognises diversity Communicates effectively
	Lives the PCT vision	Puts the patient at the heart of everything we do Understands the vision and contribution to it Manages for the future
	Develops people	Aligns and energises people to provide meaning Creates stretching targets for the people in their roles Develops self

Figure 12.1   Employee qualities framework

The levers of influence show that behavioural change around learning is the lynchpin of an effective learning organisation. The six dimensions of the EQF represent the critical success factors through which the Trust seeks to promote a working climate and culture that will support its transition from being an organisation that is 'competent' to one that is 'excellent'.

The way forward

Through the application of the EQF, the Trust will continue to create opportunities for staff to express their views and inform effective decision-making. This will be supported through the focus groups meant to gain feedback and assist in planning. In addition, the work started on key organisational themes such as 'clinical engagement' and 'decentralisation' will be continued, using the teams that considered these issues in the Programme workshops. The Trust also aims to embed a variety of the other simple organisational development tools from the Programme to encourage, enable and model the mindsets and behaviours necessary for continuous improvement. The ongoing plan includes actions that draw upon McKinsey's key traits of a learning organisation, amongst which are:

Ongoing alignment and engagement

- Disseminating the Trust vision and 'story', through a variety of media, including one-to-one meetings with the Chief Executive.
- Communicating the outcomes of the LOP.

▪ Responding to feedback from the annual Staff Opinion Survey to reinforce the vision.

▪ Completing Project tasks relating to key themes.

Focus on people development

▪ Developing an email protocol to assist staff in using email more effectively.

▪ Modelling of 'quick tools' by the Executive Team such as techniques to surface root causes of observed outcomes.

▪ Incorporating 'coaching conversations' into the PCT's training plan.

▪ Incorporating the 'problem-solving' model into the PCT's training plan.

Continuous improvement mindset

▪ Incorporating the Myers Briggs Type Indicator into team-building training.

▪ Creating Executive Team planning time.

▪ Incorporating the LOP action plan into the overall OD plan, and monitoring progress

Valuing individuals

▪ Reviewing and formalising the Trust's 'Celebrations' agenda.

▪ Embedding the EQF, through meetings with diverse staff groups.

Conclusion and learning points

The Learning Organisation Programme has been valuable to the Isle of Wight NHS Primary Care Trust in providing the opportunity to anticipate and shape the future. The success of the LOP will depend on the implementation of the action plan and EQF, and the ability to deliver cultural change. The Partnership Forum Chair was a project participant and employees were updated monthly. Critically employees were also involved in the development of the EQF. Full commitment from senior management and the setting of ambitious timescales are critical success factors. Senior management provides the leadership for the working groups and the timescales generate the momentum necessary for maximum impact.

Activities and discussion questions

1. Conduct a debate on the benefits of becoming a learning organisation. This should comprise two teams with Team One speaking **for** the motion 'the learning organisation is a useful label to aim for that encourages a sustained investment in staff development'. Team Two should speak against the motion.

2. The study of the learning organisation in the Isle of Wight Primary Care Trust describes the development of a vision for the organisation in terms of being a learning organisation. To what extent does this vision map onto the characteristics of a learning organisation as identified in the theory?

3. Identify and examine the critical success factors in promoting a climate and culture for excellence as they are described in the study and comment on the extent to which these are universal or organisation-specific.

4. The study follows the development of the framework (or vision) of the learning organisation. From analysis of this study how would you plan the implementation of this vision to achieve the transition from being competent to being excellent?

Bibliography

Argyris, C. and Schön, D. (1996). *Organizational Learning II: Theory, Method and Practice*. Reading Mass.: Addison Wesley.

Boer, H., Berger, A., Chapman, R., and Gertsen, F. (2000). *CI Changes: From Suggestion Box to Organisational Learning: Continuous Improvement in Europe and Australia*. Aldershot: Ashgate Publishing.

Department of Health (2001). *Shifting the Balance of Power within the NHS: Securing Delivery*. London: Department of Health.

Easterby-Smith, M., Burgoyne, J. and Araujo, L. (eds) (1999). *Organizational Learning and the Learning Organization*. London: Sage.

Ferguson-Amores, M.C., García-Rodrígues, M. and Ruiz-Navarro, J. (2005). 'Strategic renewal: the transition from "total quality management" to the "learning organisation" '. *Management Learning* 36(2), 149–80.

Finger, M. and Brand, S.B. (1999). 'The concept of the "learning organization" applied to transformation of the public sector', in Easterby-Smith, M., Araujo, L. and Burgoyne, J. (Eds) *Organizational learning and the learning organization*. London: Sage.

Garvin, D.A. (2000). *Learning in Action. A Guide to Putting the Learning Organization to Work*. Boston, Mass.: Harvard Business School Press.

Garvin, D.A., Edmondson, A.C. and Gino, F. (2008). 'Is yours a learning organisation?'. *Harvard Business Review* 86(3), 109–16.

Gorelick, C. (2006). 'Organizational learning vs the learning organization: a conversation with a practitioner'. *The Learning Organization* 12(4), 383–8.

Isle of Wight NHS Primary Care Trust (2008). *Operational Plan 2008/10*.

Jaw, B. and Liu, W. (2003). 'Promoting organizational learning and self-renewal in Taiwanese companies: the role of HRM'. *Human Resource Management* 42, 223–41.

Kang, S.C., Morris, S. and Snell, S. (2007). 'Relational archetypes, organizational learning and value creation: extending the human resource architecture'. *Academy of Management Review* 32, 236–56.

Lopez, S.P., Peon, J.M.M. and Ordas, C.J.V. (2005). 'Human resource practices, organizational learning and business performance'. *Human Resource Development International* 8(2), 147–64.

Marshall, J. and Smith, S. (2009a). 'Learning organisations and organisational learning: what have we learned?' *Management Services* 53(2), 36–44.

Marshall, J. and Smith, S. (2009b). 'Learning organisations and organisational learning: what have we learned?' *Management Services* 53(3), 14–19.

Marsick, V.J. and Watkins, K.E. (2003). 'Demonstrating the value of an organization's learning culture: the dimensions of the learning organization questionnaire'. *Advances in Developing Human Resource* 5(2), 13251.

Ni, W. and Sun. H (2009). 'The relationship among organisational learning, continuous improvement and performance improvement: and evolutionary perspective'. *Total Quality Management* October 20(10), 1041–54.

Ortenblad, A. (2002). 'Organisational learning: a radical perspective'. *International Journal of Management Reviews* 4, 87–100.

Pedler, M., Boydell, T. and Burgoyne, J. (1989). 'Towards the learning company'. *Management Education and Development* 20(1), 1–8.

Pedler, M., Burgoyne, J. and Boydell, T. (1991). *The Learning Company*. Maidenhead: McGraw-Hill.

Reid, M.A., Barrington, H. and Brown, M. (2004). *Human Resource Development: Beyond Training Interventions*. London: CIPD.

Revans, R. (2004). 'Accrediting Managers at Work in the 21st Century'. *Academy of Management Review* 29, 571–7.

Senge, P. (1990). *The Fifth Discipline: The Art and Practice of the Learning Organisation*. New York: Doubleday Currency.

Senge, P., Kleiner, A., Robert, C., Ross, R.B. and Smith, B.J. (1994). *The Fifth Discipline Fieldbook: Strategies and Tools for Building a Learning Organization*. London: Nicholas Brealey Publishing.

Shipton, H. (2006). 'Cohesion or confusion? Towards a typology for organisational learning research'. *International Journal of Management Reviews* 8(4), 233–52.

Smith, M.K. (2001a). 'Peter Senge and the learning organization' (Electronic version) *The Encyclopedia of Informal Education*. Retrieved on 1 July 2011 from www.infed.org/thinkers/senge.htm

Smith, M.K. (2001b). 'The learning organization' (Electronic version) *The Encyclopedia of Informal Education*. Retrieved on 1 July 2011 from www.infed.org/biblio/learning-organization.htm

Swart, J. and Kinnie, N. (2010). 'Organisational learning, knowledge assets and HR practices in professional service firms'. *Human Resource Management Journal* 20(1), 64–79.

Tippins, M.J. and Sohi, R.S. (2003). 'IT competency and firm performance: is organizational learning a missing link?'. *Strategic Management Journal* 24(8), 745–61.

Torrington, D., Hall, L. and Taylor, S. (2008). *Human Resource Management*. Harlow: FT Prentice Hall.

CHAPTER 13

Knowledge Management
Interventions for retaining human capital

David Hall

Human capital and the knowledge that contributes to this people asset has become a significant factor in many organisations' capability to create and deliver value. For many organisations today, their ability to develop and harness knowledge has become a more valuable resource than other more traditional physical resources. This chapter looks at how organisations capture and transfer knowledge to ensure sustainability and success, focusing on:

- Knowledge creation and transfer,
- Management of knowledge to support organisational learning and development,
- A case based on a knowledge transfer project at a chemicals manufacturer to retain human capital.

The value of knowledge

'Knowledge-intensive' organisations typically rely on their human capital in the form of employee knowledge, skills and experience to produce products and services that have 'tangible' value, that is value that can easily be measured and accounted for on company balance sheets. The expertise of employees or 'knowledge-workers' that enables them to create and produce tangible assets is much more difficult to measure and quantify in traditional accounting terms but can be significant in terms of its contribution to an organisation's asset base and is known as 'human capital'. Hence value associated with human capital is often described as being intangible, that is, difficult to account for by traditional financial means. Human capital is defined by Sloman (2006: 248) as 'the qualifications, skills and expertise that contributes to a worker's productivity'.

Human capital is a source of competitive advantage and many knowledge-intensive companies in technology-driven markets such as IT, pharmaceuticals, chemicals, oil and gas and others manage their human capital as a strategic asset to create value and gain leverage in highly competitive markets. This focus on human capital requires a strategic people management approach based on a business-aligned HR strategy.

Knowledge creation

Knowledge can be defined in several ways based on different perspectives. The most well-known typology of knowledge creation is Ilkujiro Nonaka's (1994) 'Dynamic theory of knowledge creation', a process model which highlights the role of tacit knowledge in organisational innovation. Nonaka and Takeuchi's (1995) theory of organisational knowledge creation distinguishes between two main forms of knowledge: tacit and explicit.

- *Explicit knowledge* is knowledge that can be expressed formally and communicated through language and documentation.
- *Tacit knowledge* is difficult to formalise and communicate because it is personal and embedded in an individual's experiences, that is, of action and context.

Tacit knowledge can be thought of as knowledge that we are not aware of having, and Polanyi (1966: 4) expressed this as 'we know more than we can tell'.

Nonaka's process model is summarised in Figure 13.1 showing four forms of interaction between tacit and explicit knowledge, which can result in knowledge creation at individual and organisational levels. This model, known as Nonaka's 'knowledge creation engine', describes four knowledge conversion or 'transfer' processes. Each process contributes to new knowledge either independently or in a 'four-stage conversion process' represented by the acronym 'SECI' (socialisation, externalisation, combinational and internalisation).

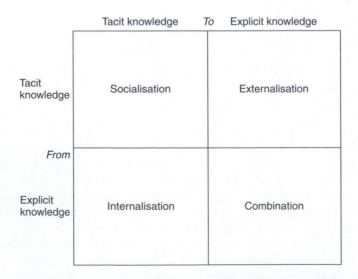

Figure 13.1   Converting tacit and explicit knowledge

The four knowledge conversion or transfer processes are as follows:

- *Socialisation*: the sharing of individual tacit knowledge with others, groups and organisations through observation, imitation and practice, that is on-the-job training.
- *Externalisation*: conversion of tacit knowledge into explicit knowledge to form codified knowledge, that is, models, theories and concepts. An example would be the writing of procedures based on experience of practice.
- *Combination*: bringing together or synthesising different bodies of explicit knowledge to form new explicit knowledge, for example research that builds on current knowledge to produce new knowledge.
- *Internalisation*: conversion of explicit knowledge to tacit knowledge; traditionally referred to as learning, for example use of theory to inform practice and the personal knowledge that results from this.

Knowledge can be translated and transferred by using any one or all of the SECI processes in combination, and a cycling or 'spiralling' of these processes can continuously create and build knowledge at individual and organisational levels. Although Nonaka's concept of knowledge has been criticised (Ribeiro and Collins, 2007) for the assumptions it makes about tacit knowledge being converted into explicit knowledge, that is that it can take place, and his lack of consideration of the politics involved in this process, nonetheless this model provides a 'blueprint' for organisational learning and knowledge management. This model of knowledge transfer was used as a framework for designing knowledge transfer processes used in the project outlined in the case that appears in this chapter.

Knowledge management

Knowledge creation, transfer and application are important elements of human capital and the effectiveness of how these processes are managed in organisations can be a source of competitive advantage. This is particularly true of knowledge-intensive organisations that depend on significant human capital contribution from employees, particularly organisations who have multi-site operations. This ability to leverage knowledge for advantage is captured by Tan (2000: 10):

> A successful company is a knowledge-creating company: that is one which is able to consistently produce new knowledge, to disseminate it throughout the company and to embody it into new products or services quickly.

Knowledge management is defined by Mayo (1998) as involving the management of information, knowledge and experience available to an organisation in order that the company's various activities can build on what is already known and extend it further. It encompasses managerial activity that is concerned with: 'the creation, acquisition, capture, sharing and use of knowledge, skills and expertise' (Swan, Newell, Scarbrough and Hislop, 1999).

This functionalist approach regards knowledge as a resource and another form of organisation asset that can be managed and utilised to sustain competitive advantage (Alvesson and Karreman, 2001). This management perspective regards knowledge as a form of commodity that can be capitalised like any other resource. This perspective assumes a unitary position based on assumptions about the nature of knowledge and how it is valued, that is knowledge is a source of value creation for the organisation. A potential source of tension in organisations is a difference in views between an employer and employee about *what* knowledge should be valued for and *how*. Knowledge management is highly contextual and contingent; it will influence and be influenced by the politics and power at play in organisations.

Knowledge management encourages and supports the creation, storage, ownership, dissemination and application of knowledge through intervention in the form of systems, policy and practice. Much of the literature on knowledge management concerns itself with the technology (methodology) of these elements, for example training and development, coaching, meetings, conferences and seminars, procedures, operating systems and manuals, intranet and internet. The case which follows describes how knowledge and 'mind-mapping' techniques were used to initially capture tacit knowledge. All of the four conversion processes described by Nonaka's 'knowledge creation engine' were employed to convert this tacit knowledge to explicit knowledge, including the use of repertory grids, 'communities of practice' involving group meetings, operational information and processes recorded and stored in databases. The 'new' explicit forms of knowledge combined existing knowledge to create organisational knowledge which could be captured and coded in the form of operational procedures stored on the company's information system. This knowledge was accessible to employees who would make use of it and to those who were interested in it. In this case Nonaka's organisation creation model provided the framework to design and implement knowledge capture and conversion techniques.

Effective knowledge management goes beyond the technicalities of specific interventions used to create and convert knowledge as there are many other considerations involved for organisations, including:

- *Valuing knowledge*: recognising what knowledge is valuable and why, and who it is valuable to. This is about the motivation that drives knowledge behaviour of individuals, groups and organisations.
- *Purpose for knowledge*: clear understanding at all levels of an organisation of why knowledge is valuable and how knowledge linked to the business objectives can be used. This is about having clear objectives and outcomes related to the application of knowledge.
- *Knowledge systems*: policies, procedures and guidelines to promote, enable and support knowledge management.
- *Knowledge culture*: promotion of attitudes and behaviours that support effective knowledge management and exploitation of knowledge, linked to people management policies, for example recruitment, retention and progression.
- *Performance and reward*: policies designed to encourage and reward employees for knowledge creation and applications that add value for organisations.

These considerations and the various factors involved advocate that effective knowledge management requires a strategic and systematic approach that is supported by values and a culture that encourages the behaviours expected of a learning organisation.

Organisational learning and the learning organisation

Organisational learning is a concept of collective learning which is different from the cumulative effect of individual learning in an organisation. Organisational learning is embedded in the routines and collective paradigm influenced by strategy, structure and culture. Easterby-Smith and Lyles (2003: 9) distinguish between 'organisational learning' and 'the learning organisation', defining the former as 'the study of the learning process of and within organisations.'

This opens the way for the emergence of the concept of a learning organisation that adapts to its surroundings, which is defined by Senge (1990) as 'a coherent social entity that can learn like a biological system to adapt and survive in its changing environment'.

Another definition of a learning organisation highlights the interventionalist and inclusive aspects which focus on behaviour: 'an organisation which facilitates the learning of all its members and continuously transforms itself' (Pedler, Boydell and Burgoyne, 1988).

A number of factors stimulated interest in the learning organisation concept in the 1980s and 1990s. The creation and production of products and services to gain competitive advantage required more sophisticated knowledge of markets, research and development, production and service, and information systems. Employees and organisations had to learn how to obtain and apply this knowledge to create value. Increasingly the scope of organisations' knowledge and learning required was becoming global to accommodate international operations and compete in these markets. This signalled a growing interest in knowledge management and learning organisations as these became sources of capital and competitive advantage.

Mike Pedler, John Burgoyne and Tom Boydell (1997) identify 11 features of the 'learning company', including a learning approach to strategy and a holistic approach to organisational learning supported by appropriate structures and self-development opportunities for all employees within a learning climate. Critics claim this is an idealistic view and it is better to think of an organisation as *developing* to become a learning organisation. A learning climate requires all employees to take responsibility for personal learning and development as part of their commitment to the 'psychological contract' with their employer. Where learning is more formalised in organisations, this commitment will feature as part of the performance management process which may be used to monitor employee progress in areas of strategic knowledge.

Organisational development

The concept of the learning organisation has strong links to organisational development (OD), where knowledge and learning play key roles in shaping an organisational culture which enables continuous and transformational change. Organisational development is a generic term encompassing a strategic and systematic approach to implementing interventions at individual, group and organisational level to influence culture through social processes.

French and Bell (1999: 25) provide the following comprehensive definition:

> Organisation development is a long-term effort, led and supported by top management to improve an organisation's visioning, empowerment, learning and problem-solving processes through an on-going, collaborative management of organisation culture – with special emphasis on the culture of intact work teams and other lean configuration, utilizing the consultant-facilitator role and theory and technology of applied behavioural science, including action research.

Knowledge management and the concept of the learning organisation are specific interventions, which play a crucial role in OD as they are people-focused and influence the social processes that shape organisational culture and facilitate change. Learning and problem-solving through collaboration play a central role in OD. One could argue that an organisation that embraces OD is on the way to becoming a learning organisation. Action-learning is a particular method of learning based on experiential learning drawing on Nonaka's model of knowledge creation, particularly with respect to the processes of 'socialisation' and 'combination'.

Competencies

The concept of competencies emerged in the 1980s as a response to organisational change and improvement in performance. 'Competency' is a combination of attitudes, behaviours and technical attributes that an individual must have or acquire to perform effectively in their job. Competencies provide an individual with an indication of what behaviours and attributes are required and valued by an employer. The term 'competence' relates competency (as a term about capability) to specified output or outcomes, providing a language or a 'code' for specifying and communicating workplace performance. Competencies and competency frameworks are widely used by organisations to provide a focus for learning and development at all levels, as they specify behavioural and technical attributes related to different levels of performance. Typical competency frameworks include people management, communication skills, problem-solving, customer service skills and team skills.

Competency frameworks focus on performance management and development but have a wide application across the people management and HRM domain, where clear criteria provide a sound basis for assessment and evaluation. Competencies can be useful in evaluating an individual's current capability and considering future performance, while helping to inform managers on how to best facilitate employee performance improvement through applying appropriate learning and development interventions. Based on specific criteria related to performance, competencies are also widely used in recruitment and selection, career development and progression, including talent management and reward management.

The competency approach has been criticised for being too 'backward looking', being based on attributes that were relevant in the past but may not be so in the future. This can be avoided if competencies are continually reviewed and refreshed to ensure they are relevant and progressive. Another criticism levelled at competencies is that they drive conformity in terms of thinking and behaviour, which can stifle individualism, creativity and diversity. The point has been made about competencies needing to be progressive if they are to remain relevant. Competencies can also lead to a 'tick box' compliance approach in their application when they are used as sole standards of performance. This potential problem can be avoided if performance outputs and outcomes are used in conjunction with competencies in performance management.

People management and the role of HRM

The strategic nature of knowledge management and the learning organisation concept require commitment from leaders of organisations that embark on this journey because of the implications it has for strategic management and investment in resources. Effective leadership in this area would address:

- clarity on the role of knowledge and learning in its contribution to the strategic direction of the organisation,
- promotion of values and behaviours which encourage a learning climate,
- supporting knowledge and learning through appropriate structures, systems and policies,
- specific people management policies that incorporate learning as a component of managing performance and reward,
- Recruitment, retention and progression strategies in line with the knowledge requirements of the organisation.

In the case study that follows, the role of leadership by the senior manager who sponsored the project and by the experienced manager at the centre of the knowledge transfer process was crucial to the outcomes and success of the project.

HRM has an important strategic role to play in the development and implementation of policies and practices which empower managers and employees to take responsibility for managing knowledge and learning. HR managers who are strategically engaged in organisational decision-making can apply their expertise in learning and development, recruitment and selection, retention and progression, performance and reward to play a key role in enabling individual and organisational learning and development – a good example of HR managers utilising their human capital to help create value for their organisations.

Knowledge transfer project at a chemicals manufacturer – a case study

'Chemcom'

Chemcom (the Company) is a 'knowledge-intensive' chemicals manufacturer producing high-specification products in a technology-driven market with more than 200 employees. The Company faced the situation of an experienced manufacturing manager approaching retirement. This individual had a lifetime's experience in his field and had been with the Company for several years. The core of the problem, identified by the Site Manager, was the potential loss of this individual's significant tacit knowledge, much of which had not yet been captured by the organisation. It was recognised that this could lead to the creation of 'knowledge gaps' in the organisation, with serious cost and opportunity implications. The challenge was to find a way of transferring this knowledge before this experienced employee retired.

Human capital, knowledge and value

For an increasing number of organisations today, 'intangible value' associated with the knowledge, skills and experience of their employees is a significant contribution to their worth and is a major contributor to their sustainability. These intangible qualities, which are embedded in people, are the essence of what is known as 'Human Capital', a term created by the economist and American Nobel Laureate W. Schultz in 1961. Human capital has gained prominence amongst academics and practitioners in recent years, as it has become recognised as a unique asset that differentiates organisations and is a source of competitive advantage. Many organisations, particularly those described as being 'knowledge-intensive' by Professor John Purcell at The Work and Employment Research Centre at Bath (Purcell, Kinnie and Swart, 2003) manage their human capital to create value-propositions for customers and other stakeholders.

It is argued that the most valuable knowledge in organisations is 'tacit' knowledge, a form of personal or 'experiential' knowledge first described by Polanyi (1966). This type of knowledge is attributed as being the source of creativity and problem-solving in individuals and is the productive force that creates value in organisations. When experienced employees with extensive knowledge leave their employers, there can be serious implications. The considerable investment an organisation has made in its people, that is its human capital, can be lost, unless interventions are in place to prevent this. Chemcom was faced with this problem as a senior employee was about to retire, and approached the University of Portsmouth Business School for assistance. This work summarises the approach taken and describes the methods used to transfer knowledge and retain human capital.

Knowledge capture and transfer

The key to effective knowledge management is encouraging attitudes and behaviours that facilitate knowledge acquisition and sharing. Leadership and culture are critical in creating an environment where this happens. A distinguishing feature of the scenario faced by Chemcom was the focus on one individual's knowledge. To address this, specific interventions were devised to assist with motivating and supporting the individual in this project, as well as with facilitating the knowledge transfer process. These are outlined below.

Motivation: The individual due to retire was motivated by the aims of the project, recognising the importance of developing knowledge transfer processes at Chemcom. This was a huge benefit to everyone concerned with this project, and it underlined the significance of motivation for individuals involved in this type of activity. To build on this, a decision was taken at the start of the project that this individual would lead this project on site, playing a significant role in defining and co-ordinating the activities of the project.

Knowledge Mapping: Knowledge mapping offers a powerful approach to capturing and transferring knowledge, producing a visual representation of knowledge based on personal experience. 'Mind Mapping' is particularly suited to capturing tacit knowledge because of its non-prescriptive approach to exploring and expressing thoughts and knowledge. This type of mapping was used to identify 'rich' tacit knowledge areas within the individual's expertise and his experience of the organisation's manufacturing activities. 'Concept mapping' is a more structured form of knowledge mapping and is particularly useful in organising knowledge and information. This mapping technique was used to develop a systemic representation of tacit knowledge areas within the manufacturing operation. This would provide the basis for developing a systematic approach to managing knowledge transfer.

Learning style and personality type

There is an inextricable link between learning styles, personality types and tacit knowledge. Learning style has been described as the way in which individuals perceive, conceptualise, organise and recall information, which shapes one's knowledge domain. Personality types, based on Jungian dimensions, as described by the popular Myers–Briggs Type Indicator (MBTI), also help to predict preferred modes of behaviour. The Paragon Learning Style cognitive typing inventory (PLSI), based on this link, identifies learning styles described by the four Jungian dimensions. Learning and personality inventories were used in this project to (a) raise the self-awareness of the client, (b) raise the awareness of the author in his role as coach and consultant and (c) aid the design of knowledge transfer activities, such as knowledge mapping and group meetings.

Knowledge group meetings

Nonaka and Takeuchi (1995) describe how knowledge creation starts with individuals accumulating tacit knowledge. Knowledge creation within organisations takes place when tacit knowledge is captured and converted into explicit knowledge and becomes 'organisational knowledge.' Knowledge group meetings, initially within one area of the manufacturing operation, were used primarily to draw out tacit knowledge not only from the central individual in this project, but also from other employees. This 'Community of Practice' approach is a form of 'best practice' for transferring knowledge and facilitating organisational learning. Employees with different roles and at different levels of seniority were included in the knowledge groups to ensure a diversity of expertise and experience was involved in the process.

The concept maps developed at an earlier stage were used to guide the content of the meetings and provided a reference framework for knowledge items. Tacit knowledge was captured and converted into explicit knowledge by a variety of means, for example written notes, file notes, knowledge maps, databases, email and intranet. Explicit knowledge 'lost' to the organisation in redundant repositories was retrieved by 'document mining', and referenced and filed within the knowledge framework developed for this project. This approach to transferring knowledge has been made 'explicit' within Chemcom in the form of an operating procedure. The feedback from the employees involved in the knowledge group meetings has been very positive. It is currently being rolled out throughout the site.

Conclusions and learning points

The significance of human capital and tacit knowledge in an organisation cannot be underestimated as these are sources of value creation in many organisations today.

Leadership is critical to shaping and encouraging a 'knowledge culture' and employees need to be appropriately motivated to actively engage in seeking and sharing knowledge. The Site Manager was instrumental in initiating this project and continued to support the development of a 'knowledge culture' at Chemcom's site.

Human resources management has an important role to play as human capital and knowledge management are strategic activities that enable organisations to differentiate themselves and create value.

Knowledge transfer strategies should be part of an organisation's 'business continuity plan'. Knowledge transfer is a process that is important at all stages in the 'life cycle' of employees, but is particularly relevant when experienced employees plan to leave their organisation.

Knowledge mapping, learning style and personality inventories are useful interventions for developing a systematic approach for knowledge transfer. Understanding how individuals prefer to deal with information, communicate and behave are important factors in designing knowledge transfer strategies.

Coaching and mentoring are helpful in supporting and facilitating knowledge transfer, particularly with key individuals who are transferring knowledge. Self-awareness plays an important role in developing and facilitating knowledge transfer at individual and group levels.

Knowledge groups meetings, a form of 'Community of Practice', involving a diverse range of participants is a powerful way of capturing and transferring knowledge.

The manufacturing manager who led the knowledge transfer activities on site at Chemcom is now enjoying his retirement with the satisfaction of knowing that his former employer and colleagues are benefiting from his legacy of knowledge transfer. His life-long knowledge and experience were not lost.

Activities and discussion questions

1. Identify three 'items' of explicit knowledge and three 'items' of tacit knowledge you have and write these down. Where did you get this knowledge? (Hint: how did you learn to ride a bike?) How have you in completing your answer converted tacit to explicit knowledge?

2. What knowledge do you value the most and why? What knowledge would you and an employer equally value and why?

3. After reading the case in this chapter, identify the knowledge conversion and capturing interventions used by Chemcom, and categorise these as types of conversion processes (main type) according to Nonaka's 'knowledge creation engine' model outlined in the chapter.

4. Provide three examples where the knowledge of employees and organisations have created value and how has this value been created? (Clue: think about your own role and that of your team in the first instance). This question could be linked to the activity in (5) below.

5. Identify how successful organisations have used knowledge and learning to become leaders in their field (Hint: think about how these organisations operate as well as the products and service they offer, for example web-based businesses).

Bibliography

Alvesson, M. and Karreman, D. (2001). 'Odd couple: making sense of the curious concept of knowledge management'. *Journal and Management Studies*, 38 (7), 995–1018.

Easterby-Smith, M. and Lyles, M. (2003). 'Re-reading organizational learning: selective memory, forgetting, and adaptation'. *Academy of Management Executive*, 17 (2), 51–55.

French, W. L. and Bell, C. H. (1999). *Organization Development: Behavioural Science Interventions for Organizational Improvement* (6th edn.). Upper Saddle River, NJ: Prentice-Hall.

Hislop, D. (2009). *Knowledge Management in Organizations: A Critical Introduction* (2nd edn.). Oxford: Oxford University Press.

Mayo, A. (1998). 'Memory bankers'. *People Management*, 4 (2), 8–34.

Newell, S. Robertson, M., and Scarbrough, H. (2009). *Managing Knowledge Work and Innovation* (2nd edn.). Basingstoke: Palgrave Macmillan.

Nonaka, I. (1994). 'A dynamic theory of organization knowledge creation'. *Organization Science*, 5 (1), 14–37.

Nonaka, I. and Takeuchi, H. (1995). *The Knowledge Creating Company*. New York: Oxford University Press.

Pedler, M., Boydell, T. and Burgoyne, J. (1988). *Learning Company Project: A Report on Work Undertaken October 1987 to April 1988*. Sheffield: Training Agency.

Pedler, M., Burgoyne, J. and Boydell, T. (1997). *The Learning Company: A Strategy for Sustainable Development* (2nd edn.). London: McGraw-Hill.

Polanyi, M. (1966). *The Tacit Dimension*. New York: Doubleday.

Purcell, J., Kinnie, and Swart, J. (2003). *People and Performance in Knowledge Intensive Firms*. London: CIPD.

Ribeiro, R. and Collins, H. (2007). 'The bread-making machine: Tacit knowledge and two types of action'. *Organization Studies*, 28 (9), 1417–33.

Senge, P. M. (1990). *The Fifth Discipline: The Art and Practice of the Learning Organisation*. New York: Century Business.

Senge, P. M. (1994). *The Fifth Discipline: The Art and Practice of the Learning Organisation*. Bantam Doubleday.

Sloman, J. (2006). *Economics* (6th edn.). Harlow: Pearson Education.

Swan, J., Newell, S., Scarbrough, H. and Hislop, D. (1999). 'Knowledge management and innovation: Networks and networking'. *Journal of Knowledge Management*, 3 (4), 262–75.

Tan, J. (2000). 'Knowledge management – just more buzzards?'. *British Journal of Administrative Management*, March–April: 10–11.

Ulrich, D. (1997). *Human Resource Champions: The Next Agenda for Adding Value and Delivering Results*. Boston, MA: Harvard Business School Press.

CHAPTER 14

Developing Leadership
Keep looking in the mirror

David Hall, Maureen Bowes, Fiona Dent and Mellissa Carr

Leadership is the most written about subject in business and management and it continues to attract the attention of academics and practitioners from all walks of life to research and write about leadership. A common theme that tends to emanate from the literature is that effective leadership *makes a difference* and is an important, even essential factor in producing desirable outcomes for people, their teams and organisations. But what makes a 'good' leader and how can organisations develop leadership capability? This chapter examines leadership and the development of leaders by:

- Reviewing theoretical perspectives on leadership,
- Examining how leadership can be developed,
- Considering two cases which describe different approaches to developing leadership.

A good starting point when discussing leadership is to describe what leadership means, which is not easy as there are many different interpretations and perceptions of leadership. There is no universal definition of leadership, even though Bass (1990: 4) describes leadership as a 'universal phenomenon'. For the purpose of this chapter, leadership is defined as *the interactions by which an individual influences followers to behave in such a way that it achieves certain goals.* This definition infers that leadership effectiveness can be determined by the ability of leaders to interact and influence the behaviours of others to achieve specific outcomes.

John Maxwell (2007: 13) attaches similar meaning when he sums up leadership as 'leadership is influence – nothing more, nothing less', which moves beyond defining leader characteristics and asserts a generalised concept for leadership based on an individual's capabilities to influence others. Definitions of leadership which centre on influencing behaviour highlight the political nature of leadership involving the role of power within an organisational context.

Perspectives on leadership

There are alternative ways of perceiving and interpreting leadership, which have been described by several writers, including Mullins (2010), Yukl (2009) as well as Huczynski and Buchanan (2007). Most offer the following framework as an approach to analysing and understanding leadership:

- The qualities or traits approach,
- The functional or group approach,
- Leadership as a behavioural category,
- Leadership styles,
- Contingency models, including the situational approach,
- Transitional and transformational leadership,
- Inspirational leadership.

In addition other leadership approaches such as authentic leadership and values-based leadership have gained recognition in this area more recently. Such a framework is helpful in exploring the meaning of leadership rather than in focusing on one particular definition. A review of each approach is summarised below.

The traits approach: This theory came to the fore in the 1920s when leadership was equated with the strength of personality of individuals who had inherited certain characteristics or personality traits (Bowden, 1926). This approach assumes leaders are born and not made and can be distinguished from their followers, and is sometimes referred to as the 'Great Person' theory of leadership. The notion that leaders are born and not bred is at the heart of the perpetual debate on whether leaders are born or made. The traits approach focuses on the individual (leader), not on the job, and does not take into account the relationship 'followers' have with the leader. This approach suggests that attention be given to the selection of leaders rather than to developing or training leaders based on the qualities and characteristics they display. The traits typically cited include self-confidence, intelligence, energy, resilience, initiative and creativity. One of several problems with this approach is agreeing on what qualities should be present in a leader and which are the most important, and this becomes more difficult when situational factors are ignored. Research that has attempted to correlate common personal characteristics with successful leadership has had little success and the qualities approach is weak at predicting effective leadership (Clegg, Hardy and Nord, 1996). The qualities approach to leadership is often dismissed as it has been superseded by several other concepts. However more recent approaches such as values-based leadership and authentic leadership echo elements of the traits approach.

The functional or group approach: This approach focuses on the functions of leadership, that is what leaders do and how a leader's behaviour influences and is influenced by the group of followers. The focus is on the content of leadership and the behaviours required to function as an effective leader. In contrast to the qualities approach, the functional approach advocates the learning and development of leadership skills. John Adair's 'action-centred leadership' (Adair, 1979) is a general theory on the functional approach, which focuses on what leaders do. The effectiveness of leaders can be determined, based on three areas of need within the group: the need to achieve the group task, the need for team maintenance and the individual needs of the group members. An effective leader will be (self) aware that their actions in one particular area of need are likely to affect the other areas, and will take this into account to achieve a high level of integration between all areas.

Leadership as a behavioural category: This approach, based on the Ohio State Leadership Studies at Ohio State University in the 1950s, identified two major dimensions of leadership behaviour described as 'consideration' and 'initiating structure' related to group performance:

- *Consideration* is what a leader shows for the group members in terms of concern, trust and support, which are factors that define the nature of the relationship between the leader and the group, that is consideration for the group.

- *Structure* is how a leader directs group interactions and activities towards achieving group goals, that is attention to the task.

Another major research project carried out at the University of Michigan at the same time as the Ohio University studies identified two similar dimensions termed 'employee-centred' and 'production-centred' supervisors (Likert, 1961). Both of these studies suggested that no one particular type of leadership behaviour is superior. To be an effective leader, a leader would have to take into account the particular situation they are faced with, including the many variables involved, and decide which behaviour or combination of behaviours was most appropriate. This approach to leadership lends itself to training and development, starting with awareness (self and others) and learning how to modify behaviour. The case towards the end of this chapter describes how applied emotional intelligence (EI) was used to develop self-awareness and awareness of others as an intervention to improve leadership and group performance in a team.

Leadership styles: Research from the late 1930s through to the 1950s considered the importance of leadership style, which Mullins defines as: '. . . the way in which the functions of leadership are carried out, the way in which the manager typically behaves towards members of the group' (Mullins, 2007: 371). Leadership style is relevant because of the type of influence a leader or manager will have on employees, based on how they (leader) behave. If a manager wishes to have a positive effect on a group, they need to consider their behaviour and adopt a style that is likely to produce desired outcomes for a group. Classification of leadership styles can be summarised by three broad headings:

- *Autocratic (or authoritarian)*: centralised (leader) authority and decision-making,

- *Democratic*: consultation between leader and group, and shared decision-making,

■   *Laissez-faire*: employees given freedom on what to do and on how to work, and are supported by the leader to do so.

Another well-known classification of leadership styles is that by Tannenbaum and Schmidt (1973), describing four main styles of leadership characterised according to the degree of control the leader exerts over employees:

■   *Tells*: manager announces decisions with no participation from employees other than an expectation that employees will follow instructions (highest degree of leader control).

■   *Sells*: manager makes the decision but attempts to persuade employees to accept it.

■   *Consults*: manager discusses problem with employees and takes on their views in making a decision.

■   **Joins**: employees are given boundaries within which they can make the decisions (lowest degree of leader control).

This continuum of leadership styles can be related to McGregor's '**Theory X**' (manager-centred) and '**Theory Y**' (employee-centred) concepts of management (McGregor, 1960).

Contingency models, including the situational approach: This approach asserts that the environment or situation in which leader–group interactions takes place is the dominant factor in determining effective leadership. Some of the main contingency models and theories include:

■   *The situational leadership model* by Hersey, Blanchard and Johnson (2001), who advocate that leaders adopt certain styles (modes of behaviour) that are most appropriate to the group or individual 'followers', based on the group members' state of 'maturity' or 'readiness' to achieve tasks. Maturity can be defined as a combination of ability, willingness and confidence to carry out a particular task. The group members' readiness to achieve specific tasks will vary over time, so it becomes important that a leader or manager is aware of the specific nature of situations and learn to adapt their style as necessary.

■   *Contingency theory of leadership effectiveness* by Fiedler, which suggests that leadership effectiveness is determined by the favourability of the leadership situation, which depends on leader–member relations, task structure and position (leader) power. Based on a combination of the variables, Fiedler constructed combinations of group-task (leadership) situations which lent themselves to different leadership styles (Fiedler, 1967).

■   *Path–goal theory* by House, based on the 'expectancy' theory of motivation, suggests that the performance of individuals is influenced by the extent to which a manager or leader supports them in achieving their goals, expectations and satisfying their needs in terms of performance (House, 1971). The two main situational factors are the personal characteristics of group members and the nature of the task. House identifies four main types of leadership behaviour: directive leadership, supportive leadership, participative leadership and achievement-orientated leadership.

Transactional and transformational leadership: two fundamentally different types of leadership, based on influencing motivation of employees.

- *Transactional leadership* is a form of 'leader-centred' or 'power-centred' control based on the transaction of rewards and punishments for the completion of tasks. The source of influence is formal power and authority which facilitates the leader's ability to enter and fulfil such transactions with group members. Transactions of this nature would tend to focus on lower-level psychological needs, which are typically met through extrinsic rewards, for example bonus, overtime and time off.

- *Transformational leadership* is 'follower-centred' and is based on the leader motivating employees through their higher-level psychological needs of intrinsic rewards and, in this way, facilitating trust, commitment and loyalty. The emphasis is on generating a vision or a 'big idea' that appeals to the values and ideals of followers, which provides direction to help 'mobilise' employees to transform the fortunes of an organisation (Bass, 1985).

Inspirational leadership is concerned with the skills of leaders to motivate and inspire people. Transformational leadership could be considered as a form of this type of leadership. Charismatic leadership is another name given to a form of leadership that inspires and mobilises people, but if one considers charisma to be a type of personal quality – could this be considered as a trait theory of leadership? Many writers claim that transformational, charismatic and visionary leadership are all forms of the same type of leadership approach which focuses on motivating and mobilising employees through the use of a vision, values and a 'higher purpose' for the team beyond individual self-interest. Authentic leadership and values-based leadership can be regarded as other forms of inspirational leadership, which are based on the promotion of certain values, and leader (and employee) behaviours that support those values, that is what a leader (genuinely) stands for, as the source of motivation. The use of vision ('where we are going') and values ('how we will get there') together is used extensively in transformational and other forms of leadership which focus on motivating people at an emotional or a psychological level.

Leadership learning and development

How do leaders learn and what can be learnt to become an effective leader are important questions, particularly for organisations and aspiring leaders. These questions assume that leadership can be learnt, but there is an opposing view that 'leaders are born, not made' supported by the traits approach, which suggests that leaders are born with certain inherited qualities that shape their personalities to become leaders. Personality traits and aspects of character may be inherited to some extent but are developed throughout life, particularly in the early stages, as individuals learn and develop through their experiences. Individuals interact and influence others from an early age, and continue to develop this capacity as they learn and grow. Kouzes and Posner (2002: 386) cited by Sadler-Smith (2006: 314) express the view that leadership is an 'observable set of skills and abilities . . . and any skill can be strengthened, honed and enhanced, given the motivation and desire, the practice and feedback, and the role models of coaching'. Leadership capability is an outcome of an individual's inherited qualities and what they learn – a combination of nature and nurture.

From a learning and development perspective, Sadler-Smith (2006: 317) drew the following inferences from various leadership models:

1. Leaders need to be sensitive to the readiness ('maturity') of followers to behave in particular ways.

2. Leaders should have or acquire the skills of being able to identity followers' readiness.

3. Leaders must be aware of their own leadership style and have the capacity to vary their style in accordance with the circumstances.

4. Leaders must be attentive to the context in which they operate and their capabilities to lead within that context.

5. Leaders must be responsive to the dynamics of the leader–follower relationship and the extent to which followers are developing new skills and competencies. Leader behaviour should reflect these changes.

6. Leaders must exhibit modesty to the extent that they are prepared to relinquish their leadership role and hand over authority to others more suited to the task or the context; hence for leadership development to be effective there needs to be succession planning.

This distillation of capabilities provides a useful framework for the design and implementation of learning interventions to develop leadership. Other frameworks based on a competency approach have been specifically developed for the purpose of facilitating leadership (and management) learning. These include the National Occupational Standards in Management and Leadership published by the Management Standards Centre. These occupational standards were developed to benefit employers by improving access to high-quality managers and leaders, and individuals seeking ongoing self-development. These standards provide a framework for the design of educational and training interventions for developing potential managers and leaders, and are used extensively by awarding bodies and institutions.

Individuals have different development requirements, depending on their experiences and skills, meaning that a 'one-size fits all' approach to leadership learning is often inappropriate. A good starting point is the use of diagnostic methods and feedback to establish what knowledge and skills need to be developed on an individual basis. A 360-degree feedback, psychometric assessments and simulation techniques can be useful tools for this purpose. There are a range of learning and development interventions available, including leadership programmes, leadership activity centres, special projects and coaching. A 'blended' learning approach, with a range of development methods, is effective in facilitating individual learning.

The two cases which follow are about learning and developing leadership with a focus on self-awareness. The first case looks at the importance of role of emotional intelligence in developing a team of surgeons. The second case reports on a leadership research project and how the findings led to the design of a Future Leadership programme. The conclusions in both cases agree that self-awareness is a crucial factor in leadership learning and development, and effective leaders typically exhibit this to a high degree. The message seems to be clear – if you want to be a leader, keep 'looking in the mirror'.

Applied Emotional Intelligence and a team of surgeons – a case study

What is EI?

Since Goleman's 1998 *Harvard Business Review* article 'What makes a leader?' and his books *Working with Emotional Intelligence, The New Leaders* and *Social Intelligence*, Emotional Intelligence (EI) has become recognised as an HR intervention with potential for improving individual and team performance. This article describes the application of EI to the professional relationships of a dysfunctional team of surgeons. Sparrow (2005) sees EI as a subdivision of cognitive intelligence – the application of thinking to feeling, and according to Sparrow and Knight (2006) a different understanding of EI has evolved in the UK over the past six years known as Applied Emotional Intelligence – the practice of managing the relationship between our thoughts, feelings and behaviour, with particular emphasis on how feelings affect behaviour. This approach develops earlier EI concepts through recognising the importance of attitude. Using a diagnostic profile, part of which is based on the OK Corral Model of Transactional Analysis, insights into personal attitudes can be gained by measuring how much or how little we value ourselves compared with how much or how little we value others. Unlike IQ, individual attitude and levels of Emotional Intelligence can be developed. Self-perception and 360-degree feedback form the starting points, and areas for personal development can be contrasted to provide valuable perspectives for performance improvement and cultural fit.

The surgeons and key features of the EI process

In March 2005 a team of four surgeons described themselves as 'dysfunctional, infighting and untrusting'. A benchmark questionnaire revealed the three key team development areas as *Co-operation and Conflict, Support and Trust* and *Clear Objectives and Agreed Goals.* The benchmark questionnaire for March 2006 records a 70–90 per cent improvement in these areas. The surgeons describe themselves now as 'effective, co-operating and directed'. A significant turnaround – so what happened? There is no quick fix for a dysfunctional team. Even aspirational teams have to factor in ways of sustaining success. Lasting change requires commitment and levels of commitment, like so many aspects of behaviour, are influenced by attitude. Success cannot be sustained by a single training intervention; success depends on increased knowledge, skills development, a shift in attitudes and new habits to replace old, limiting patterns of behaviour. The approach taken with the surgeons integrated these four areas and spanned one year.

Self-development starts with self-awareness and therefore each surgeon completed the JCA on-line self-perception questionnaire to assess the levels of emotionally intelligent behaviour and to find out what this revealed about his (they were all men) attitude. In addition, each surgeon chose six people, including the other three team members, to complete a shorter 360-degree version of the questionnaire, and as a consequence each surgeon was able to compare his self-perception with the perceptions of others. Both questionnaires measured a Self-Regard, Regard for Others, Self-Awareness, Awareness of Others, Emotional Resilience, Personal Power, Goal Directedness, Flexibility, Personal Openness, Trustworthiness, Trust, Balanced Outlook, Emotional Expression and Control, Conflict Handling, Interdependence and Self-Assessed EI. The surgeons received a personal, narrative report and had a one-to-one feedback session to identify, first, which area of development was most important and, second, how to translate that priority area into specific actions or behaviours. They each committed to practising their action points regularly. To assist in ensuring the action points happened, each surgeon chose another team member as a support both to discuss and to receive feedback on progress. While the Individual Effectiveness Profiles were confidential, the action points were not. A list of the action points was circulated within the team to raise awareness and accommodate personal change.

One-to-one coaching contributed to meeting individual development needs and facilitated meetings between pairs of surgeons, thus resolving conflicts and clearing tensions. The whole team participated in a monthly, half-day group intervention where key learning points for the team were introduced, current issues were identified and addressed and emotionally intelligent behaviour put into practice. Group intervention foci included 'I'm OK. You're OK', 'You get what you tolerate' and 'Open and honest feedback'. The repeat of the benchmark questionnaire at the end of the intervention built in accountability. It showed the team's progress to be sustained within an effective team climate, open and honest verbal communication (featuring reduced email communication between each other), increased mutual respect, ease in giving and receiving feedback, trust in individual roles, clarity of goals and team identity as well as increased knowledge and confidence to address conflict. As a result the surgeons report that the efficiency and effectiveness of the service has significantly improved.

Three key differentiators when interventions focus on attitudes and habits

Responsibility to change: Attitude determines how each individual embraces change and reveals the degree of willingness or reluctance to engage with different approaches and new habits. To make the team work, the surgeons had to change. In any team the difficulties result not just from one person's attitude or behaviour, but from how everyone else responds to that behaviour and how the group behaviour is managed. The surgeons made choices about which limiting patterns of behaviour to replace, and the facilitated sessions and group interventions introduced new ways of working, including the practice of 'I'm OK You're OK' behaviours, which raised individual levels of self-esteem and created healthy interpersonal dynamics.

Clearing feelings: Achieving a willingness to change means substituting feelings that motivate for feelings that de-motivate. The surgeons did not trust one another, but recognised that trust was a vital ingredient if they were to work together effectively. They knew rationally that they should demonstrate trust for one another but found themselves emotionally unable to do so. They were at a dead end. Turning this around is not a quick, easy or rational process. Workable solutions required 'give and take', a recognition of personal vulnerability, a willingness to behave differently plus time and evidence to feel that it was safe to trust again. They did achieve this, not in a soft and fluffy way, but with courage, commitment and integrity. These individuals shared their self-development through action points and team sessions and in doing so increased their self-awareness and personal openness, and improved interpersonal relations. The surgeons became more connected, got to know one another better and respected their differences. Consequently team member commitment grew with the momentum of the programme, making it more difficult not to deliver on the consensus they had achieved as peers.

Sound development processes: Emotionally intelligent behaviour consists of intrapersonal and interpersonal intelligences. To be effective in these areas we need to start with 'awareness' and progress through 'reflection' to 'knowledge' and 'management'. These steps are exposed in Figure 14.1 below.

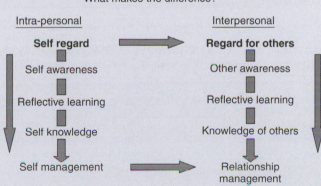

What makes the difference?

Intra-personal	Interpersonal
Self regard	**Regard for others**
Self awareness	Other awareness
Reflective learning	Reflective learning
Self knowledge	Knowledge of others
Self management	Relationship management

Figure 14.1   EI awareness model

Source: © Centre for Applied Emotional Intelligence 2006 (published with permission of Amanda Knight)

EI potential impact and conclusions

Sparrow (2006) suggests that there are many reasons why organisations do not apply the above processes – a lack of awareness of the potential of applied EI, time pressures and financial cost. Whilst qualitative results are challenging to quantify, what would the following outcomes be worth to your team or organisation?

1. Team members solve a problem from a basis of accepting difference – different needs, wants and styles – and role-model authenticity. This level of congruence at the core of an organisation or team is what creates a change in culture.

2. Authentic leadership, peer commitment and strong communication processes – the right people talking, engagement and the will to make things happen.

3. The right people meeting and efficient processes in place to facilitate open and honest communication, saving time, increasing trust and improving decisions.

4. Targets met because of transparent communication, respect for true deadlines and negotiation between people and departments.

5. Improved team communication, staff finding their own solutions with more face-to-face communication, resulting in fewer conflicts and demands on management time to solve people problems.

The extent to which an individual or team is motivated to change, to develop or to continuously improve is directly influenced by each person's feelings. Rational argument or persuasion may win over the sceptical, but most people are moved to action through feelings. In turn feelings are rooted in personal attitudes (the extent to which people value themselves and others). Individuals may be told they need to change their attitudes, or trust more, or be more positive; they may be aware of this themselves and then falter as they do not know how to apply this to their behaviour. Personal development or team interventions can bring sustainable success when they address individual attitudes; make the connections between feelings, thoughts, behaviour and attitudes; and facilitate real opportunities to practise 'how to'.

If I knew then what I know now: new thoughts on leadership development – the Ashridge case

The Ashridge Business School was established by Royal Charter in 1959 to provide Executive Education to practising managers. Ashridge now offers a full range of consultancy and development services, including customised programmes, open enrolment programmes, OD consultancy, post-graduate qualifications and other learning services. The School works with a broad range of national, international, public and private sector businesses, primarily in the areas of leadership, strategy, change and general management.

Leadership development and future leaders – two key questions

What do you wish you had known 10 years ago? This was the question that a group of faculty members pondered in the quest to identify the key issues for 'leaders-in-waiting'. Ashridge has for many years run successful leadership programmes mainly targeted at experienced business leaders. However, in recent years, many organisations have also asked us to help them to identify their future leaders. The question was – do new leaders require the same development processes as existing leaders or are there different needs and demands and therefore different possibilities?

In a typical academic fashion, a research project was formed where a group from the leadership faculty gathered together to share and develop ideas about the topic itself and the research process. Quickly it was found that many of the same stock answers were emerging and nothing significantly new coming up, except that many of the existing leaders questioned suggested that they wished they had known more about themselves. This prompted us to try a different approach. We asked existing leaders two key questions. First *what have been the critical incidents that have shaped your leadership development?* And second *what do you wish you had known 10 years ago?*

The answer to the first question was illuminating and identified critical incidents which were categorised under seven major themes. The first four themes relate to the job role and the work itself and the other three themes relate to the individual and how they lived their life:

1. *Being a manager* – the range of experiences that people take on when they are in charge, for instance, promoted to manage peers and manage a relationship with a PA.

2. *Managing others* – the everyday people-related challenges that the new manager faces, for instance dealing with demotivated colleagues and disciplining someone.

3. *Being managed* – the impact of the boss and other more senior colleagues, for instance disagreeing with the boss and finding a good mentor.

4. *Fulfilling the management role* – the functional responsibilities that a manager takes on as part of their role, for instance preparing budgets and making someone redundant.

5. *Developing corporate awareness* – this relates to many of the organisational, cultural and political processes that managers find themselves involved in, for instance, attending the first board meeting.

6. *Where work and life meet* – the challenge of the work–life balance.

7. *Self-insight* – raising personal awareness and understanding.

One of the 'light bulb' moments during the research process came when the link was made between what was now being termed as 'hindsight' learning and the response to the second question 'what do you wish you had known 10 years ago?', as there was a link between the critical incidents and the answers to the hindsight question. The seven themes that emerged in response to the hindsight question are:

1. *Building a career* – taking opportunities, preparing for something new and being willing to take unexpected routes and diversions in your career path;

2. *Relating to others* – understanding the two-way process of self-awareness and awareness of others;

3. *Personal learning* – this is more about the learning relating to the job and role;

4. *Stepping outside the box* – recognising that rules are for guidance only;

5. *Power and politics* – the importance of networking and political savvy;

6. *Focus of energy* – priorities, use of time and stress management;

7. *Sense of self* – developing competence, authenticity and recognising strengths and weaknesses.

The linkages between the critical incidents and the hindsight learning are:

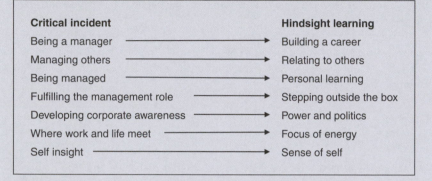

The most important themes to emerge were self-insight and sense of self, a view represented by recent leadership research (Velsor, 1996; Goffee, 2006). The response was to create something completely different that satisfied both the needs of clients and took account of the research findings, which led to the development and launch of the *Future Leaders Experience*. This new programme is represented in the model shown in Figure 14.2 below:

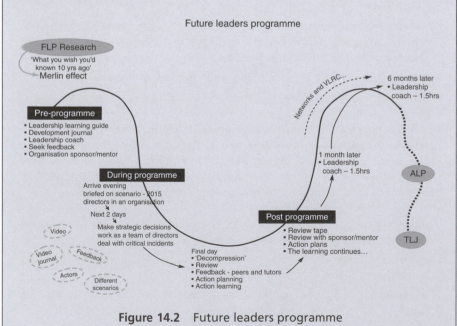

Figure 14.2   Future leaders programme

The Future Leaders Experience

The overall purpose of the *Future Leaders Experience* is to provide the participants with the opportunity to accelerate their leadership development by enabling them to encounter a range of critical incidents, giving them experiences during the development process that will trigger their 'muscle memory' when they are faced with the challenge in the workplace. During the three-day experiential workshop participants have the opportunity to receive both feedback and coaching on their ability to deal with the incidents they face. This, together with the pre- and post-programme learning processes, provides a very different type of 'programme' for 'leaders in waiting'. The *Future Leaders Experience* was piloted in 2004 and has been delivered eight times. Further research was conducted with 20 of the participants to review what they recalled, applied and learned from the experience and also to explore their critical incidents and what they believe enabled effective long-term learning.

Real emotional experiences and the opportunity to reflect – the key to future leadership challenges

Being a leader is a challenging and often lonely job and those who are identified as 'leaders in waiting' need to be prepared for this potentially tough ride. Conventional development programmes can only prepare people for certain eventualities but by providing participants with an experiential and emotionally intense event they can truly feel what it could be like to take on the leadership role in reality. One of our major learning points from this project work has been the experience of running the workshop. In equal measure it has been as emotionally challenging, intellectually stimulating and uncomfortable for the tutor group as it tends to be for the participants.

In summary, building the self-awareness and confidence of 'leaders-in-waiting' is paramount, and by providing them with 'real' emotional experiences, balanced with the opportunity to reflect thoroughly and make sense of the process, they are more effectively prepared for future leadership challenges.

Activities and discussion questions

1. Who you do regard as a good leader and why? What have they done that makes them such a good leader and can you relate this to any leadership theories? *(Your choice of leader could come from the workplace, sport or any other walk of life).*

2. Can you think of any examples where the 'followers' decided not to follow their leader any longer and found a new leader? Why did they decide not to follow their leader?

3. Do you believe the type of military leadership that is found in the Armed Forces would be effective in other organisations? Explain, referring to leadership theory.

4. After reading the first case in this chapter, discuss the types of interventions used in applied emotional intelligence and the benefits these could bring to other teams in the organisation?

5. After reading the second case in this chapter, discuss the importance of reflection (critically looking back at experiences) in supporting leadership learning and development. What is its relevance to the development of the 'Future Leaders Programme' described in the case? *(Hint: you may wish to look at Kolb's learning cycle mentioned in Chapter 1).*

Bibliography

Adair, J. (1979). *Action-Centred Leadership*. Aldershot: Gower.

Bass, B. M. (1985). *Leadership and Performance beyond Expectations*. New York: Free Press.

Bass, B. M. (1990). *Handbook of Leadership: Theory, Research and Managerial Applications* (3rd edn.). New York: The Free Press.

Binney, G. and Williams, C. (2005). *Living Leadership: A Practical Guide for Ordinary Heroes*. Financial Times/Prentice Hall.

Blass, E. and Carr, M. (2006). 'Learning for the future from hindsight: the core-periphery model of leadership and management development', in Mack, T. C. (Ed.), *Creating Global Strategies for Humanity's Future*. Bethesda, USA: World Future Society, 120–140.

Bowden, A. O. (1926). 'A study of the personality of student leaders in the United States'. *Journal of Abnormal and Social Psychology*, 21, 149–160.

Bryman, A. (1999). 'Leadership in organisations', in Clegg, S., Hardy, C. and Nord, W. (Eds.), *Managing Organisations: Current Issues*. London: Sage, pp. 276–292.

Carr, M. and Poole, E. (2005). 'If I knew then what I know now!'. *360°: The Ashridge Journal*, Spring, 46–50.

Carr, M. and Poole, E. (2005/2006). 'What I wish I'd known 10 years ago'. *IEE Engineering Management*, December/January, 36–39.

Clegg, S. R., Hardy, C. and Nord, W. R. (1996). *Handbook of Organization Studies*. London: Sage.

Fiedler, F. E. (1967). *A Theory of Leadership Effectiveness*. New York: McGraw-Hill.

Goffee, R. (2006). *Why Should Anyone Be Led by You? What It Takes to Be an Authentic Leader*. Boston, MA: Harvard Business School Press.

Goleman, D. (1998). *Working with Emotional Intelligence*. London: Bloomsbury.

Goleman, D., Boyatiz, R. E. and McKie, A. (2002). *The New Leaders: Transforming the Art of Leadership*. London: Sphere.

Hersey, O., Blanchard, K. and Johnson, D. (2001). *Management of Organisational Behaviour: Leading Human Resources* (8th edn.). London: Prentice Hall.

House, R. J. (1971). 'A path-goal theory of leader effectiveness'. *Administrative Science Quarterly*, 16, 321–338.

Huczynski, A. and Buchanan, D. (2007). *Organisational Behaviour: An Introductory Text* (6th edn.). Harlow: Pearson Education.

Kouzes, J. M. and Posner, B. Z. (2002). *The Leadership Challenge*. San Francisco: Jossey Bass.

Likert, R. (1961). *New Patterns of Management*. New York: McGraw-Hill.

Maddocks, J. and Sparrow, T. (2000). *The Individual and Team Effectiveness Questionnaires. Users Manual*. Cheltenham: JCA (Occupational Psychologists) Ltd.

Maxwell, J. C. (2007). *21 Irrefutable Laws of Leadership* (2nd edn.). Nashville, TN: Thomas Nelson.

McGregor, D. (1960). *The Human Side of Enterprise*. New York: McGraw-Hill.

MSC (2004) *National Occupational Standards in Management and Leadership*. Management Standards Centre. Available online at: www.management-standards.org.

Mullins, L. J. (2007) *Management and Organisational Behavior*. Harlow: Financial Times Prentice Hall.

Mullins, L. (2010) *Management and Organisational Behaviour* (9th edn.). Harlow: FT/Prentice Hall.

National Occupational Standards in Management and Leadership (2004). Retrieved 13 October 2011, from the Management Standards Centre website: http://www.management-standards.org/standards/standards.

Northouse, P. (2009). *Leadership: Theory and Practice* (5th edn.). Thousand Oaks, California: Sage.

Sadler-Smith, E. (2006). *Learning and Development for Managers*. Oxford: Blackwell Publishing.

Sparrow, T. (2005). *How the CAEI approach to EI differs. AppliedEI ezine.*, 7, Retrieved from http://www.emotionalintelligence.co.uk/ezine/issue07.html.

Sparrow, T. (2006). *Why Development Training Doesn't Work. AppliedEI ezine., 20*, Retrieved from http://www.emotionalintelligence.co.uk/ezine/downloads/20_Why.pdf.

Sparrow, T. and Knight, A. (2006). *AppliedEI – The Importance of Attitudes in the Development of Emotional Intelligence*. San Francisco: Jossey-Bass.

Tannenbaum, R. and Schmidt, W. H. (1973). *How to Choose a Leadership Pattern*. Boston, MA: Havard Business School Press.

Velsor, J. (1996). 'A look at derailment today: North America and Europe'. Greensboro, North Carolina: Center for Creative Leadership.

Yukl, G. (2009). *Leadership in Organizations* (7th edn.). Harlow: Pearson International.

CHAPTER 15

Employee Development
A journey towards competence

David Hall, Clare Matton and Gary Rees

Strategic people management is a range of strategies designed to ensure organisations have in place the people capabilities to meet their business goals. Typically strategic HRM is the focus of this activity as it aligns people management strategies with business objectives, and employee development is a key part of this integrated approach. Employee development has wider implications for the recruitment and retention of employees, playing a crucial role in the 'war for talent' (Chambers, Foulon, Handfield-Jones, Hankin and Michaels, 1998). This chapter examines:

- Strategic relevance of employee development,
- Interventions for employee development, focusing on the use of competencies,
- A case that examines employee development based on a competency framework in a UK uniformed service organisation.

Definitions of 'employee development' are relatively few and far between, although Noe (2004) describes it as a combination of education, experiences, relationships, assessments and abilities that help employees perform in their job. 'Personal development', 'training and development' as well as 'learning and (talent) development' are more commonly used terms, which encompass the meaning of employee development. Descriptions of these terms emphasise the role and importance of ongoing learning as the key development intervention, indicating the strategic approach that many organisations take towards 'employee development'.

Strategic relevance of employee development

Early HR theory and models identified employee learning and development (L&D) as an important function of HR management (Fombrun, Tichy and Devanna, 1984). Research on the connection between HR policy and employee (and organisational) performance has consistently identified training and development as a key component of this relationship. It is one of the 11 areas of HR policy and practice that were found to be influential in facilitating discretionary behaviour in employees, leading to high levels of performance (Purcell, Kinnie, Hutchinson, Rayton and Swart, 2003). HR policies applied to improve performance are described as 'High Performance Work Practices' (HPWPs). Sung and Ashton (2005) identify 35 HPWPs and categorise these as: high involvement, human resource practices, and reward and commitment. Of the 14 HPWPs that feature under 'human resource practices', nine involve employee L&D in some form.

Chartered Institute of Personnel and Development (CIPD) identifies 'capability-building' as one of eight strategic themes that are important for the long-term sustainability and performance of organisations, defining it as 'equipping the people in the organisation with the skills and knowledge they need to meet both present and future challenges. Also identifying existing necessary and potential capabilities, ensuring they are accessible across the organisation. Capability-building applies not only to individuals but also to teams and organisations' (Miller, 2011).

Capability-building is a continuous process that is an integral part of organisational development (OD) and change is highlighted, emphasising its strategic nature. This type of capability-building that centres on people is human capital management and is a key component of strategic HRM. A human capital perspective views employees as assets that bring value to organisations and should be invested in as any other resource. Amir and Livine (2001) propose that investing in employee training and learning might be usefully viewed as an investment in human capital.

Talent management is another concept that provides a framework for strategic intervention in developing employee capability. However it goes further to include how employers attract, develop, engage and retain people to build their human capital asset. A broader concept than (employee) learning and development, talent management considers peoples' potential in terms of the value they could offer organisations in the future and includes workforce planning and succession planning (McCartney and Garrow, 2006). Clearly talent management has to be closely aligned to the business strategy and may be one of several HRM strategies.

The case that follows illustrates the strategic approach taken by the UK Fire and Rescue Service in implementing The National Fire and Rescue Service Learning and Development Strategy.

Interventions for employee development

In the literature, some authors differentiate the terms 'development' and 'learning' while other authors argue that such distinctions are futile (Stewart, 1999). It is generally accepted that learning is the 'core process' at the centre of learning and development (see definition below), whereas development tends to be focused on the direction the learning takes, usually in the context of job or organisational outputs. A 'developed' individual also suggests a state of preparedness or readiness to undertake certain tasks, based on their learning. Talent management has a broader remit, which incorporates an external strategic view of people-skill resources. One definition of learning is: 'Learning is the longer-term change in the knowledge possessed by an individual, their type and level of skill, or their assumptions, attitudes or values, which may lead to them having increased potential to grow, develop and perform in more satisfying and effective ways' (Sadler-Smith, 2006: 4).

Learning can be planned or unplanned, but an individual usually has to complete a learning process, such as the learning cycle (Kolb, 1996) described in Chapter 1, to enable learning to take place. In the workplace, most forms of employee development (including leadership and management development) tend to be based on some form of directed or supported learning to develop individuals in their current job or for potential future roles. In terms of direction at a high level, employee learning and development should align with the needs of the organisation, the group and the role. HRM, L&D, talent management, human capital management, management development and performance management are all 'higher level' interventions that can form part of an integrated and coherent strategy for team and organisational development. HR managers and line managers, sometimes supported by learning professionals, have a crucial 'business partnership' role to play in shaping and supporting employee L&D interventions. Performance management is a key intervention as it provides the line manager and employee with an opportunity to assess progress and development needs. However the role and responsibility of the employee cannot be over-emphasised because of the importance of motivation in learning, that is individuals have to be self-motivated to learn. The role of management is to create an environment that encourages and supports motivated employees to learn, develop and progress in their careers.

L&D interventions, which are not strategic in nature but are operational, can be defined as events or activities that are planned and are deliberately undertaken to facilitate learning. Popular forms of employee (and management) L&D interventions include:

- **On-the-job training**: planned and structured learning while doing the job supported by one-to-one instruction.
- **Action learning**: usually project-driven learning on and in the job based on the principles of continuous learning and reflection aimed at problem-solving and improvement. This form of learning uses small groups or 'learning sets' to support the learning process of individuals in the group (Revans, 1998).
- **Work-based learning**: learning in the workplace which is self-directed, usually under the guidance of a mentor, and is supported by some form of internal and/or external learning provision, for example an in-house development programme or external conference. Learning institutions such as universities and FE colleges can be partners in work-based learning and provide accreditation towards formal awards.
- **Coaching and mentoring**: aimed at supporting the L&D needs of individuals to improve their skills and performance in their current role but can also have a developmental emphasis aimed at future career roles. The coach usually comes from outside the coachee's organisation. Mentoring can be a

longer-term intervention than coaching and is provided by an experienced internal manager. The emphasis has more to do with personal guidance in the organisational setting.

- *Knowledge management*: specific interventions or learning tools based on imparting and sharing knowledge within a team or organisation, which are typically web-based (intranet) and often interactive to assess knowledge and learning.

- *Training*: instructor-led learning based on specific content relating to the job or activity. Can be led by an internal (from the organisation) or external trainer.

- *Education*: course-based vocational and management education which is hosted by a learning institution, FE college or university and is recognised by the award of a qualification. This is a common route to gaining professional management awards based on occupational standards underpinned by competency frameworks. It can incorporate action learning, work-based learning and distance learning methods.

- *E-learning and blended learning*: learning using computer-based technology to access electronic sources of learning. Organisations may have a specific web-based learning resource to support e-learning. Blended learning is a method of using a range of learning interventions based on different modes of delivery, for example web-based resources and work-based learning or classroom training.

Many of the above interventions are used in management development and are complemented by a range of analytical or 'diagnostic' techniques to help individuals identify their development needs. For example, 360-degree feedback, psychometric profiling, business simulations and development centres are all helpful methods to identify individual training needs as part of the training needs analysis. Management development methods typically draw on the use of competencies as a basis for defining technical and behavioural attributes individuals need to demonstrate to perform effectively in their roles, and this will be discussed in more detail below.

Competency-based learning and development

Competencies and competency frameworks are widely used to define standards of expected performance based on skill sets and behaviours specific to certain roles. The UK National Vocational Qualifications (NVQs) were established in the 1980s to coordinate the development of occupational standards in the UK, in response to the British government's desire to improve competitiveness by raising the level of training in the workplace. An NVQ comprises units of competence, which can be specified in terms of the skills and behaviours needed to do an effective job. Competence can be assessed in various ways which provide a basis for recognition and award of NVQs and other qualifications linked to competencies. The Management Standards Centre developed the National Occupational Standards for management and leadership in 2004, which were revised in 2008 (MSC, 2004); they are statements of best practice outlining the performance criteria, related skills, knowledge and understanding required to effectively carry out various management and leadership functions. The core standards cover managing self and personal skills, providing direction, facilitating change, working with people, using resources and achieving results. A competency framework underpins these standards, comprising units of competence in each of these areas at four different levels of responsibility: team leader, first-line manager, middle manager and senior manager. These units can be used to design workplace L&D interventions, which can be assessed in several ways. They also provide a basis for designing educational courses, which can be assessed for awards. The professional management institutions, such as the Chartered Management Institute (CMI) and Institute of Leadership and Management (ILM), use this competency framework to design and assess a range of awards at different levels.

Many UK organisations have used this framework to assist with the design of their own competency frameworks. Other organisations have developed their own frameworks, including The NHS Leadership Qualities Framework, launched in 2002, to describe the qualities expected of the existing and aspiring NHS leaders. It comprises 15 leadership qualities organised in three clusters: personal qualities, setting direction and delivering the service. Each leadership quality is broken down into several levels, which help to define competence in terms of the key characteristics, attitudes and behaviours required of effective leaders at any level of the service. The new NHS Leadership Framework was launched in 2011.

Although the competency approach to management standards has broad appeal because of the consistency-related benefits it offers, it has attracted criticism for being applied in a deductive way (by prescription) rather than inductively to describe effective management and leadership (Bolden and Gosling, 2004). In other words, if competencies are used in a compliant 'tick box' fashion and the dialogue does not extend beyond the limited definitions of the competencies, then the true nature of what management and leadership means can be lost, leading to a static and sterile situation. There has to be room to move beyond the strict 'specification' of competencies to ensure that the process of individual and organisational development is a dynamic and progressive one, which reflects the challenges that organisations face in a changing business environment.

The case which follows describes how the UK Fire and Rescue Service (FRS) implemented its competency framework: the Integrated Personal Development System (IPDS) to facilitate the development of FRS employees. Research into employee perceptions of this system and its application are discussed.

The effectiveness of employee development at West Sussex Fire and Rescue Service (WSFRS) – a case study

The UK Fire and Rescue Service is undergoing a modernisation programme, an element of which is the adoption of a national framework of skills and competencies, known as the 'Integrated Personal Development System' (IPDS), to be used at all stages of employees' careers, from selection, through training and development and performance management to retirement.

Integrated Personal Development System (IPDS): an employee competence framework

The IPDS implementation has caused employee development to change beyond all recognition. The National Fire and Rescue Service Learning and Development Strategy provides a framework for a decade, spanning 2005–2015, whereby implementing IPDS supports modernisation of the Fire and Rescue Service. However concerns have been expressed about the degree of progress made by individual Fire and Rescue Services in their implementation of IPDS relating to issues such as whether each of the elements that make up IPDS fit together effectively, whether the tools are being utilised for their intended purpose and whether IPDS is delivering results.

Published reviews focus on the management perspective, but given that IPDS is a system implemented *by* fire service employees *for* fire service employees, success is reliant on employee buy-in. Without support from everyone, from fire-fighters to chief fire officers, it cannot succeed in achieving its aims as a fundamental component of the Learning and Development Strategy. Therefore this research focused on the employees within one UK Fire and Rescue Service, WSFRS, and how they perceived its effectiveness in relation to the IPDS strategic objectives, which are:

1. To provide a clear and distinct career path for every individual in the fire and rescue service, regardless of whether they are uniformed or support staff, full- or part-time.

2. To ensure all staff receive role-specific development and lifelong competence.

3. To enable people with the appropriate skills and experience to enter the service at the most suitable level, increasing professionalism and effectiveness.

The main elements of IPDS, in terms of employee development, are:

- Assessment and Development Centres (ADCs),
- Personal Development Plans and Records – including NVQs, National Occupational Standards, other qualifications and work-based learning and assessment,
- Performance Appraisals.

The research centred on understanding employees' perceptions of a variety of factors within the context of their organisation. The research methodology adopted two key strategies, a case study and a survey, to explore past and present issues and to focus on the findings within a single environment, the WSFRS. A questionnaire was used to gather data from a representative organisational sample, followed up by structured interviews with individuals to elicit deeper meaning and understanding of the questionnaire data. In addition the ex-director of the IPDS hub was interviewed and a variety of secondary data were also used in the form of organisational policies and procedures, employee data from ADCs and appraisal processes.

Development and career progression

A key finding was that employees' understanding of IPDS varied considerably. At middle-manager level the majority demonstrated a good understanding of IPDS.

However at fire-fighter level most employees understood it was focused on the individual but often thought it was a system purely for recording their training activities. When asked whether they felt they would have opportunities to progress in their careers within the Service, 60 per cent of the middle-manager population either disagreed or were unsure. Supervisory managers appeared to be the most optimistic group of employees, with 61 per cent agreeing they would have opportunities to progress in the future, followed closely by the fire-fighters, with 57 per cent.

The data suggest that there are gaps within the competence assessment and development processes, with inconsistencies in the sign-off of individual competence status. There were clear systems in place for maintenance of competence at fire-fighter level but there was room for development of this area for management levels. NVQs were in place for fire-fighters, with plans to expand these to other levels, including management. There were mixed feelings about opportunities to access development, with only a half of fire-fighters and supervisory managers agreeing that they had access to development opportunities – the majority of the remainder being unsure. However the pyramid shape of the organisation, which reduces the opportunities for career progression, may have affected this response. An important point to note here is that individuals are only placed on formal development programmes once they have secured a post at a more senior level, as resources do not allow significant investment in development before this stage.

From single-point to multi-tier entry into the FRS management structure

Until the introduction of IPDS and multi-point entry, all uniformed staff joined as fire-fighters – the most junior rank. The introduction of multi-tier entry aimed to improve equality of opportunity by increasing diversity in the workforce and to ensure future sustainability. Nationally there are concerns about the effectiveness of the development programmes being provided by individual Fire and Rescue Services to direct entrants, in that they concentrate too much on quantity rather than on quality of outputs. Although generally employees were supportive of the principle of direct multi-tier entry, a recurring theme was a feeling that people not considered to be adequately qualified currently occupied many senior management posts primarily because these senior managers would have been selected at the start of their career by using the entry standards for a fire-fighter, and assessed for their senior management potential.

A typical response from a fire-fighter was, 'I agree with the tiered entry approach for managers. When I joined it was just about moving up the ranks'. Several employees felt that senior management positions should be opened up to external applicants, who were more likely to have the appropriate management training and experience. A typical quote from a Supervisory Manager was, 'The service is being run by fire-fighters with an appropriate number of years service under their belts... external candidates should be given the opportunity to apply for managerial positions, who would probably have the relevant and appropriate training to undertake the role, better than a fire-fighter'. The employees' views were mainly based on perceptions, rather than experience, as at the time of the research WSFRS had not employed anyone via direct entry methods.

Assessment Development Centres (ADCs) and the Personal Development Planning (PDP)

ADCs are designed to measure an individual's development needs against a set of management competencies in advance of their progress to a higher role. This enables the design of individually tailored programmes. Employees generally supported ADCs as a method to assess development needs prior to moving into a new role, with confidence higher among those who had taken part in ADCs. Previously a system of knowledge-based examinations prevailed as the means to promotion. These examinations represented the system of learning-based assessment, whilst IPDS fits the model of competence-based assessment (Fletcher, 1997). IPDS combines ADCs with competence-based training to ensure a link between competence gaps and development programmes. A major concern regarding ADCs was the financial costs associated with the large numbers of people being allowed to attend, without an effective mechanism to sift or recommend individuals for development to the next role. Although some employees viewed this as positive because it opened up opportunities, it resulted in a disproportionate number of people going through the process in relation to the numbers of vacancies projected at each level. For example just 18 per cent of employees who entered the first stage of the ADC (designed to assess potential for development to the next level) actually progressed to the next stage, indicating that over 80 per cent of those who accessed the first stage were not 'ready' to do so.

The PDP process establishes a mechanism by which individuals starting in a new role join a development programme to facilitate competence acquisition. Personal Development Records (PDRs) enable progress to be assessed and recorded throughout the journey to competence, as measured against the occupational standards. Although few employees found the process useful, a major finding was that over 70 per cent of respondents reported a lack of support throughout the development process. The majority of employees agreed that the appraisal process identified their development needs, with 89 per cent of all respondents agreeing that their appraisal provided an opportunity to discuss their performance. However there was less confidence in the guarantee of receiving the support they needed to address the development needs identified at the appraisal.

Addressing the challenges

In order to address the lack of support in the employee development phase, the Learning and Development Department has been re-structured into two distinct functions – organisational development and training delivery. The Organisational Development team will focus on providing dedicated support to individuals in the development phase of their roles, for example whilst they are completing NVQs. A new post of Organisational Development Trainer has been established, which will provide direct support both to individuals working towards competence status and to the line managers and workplace assessors responsible for those individuals.

Additionally there are plans to enhance the current appraisal process by making it competence-based so that it can support and complement the other competence-based tools. By aligning the performance measures, development measures and competence measures, based on National Occupational Standards in line with roles, the system will become holistic and will provide a common 'language' that all employees are able to understand. Additionally by basing appraisals on competence, line managers will be better placed to recommend and support employees when they are ready for development to a new role, because they will have an accurate picture of the individual's current position and readiness to progress, using common measures.

Developing a competent workforce will demonstrably add value to the organisation, but in order to monitor this value it must be continuously measured to allow refinement to the processes. The HRD strategy of IPDS can then be reviewed to ensure it continues to support the overall objectives of the National Fire and Rescue Service for the future.

Activities and discussion questions

1. Consider the learning you have experienced in the workplace and/or in an educational institution. Identify the interventions/methods used in the learning process that took place, for example was the learning planned or unplanned? How was the learning supported and who was involved? Why did the learning take place in the way it did?

2. Based on the learning identified in (1) above, what competencies (knowledge and skills) were developed as a result of the learning that took place, and how did this learning impact on how you performed your role at work or on your course?

3. What learning would you have to undertake to be in the position you would like to be in three to five years from now. Why would you have to undertake this learning? How will you acquire this learning and who will provide it?

4. Can you identify the competencies required of you in your current role (or a former role)? If these are documented, would you agree that they cover your role based on your experience in the job? What are the potential consequences if they do not, for example for performance reviews, rewards and career progression?

5. Discuss the 'positive' and 'negative' perceptions of employees of the competency-based Integrated Personal Development System (IPDS) discussed in the case above?

Bibliography

Amir, E. and Livine, G. (2001). *Accounting for Human Capital When Labour Mobility Is Restricted*. London: London Business School.

Bain, G., Lyons, M. and Young, A. (2002). *The Future of the Fire Service: Reducing Risk, Saving Lives. The Independent Review of the Fire Service*. London: ODPM.

Bolden, R. and Gosling, J. (2004). 'Leadership standards: pros and cons of a competency approach'. A paper presented at the *SAM/IFSAM VIIth World Congress: Management in a World of Diversity and Change*. 5–7 July, 2004, Göteborg, Sweden. Academic stream: Management education.

Chambers, E.G., Foulon, M., Handfield-Jones, H., Hankin, S.M. and Michaels, E.G. III (1998). 'The war for talent'. *McKinsey Quarterly*, 3, 44–57.

Department for Communities and Local Government. (2007). *Fire and Rescue Services National Framework 2008–11 Consultation*. London: Communities and Local Government Publications.

Fletcher, S. (1997). *Competence-Based Assessment Techniques* (2nd edn.). London: Kogan Page.

Fombrun, C.J., Tichy, N.M., and Devanna, M.A. (1984). *Strategic Human Resource Management*. New York: Wiley.

Kolb, D. (1996). 'Management and the learning process', in Starkey, K. (ed.), *How Organisations Learn*. London: ITP, pp. 270–287.

Leishman, F. and Savage, S.P. (1993). 'Officers or managers? Direct entry into British police management'. *International Journal of Public Sector Management*, 6 (5), 4–11.

Management Standards Centre (2004). *National Occupational Standards in Management and Leadership*. Retrieved from the Management Standards Centre website: http://www.management-standards.org/standards/standards on 1 November, 2011.

McCartney, C. and Garrow, V. (2006). *The Talent Management Journey*. Research reports. Horsham: Roffey Park.

Miller, J. (2011). *Sustainable Organisation Performance: What Really Makes the Difference?* London: CIPD.

NHS (2011). *Leadership Qualities Framework*. Retrieved from http://www.nhsleadership qualities.nhs.uk/ on 1 November, 2011.

Noe, R.A. (2004). *Employee Training and Development* (3rd edn.). Toronto: Irwin.

Purcell, J., Kinnie, N. Hutchinson, S., Rayton, B. and Swart, J. (2003). *Understanding the People and Performance Link: Unlocking the Black Box*. London: CIPD.

Revans, R.W. (1998). *ABC of Action Learning*. London: Lemos and Crane.

Sadler-Smith, E. (2006). *Learning and Development for Managers*. Oxford: Blackwell Publishing.

Stewart, J. (1999). *Employee Development Practice*. London: FT Pitman Publishing.

Sung, J. and Ashton, D. (2005). *High Performance Work Practices: Linking Strategy and Skills to Performance Outcomes*. London: Department and Trade and Industry.

CHAPTER 16

Approaches to Workplace Learning

Learning on-demand and work-based learning

Marjorie Corbridge, Natalie Macaulay, Julia Barton and David Hall

Learning theory exposes the idea that there are different approaches to learning, which should be made available in the workplace if an organisation is to match the variety of learning styles that will be prevalent among the employees. More than ever, changes in technology, changes in how we work and changes in lifestyle impact on how the employee may think about his or her own personal development. According to Miller (2008: 18), 'Over the last few years, we have transformed into a society that wants everything on demand – from the TV shows and movies that we watch, to the radio programs and music we listen to. So why shouldn't learning be the same way? . . . as each generation becomes more technically savvy . . . it has come to expect a learning environment where content is available anytime, anywhere, at the click of a button.' Employers are able to capitalise on the flexibility that many employees are happy to display by providing a variety of approaches to workplace learning.

Employee development is a key activity to make sure that staff have the right skills and knowledge to ensure the level of performance needed to achieve the strategic vision for the organisation. In Chapter 12, the concept of the learning organisation and organisational learning were examined and the processes for developing and sustaining learning explored. This chapter focuses o on two different approaches to learning and development, which enable organisations to examine some of the options available in developing their employees. The first part looks at learning on demand and examines the role played by technology in maximising employee engagement with learning and development. Second is an opportunity to examine the ideas that bring education institutions and employers together in exploring work-based learning and the opportunities that can be derived from demand-led development.

Learning on demand

The challenges facing today's organisations, in particular those operating in the global market, mean that information and organisational knowledge, usually held by the employees or distributed around organisational systems, are key ingredients in ensuring that organisations stay at the top of their game. The early twenty-first century has seen a knowledge and information explosion, with seemingly unlimited information available on demand. Customers can access product and service information not just from one organisation but also from competitors at the touch of a button. So the challenge is not the availability of information; it is, as indicated by Trondsen and Vickery (1998: 169), 'despite the dazzling array of technology now available to create, store, organize, manipulate and transmit information – companies must rely on the ability of their employees to absorb information, make it part of their knowledge base and apply it effectively in their work'. They go on to assert that at a time when information technology can transmit millions of bits of data in seconds, old learning paradigms 'I teach, you learn' are no longer sufficient. Technology is now mobile, which makes it easy for the employee to access company data remotely, either through accessing the organisations' servers or by using cloud computing. This technology allows the cloud provider to make sure that the infrastructure is in place and works and that the organisation can work seamlessly on any document in any location. All that is required is Internet access. However, whilst investing in the cloud may still be a little way off for some organisations, this does appears to be the 'next big thing'. Further development of cloud computing, both public cloud and private cloud, has the potential to boost learning on demand.

Technology is at the source of the success of learning on demand, and it enables a new model of learning to be explored. Learning is often seen as an information flow from the teacher to the learner with the time, place and pace dictated by the teacher. The ability to provide a virtual learning environment (VLE) encompasses information flow from the teacher to the learners, information from learner to learner and direct access to a variety of learning media, including online tutorials and webinars, but there is more control by the learners, who are able to manage their learning by engaging with it at a time and a place suited to their work schedule and home commitments and at an individual pace which suits their learning style. The range of material that can be sourced for this type of learning is significantly broader than that which would be available within a formal training situation. Multimedia presentations, individualised discussions between mentor and mentee, small-scale discussion groups all allow an individualised approach to learning on demand. Rather than the teacher making the decision on what the learners know (or need to know) the learners have the opportunity to reflect on the level of their current knowledge and skills, identify the gaps and seek the appropriate 'bundle' of learning to meet those gaps. At this stage of development learning on demand is probably best suited to knowledge updates, legal changes, new product details, the knowledge aspects of staff induction, technical updates and knowledge sharing in geographically dispersed organisations. The development of soft skills may be more of a challenge for learning on demand as this type of skill development is more suited to face-to-face communication so that any idea that learning on demand is the answer to all employee development needs is fallacious.

Benefits of learning on demand

The first key benefit of learning on demand is the flexibility, which enables the organisation to bring both existing and new employees up to speed quickly and to derive a benefit from a fully skilled workforce. Trondsen and Vickery argue that (1998: 171) 'multimedia based learning on demand can compress the time necessary to move people through the four stages of learning – progressing from an unconscious incompetent state to an unconscious competent state. Because employees learn in a situational format, they master material more quickly and retain it better'. The flexibility offered by learning on demand often means that employees get instant feedback on their learning, and this increases their confidence and motivation and is likely to impact positively on their job performance. The second key benefit is the impact on the costs of employee development. Improvements in technology have made learning on demand, using intranets and cloud computing to deliver multimedia training material, a more cost-effective option than text-based development options. This brings an alternative dimension to employee development, enhancing the training opportunities for employees. Third is the ability to ensure that all employees have access to high-quality training material. Traditional organisational in-house training may be of mixed quality and the development of material for learning on demand enables the organisation to both standardise and customise material, to capture the best trainers, on their best days and hence provide a more consistent and high-quality learning opportunity for all staff. Fourth organisations can use their staff developers and trainers in a different way by enabling them to act as internal consultants, seeking views on training needs from a variety of sources, developing appropriate material and disseminating this widely through the learning-on-demand network. This may put the developers closer to the business and better able to understand the skills and knowledge needed to enhance overall performance and better able to develop new and creative ways to facilitate that learning.

What are the triggers for expansion of learning on demand?

The *increase in globalisation* and the 24/7 society mean that competition for provision of products and services is significant and the buyer is no longer limited to a supplier at local level; in order to retain a competitive edge organisations must ensure that they have the best talent with the best knowledge and skills to deliver the best products or services to the global market. Staff will need to be more knowledgeable to compete in this market. This may be a trigger to the further development of high-quality education and training on demand. Many organisations are recognising the *need to be nimble*, to work smarter, to be more efficient and to respond to market changes more quickly than perhaps they did in the past. In order to reflect these changes, *organisational structures have become flatter*, the span of control has increased and managers are looking for value added from each employee: this means that employees need improved cognitive skills to identify, address and solve problems quickly and effectively. Finally, as Trondsen and Vickery (1998: 175) put it, 'The new work environment is one of 'less': less time to solve problems; less time to learn (especially to attend time consuming training sessions off site); less time available off the job; less time for administration; less time to help colleagues; less time to manage and less time to receive management guidance or supervision.'

What are the barriers to learning on demand?

Several organisations (Lockheed Martin, Hewlett-Packard) that embraced learning on demand at the early stages are unsurprisingly in the technology industries, where there is likely to be a culture that embraces technological change and a familiarity with technology that excites them to adopt new ways of learning. One of the barriers to moving forward on the take up of learning on demand is the culture of the organisation and the extent to which there is a culture that welcomes change and one that is not fearful of technology. An organisation with a culture that is more traditional, slow to change and cautious in its decision-making will want to see how this works in practice before it takes up this approach. The level of uncertainty and in many instances the lack of clarity on the costs and benefits may act as a barrier to taking up learning on demand.

However, while the case for learning on demand – the speed, flexibility, accessibility, customisation and standardisation – is a compelling one it is unlikely to be the only way forward in employee development. There is much talk about blended learning, and this openness to bringing together a range of alternative approaches to employee development to maximise the benefits of each may be the way to develop the workforce to its potential for the benefit of both the organisation and the employee. The first case study in this chapter looks at the development of e-learning and learning on demand and examines how this worked in a geographically dispersed organisation operating in different counties and using different languages. This highlights very effectively the need for timely design, development and delivery of learning on demand to ensure that staff have the necessary knowledge and skills in time for the launch of a new product to market.

Work-based learning – an alternative approach to employee development

It is several years since the publication of the Government's Competitiveness White Paper, which identified the knowledge economy as a significant factor in contributing towards business competitiveness and national prosperity. The 2001 White Paper on Enterprise, Innovation and Skills emphasised the importance of people, their skills, knowledge and creativity as the key to improving productivity in a knowledge economy. The first and second editions of the UK Competitiveness Indicators in 1999 and 2001, respectively, identified a shortfall in UK productivity when comparing the UK economy and other G7 economies. The link between UK competitiveness and employee and management skills was made, as skills were identified as one area where the UK was behind, the others being research and design, innovation, enterprise and investment. Poor literacy and numeracy, a shortfall in intermediate and vocational skills, compounded by a shortage of skilled managers in the workforce were cited as the underlying problems. Although there have been improvements in UK productivity, the UK still lags behind that of the USA and France. At least 20 per cent of the productivity gap has been attributed to a weakness in skills in the UK.

In recent years there has been a considerable increase in bringing together the planned, and sometimes unplanned, learning that takes place within the workplace and educational institutions, which can accredit the work and make the award of a qualification. This is termed work-based learning (WBL), which is described by Boud and Solomon (2001: 4) as 'a class of university programmes that bring together universities and work organisations to create new learning opportunities in workplaces. Such programmes meet the needs of learners, contribute to the longer term development of the organisation and are formally accredited as university courses'. There has been a long history of flexibility in the delivery of higher education in the UK from correspondence courses through to the Open University, which provided a mechanism to access learning for those who were unable to access through more traditional routes. The SCQAA (2008: 3) contend that WBL 'is seen as part of the access tradition. For people at work, accessing Higher Education (HE) through traditional routes can either mean sacrificing an existing job or trying to fit in part-time education with increasingly demanding patterns of work...principally [it is] a new form of access aimed at employees facing considerable barriers...and consequently excluded from important learning opportunities'. The distinction between WBL and 'traditional' learning is that WBL is the means by which a discipline is delivered, not the discipline to be studied. In other words, WBL is not 'content' driven by any specific curriculum, but it provides a formal, structured process for learning.

Learning outcomes, which are agreed to between the employee, employer and the educational institution assessing the work, provide a means to accredit and award qualifications. The learning outcomes are often used to generate a learning contract, which is a document used to help in framing the workplace projects that will guide the learning. As Anderson, Boud and Sampson (2004: 2) state, 'the use of a learning contract is based upon a number of assumptions about nature of learning and learners. It derives largely from the ideas of educators such as Malcolm Knowles [(1980)] who believe that as autonomous human beings adult learners should be encouraged to take more responsibility for their own learning and to use their existing skills and experiences as the basis for new learning, and that they should be allowed in formal educational settings to learn things which are of importance to them'. Learning contracts provide for the formal recording of the learning objectives of the project (or projects); the strategies and resources available to achieve the objectives; the evidence that will be produced to show that the learning outcomes have been met and the criteria that will be used to assess this evidence. In this way, WBL provides a mechanism for personal and workforce development based on accreditation and the award of qualifications. This model works and is applied by many institutions within the Higher Education (HE) sector. However the model tends to focus on the needs of the employee as the learner. There is an opportunity to develop this 'partnership' model to meet the wider needs of employers who wish to take a strategic and coherent approach to develop a skilled and qualified workforce, in line with business aims, that is 'work-based learning partnerships'.

Work-based learning partnerships

There are many examples of a partnership model in operation in Higher Education institutions. For example one model is the partnership forum for leadership and management, which has recently been established, consisting of the Portsmouth Primary Care Trust, South Central Strategic Health Authority, Portsmouth City Council and the University of Portsmouth, with the aim of developing learning and development solutions that meet these organisations' needs and provide opportunities for accreditation towards qualifications. The University of Portsmouth is also the preferred supplier for academic accreditation for leadership and management with the Fire and Rescue Service, providing a WBL qualifications framework from the Foundation degree to the postgraduate degree level. This framework is based on the National Occupational Standards in Management and Leadership and mapped against the FRS 'Aspire' leadership model. Another example is the involvement of the Sector Skills Council for Retail that works with a Consortium of Retail universities to develop a Foundation degree in retailing, which allows large employers to develop modules that meet their particular needs. Employers such as Tesco, Henderson's, The Cooperative and Morrisons, among others, now work closely with universities such as Manchester Metropolitan, Middlesex and Derby to offer WBL degrees, in some instances from Foundation degrees to professional doctorates.

The future

There are opportunities for HE institutions to work with employers and other organisations to shape the future of employee development and management learning and to play an important role in developing the UK workforce. WBL Partnerships involving key stakeholders provide a compelling case as a model for delivering and accrediting learning at the workplace. This model is currently playing a role in delivering high-level skills to employers and employees, and the indications are that it will become more widely adopted in the future. The UK skills agenda presents 'new horizons' for the HE sector, and leadership within universities will be a crucial factor in how this sector rises to the challenge.

Study 2 in this chapter examines the application of work-based learning to a health care institution and the development of a work-based learning continuum. This continuum seeks to identify the roles played by different parties in developing work-based learning opportunities. The health care institution suggests that this helps in discussions with educators when looking to provide work-based learning.

Learning on-demand – the case of the sales training

Video on demand, TV on demand, Publishing on Demand – are these terms you are familiar with? Gone are the days of only four TV channels operating within set hours. Our lives are an ongoing exercise in customisation to meet our own unique needs, wants and desires, and technology is helping us. How then might 'customisation' be revealing itself in learning and development? This study takes a brief look at the history of learning supported by technology. It looks at how learning budgets are faring in difficult economic conditions, what constitutes good learning with technology and shares a recent application of 'learning on-demand' in one organisation. The goal is to promote thinking about how easy or easier it could be to implement technology into your organisational learning.

Resilience in learning

The global economic downturn which started in 2008 produced some interesting trends in training budgets. In the UK the CIPD Learning and Development Survey (2009) reported that the average training spend per employee was £220. Overall training spend was declining, but in absolute terms by only seven to 10 per cent – far less than in other recessions. Have organisations finally understood the benefit of learning? What might this 'resilience' in learning budgets be attributed to? Half of the respondents to the Learning and Development Survey confirmed that funds for learning and development remained the same in 2008. Three-quarters of respondents agreed that learning and development continued to be perceived as an important part of business improvement, despite the challenging economic times. The areas within the learning and development budget experiencing the most significant growth are in-house development and e-learning, with more than half of respondents reporting a greater focus on in-house development and 42 per cent responding that the use of e-learning had also increased.

The evolution of e-learning

The 1980s saw the introduction of Computer-Based Training (CBT). This was a genuine attempt to harness the potential of technology, with the technology movement leading the charge, but often with learning interventions that were poorly designed, and slow. In the 1990s e-learning progressed with instructors taking back the role of designing learning online, in order to ensure that the content reflected learning needs. Over the past 10 years learning specialists have begun to harness the capabilities of modern technology to enhance the response to user needs and create better learning experiences. The advent of Web 2.0 and social media has spawned Learning 2.0 and 'learning on-demand'. No longer is e-learning available solely on the computer terminal – we are now able to access learning on the go and from virtually anywhere in the world. Individuals can now 'demand' how they want their learning delivered – online, classroom-based, blended or mobile. Regardless of how learning is delivered, one constant exists – it has to be delivered quickly. Design, development and delivery of learning life cycles have been dramatically reduced. People want customised learning delivered by using a variety of media and they want it NOW! Given the resilience of learning budgets in organisations and the growth of e-learning, how has technology enabled this?

Learning on demand

Howard (2008: 1) highlights the changing requirements for training by stating that: 'learning on-demand sets the stage for a new role for corporate learning and development organisations that allows a more rapid and flexible approach to enhancing corporate performance'. The development of Web collaboration technologies allows the organisation to facilitate the exchange of information and ideas between employees, customers and partners in real time, using readily accessible media such as blogs, wikis, podcasts and streaming media, discussion rooms, communities of practice and social networking tools. Learning on demand is different from other e-learning approaches in that it relies heavily on the following key features identified by Howard (2008: 5):

> *The portal as the gateway*: the portal provides the 'place to go' for the training resources and the flexibility that was not available with earlier technology.
> *Flexible technology architecture*: a content management system alone is not sufficient to maximise the benefits of learning on demand. Rather a collaborative network is required to enable the learning community to exchange information, as well as to capture knowledge about relevant subjects.
> *Personalisation* allows the capture of user data, such as geographical location or language, to ensure the appropriate learning is delivered in the language of the user.
> *Contribution from the learning community*: learning on demand enables a contribution to be made to the collective knowledge on a course or topic. Learning on demand is one way for an organisation to capture the collective knowledge that would otherwise disappear as experienced workers leave the organisation.
> *Ownership of the content*: the content of the learning on demand is assigned to 'content stewards', who are responsible for the accuracy and relevance of the content, as well as the personalisation and monitoring of usage.

Rapid, relevant and real easy . . .

One such company that has recently embraced learning on demand did so as a way to disseminate new sales product information to their sales teams. The organisation has a collection of eight companies spread across the EU, operating in multiple markets, segments and languages. These companies experience relatively high staff turnover amongst their sales teams. A major challenge is that the markets are changing rapidly and in order to remain competitive they need to constantly develop new products and bring them to markets quickly. The new products require intensive sales training in order to capitalise on their introduction, and the logistics involved in training individuals on a traditional face-to-face basis was proving too costly and too slow. The ability to leverage the route to market was being compromised by local differentiation caused by the highly subjective involvement of local training teams. The organisation wanted to maximise access to learning online, thereby enabling the sales staff to undertake the training whenever and from wherever they choose.

This means that the requirement to be 'off the job' was not necessary to complete the learning. Even though there was a clear need to embrace learning on demand there also had to be a clear and robust financial business case. This was achieved by a learning on-demand return on investment plan developed using existing training metrics and costs. The plan generated a strong financial case to embrace learning on demand.

The organisation started with its first product to be designed centrally. This made sense as the product was not to be further differentiated for its different markets, which meant the learning strategy could also be set. The design of the learning began by capturing the input from a cross-cultural group of subject matter experts. An instructional designer took the inputs and created the detailed instructional design to provide the detailed framework for the transfer of learning objectives to the learner. The primary benefit of this project was the functionality to discover, design and deliver the learning rapidly. Advances in access to e-learning authoring tools enabled fast distribution of learning to learners. The online authoring tool adopted as the input method used PowerPoint, but simply placing PowerPoint presentations into an authoring tool does not constitute learning design. While good technology is now widely available, good instructional design remains elusive. Good instructional design requires a combination of context, challenge, activity and feedback. An instructional designer can make the learning fun and when learning is fun it can also be engaging. An effective way to engage people in terms of learning on demand is to ensure the learning is interactive. Once the learning modules were created, the challenge was then how to disseminate them across eight geographical locations, each with disparate HR Information Systems and different IT architectures. However there was no budget for the purchase of a custom-built learning management system. This was resolved using a freeware, open-source learning content management system. Open source resources have their base code 'unlocked' to enable developer collaboration, globally. The owner unlocks the code in the hope that others will enhance and contribute to the product. This freeware is easy to use and can be customised to look and feel like a bespoke built system for the organisation. The development and accessibility of these platforms generate opportunities for rapid and engaging dissemination of learning and development to small and medium companies, and enable larger organisations to bring a significant proportion of their development in-house. Learning and development professionals now have the opportunity to design and deliver their own materials, rather than having to rely on project-managing expensive IT support to programme their content on slow and inflexible learning or content management systems. The organisation's first two modules were delivered in multiple languages to eight different European countries, and from inception to delivery the whole project took just six weeks. The success of the first two modules meant that a further two modules were commissioned, with the third module taking just four weeks to design and deliver. In six months the organisation has moved from reliance on a traditional model of training delivery to one that now harnesses the rapid ability to deploy learning on demand. Further modules are planned for early in 2010, and having trained internal people to use the authoring tool, the organisation is now only relying on external support for their instructional design, and technical support for the freeware.

The future

Is this the end of traditional classroom-based delivery? Not at all. Learning on demand is even more powerful when used as part of a blended learning strategy. This is a cost-effective way to deliver learning, whilst harnessing the benefits of both e-learning and face-to-face presentation, and it is becoming increasingly popular as a total learning solution. Whether learning strategy has driven the growing trend for learning on-demand or vice versa is irrelevant. What is important is that learning and development professionals have an unrivalled opportunity to deliver great learning in their organisations; to make it engaging and interactive, customised when, where and how it fits for learners, which in turn means a better return on results for the organisation and greater demand. Try it . . . you may be amazed at the response.

Demystifying work-based learning: developing a work-based learning continuum and accrediting work-based learning in a health care institution – a case study

Defining work-based learning

In their survey of 270 employers, Glass, Higgins and McGregor (2002: 5) suggest that over 70 per cent of employers have increased their volume of work-based learning over recent years. Work-based learning is on the increase but what exactly is it and how can organisations maximise the benefits for both the employer and employee? Boud and Solomon (2001) propose that the defining characteristic of work-based learning is that 'working and learning are coincidental and complimentary'. Following an audit of workplace learning opportunities in a large health care institution, it became apparent that work-based learning could encompass four distinct elements – *learning about work, learning from work, learning in work and learning for work*. The term can refer to informal, or formal, structured learning experiences. Where learning is informal, lack of recognition of achievements is common. Figure 16.1 shows examples of informal learning opportunities in a health care setting, which are transferable to other work environments.

Mentoring	Sabbaticals	Acting in a specialist or link role
Coaching	Developing new skills/competencies	Developing teaching resources
Secondments	Teaching others	Handovers
Shadowing	Undertaking project work	Supervision sessions
Rotations	Writing policies or procedures	Writing reports, bids or business cases
Audit	Appraisal	Personal development plans
Evaluation	Action Learning	Peer support groups
Newsletters	**Presentations**	**Conferences**

Figure 16.1   Examples of informal work-based learning opportunities in a health care setting

Boud and Solomon (2001: 5) suggest that work-based programmes typically have six characteristics:

A partnership exists between an employer and an education institution.

Learners are employees of the partnership employer organisation.

A learning programme is derived from the needs of the workplace and learner.

The starting point and level of the programme are established following the determination of current competencies and learning needs.

Learning projects are undertaken in the workplace.

To warrant the award of academic credit, the education institution assesses the learning outcomes according to a transdisciplinary framework.

The potential impact of work-based learning

Pedlar and Aspinwall (1998) suggest that 'learning has become the key developable and tradable commodity of an organisation'. They describe 11 characteristics of a learning organisation, two of which relate specifically to work-based learning. First do leaders and managers facilitate their own and other's learning from experience? Second are self-development opportunities available for all, not just the favoured few? A learning culture facilitates personal growth and satisfaction with work, and the organisation can become more flexible, adaptive and responsive to change. In the Glass et al. (2002) study, employers cited many reasons for supporting work-based learning initiatives, including improvements in quality of service or product, making the company more competitive, improving job competence, keeping up with technological developments, increasing productivity and increasing employee flexibility. Learning opportunities can be linked to staff reward and recognition, and therefore retention schemes. However empowering an employee through learning achievements can lead to dissatisfaction if they are not able to implement their new learning, innovate and make changes. Work-based learning has the potential to minimise the gap between theory and practice through the practical application and examination of theory. In work-based learning systems, the role of the teacher adapts to become more learner-centred, where facilitation of learning and direction to appropriate learning resources are of greater value than the direct transfer of expert knowledge. Employees may develop greater skills of reflection (Schon, 1983) and self-awareness through the exploration of their own and others' practice. Employees benefit from more meaningful appraisal and development planning. Increasingly development plans are based on role competencies, and the manager navigates through an array of learning interventions to plan how staff will meet their learning needs. An effective work-based learning system assists with this planning process by providing frameworks and structures for achievement.

A proposed model for the development of work-based learning programmes

Knowledge related to work has traditionally been determined, delivered and assessed by academic institutions, with influence from professions or disciplines. Increasingly more integrated partnerships are being developed to ensure that learning meets the changing needs of the workforce and has a productivity impact. Following an audit of work-based learning opportunities in a large health care institution, a Work-based Learning Continuum was developed. This has assisted discussions with education providers in planning new approaches to learning (Figure 16.2).

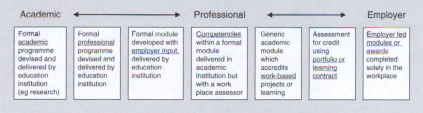

Figure 16.2   A work-based learning continuum

Accreditation of work-based learning can be academic and/or professional. The Glass et al. (2002) study found that 87 per cent of employers considered accreditation to be of some benefit and that accreditation influenced 40 per cent of employees' training decisions. Accreditation can improve staff morale, raise quality, enable achievement of national benchmarks and improve the organisation's product, service and image. Employees believed that accreditation enhances their curriculum vitae (CV), increases their confidence and helps them gain promotion and higher pay. Experience has highlighted some challenges when seeking to implement accredited work-based programmes. Employees may not perceive value in accredited programmes if they have prior credits or awards. However without assessment for credit there is no evidence for the achievement of learning outcomes, so employees should be encouraged to complete all assessed elements. Some employees may not have sufficient study skills therefore confidence and competence to study should be established before an employee commences a programme.

Education institutions need to be flexible in their assessment strategies and processes and the key is to devise work-based assessments, which are contextual and reflect the real-life requirements of the job. Many employers provide a range of in-house and on-the-job training programmes, particularly in areas such as health and safety, where updating requirements are statutory (legal requirement) or mandatory (national, professional or employee requirement). Traditionally these require employees to attend taught sessions delivered in the organisation but away from the employees' usual workplace. In order to enable meaningful learning during these updates and prevent impact on services through staff absence, trainers have been experimenting with alternative approaches. These can range from use of new learning technologies such as e-learning, simulation and provision of training in the actual work setting. Traditionally these programmes are not accredited and learning goes unrecognised. A robust work-based learning approach utilising kite marking principles could counter this. In-house training can be assessed against quality education standards, and bite-sized learning elements built into larger ones, for example fire safety built into a larger module about identifying, preventing and managing risk.

Implementing an effective work-based learning system and conclusions

In the Glass et al. (2002: 42) study, the main constraint on the provision of work-based learning was time off the job to participate in or facilitate learning activities. Other resource constraints were limited training budgets, the cost of education fees, lack of backfill for replacing staff and the lack of financial incentives. Staff must also have access to up-to-date learning resources. Use of new learning technologies require IT support and infrastructure because system incompatibility can thwart work-based learning endeavours. Work-based learning is rarely the 'cheap option'. Staff still need sufficient time to undertake learning although this can often be allocated more flexibly. There may also be hidden costs in terms of manager and workplace mentor and assessor support. One of the most challenging aspects of work-based learning is when an employee is required to frame their learning needs in a learning contract. Here learning outcomes must be articulated, and a plan developed as to how these will be achieved and measured. Support from an experienced educator can provide much needed direction and guidance.

Work-based competencies can stem from national or local frameworks. Whilst these may lead the employer to feel confident in their employees' skills, there is a danger that they can become overly technical and reductionist. The successful application of competencies to a range of contexts and settings, and evidence of underpinning knowledge should be sought, rather than the single observation of a task. Some work-based learning systems create very individual learning journeys, on which the employee travels alone. Recognising the need for peer support and re-creating this through communities of practice, informal networks or online discussion groups can help prevent isolation. To enable effective learning, *the employee, line manager, education facilitator and workplace mentor* are essential and interdependent partners in determining what, how and when learning is to take place. This chapter has offered the reader an insight into some of the key aspects of work-based learning. In proposing a simple model for implementation, it aims to capture the interest of those who have not yet considered work-based learning approaches in their own organisations.

Activities and discussion questions

1. You have been asked by your Head of Employee Development to prepare a presentation for your senior management team, which:

   a. Examines the concept of learning on demand
   b. Discusses the advantages and disadvantages of learning on demand for your organisation
   c. Makes recommendations of how to move forward with the idea of learning on demand

2. Examine the provision of a collection of focused training activities within your organisation (this should be any area of training that is core

to your business activity. For example product training, IT training, management development and sales training)

- List the training that is currently on offer in this group.
- Examine how this training is offered and to whom.
- Comment on the effectiveness of the training offered.
- Explore the option of offering this training 'on-demand'.
- Develop a business plan to offer learning on demand or blended learning as an alternative approach to offering this learning.

3. Examine the first case, learning on demand. Identify the **critical success factors** in the development and delivery of the learning on demand example in the study. Give reasons for your choices and indicate what metrics you would use to measure success.

4. Conduct a debate on the benefits of introducing formal work-based learning into your organisation. This should comprise two teams with Team One speaking **for** the motion 'Work-based learning offers benefits to both the employer and the employee'. Team Two should speak against the motion.

5. Examining the second case, 'Demystifying work-based learning', examine the extent of work-based learning in your organisation. This may include:

   a. Individuals following accredited university or college courses with components of work-based learning such as Foundation degrees, degrees in management or leadership, technical subjects or professional qualifications.
   b. Formal partnerships with academic institutions that provide courses of applied study tailored to your needs.

   How much control does the learner or the learner's manager have over the content or the application of the learning to the workplace? What additional role might be played by key players in your organisation to maximise the benefits of this approach to employee development learning?

6. Consider the work-based learning continuum shown in Figure 16.2 and apply it to your organisation. What professional groups, educational institutions and employers might come together to develop work-based learning opportunities for your employers and managers? What roles would they play? What challenges have you had to overcome to apply this continuum to your organisation?

Bibliography

Anderson, G., Boud, D. and Sampson, J. (2004). *Learning Contracts: A Practical Guide*. London: Routledge Falmer.

Annual Survey Report, Learning and Development (2008). London: CIPD.

Armstrong, S.T and Sadler-Smith, E. (2008). 'Learning on demand, at your own pace in rapid bite-sized chunks: the future shape of management development'. *Academy of Management Learning and Education* 7 (4) 571–86.

Arnold, J.T. (2007). 'Learning on the fly'. *HR Magazine* September 2007: 127–31.

Bersin and Associates (2007). *A New Organizational Model: Learning on Demand.* Retrieved from http://joshbersin.com/2007/10/01/a-new-organizational-learning-model-learning-on-demand/

Boud, D. and Solomon, N. (Eds) (2001). *Work-Based Learning: A New Higher Education?* The Society for Research into Higher Education. Milton Keynes: OU Press.

Brennan, L. (2005). *Integrating Work-Based Learning into Higher Education.* London: UVAC.

Cannon, F. (2003). 'Organisational climate: a tool for improving business performance'. *Human Resources and Employment Review* Croner, 1(1): March.

CIPD (2009). *Learning and Development: Annual Survey Report.* London: CIPD.

Dealtry, R. (2008). 'Global corporate priorities and demand led learning strategies'. *Journal of Workplace Learning* 20(4): 286–92.

Durrant, A., Rhodes, G. and Young, D. (2011). *Getting Started with University Level Work Based Learning.* Farringdon: Libri Publishing.

Fink, F.K., Rokkjær, O. and Schrey, K. (2007). 'Work based learning and facilitated work based learning'. TREE retrieved from http://www3.unifi.it/tree/dl/oc/d8.pdf

Garnett, J., Costley, C. and Workman, B. (2009). *Work Based Learning in Higher Education.* London: Middlesex University Press.

Glass, A., Higgins, K. and McGregor, A. (2002). *Delivering Work-Based Learning.* Scottish Executive Central Research Unit. www.scotland.gov.uk/publications/2002/06/14558/3244

Hartley, D.E. (2000). *On-Demand Learning: Training in the New Millennium.* Amhurst: HRD Press.

Helyer, R. (2010). *The Work-Based Learning Student Handbook.* Basingstoke: Palgrave Macmillan.

Howard, C. (2008). *Learning On-Demand: A New Role for Enterprise Learning.* www.hrzone.co.uk/files/siftmedia-hrzone/bersin.pdf

Knowles, M.S. (1980). *The Modern Practice of Adult Education: From Pedagogy to Andragogy.* Englewood Cliffs: Prentice hall/Cambridge.

Leroy Ward, J. and Riley, M. (2008). 'E-learning: the cost effective way to train in tough economic times'. *Employee Benefit Plan Review* 63(2): 12–4.

Lester, S. and Costley, C. (2010). 'Work-based learning at higher education level: value, practice and critique'. *Studies in Higher Education* 35(5), 561–75.

Mabey, C. (2005). 'Management development works: the evidence'. *Achieving Management Excellence Research Series 1996–2005.* London: CMI.

McLean, C. (2006). 'Blue cross and blue shield of Florida: rapid learning on demand'. *Chief Learning Officer* 5(5): 55–6.

Meawad, F. and Stubbs, G. (2008). 'A framework for enabling on-demand personalised mobile learning'. *International Journal of Mobile Learning and Organisation* 2(2): 133–48.

Miller, M. (2008). 'Learning on demand'. *The THE Journal* 33(11): 18–21.

Pedler, M. and Aspinwall, K. (1998). *A Concise Guide to the Learning Organisation.* London: Lemos and Crane.

Pollitt, D. (2005). 'Scottish water employees get learning "on tap"'. *Human Resource Management International Digest* 13(7): 25–7.

SCQAA (2008). *Emerging Models of Work Based Learning in Scottish Higher Education.* Mansfield: ScQAA.

Schon, D. (1983). *The Reflective Practitioner: How Professionals Think in Action.* London. Jossey Bass.

Tapscott, D. (2006). *Winning with the Enterprise 2.0.* New Paradigm Learning Corporation. www.newparadigm.com

Trondsen, E. and Vickery, K. (1998). 'Learning on demand'. *Journal of Knowledge Management* 1(3): 169–80.

Ward, J.L. and Riley, M. (2008). 'E-learning: the cost-effective way to train in tough economic times'. *Employee Benefit Plan Review* 63(2): 12–4.

Wilton, P., Woodman, P. and Essex, R. (2007). *The Value of Management Qualifications: The Perspective of UK Employers and Managers*. London: CMI.

CHAPTER 17

Coaching for Employee and Organisational Performance
A strategic intervention

Stephen Pilbeam, Valerie Anderson, Sara Hope and Alistair Campbell

This chapter introduces the strategic people management discipline of coaching for performance, and examines:

- Research into the role of line managers in coaching at work – a coaching style of management at the sharp end of business,
- A case study focused on the role of the internal coach in a complex, multidisciplinary, international organisation of 10,000 employees,
- A case study where external coaches were used by a major UK financial services provider to improve the success rate in winning competitive bids.

We start with an assertion – coaching for performance is a fundamental component of strategic people management. Coaching goes to the heart of managing people effectively because the focus is on future potential, rather than just on past performance, although clearly the analysis of past performance is instructive in identifying potential. Coaching is an increasingly popular tool for supporting personal development. Eight out of 10 respondents in the *CIPD Learning and Development survey* (2010b) reported using coaching in their organisations. Over one half of survey respondents identified coaching as the most effective approach to development, closely behind 'in-house development programmes', which tended to include a large coaching element. It was evident that coaching is formally embedded within talent development programmes, with coaching interventions linked to corporate strategy through performance management and review, management development processes and the development of leadership capability.

It is argued by Whitmore (2009) that less than 50 per cent of employees' potential manifests itself in the workplace, with the most frequently cited blocks to developing potential, which are external to the individual employee, being the restrictive structures and practices of the employing organisation, the lack of encouragement by managers and the lack of opportunities to self-actualise. The most significant internal blocks to developing potential are clustered around fear of failure, lack of confidence and self-doubt. Consequently building both contextual and self- awareness, encouraging the acceptance of personal responsibility and engendering self-belief are primary goals of a coach, whilst at the same time being able to evaluate the prevailing management styles and organisational structures and the impact they might have on individual and team performance.

What is coaching?

So, what is coaching and what is the role of the coach in an employment situation? Clearly there are parallels with sports coaching, but for our purposes 'coaching is the unlocking of an employee's potential in order to maximise not only their performance, but also that of the team and the organisation', and the role of the coach is 'to enable the learner to learn, rather than teaching the employee'. According to the CIPD (2009b) the characteristics of coaching include:

- It is essentially a non-directive form of development.
- The focus is on developing individual knowledge and skills and improving performance.
- Personal issues may be incorporated but the emphasis is on performance at work.
- Coaching activities have both organisational and individual goals.
- Feedback on strengths and their weaknesses is garnered.
- There is an assumption that the individual is psychologically well and does not require a clinical intervention; coaching is not psychoanalysis.
- Skilled coaching needs to be delivered by trained coaches.

Coaching is helping another person to work out the best way to achieve their goals, build skill sets and produce the results that the organisation needs; it is not restricted to formal or scheduled discussion and it is not telling someone what to do.

As the research and the cases that follow will demonstrate coaches can be internal to the organisation, either separate from or integrated within the line management role, or coaching may be better performed by an external coach. Whether coaching is provided internally or externally, it is necessary for the coach to adopt an optimistic view of dormant capability and also to recognise that coaching activity is on various continuums from unstructured to structured, spontaneous to pre-planned and short term to long term, and the cases that follow illustrate that there is no single best way. There is no escape from contingency, even in the art of coaching; it all depends on the circumstances of the individual and the organisation.

It is beyond the scope of this chapter to aspire to develop coaching skills but there is a well-trodden model that seeks to give some structure to the necessary questioning and feedback that is part of any coaching intervention. Familiar to all coaches, it is Whitmore's *GROW* model (2009), a simple model that consists of four elements – *Goals, Reality, Options and Wrap-up*. The *Goal*-setting stage is about agreeing on topics for discussion, agreeing on session objectives and identifying longer-term goals, and whilst this precedes the *Reality* check, in what may appear to be a continuous cycle model, it may be necessary to undertake the *Reality* check first by inviting self-assessment, checking out assumptions and what barriers there might be to realising potential before the Goals questions can be answered. Therefore rather than being a one-way continuous cycle the *GROW* model will necessarily include elements of oscillation, as the coaching conversation develops. The third element is *Options*, where options are explored and suggestions are developed before the final stage of *Wrap-up*, where commitment is made to actions, obstacles are identified, training needs are recognised and support agreed to, prior to agreeing on the next Goals session. Whitmore is at pains to point out that the model is no more than a model to provide some structure, and it remains essential for the coachee to have a sophisticated awareness of the organisational context and to develop high levels of self-awareness, which may benefit from some form of 360-degree feedback, and to take responsibility for self-actualising and unlocking latent potential, together with the personal responsibility for thoughts and actions.

Coaching is a widespread development tool and performance management technique and is being used by organisations across the UK, and increasingly, worldwide. However two factors are crucial to coaching success. First coaches must be developed and skilled, and second effective evaluation of coaching interventions needs to be further developed. Organisations therefore need to:

- understand the context and potential of coaching,
- identify the objectives of coaching,
- evaluate coaching through aligning it with strategic objectives and deploying appropriate metrics.

Survey research – Coaching at the sharp end: The role of line managers in coaching at work

In 2008, the CIPD commissioned researchers from the University of Portsmouth Business School to assess the implications of the devolution of coaching to line managers. A full research report was published by the CIPD (Anderson, Rayner and Schyns, 2009) and an online practical tool was also made available (CIPD, 2009a). What follows is a summary of the work that was undertaken and is based on the research commissioned by the CIPD, whose contribution is gratefully acknowledged.

Line managers have a crucial role to play in people management and development and the 'line manager as coach' role is increasingly being advocated as an important part of line managers' responsibilities. Coaching involves processes that are essentially non-directive, goal-focused and performance-driven. Coaching in organisations can deliver a range of benefits that include enhanced individual performance, improved communication processes, higher productivity, greater clarity about goals and objectives, effective knowledge-sharing processes, increased creativity, enhanced staff engagement and the development of an effective leadership style. However the expectation that line managers can fulfil all the functions of a specialist coach is not realistic, and probably not desirable. The manager-as-coach role is better described as a coaching style of management, which itself forms part of the wider development of a participative approach to managing people. Although the idea of a coaching style of management is attractive little research into what is involved has been undertaken, and this particular study was the first systematic assessment in the UK of these important issues.

A 'mixed methods' approach was taken to the research; three different types of data informed the analysis. First discussion group data from 95 people representing 69 different organisations who participated in the CIPD Coaching at Work conference in November 2008 were analysed; second in-depth interviews were undertaken in four organisations that had already gone some way towards developing an organisational 'coaching culture'. Data from the interviews and discussion groups, as well as insights from the coaching literature, informed the development of the third strand of the research: an online survey was completed by over 500 line managers from 12 organisations drawn from the public, private and not-for-profit sectors.

A number of key principles underpinned the design of the online questionnaire. First it was acknowledged that line managers may not all agree on the value of coaching and its relevance to them. Some managers may be convinced of the benefits and make use of a range of coaching behaviours as part of their management style. However, others may be 'agnostic' at best, and some are likely to be hostile to the idea. A 'coaching questionnaire' is unlikely to be completed by 'coaching sceptics' and so the word 'coaching' was not used in the survey – rather its language focused on 'managing' at the sharp end. Second line managers may view (or 'rate') their own patterns of behaviour 'in general terms' more positively than others might do, and so respondents were asked to reflect on behaviours during the previous three-month period, rather than on their 'general behaviour'.

Statistical analysis of the questionnaire data, using a technique known as principal component analysis, identified two related features of coaching, as undertaken by managers.

1. **Primary coaching characteristics** have a focus on individual performance, and comprise:

   - a development orientation,
   - a performance orientation,
   - effective feedback processes,
   - successful planning and goal-setting activities.

2. **Mature coaching characteristics** have a broader focus on empowerment, and comprise:

   - using ideas from team members,
   - powerful questioning,
   - team-based problem solving,
   - shared decision-making.

An assessment of the correlation between various responses to different survey questions also indicates that coaching characteristics are not associated with determinants such as a manager's age, experience or gender, suggesting that all managers have an equal chance of being able to develop and implement a coaching style of management. In addition to the correlation analysis, the qualitative data from interviews and discussion groups also showed the close links between the extent to which line managers engage in coaching behaviours and factors such as manager self-confidence and manager–team relationships. This means that coaching by managers can be part of a 'virtuous circle'. Coaching results in better manager–team relationships and improved levels of manager self-confidence. At the same time, these factors also tend to encourage managers to engage more often in coaching behaviours. Although a management style of coaching can be part of a 'virtuous circle' the research also identified a number of obstacles, or inhibitors, to the development of coaching characteristics by line managers. Concern about the time implications of coaching was by far the most significant barrier identified by the questionnaire respondents. In addition organisational culture ('it's not the style in our organisation'), a lack of confidence to deal with difficult people and a perceived lack of coaching skills were further inhibitors.

Given the inhibiting nature of a lack of confidence and of skills to underpin coaching characteristics, the analysis also assessed perceptions about support and development reported by the questionnaire respondents. The analysis showed that all types of learning and support opportunities – formal and informal, work-based and off-the-job – are perceived by most managers to be helpful in developing coaching behaviours. Importantly the analysis demonstrates that training and support can be both an 'input factor' and an 'output factor' relating to coaching by line managers. Training is essential to help managers develop the confidence to implement coaching. Furthermore as managers adopt coaching characteristics, they are more likely to appreciate and participate in different learning and support activities.

The research also established the wider influences that affect the extent to which a coaching style of management can be achieved in organisations. The senior management's ownership of coaching as a business issue and the top management's role-modelling of coaching characteristics are necessary. In addition clarity about coaching roles and expectations, combined with a clear acceptance of the time and resource constraints on the extent to which managers 'at the sharp end' can develop and sustain coaching characteristics as part of their role, are needed.

Coaching in adversity

This systematic research into the role of the line manager as coach suggests that a coaching style of management is as appropriate for organisations facing the challenges of hostile economic conditions as it is for those enjoying business growth and development. Although there may be a danger of a return to 'macho management' during an economic recession, the business case for a sustained coaching style of management remains. First, primary coaching characteristics relate to a performance orientation, and coaching by line managers can enhance the development and retention of high performers such that a sufficient number of people of good quality will be in place to ensure a 'head start' when economic recovery begins (of course coaching also provides a robust and proactive approach to managing poor performance). Second, the coaching of managers by managers can contribute to the development of newer management capabilities that individuals require if they are to make the transition from managing in a growth situation to managing in a 'slimmed down' organisation. Third, employee engagement and commitment are key variables for organisations during difficult times; the research shows that a coaching style of management delivers benefits that are manifested in better team relationships, enhanced levels of self-confidence and more general improvements in engagement, flexibility and commitment.

Coaching as 'business as normal'

The successful implementation of coaching by line managers requires HR professionals to work with their line management colleagues to diagnose the most effective way forward in implementing and embedding coaching, so that it becomes part of 'business as normal'. A coaching style of management is not something that can be achieved in isolation. Coaching has to be seen by top managers as a business issue rather than as an HR department initiative, and senior managers must communicate their commitment to coaching and role-model coaching characteristics in a consistent way. HR professionals must work to ensure that clarity about coaching roles and expectations is achieved and clearly communicated, training and support is provided, and that managers gain personal confidence in their abilities. In addition coaching as a style of management has to be grounded in constructive relationships, both within and between teams. This involves giving consistent attention to the time and resource constraints facing all managers, particularly those closest to 'the sharp end'; providing appropriate and relevant training and support; fostering effective team working and relationships; and encouraging managers to develop confidence in their coaching capability.

An examination of the role of the internal coach: is the internal coach there for the coachee or for the employer? – a case study

Until recently little has been researched or written on the topic of the internal coach, which has been 'flying under the radar' of mainstream coaching (Frisch, 2001: 241), and there is little theoretical research examining how or why the internal coach should work and when they will be most successful (Feldman and Lankau, 2005). Internal coaching has not 'garnered' the cachet of external coaching, and as a result little has been openly discussed about it (Frisch, 2001; Wilson, 2009). This unique form of coaching practice warrants special attention as a business practice, because it has been suggested (Jarvis, 2007; Wilson, 2009) that it brings unique benefits and potential pitfalls compared with other kinds of coaching and development activities. The aim of the research was to increase understanding of internal coaching and add breadth to the debate about how the role of an internal coach progresses.

An inductive approach was used to explore the research questions within a single organisation: a complex, multidisciplinary, international organisation of 10,000 employees. To bring a greater breadth to the body of knowledge on internal coaching the research sought to provide a unique insight into how the role of the internal coach is experienced by internal coaches, coachees, business leaders and HR professionals. The key issues emerging from the research were that the role of an internal coach appears to be ambiguous and subjective, as a result of participants' differing individual experiences, perceptions and beliefs. There are substantial gaps in our knowledge and understanding of the internal coach because the majority of the empirical research to date is anecdotal, or based heavily on opinions and self-reported benefits. Many of the articles written about internal coaching have not adopted a holistic view; they have failed to take into account the experiences of the wider stakeholders within an organisation, in particular, the 'buyers' of internal coaches, namely business leaders and HR managers. The research strategy consisted of a case study within an organisation that has used full-time internal coaches for ten years. The internal coaches coached on a full-time basis, rather than coaching in addition to other activities. The data were gathered using semi-structured interviews, during which participants were encouraged to describe their experiences of internal coaching in order to provide new insights and to increase understanding. Bearing in mind there is little theory relating to the internal coach, the data were used to generate themes and further understanding based on the experiences of the participants. The research was revealing in the following areas.

The purpose of the role of an internal coach

The findings suggest that the purpose of the role of an internal coach within the organisation is to support the personal career development and performance of employees through coaching and giving advice. The primary reason for employing an internal coach appears to be because they understand the business, the promotion process and the organisation. However, whilst the purpose of the role is specific to the organisation and had been communicated to its employees via the intranet, the way in which participants perceived the role appeared to be based on individual experiences, personal beliefs and the context in which they operate.

The empirical evidence suggests that whilst an organisation can have a prescribed role for an internal coach, the way in which the role is experienced and used by employees depends on the individuals and the meanings they associate with internal coaching. This results in ambiguity about the role and the development of perceptions based on subjective experience. The consequence of this ambiguity appears to be a sense of frustration from the internal coaches, business leaders and HR professionals. This supports the literature suggesting internal coaches may find it challenging when they have to manage the expectations of employees regarding what coaching actually is. The research also provides evidence about the 'conceptual confusion' (D'Abate, Eddy and Tannebaum, 2003) associated with the internal coach. Linked to this ambiguity about the role, the findings also reveal a tension between the personal and organisational dimensions of internal coaching. The coachees see the role as supporting them personally, whilst the HR professionals and business leaders see it as primarily supporting the organisation. The findings suggest that HR professionals appear to be more concerned with being able to demonstrate the return on investment in internal coaches compared with the experiences of the other populations such as internal coaches, coachees and business leaders. This could be because the world of the HR professional is more focused on demonstrating a clear benefit to the realisation of business goals and objectives.

If one subscribes to the view that coaching requires one essential 'ingredient that cannot be taught: caring not only for external results but for the person being coached' (Gallwey, 2003: 177), then it could be suggested that focusing too much on measuring the results of internal coaching may result in losing the essence of learning. The research outcomes suggest that one of the challenges for an organisation is achieving a balance between being able to articulate what the purpose of the role of an internal coach is, being able to measure the impact of the role on the bottom line and being able to maintain the quality and value of the coaching relationship. There appears to be a pull to have clarity, and yet the evidence from the experiences in this case study suggests this is difficult to achieve in practice. Whilst one can place structure around it, the question becomes 'what are you doing that for, and what are you hoping to achieve from it'?

The attributes required of an effective internal coach, and who is the client in an internal coaching relationship?

The findings suggest that the attributes required for an internal coach to be effective include technical coaching skills (listening, questioning), understanding the organisation and credibility. Credibility is seen as a function of being 'business savvy'. The attribute cited as most important to the effectiveness of the internal coach is experience, which is referred to as coming from doing the role full-time or working in other organisations as an internal coach. The challenge for an organisation then becomes how to recruit, train and develop internal coaches that have the necessary level of experience to be effective, particularly if they are fulfilling the role in addition to their 'day job'. Another key factor enabling internal coaches to be effective is that, since they are not part of the HR function, they are therefore seen as more independent, which serves to reinforce the value of confidentiality.

From the coachees' perspective the internal coaching relationship is very much about them as individuals, and so their particular needs take precedence. Although the internal coaches all put their coachees' needs first in their internal coaching relationships, they did recognise they have other stakeholders and therefore feedback given to the latter was of importance to the business. The experience of the coachees in this case suggests that confidentiality with an internal coach was not an issue of concern. This is in contrast to the literature suggesting that coachees may not fully trust the relationship is confidential because internal coaches are employed by the same organisation. What becomes apparent is the notion that perceptions exist about the internal coach and that assumptions are made about confidentiality by those who may not have experienced coaching by an internal coach. This is linked to the assumptions relating to the challenges for an internal coach. The coachees see themselves as the most important persons in the internal coaching relationship, they trust that the conversations are confidential and they gain value from the relationship.

The research findings support the notion that, from the perspective of the HR professionals and business leaders, the internal coach may be restricted to some extent by the organisation framework and focus on delivering skills, performance and development coaching. However what has also been shown through the experiences of the internal coaches and coachees in this study is that the agenda can develop more widely in the coaching relationship. It could be suggested that the coach might be able to coach at a deep and transformational level if the capability and matching are right. However from an organisational perspective, it appears the perception is that the purpose of the internal coach is to provide skills, development and performance coaching.

Conclusions

The research suggests that even if an organisation clearly describes the intended role of an internal coach and communicates the kind of coaching someone can expect to receive from a coaching relationship, participants are still likely to attribute their own meanings to the role on the basis of their perceptions and experiences. Paradoxically, there appears to be a tension between the coachees saying that they are the clients and the HR professionals and business leaders reflecting different demands. The question then becomes: to what extent is the organisation ready to acknowledge the ambiguity and subjectivity, and trust the experience and ability of the internal coach in creating a learning opportunity for the coachee that translates into enhanced business performance? Whilst an organisation employing internal coaches can put the structures and frameworks in place to recruit and develop the most appropriate people, provide them with supervision and enable them to have the right experience as an internal coach, there still needs to be recognition that the role is ambiguous and subjective.

The findings in this case study suggest that the coachee receives value from the coaching, and the management challenge is to trust that this translates into enhanced performance. If one adopts Gallwey's (2003) view that the focus within organisations is too much about coaching and too little about learning, then the danger of organisations focusing too much energy in assembling frameworks and structures around internal coaching is that these may obscure the true value of the learning and development.

The aim has been to use empirical evidence to help increase understanding about internal coaching, and that by understanding how different populations experience the role of an internal coach, effective practices can then accumulate as the dialogue progresses, benefiting internal coaches and those organisations planning to offer such services. It appears to point to the need for a further debate about what is a commercially viable and ethical way of structuring internal coaching.

Coaching for success: using behavioural analysis to drive performance improvement – a case study

A major UK financial services provider wanted to improve its success rate in winning major competitive bids – a situation where it would tender against competitors to win a contract for services to a large client. The bids for services were for insurance broking, strategic risk consulting, outsourced risk management and HR services. Because of the high costs in bidding and comparatively low profit margins, a small increase in bid win rate makes a disproportionate impact on the total profitability of the business. About 100 bids per year were being submitted, with a steady win rate of 40 per cent. The question was: what could be changed to increase the win rate? Typically between seven and 20 people were involved in any single major bid team. Of these, most were highly experienced and had managed or supported dozens of bids, and many had managed hundreds of bids. The organisation decided to employ external consultants, Campbell Management Consulting, to investigate, diagnose and coach for success.

Identifying the bid behaviours – diagnostic activity

Each bid had a clear outcome within a comparatively short period of time. A large number of people were involved, and therefore a diverse range of behaviours existed, and in addition there was a high volume of bids. This situation presented an excellent opportunity to study the behaviours exhibited by teams and to start to correlate the behaviours with bid outcomes, potentially enabling the identification of a trainable set of behaviours most likely to lead to success.

A list of 16 behaviours that could be adopted by bid teams was created. This was based on the views of experienced practitioners, including some from outside the organisation being studied, of what they believed would correlate with success in bidding. The work of 42 bid teams was observed and the adoption or non-adoption of each of the 16 behaviours was tracked. The behaviours were recorded for each bid before finding out the bid result to avoid the researcher's prejudice relating to successful behaviours influencing the research. A powerful feature of this approach was how fast, simple and cheap the data gathering was.

Implementing a change in behaviours through coaching

Although many of the practitioners were highly experienced, they had a wide range of views about the 'bid behaviours' that were most likely to lead to success. It is notable that there was no major difference in bid success rates achieved by individual practitioners. No practitioner could point to any data to support their arguments in favour of their perceived view of 'best practice' in bid behaviour. For example, some would always use an external consultant to coach their presentation team and some would vehemently oppose the idea. Anecdotal evidence was normally quoted by an individual to point to situations where the behaviour they were advocating had been used in a successful bid or where it had been absent in a losing bid. Attempts to identify good practice in a particular process often rely on asking a panel of experienced practitioners to provide an opinion; this is often described as a 'Delphi Study', a technique developed in the 1940s to predict future outcomes in complex situations. Such an approach to this problem with these practitioners would not have yielded a clear answer as to the behaviours correlating with bid success. During the study period individual practitioners were very likely to repeat their preferred behaviours in each bid situation they came across. Figure 17.1 shows the distribution of behaviours across all 42 bids based on how often they were used and how far they correlated with success – that is the proportion of bids where this behaviour was used that were successful. Few of the behaviours most correlated with success were used frequently.

Groups of behaviours were defined as:

- 'best practice'*behaviours – often-used and under-used*: a greater than 80 per cent correlation with success

- 'good practice'*behaviours*: a 60–80 per cent correlation with success.

- 'potential time-waster'*behaviours*: a less than 60 per cent correlation with success.

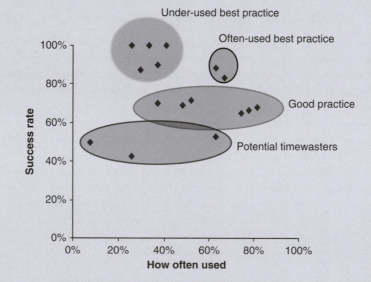

Figure 17.1   Distribution of behaviours and titles allocated to each group

The working hypothesis was that there was likely to be an opportunity for significant performance improvement if the frequency of use of the behaviours most highly correlated with success could be increased. Figure 17.2 illustrates the list of behaviours in each of the groupings. This demonstrates that there was nothing revolutionary in the list of behaviours; no new 'Big Idea' was evident.

Coaching for success

Bid teams were subsequently coached in adopting the behaviours most highly correlated with success. This was primarily through on-the-job support by a coach

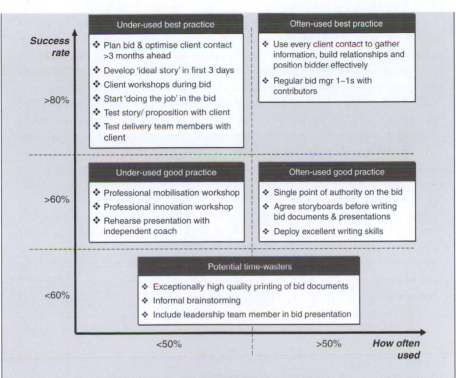

Figure 17.2   The behaviours in each group

becoming involved in the early planning phase or by a kick-off team meeting and then trying to build the target behaviours into the approach of each bid team. The involvement of the coach was not imposed by top management, but rather an option that was made available and then taken up or not by individual bid sponsors. While many individuals and teams resisted the idea of challenges to their own preferred practice, teams did start to adopt new behaviours and the average win rate across the coached teams increased. For some bid teams, the use of quantitative evidence was powerful in influencing them to change behaviour. For others, it merely seemed to increase their desire to challenge the data. Less experienced practitioners appeared to be most willing to change their behaviour, based on the evidence provided by this research. The final outcome was an increase in bid win rate for coached teams from 40 to 60 per cent. Because of the disproportionate impact of bid win rate on profit, this equated to an increase of 100 per cent in profit contribution for this part of the bid pipeline. Yet, despite this remarkable improvement, the fact that adoption of the 'best practice' behaviours was not complete indicates there is further opportunity. A comprehensive change management programme focused on increasing the adoption of the target behaviours could be justified on this basis.

Conclusions

This work suggests that radical performance improvements are obtainable from simple but systematic changes to behaviour, using techniques that are already in use in the organisation – a major performance improvement does not necessarily require a new 'Big Idea' or the imposition of external notions of 'best practice'. Simple, quick analysis of behaviour, in 'real time', as processes unfold, and tracking against success is a powerful means not only to determine desirable practices, but also to implement major performance improvements associated with the wider adoption of these practices. The behaviours most likely to lead to success are not necessarily best identified solely by studying the behaviour of those practitioners achieving the highest success rates. High performers have their own practitioner bias and the smaller sample such an approach would imply leads to a higher probability of 'luck' or 'hard work' influencing the study. Higher performance improvements can potentially be achieved by studying all practitioners and correlating behaviours with success on a situation-by-situation basis. Experienced practitioners can have strong, competing views of the behaviours most likely to lead to success in their domain of expertise and these may not be borne out by data. This can make it difficult to give clear evidence-based advice to a new practitioner, whilst also challenging the notion of using Delphi studies or similar techniques to establish 'best practice'. The achievement of benefits from this approach to performance improvement is subject to good change management practice.

Activities and discussion questions

1. First, using the GROW model of coaching identify three key questions that can be asked at each of the four stages of the model. Second, it is argued that the coachee needs to have '*a sophisticated awareness of the organisational context*' and also '*high levels of self-awareness*' – discuss these two concepts and examine how the coach can help the coachee to achieve this double awareness.

2. What characterises a coaching style of management and how can management development support line managers in developing this style? Make a case to 'agnostic' and 'hostile' line managers that a coaching style of management will generate benefits for the manager and the organisation, and rewards for the individual employee. As part of your case explain what is meant by the 'virtuous circle'.

3. In the first case it is argued that whilst the organisation may prescribe a role for the internal coach, the role is perspectival. Identify the different participant perspectives and the meanings associated with these different perspectives, and the ambiguities this can create. How can the expectations and conceptual confusions of employees and other participants be managed?

4. What are the arguments 'for' and 'against' using 'internal' or 'external' coaches'? Tabulate your responses in a 2 × 2 grid.

5. What characteristics are necessary to be an effective internal coach? How should an internal coach manage issues of confidentiality concerns that may be expressed by the coachee in relation to the sharing of information with the organisation?

6. In the second case what research was undertaken by the external consultants prior to the coaching activity and why was this diagnostic activity an important precursor to coaching activity? Discuss three critical success factors for the effectiveness of the coaching interventions, and the barriers that have to be overcome.

Bibliography

Anderson, V., Rayner, C. and Schyns, B. (2009). *Coaching at the Sharp End: The Role of Line Managers in Coaching at Work*. London: CIPD. *www.cipd.co.uk/Bookstore/_catalogue/ Coaching/9781843982388.htm*

Bono, J. B., Purvanova, R. K., Towler, A. J., and Peterson, D. B. (2009). 'A survey of executive coaching practices'. *Personnel Psychology*, 62, 361–404.

Carroll, M. (2009). 'Preparing employees to become effective coaches'. *Training Journal*, March, 62–6.

CIPD (2009a). *Coaching at the Sharp End: Developing and Supporting the Line Manager as Coach*. A Practical Tool. London: CIPD.

CIPD (2009b). *CIPD Taking the Temperature of Coaching Survey*. London: CIPD.

CIPD (2010a). *Coaching Guide*. London: CIPD.

CIPD (2010b). *CIPD Learning and Development Survey*. London: CIPD.

CIPD (2011). *Coaching Factsheet*. London: CIPD.

Clutterbuck, D. and Megginson, D. (2005). 'How to create a coaching culture'. *People Management*, 11 (8), 44–5. 21 April.

Coaching Conundrum (2009). *Building Coaching Culture That Drives Organisational Success*. Princetown, NJ: Blessingwhite [Electronic version] https://cms.mysmarterwebsite.co.uk/bluegreenlearning-com/_img/Global_Coaching_Culture_Survey_2009.pdf

D'Abate, C., Eddy, E. R. and Tannenbaum, S. I. (2003). 'What's in a name? A literature-based approach to understanding mentoring, coaching and other constructs that describe developmental interactions'. *Human Resource Development Review*, 2 (4), 360–84. December.

Feldman, D. C. and Lankau, M. (2005). 'Executive coaching: A review and agenda for future research'. *Journal of Management*, 31, 829–48.

Frisch, M. (2001). 'The emerging role of the internal coach'. *Consulting Psychology Journal: Practice and Research*, 53(4), 240–50. Autumn.

Gallwey, T. (2003). *The Inner Game of Work*. New York: Texere Publishing.

Hargrove, R. (1995). *Masterful Coaching: Extraordinary Results by Impacting People and the Way They Think and Work*. San Francisco, CA: Jossey-Bass Pfeiffer.

Incomes Data Services (2009). 'Coaching and mentoring'. *HR study 897*. London: IDS.

Jarvis, J. (2007). 'Insider knowledge'. *Coaching at Work*, 1 (3), 26–8. London: CIPD.

Knights, A. and Poppleton, A. (2008). *Developing Coaching Capability in Organisations: Research into Practice*. London: CIPD.

Lampshire, J. and Lewis, L. (2008). 'Coaching'. *CIPD toolkit*. London: CIPD.

Matthews, J. (2010). 'Can line managers ever be effective coaches?'. *Business Leadership Review*, 7 (2), 1–10, April. Association of MBAs.

McDermott, I. and Jago, W. (2005). *The Coaching Bible*. Piatkus, London.

Megginson, D. and Clutterbuck, D. (2009). *Further Techniques for Coaching and Mentoring*. Oxford: Butterworth Heinemann.

Whitmore, J. (2009). *Coaching for Performance*. London: Nicholas Brealey Publishing.

Wilkinson, J. (2007). 'Managing to coach'. *Coaching at Work*, 2 (5), 9–14. September/October.

Wilson, C. (2007). *Best Practices in Performance Coaching: A Handbook for Leaders, Coaches, HR Professionals and Organizations*. London: Kogan Page.

Wilson, S. (2009). 'True dilemmas'. *Coaching at Work*, 3 (3), 44–7. London: CIPD.

www.cipd.co.uk/Bookstore/_catalogue/Coaching/9781843982388.htm

CHAPTER 18

Mobile Technology
Maximising its benefits to the management of organisations

Marjorie Corbridge and Linda Carter

Maximising the strategic benefits of technology

Both employers and employees in twenty-first century organisations rely heavily on modern and mobile technology to enhance individual and organisational performance in an increasingly globalised world. A range of technology is needed to engage with suppliers and customers who may be located anywhere in the world, working in different time zones and expecting instant answers to their questions. This is also true when considering communication with employees. Undoubtedly many of us would find it difficult to function without the support of our Smartphone, our mobile tablet or our laptop, connected to the Internet, Facebook, Twitter or instant messaging. However this technology can provide an easily accessible mechanism for staff engagement and staff development. As Ashworth (2006: 42) explains,

> The increased flexibility offered by [mobile] technology is changing the structure of employees' lives, gone are the days of sitting at the same desk each day...instead people are splitting their time between clients and customer premises or working while travelling.... The new age of mobility and flexibility undoubtedly brings a wealth of opportunities and benefits. It also brings with it a revolution in working life and a requirement for new skills that must be supported and developed.

Mobile technology is a readily available tool that leaders and managers should be exploring and exploiting to the maximum for the benefit of the organisation. Many employees are already familiar with this technology in their personal space and their private lives and to ignore the technology would be an oversight in today's businesses. However there are potential threats and issues associated with technology which also need to be addressed.

The harnessing of technology for organisational benefits

Communication technologies are useful in *engaging staff* in the life of the business and in informing them about the vision and values of the organisation. For example podcasts can be used as a mechanism to inform about new services or new products, new markets or about how the business is performing and what it may mean to employees. Podcasts are of course one-way communication but if supplemented by the use of webinars, allowing staff to participate, seek clarification or submit ideas, then two-way communication can take place. These technologies can help to build communities within the organisation, facilitate engagement and enable increased understanding of how different parts of the business function and synergise. Networking sites such as Facebook and Twitter are also increasingly used by businesses to inform different interest groups, such as employees and customers, about organisational developments. These can also be set up internally with subsections of the business using these as a way of engaging interested parties. The advantages are that these use technology which is in popular use and therefore tap into everyday activities of staff, increasing the likelihood that they will be accessed.

These technologies can also be used for *staff development*, allowing the 'anytime, anyplace, anywhere' concept to be applied to learning. Learning and development can be provided in many ways from traditional classroom activities or one-to-one sessions at one end of the spectrum where participants have to be in one place at one time, through webinars, which allow participants to be in any place but at one time, to interactive 'learning on demand' packages or podcasts which can be developed and made available for use anytime, anyplace, anywhere. Distributed learning is particularly beneficial for staff development aimed at staff who are geographically or time dispersed and who may need regular training or updating in order to maintain or improve performance. In particular it is aimed at sales teams who may need to be constantly updated on new products to enable sales targets to be met without taking the sales people out of the field. Easily accessibly development encourages employees to be proactive in their own development and maintain their knowledge and skills both for their own benefit and for the benefit of the business. Technology also has the potential to impact on the culture of the organisation and in particular on 'how things are done around here'. Those leaders who embrace technology and seek ways of capitalising on the benefits that mobile technology offers to an organisation are likely to be the ones that generate a 'buzz' in the workplace and encourage the middle managers to look for ways of identifying the value that can be added by maximising the benefits of the technology in communication with the organisation's stakeholders.

Leadership and the challenges of technology

But does this technology always enhance business performance or might it reduce it? To what extent do constant interruptions interfere with individual and organisational effectiveness? Are employees placed under increasing pressure to be available 24/7? If this is the situation what role can business leaders play in setting the cultural expectations of how personal technology should be used at work? Mindrum (2011: 20) contends that an 'always on, always reachable' electronic communication environment has devastating effects on employees' work-life balance, engagement and productivity. New behaviors modelled by leaders, and updated cultural presumptions can lessen the negative impact of technology.

He goes on to say (Mindrum, 2011: 25), 'The burden falls on influential leaders in an organization to set expectations and model the behaviors needed to deal with interruptive technologies'. It appears from this that it is not what is said in terms of policies and procedures that will have the most impact on the relationship with the technology but the behaviour of the leaders in the organisation and the dominant organisational culture that will have the most significant impact.

There are many theories and models of leadership, but one that has stood the test of time is the work done by Kouzes and Posner which goes back to 1985. The term 'leadership' is to some extent a value-laden term which historically has carried with it the view that leaders somehow have a distinctive personality that enables them to be leaders. In asking people to list the names of leaders, the same names will appear and the question will also be asked 'can leadership be learned (developed)?'. It is interesting to examine these ideas. Dixit (2011: 1) contends that 'successful leaders possess certain distinguishing qualities like intelligence, emotional balance, technical skills, communication skills, inner drive, high energy levels and human relations skills'; clearly when these qualities are examined they are a collection of personal attributes and skills and as such many of these can be developed. Leaders are seen to be people who 'get things done', which usually means inspiring or motivating staff to do what is required to ensure an effective and successful organisation. Employees need to know and understand the vision, know what they have to do to achieve the vision and importantly to see what their leaders **do** to develop a successful organisation. Kouzes and Posner (2007: 60) talk about the 'leadership challenge' that requires the use of five practices. These are first 'model the way', which includes putting in place standards which address how people should be treated and how aims should be pursued, setting an example of behaviours that others can see and follow as well as making sure that processes support the behaviour needed to succeed. Second 'inspire a shared vision', which requires the leader to communicate a clear vision of the organisation not just in terms of aims and objectives, which tend to be short-term, but also in terms of values and beliefs, which are the factors that can make the organisation and its leader distinctive. This clarity of vision can create opportunities for others to follow and instil in them the confidence to do 'extraordinary things'. Third 'challenge the process', which means that leaders should seek out new opportunities and new ways of doing things by taking risks and testing the systems and processes to ensure that they are 'fit for purpose' in terms of supporting creativity and innovation. Leaders embrace learning and accept that not everything will succeed; they learn from mistakes and through that build the steps to success. Fourth 'enable others to act', means that leaders recognise that success comes through team effort. They are capable of building strong teams and giving members of the team power to act and recognition for achievement. This helps by contributing to building confident individuals and confident teams. Fifth 'encourage the heart' requires the leader to instil in the staff passion for what they do; this increases enthusiasm. However, achieving 'extraordinary things' in organisations is hard work; leaders are the ones who keep the staff motivated, hopeful of success and striving to succeed through recognition and through the sharing of rewards for success. An important aspect of the Kouzes and Posner principles is the 'telling of stories', as this is a way of spreading the word on success and also of allowing discussion of failure, thus facilitating organisational learning. This storytelling and sharing of experiences also reinforce the organisational culture by supporting the development of a common understanding of the organisation and how it works. So how can these five principles of leadership support the positive use of technology? Examining these we can see that the way in which the leader uses and responds to the use of technology sets the standard or 'models the way', and it is in seeing the behaviour of the leaders that the staff learn what is expected.

Mindrum (2011: 20) looks at the 'involuntary response human beings have to the constant pull and interruptions of communications technology', stating that research shows that 'interruptions take up more than a quarter of the typical worker's day', with the research also showing that these interruptions have a significant effect on performance, and its consequential financial impact. He suggests that we need to develop strategies to deal with the negative aspects of interruptive technologies. First we should 'be honest' in acknowledging that we need help in managing the demands of interruptive technologies. It is easy to see in many organisations that people are distracted at meetings and pulled away from tasks by the 'ping' of the Smartphone, but what are organisations doing about it? Second, 'set rules' such as no Smartphones in meetings or when doing key tasks, and stick to these by making sure that there are very effective messaging systems. However, above all, work with leaders in setting standards: 'If executives make clear that an e-mail sent to them will not be treated as urgent, but in fact will result in a response some hours later – and then treat other employees with similar expectations – presumptions will gradually change'. This leadership behaviour will impact positively on the organisational culture.

Organisational culture and technology

Organisational culture or as Mullins says (Mullins, 2010: 740), 'the way we do things around here', is a mechanism for reinforcing positive behaviours. The leadership in organisations is a key influence in determining and maintaining the culture, and gives credence to the behaviours that dominate organisational life. There are many models of organisational culture but the one of interest in this context is the cultural web presented first by Johnson (1992: 31). The cultural web includes six aspects, which together identify the paradigm that brings together the behaviours that are valued in the organisation. The six aspects are stories and myths, rituals and routines, symbols, power structures, organisational structures and control systems. Together these define and bind the culture and set the framework for how things are done. For the purposes of this study the three aspects useful for further exploration are *stories and myths*, *symbols* and *rituals and routines*. These can help to define what is acceptable in terms of interruptive technologies. The stories and myths concerning technology and how it is used in the organisation can help establish the cultural norm. *Stories* circulated within the organisation about managers who expect responses 'by return' to e-mails, instant messages or calls are establishing this as the requirement and sending out a strong message that this is 'the way we do things here'. Likewise positive *stories* about the use of blogs, podcasts and networking sites to communicate widely with all staff, keep them informed or include them in decision-making establish a role for the technology, acknowledge the benefits that technology can bring to the organisation and positively reinforce the culture. In terms of *symbols*, providing individual technology such as cell phones to all managers may act as reinforcement that 'you must be available when *I* want to contact *you*' or can be a sign that the leadership team is available to the managers when they are needed. The message sent out depends on the behaviour of the users. If the manager *demands* immediate responses and availability of staff 24/7, but is never available to take a call from a members of staff, then the messages that 'I am in control' and that 'my time is of more value than yours' are the ones received, and the staff are likely to experience stress. In considering 'rituals and routines' it is interesting to see how technology is used in public spaces or in meetings: is it the norm that phones are turned off? If staff see leaders and managers responding – even with a glance – to a connected device whilst in a meeting it does not go unnoticed and raises questions as to what is acceptable. If instead staff can see at those times that they have the undivided attention of the manager, then those members of staff are more likely to give full attention to the work that they are employed to do. Whilst it is important to have policies in place related to the use of communication technologies covering computer and software use; personal use of e-mail; instant messaging (texting); Internet use and Internet shopping; blogs, social media and cell phones; as well as privacy, it is the practice that will determine the positive or negative impact of these technologies.

Additional considerations: work–life balance and stress

This is a wide-ranging and complex area of leadership and management, as it impacts on many areas of working life. Whilst the benefits can be extensive and far-reaching if the technology is exploited in a thoughtful and balanced way, there is the potential for it to become invasive and blur the boundaries between working life and private life, with a consequential impact on stress, if care is not taken. The first factor for consideration is the impact of poorly managed technology on the work–life balance. According to Brough and O'Driscoll (2010: 280) failure to manage the work–life balance can have 'a significant effect on workers' health and performance'. However there is evidence that some employees may value the blurring of these boundaries with Holmes (2010) identifying the rise of 'a new group of workers – "Generation Standby" – who never seem to fully switch off from work or home'. These workers are regularly 'home-ing' from work and 'working' from home. This raises new challenges for leaders as these employees might expect increasing flexibility from their employers to enable them to work in this way. Anonymous (2010) also describes generation standby and states:

> Call it multi-tasking or life-splicing but increasingly, fuelled by advances in technology, employees are blurring the boundaries between home and

work.... 'Generation Standby' employees are now enjoying, and expecting, greater levels of flexibility and mobility than ever before – but this cultural shift raises new questions about trust in the workplace, the use of new technologies, the balance of power in the employer vs. employee relationship and levels of control that businesses now have over people and content.

Failure to deliver on these employees' expectations may lead to recruitment and retention issues, which can equally challenge organisations. So there is no 'one size fits all' solution to the issue of work–life balance related to technology as different employees define this differently. Do leaders need to respond to changing expectations, recognise the importance of trust in the culture and build an organisation that meets these needs? Research shows (Cooper, 2002; HSE, 2010) that a significant cause of workplace stress is associated with a lack of control over the working environment, and how the employee experiences this. Technology that is 'always on, always reachable' (Mindrum, 2011: 20) can leave employees feeling out of control, pressurised into leaving technology switched on and hence experiencing stress or turning off the technology and also experiencing stress; they feel this is a no-win situation. Leaders have a responsibility to 'model the way', 'set the standard' and provide a working environment in which all can flourish.

The case study below explores the use of technology in the Further Education (FE) sector, showing the way that technology can enhance the culture of the organisation and the behaviours of the employees for the benefit of the students. The implications for leadership and leadership development are explored, and the study provides an opportunity to consider the issues raised by technology and how it is used in the organisation, and how these may be addressed.

Anytime, anyplace, anywhere ... leading the benefits and understanding the tensions of the 'Martini' culture – a case study in the FE sector

This study examines the impact of information technology on leadership and draws on research carried out on behalf of the British Education Communication Technology Association (BECTA) with leaders in the further education (FE) sector. Its key messages may be relevant for any leader and professional who carries a mobile device and lives in a technological world. The vintage advertising slogan from the Martini advert sums up the enormous potential of technology to connect with others at *any* time, *any* place and *anywhere*. It also signals the tensions and dangers of the 24/7 working culture.

With technology comes emotion – love and despair in equal measures. Technology has transformed the way we work and the way work is done. Whilst we can catalogue its benefits we can also feel the frustration and tensions it brings in its emotional wake. Technology is important to everyone – it would be rare indeed for an employee not to have a stake in its capabilities; the absorption of technology into routine tasks has steadily increased everyone's expectations of what can be achieved.

The technology we experience outside of 'work' is also fuelling our excitement of what is, and what might be possible. The revolution in our communication habits is also well documented. We anticipate a reaction to our email messages and may be surprised that a reply has not been immediate. The rise of expectations and the 'anytime, anyplace, anywhere culture' is blurring work and home boundaries, and sending out challenges to leaders in all organisations. The call of leadership is to 'model the way' (Kouzes and Posner, 2007), and to facilitate cultures in which the advantages of technology can benefit rather than exhaust, and excite rather than depress, their stakeholders. Using FE colleges as an illustration, this study explores the challenges and possibilities of technology for leaders and suggests lines of enquiry which managers within organisations can use to examine the 'digital health' of their culture.

Harnessing technology and realising its benefits

In further education, evidence exists which shows how technology is enhancing the learning experience. Colleges, confident in the use of technology, are creating stimulating learning environments where staff and learners can see and feel the benefits. Real and tangible digital dividends have been achieved. These benefits may be related to enhancing teaching, conducting a tutorial or interrogating the system for learner data. In these e-confident colleges, staff cannot imagine life without technology. Leadership and power in these colleges are distributed. Senior leaders and governors are optimistic about the future, have a realisation of the power of technology and a vision that embraces the uncertainties of change. But the middle managers are key change agents for advancing the take-up of technology; they demonstrate both intra- and entrepreneurial skills. This means they know where they are able to source extra funding for technological projects, know which members of staff to contact to make the projects 'buzz' and have the negotiation skills to broker deals between departments. Other qualities found in these successful colleges include visible and tangible resources and actions (e.g. distribution of laptops to all staff, interactive whiteboards in all classrooms and distribution of digital recorders to all media students), and technical staff who are proactive and take pride in their robust and reliable system. However technology has not replaced personal relationships or face-to-face communication in these institutions, far from it; they place high value on relationships and the creation of new working teams. Collaborative work across curriculum areas and between curriculum and technical areas is encouraged in the search for innovative ways of improving learning environments. Furthermore colleges report that releasing and sharing data has led to new behaviours and new understanding between staff from different departments. Managers from finance, quality and curriculum are more likely to understand each others' perspectives when faced with shared and open information. In this way technology is a driving force for changing work cultures. Students are also benefiting from the speed and ease of submitting work via email and tutors too are experimenting with the new technologies – blogs, podcasts and networking sites are enabling new ways to collaborate and interact with learners. Furthermore as new tutors use their e-expertise to help and support their colleagues, new opportunities for leaders to identify talent and encourage peer development are occurring and power shifts are happening.

Perhaps, surprisingly, technology is seen as a catalyst for encouraging connections between people and as a way of promoting college values. Colleges confident in the use of technology share key values (e.g. a desire to improve the life chances of others), and technology can help to underline and reassert this philosophy. By encouraging an experimental approach colleges can 'walk and talk' their passion for learning. An open-minded approach to technological change and an ease with uncertainty and ambiguity can lead to a self-critical culture in which quality is constantly examined and ways to improve/develop are assessed as a matter of course. What is important here is that the college leaders use every opportunity to communicate these shared values of the colleges to reaffirm their purpose. The values permeate the organisation and help to create a culture where technology drives organisational and staff development. Technology is used as both the driver for change and a lever to help reaffirm key shared values.

Identifying the challenges and pressures of technology

For the tutors and leaders challenges exist to get the best out of the new generation of learners who have never known a world without a mobile phone and the World Wide Web. The use of technology is not only affecting the way that people learn, it is changing mindsets. The ability to share data or information on an intranet makes resources easily available to learners and staff alike, and also speeds up paperwork. The speed, accuracy and accessibility of information are real strengths for the organisation, but effective leadership is essential to maximise its full potential. It is possible for all staff to be part of the development of data histories and for managers at all levels of the organisation to be able to make informed decisions about the experience of the learners. Managing information and balancing the 'load' is, and has always been, a leadership skill. For many, there are new challenges associated with the sheer amount of information available. The language typically used to describe the feelings that arise is 'water-laden', 'being submerged' and 'feeling drowned'; these explain the sense of powerlessness that is often evident. Managers may need help in facilitating the ability to 'swim' rather than 'drown' and to 'dive' rather than 'sink' in the data pools. There are also dangers in data being the sole driver of decision-making, and effective leadership must take balanced decisions that not just maximise the use of the technology but also encompass personal, social and educational values. Whilst there are numerous benefits associated with responsive and fast communication there are real concerns of email overuse, leading to unreasonable pressures of keeping up with the volume of messages. The leadership challenge of communicating has always existed and technology has been added to the mix. Mobile technologies are a major cause of the blurring of boundaries between work and home, and it seems that people have lost sight of the fact that email is asynchronous, believing instead that a response should be immediate. Such expectations lead to stress and an undervaluing of people's time. Concerns have been expressed relating to the emergence of gluttony of communication and at the other end of the spectrum the awkwardness and guilt that people feel if they decide to switch off their mobile devices when away from their workplace. Setting boundaries and creating policies and guidelines for the reasonable use of mobile technologies are key leadership issues requiring leaders to role-model behaviour.

Implications and questions for organisations and leadership development: developing people, creating spaces

So what does this imply for leaders in organisations across all sectors? The continuing development of leaders needs to take into account the way technology is shaping behaviour and culture. What values are being underlined or undermined? The following suggestions identify headline issues that may be relevant to managers and leaders and that could start different lines of enquiry:

- The research suggests there are real opportunities for using technological change to drive organisational and staff development. Exploring the use of more informal social spaces in organisational life could be one such opportunity. Creating spaces for people to come together, explore and coach each other not only generates ideas but it also builds relationships and energy. Inspiration can happen, one conversation at a time, in a climate in which new networks are encouraged, whether these are virtual or real.

- Technology can model leadership behaviours that are inclusive and reflective, by using tools such as blogs and podcasts that enhance these qualities of leadership. It also offers easy ways of keeping in touch with professional networks and sharing information.

- A challenge for leaders is managing expectations and co-creating a climate of innovation and possibilities. Technology is challenging the traditional decision-making models and opening out new possibilities of empowering others. The speed, accuracy and accessibility of information offers the possibility of shifting power and devolving decision-making, but it requires appropriate diagnostic and planned development for effective leadership.

- Technologies insist that leaders project into the future and imagine what might be possible for new environments; opportunities now exist for different kinds of leadership.

- Technology offers new ways of working and new and different styles of connecting, but if the purpose of the business is clear there are opportunities to reaffirm its shared values and promote its raison d'être.

What issues does this study raise for managers in organisations?

It is interesting to consider the extent to which leadership teams within organisations regularly examine their cultures in the light of technological advancements and are therefore able to maximise the possibilities of technology and minimise its dangers. How often do managers use scenario planning to model alternative situations and examine alternative solutions? What aspects of technology feature in development schemes for middle managers and how are they encouraged to search for opportunities to enhance communication through its use? These and other questions are also important in feeding the guidelines that are provided in the organisation and the cultural norms that are established for the use of mobile technology.

Activities and discussion questions

1. To what extent do leadership teams within your organisation analyse the culture of the organisation in the light of technological advancements? What should the leadership team do to ensure that the culture reflects the practice in terms of the use of technology?

2. Plan an 'away day' for your leadership team aimed at developing and using scenario planning to explore different futures for communications technology and examine their implications for your organisation.

3. This study contends that 'middle managers are key change agents to progress the take-up of technology' in the FE colleges. Why do you think this is so and what should middle managers be doing to progress the take-up of technology?

4. Examine the role of middle managers in your organisation and explore:

   a. the role that middle managers play in embedding technology effectively in the operation of the business,
   b. the extent to which middle managers are searching for ways to enhance communication possibilities,
   c. how middle managers are embracing technology to enhance management development initiatives.

5. What guidelines (or policies) are provided in your organisation for the reasonable use of mobile technologies inside and outside the work boundaries, and importantly what are the cultural norms in practice?

Bibliography

Anon (2010). *Generation Standby on the Increase.* Retrieved on 10 June from http://www.clearswift.com/news/press-releases/generation-standby-on-the-increase.

Ashworth, L. (2006). 'Technology is developing – and so must HRs methods of supporting mobile workers'. *People Management*, 15 June 2006.

BECTA (2009). 'Has the role and function of leaders changed as a result of technology?' March.

Brough, P. and O'Driscoll, M. P. (2010). 'Organizational interventions for balancing work and home demands: an overview'. *Work and Stress* 24 (3), 280–97.

Carter, L. (2008). *Harnessing Technology; Realising the Benefits: The Cultural Landscape of Successful Colleges.* London: BECTA. November.

Chermack. T. (2011). *Scenario Planning in Organizations: How to Create, Use, and Assess Scenarios.* San Francisco: Berrett-Koehler.

Clark, D. (2007). *Podcasts and Learning.* (Electronic version) Line Communication.

Dixit, V. (2011). 'The leadership challenge'. *Journal of Education and Vocational Research* 1(1), 1–3.

Guerin, L. (2011). *'Smart Policies for Workplace Technologies: Email, Blogs, Cell Phones and More'*. Berkeley: SHRM and Nolo.

Holmes, B. (2010). 'Web 2.0 in the workplace'. *Personnel Today*, 20 May 2010.

HSE (2010). *The Generation Gap: Towards Generation Z Horizon Scanning SR024*. Retrieved from http://www.hse.gov.uk/horizons/downloads/generationz.pdf.

Johnson, G. (1992). 'Managing strategic change – culture and actions'. *Long Range Planning* 25(1), 31.

Kouzes, J. M. and Posner, B. Z. (2007). *The Leadership Challenge*. San Francisco: Jossey-Bass.

Lindgren, M. and Bandhold, H. (2009). *Scenario Planning*. Basingstoke: Palgrave Macmillan.

Maag, M. (2006). 'iPod, uPod? An emerging mobile learning tool in nursing education and students' satisfaction'. (Electronic version) *From Proceedings of the 23rd Annual Ascilite Conference: Who's Learning? Whose Technology?*

Mindrum, C. (2011). 'The twitching organization'. *Chief Learning Officer* 10(3), 20–25.

Mullins, L. (2010). *Management and Organisational Behaviour*. Harlow: FT Prentice Hall.

Rhydderch, A. (2009). *Scenario Planning*. London: Government Office for Science.

Sirkka, L., Lang, J. and Lang, P. (2005). 'Managing the paradoxes of mobile technology'. *Information Systems Management* Fall, 7–2.

CHAPTER 19

The Strategic Value of maximising the benefits of Employee Well-being

Marjorie Corbridge and Bridget Juniper

Employee well-being is on the agenda in many organisations, and there are different approaches to this strategic people management issue. Smethurst (2007: 24) forces us to reflect on just what range of initiatives organisations might consider when thinking about employee well-being.

> Let's get one thing straight. . . . Wellness is not some woolly fad about installing gyms and ensuring that there are carrots on the staff canteen menu. It's about better management, improving the productivity of the business and ensuring individuals are able to perform to their full potential. That's how the agenda should be seen. . . . There is no point in providing subsidised gym membership if people are coming in [to work] afraid that they're going to be bullied by their manager. . . . People feel at their best when they have completed a difficult challenge and received good external feedback.

Leaders and managers should be taking a strategic look at what they are doing to provide a working environment where employees are able to maximise their potential in a supportive environment.

Different terms are used when discussing employee well-being: wellness management, employee wellness, employee health and well-being as well as wellness at work. Generally all of these terms come down to a definition that encompasses a positive approach to providing a work environment in which employees can take responsibility for their own health and well-being with the support of their employer. The CIPD (2007a: 4) defines employee well-being as 'creating an environment to promote a state of contentment which allows an employee to flourish and achieve their potential for the benefit of themselves and their organisation'. This is in stark contrast to an approach that places the emphasis solely on absence and attendance management and monitoring, which in many ways deals only with employee sickness and the symptoms of a lack of motivation to come to work. Employees do and will continue to get sick and to take time off from work and that is to be expected, but employee well-being is about engaging with employees and motivating them to attend work when they are fit to do so, and dealing with aspects of working life that interfere with their ability to attend and their motivation to come to work. Employee well-being focuses on the employees' physical, mental and social health, with the employee and the employer working together to address lifestyle- and work-related issues that impact negatively on the employees' ability to come to work or to perform to their potential when they are at work. It is concerned with the whole person and their physical and mental well-being both inside and outside of work. One of the challenges facing organisations is the difficulty associated with the recognition that well-being is a subjective feeling as stated by the CIPD (CIPD, 2007a: 4) – 'for some people the ability to do 50 press-ups may be a sign of well-being, while for others the intellectual challenge of handling a difficult meeting well may provide a positive experience of well-being'. This diversity of employee experience and expectation means that the employer has to develop a strategy and an approach that meet these differing requirements.

Developing an employee well-being strategy

To develop and put into place an employee well-being strategy it is important that the organisation is clear about what it is working to achieve, the business benefits that it is seeking to derive from an effective employee well-being strategy and the requirement to embed its actions within the organisational culture. It may be useful here to look at the idea of employee well-being alongside that of organisational well-being. The definition above places both the employee and the organisation at the heart of the debate, but what are the factors that lead to a state of well-being and are these factors common to both the organisation and the employee? Kraybill (2003), quoted in CIPD (2007a), identifies

> multiple aspects of the workplace that affect employees' ability to function well in order to accomplish the goals of the organisation. These aspects include: the organisational culture; relationships with other agencies; personnel policies (including pay and benefits); supervision; quality and structure of decision making; communication and its effectiveness; conflict resolution; cultural diversity and sensitivity; opportunities for advocacy; the physical working environment and support for personal wellness.

It can be argued that these factors are a prerequisite to the development of a workplace that has an inclusive culture where all workers feel valued, where there is mutual respect, where staff are engaged and take personal responsibility for what they do at work and where they feel that they are able to contribute effectively to the performance of the business. There are also factors that employees must work towards in order to ensure that they are able to maximise the positive aspects of the work environment, and these include taking responsibility for their health; developing positive attitudes that support self-respect and self-confidence; being open to change, curious about organisational developments and having a strong support network. It is the interface between these two parties and the interaction between them that determines the development of effective employee well-being. Jack (2004) identifies the importance of the work environment in the recruitment and retention of talent and the perceptions that both applicants and employees have of how an organisation measures up to being an 'employer of choice'. She goes on to explain that one way to differentiate your organisation from your competitors is in its attitudes and practices related to employee well-being. Jack identifies five aspects that might have a negative impact on employee well-being. These are first the organisation itself and the employees' understanding of its purpose, its culture and values, how well it is managed and the way it handles communication and conflict. Second are the job the employee is doing and the extent to which they have scope to influence the work as well as the feeling of how realistic the demands of the job are. Third are the physical working environment and the feeling of a sense of security. Fourth are empowerment and the extent to which the employees feel able to influence their sphere of work, raise concerns about work issues and whether they feel they are managed well. Finally the health and personal life of the employee are in balance. The reason for exposing these factors is to provide a framework in which an organisation can explore its rationale for developing a well-being strategy and investing in its employees. In summary in order to develop and implement a well-being strategy the organisation needs to take on board all of the factors that are brought to play on the issue.

Business in the Community (BITC) (2011: 7) has produced reporting guidelines on employee wellness and engagement with the aim of

> moving the agenda on from basic health and safety compliance to elevating wellness and engagement to becoming a boardroom issue'. This work includes the 'development of a toolkit for ... companies on health, safety and well-being management ... to stimulate debate and innovation and lead to continuous improvements in human capital management ... and as a consequence to better business performance.

BITC express their conviction that employee well-being is a 'key challenge' for organisations that needs 'a strategic response in terms of board commitment [and] integration into core business processes'. The benefit as they see it is 'not just to stop the waste that ill health and low motivation represents but to grasp the business potential of enhanced employee engagement and productivity'. This report introduces the BITC WORKWELL model based on five principles (2011: 13). First the organisation needs to show that it has in place a vigorous employee wellness and engagement strategy that is linked to the business objectives. Second it has to take a strategic approach to skills and talent to meet both present and future needs. Third it has to ensure that employees have a voice in the business and that effective communication takes place. Fourth is the requirement that the organisation take a positive approach to 'building physical and psychological resilience to support sustainable performance'. Fifth it is important that the organisation has in place a working environment that embraces well-being and productivity. The model points out that the business benefits include better engagement, better attendance, better retention and recruitment, better brand image and higher productivity. However in order to achieve these benefits there are actions that employers need to take, which include better work (create a happy and creative workplace), better relationships (provide communication and social connections), better specialist support (good interventions to manage employee well-being) and better physical and psychological health (create an environment in which healthy behaviours are expected). The model also explains that expectations are also placed on the employee, namely to keep learning, to connect with others, to be a giver and volunteer, to take notice and to be active. This model is a useful way of exploring the parties that are critical in the successful management of employee well-being, and of recognising the link with the performance of the business.

Measuring and monitoring employee well-being

Having looked at the importance of the well-being strategy and the role it can play in the employer–employee relationship it is only appropriate to address what is probably the single biggest challenge facing the employer on the management of employee well-being and that is the issue of measurement and monitoring. To build a business case for investment and to get any issue onto the strategic people management agenda it is absolutely critical to be very clear about what it is you are striving to achieve, what the critical success factors are and how these will be measured. BITC (2011) includes several case studies that give examples of metrics that may be appropriate in various businesses, including Nationwide, BT Openreach and RBS, among others, and reports on their activities; these can be examined in the BITC paper. The metrics selected are deliberately generic in nature so that they can be applied to a variety of organisations. These organisational studies are helpful in looking at how businesses are actually applying the knowledge about this potentially complex area of people management and measuring its impact. Each of the employer actions named above has metrics identified at the entry level, intermediate level and mature level, enabling the organisation to assess where they are in terms of their approach to employee well-being. For example, on the 'better physical and psychological health employer action', BT Openreach have identified a specific issue of 'promoting emotional resilience through change management' (BITC, 2011: 23). The rationale behind this is that 'BT has developed an integrated approach to well-being that links health and safety with managing change well, and protecting [the] mental health [of their employees]'. The metrics used are the level of sickness absence, the number of incidents of bullying and harassment and the number of grievances brought by employees. These figures are produced on a regular basis and published internally for managers at the level of each unit. There are other examples of the metrics in the BITC paper.

A clearly articulated employee well-being strategy requires aims and objectives to be set, together with the identification of measurable outcomes, in order that the impact of the strategy and the investment that supports the strategy can be assessed and the return on investment examined. Berry, Mirabito and Baun (2010: 105) contend that 'wellness programs have often been viewed as a nice extra, not a strategic imperative'. They go on to say that 'newer evidence tells a different story ... healthy employees cost you less'. This research, which took place in the US, shows that employers taking part in the research saw a reduction in labour turnover, in one case 'the rate was 9 per cent in 2009, down from 19 per cent in 2005' (Berry et al., 2010: 106). However the thrust of much of the US research is on the benefits of wellness programmes and this raises the issue of looking at the difference between wellness programmes and a well-being strategy. Does an organisation that offers a collection of wellness programmes have a well-being strategy? The answer may be, 'well it all depends'! If a strategy requires aims, objectives, initiatives, measurable outcomes and regular review, then perhaps a collection of initiatives that are coherent, monitored and measured as well as reported upon might be deemed a strategy. However it could be argued that a key dimension is missing. That dimension is the need for some focus on employer actions that address internal aspects of the work, the job and the management, which are seen to be an important aspect of a well-being strategy. The focus on wellness initiatives requires that the employee must be proactive in participating in these initiatives if the organisation is to derive a benefit. Whilst some employees will do this to derive personal and also organisational benefit, there is nothing to address what actions will be taken with the internal, work-related factors, which we have seen may be equally important.

In summary to maximise the benefits of employee well-being requires a strategic approach with commitment from the boardroom to the investment that may need to be made. To get that commitment, the proposers of the strategy need to have a focused view of what it is that they want to achieve, the measures they will use and the monitoring and reporting that will take place. BITC (2011: 7) makes an important point in saying, 'so often companies proclaim in their annual report that "employees are our most important and valuable asset" and "our staff are critical to our success" yet most fail to elaborate on this asking ... stakeholders to take it on faith that they are managing this effectively'. The case research below takes a very strong approach to working on robust metrics that can identify where organisational factors are contributing to employee well-being or indeed where they may be having a negative impact on well-being. This then allows the organisation to take action to address these negative factors. This case does not address wellness programmes, but clearly any well-being strategy can and perhaps should encompass both aspects: employer-led organisational aspects and employee participation in wellness programmes.

Measuring employee well-being: you can only manage what you measure – case study research

Based on a study within Portsmouth City Teaching Primary Care Trust the research explores a new approach to employee well-being, and the findings provide HR professionals with new thinking by challenging conventional practice. The research redefines what is meant by employee well-being and proposes a new way to manage it strategically. The well-being needs of staff are assessed directly and empirically, thus providing solid evidence for what is required on the basis of fact rather than management 'hunch'. The work supports the view that a strategy that is evidence-based is more likely to be relevant to staff needs and therefore more likely to succeed.

This study therefore considers the case for the new approach and outlines the study. Part Two of the case study applies the measurement tool to the PCT, provides the findings and discusses the implications.

Employee well-being: growth in interest, definition and measurement

Interest in employee well-being (EWB) is rising. This is reflected not only in HR practice, but also in wider management behaviours and policy work at government levels. The prime driver for this phenomenon is the growing compendium of research that indicates a keen relationship between people's wellness and their output in the workplace. This has major implications for performance and cost to employers, as well as the actual health of workers themselves (Mills, 2005). With organisations under relentless pressure to improve efficiency, cut costs and deliver better returns to shareholders, many workers are finding themselves under continual pressure and strain as the nature of work transforms and roles are required to undergo far-reaching changes (Sparks, Faragher and Cooper, 2001; Faragher, Cooper and Cartwright, 2004). This is especially pronounced in today's economy, which has to rely more on services than industry, bringing with it an inherent reliance on improving and sustaining the efforts and outputs of employees (Mills, 2005). As a consequence of these factors, many organisations channel considerable resources towards enhancing EWB, or at least mitigating against its declining further. According to the CIPD, nearly one-third of employers who responded to a survey indicated they now have a well-being strategy or something similar in place (CIPD., 2007b). The most commonly provided well-being benefits to the staff that were cited included access to counselling, smoking cessation initiatives, employee assistance programmes and healthy eating options in restaurants. Conceptually these efforts are to be encouraged but most are destined to fail because they do not address the fundamental problems that impair employee well-being. This inability to evaluate the main drivers of EWB means that programmes are transacted in a vacuum, with little chance of success however defined.

The starting point for an employer interested in this area is to define exactly what they mean by the term EWB. Based on a comprehensive literature review of the construct, a suggested definition is

> that part of an employee's overall well-being that they perceive to be determined primarily by work and which can be influenced by work-place interventions.

This definition is important because it highlights the significance of employees' *own* perceptions of how work impacts on their well-being, and it focuses only on those aspects that can be addressed by the employer. If organisations are serious about EWB, it is also recommended that they evaluate the needs of their workforce at the outset. Only by doing this can leadership teams develop an evidence-based strategy that will address what is most important to their staff so that they avoid the usual pitfalls of instigating elaborate programmes that are ineffective and wasteful.

To address this need, a new, clinically based instrument has been developed that measures the well-being of employees. Called the Work and Well-Being Assessment (WWBA©), it is a standardised questionnaire completed by employees to assess their work-related well-being. The questionnaire is available online and takes approximately six minutes to complete. Its development is based on proven methodologies that have been used for the past 25 years to measure the impact of disease on patients' well-being and evaluate the effectiveness of new drugs (Guyatt, Veldhuyzen Van Zanten, Feeny and Patrick, 1989). The instrument comprises 10 different work and non-work domains that have been shown to impair EWB (see Figure 19.1). Each domain consists of a number of questions that relate to EWB. For example the Advancement domain contains questions regarding opportunities for development while the Impact Outside of Work domain includes items concerning how work impacts on family life.

WWBA (general) 10 domains

- Advancement (ADV)
- Psychological (PSY)
- Direction & understanding (DIR)
- Engagement (ENG)
- Physical (PHY)
- Impact outside of work (OUT)
- Control (CTL)
- Relationships at work (REL)
- Workload (WL)
- Workplace environment (WE)

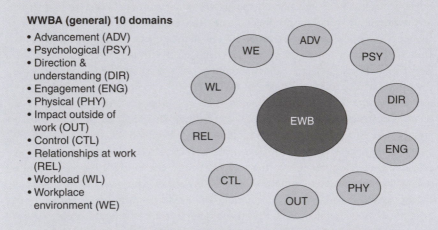

Figure 19.1   The Work and Well-Being Assessment domains ©

Portsmouth City Teaching Primary Care Trust – background

Portsmouth City Teaching Primary Care Trust (PCT) recognises that the well-being of employees is a key factor in the delivery of quality services to patients and is therefore committed to developing and maintaining a workforce that is well in its most holistic sense. Like many organisations, the PCT's approach to wellness included over 20 initiatives such as pilates classes, pool bikes and childcare assistance. However faced with high-sickness absence of up to 12 per cent in some services it recognised that it lacked a clear evidence base for its EWB strategy and investment programme. Although the PCT participates in the mandatory annual NHS staff survey, the results, to date, have failed to provide a comprehensive measure of EWB. The PCT was therefore attracted to using the WWBA; it was hoped that the instrument would generate robust data that would inform and shape its overall approach to EWB and ensure the programme met the needs of its workers.

Research objectives and methodology

The research had three main objectives.

- Compare the perceptions amongst senior managers of the well-being of their staff with the actual experiences reported by staff themselves.
- Identify any significant differences in the reported well-being profiles across sub-groups.
- Determine the key drivers of employee sickness absence and commitment to the PCT, based on the 10 domains shown to be associated with EWB.

The research was conducted at the end of 2008 and comprised two main stages. The first stage focused on garnering the views of senior management on the current status of EWB. This involved semi-structured interviews with seven PCT senior managers, including the Trust's CEO. Interviewees were invited to 'score' overall EWB for their respective teams and volunteer their views on EWB within their departments and service lines. The second stage of the research was quantitative and involved the deployment of the WWBA to six services and departments within the PCT. Recognising the desire to determine drivers of absence and commitment, four supplementary questions regarding absence and commitment were added to the WWBA. An online link to the WWBA was then emailed to all staff within the identified teams, inviting them to complete the questions. Employees were given a three-week completion period, and all responses were anonymous. Data collected during the two stages were then examined and analysed according to the three objectives identified.

Emerging themes

Detailed findings from the study will be explored in the second part of this case study. However a preliminary analysis of the findings points to a number of emerging themes, which are summarised as follows:

Taken as a whole, EWB levels at the PCT were within acceptable limits. However certain teams and staff groups displayed significantly lower EWB, which was surprising to senior management and raised some concerns. Overall the WWBA indicated two main areas of work that impaired EWB. The first was the stress and frustration experienced with heavy workloads. The second was employees' general unease with organisational change. On the positive side, opportunities for advancement, the impact of work on family life and relationships with colleagues and supervisors scored very favourably. The ability of the PCT's senior managers to successfully forecast the EWB problems of their staff was mixed. A number of managers participating in the qualitative interviews identified some problem areas that they perceived as adversely impacting EWB, which were consistent with the empirical data collected using the WWBA. However other managers, including those responsible for teams with high absence rates, showed clear gaps in their appreciation of the EWB issues faced by their staff. No manager was able to predict with a high degree of accuracy all the factors highlighted by WWBA findings.

These top-line findings reveal new insights on EWB. They show the value of assessing EWB directly, such that the most important issues can be identified and therefore addressed effectively. The alternative is to rely on management to second-guess the problems. The early findings from this study suggest that this is not a viable option.

The measurement of employee well-being at Portsmouth City PCT – case study results

This stage reports the finding of the research. The PCT has used the data to update its Wellness Strategy and inform specific actions to address the main issues identified. The PCT commissions and provides NHS services for the people of Portsmouth and those who live in surrounding areas. The PCT employs about 2,000 staff and, like many parts of the NHS, is undergoing significant change as it restructures to become a commissioning organisation and allows the provider function to operate at arm's length.

All staff within the six PCT teams identified for the research were invited to complete the Work and Well-Being Assessment (WWBA), which presents an approach to measuring EWB based on a methodology used to evaluate the health and well-being of patients in clinical settings (Juniper, Guyatt and Jaeschke, 1996). Teams were a mix of patients facing services and support functions, and they were also asked to answer questions regarding sickness absence and general commitment levels to the PCT. Separately managers of each team were asked to anticipate the well-being issues of their respective departments so that a comparison between manager perceptions and empirical, employee-driven data could be drawn. All staff within three teams completed the WWBA, and the overall response level was 67 per cent. The WWBA measures EWB across 10 different domains (Figure 19.1). Each domain comprises a number of questions relating to well-being within that particular construct. Scores range from 0 to 6.0, where 0 indicates no impairment to work-related well-being and 6.0 indicates extreme impairment. Overall the six PCT teams showed a score of 1.68, indicating the impact of work on EWB was low. The highest scoring domains were impact of work on psychological health and impact of organisational change on staff (Direction) (Table 19.1). Opportunities for training and development (Advancement) were positively perceived. How work interfered with home life (Impact Outside) was considered by respondents to be minimal.

The results by department and services

When findings were broken down into different departments and services, analysis revealed some significant differences ($p < 0.05$) between teams (see Table 19.2).

Community Children's Nursing showed the most favourable EWB score (0.97), while employees working in Adult Mental Health (AMH) indicated the highest levels of impairment (2.46). AMH scored highest on all domains but three. People working in the Podiatry service also showed relatively high scores across all domains. The ability of managers to predict how work affected EWB was patchy. All managers were able to identify correctly some areas of cause and effect. However none was able to provide

Table 19.1   Overall EWB scores for PCT

Rank	Domain	Domain score
1	Psychological	2.08
2	Direction	2.06
3	Workload	1.82
4	Physical	1.78
5	Control	1.73
6	Engagement	1.51
7	Workplace environment	1.49
8	Relationships	1.43
9	Impact outside	1.33
10	Advancement	1.32
Overall score		1.68

Table 19.2   EWB scores by team

Code	Substance misuse	Children's nursing	Finance	Adult mental health	Podiatry	Public health
PSY	1.47	1.22	1.55	3.24	2.70	2.06
DIR	1.94	1.32	1.48	3.05	2.80	1.63
WL	0.85	1.30	1.43	2.79	2.15	2.18
PHY	1.14	1.02	1.29	1.93	2.64	1.70
CTL	1.35	0.84	1.29	2.95	2.35	1.48
ENG	1.33	0.77	1.08	2.20	2.16	1.19
WE	1.62	0.52	1.11	1.70	2.42	0.89
REL	0.89	0.88	0.78	2.45	2.05	1.33
OUT	0.95	0.75	0.88	1.96	1.83	1.33
ADV	1.12	0.98	1.04	1.55	1.82	1.04
Score	1.29	0.97	1.21	2.46	2.32	1.51

a comprehensive account of all issues subsequently revealed by the quantitative analysis, and some managers' views and opinions were diametrically opposed to the data findings. The study also identified the main predictors of key outcomes for the PCT, namely sickness-absence levels and commitment to the organisation. Regression analyses indicated that sickness levels were mainly due to issues regarding Engagement and Control. Employee commitment levels were driven largely by variables within the Engagement, Control and Workload domains.

Findings from the WWBA showed that, overall, EWB within the PCT was at an acceptable level, but at the team level there existed some notable differences. Experiencing high levels of stress and frustration at work and being concerned about organisational change at the PCT were clear sources of impaired EWB. Some of these sources were felt more acutely at the team level. Rather ironically, AMH employees recorded considerably higher levels of impaired psychological health than their colleagues in other teams. Interestingly the main predictors of sickness absence were not related to physical health but to Engagement and Control levels. As its name suggests, the Engagement domain determines the level to which employees feel valued for their contribution and their confidence in leadership. The Control domain evaluates the level to which staff can exert influence over their goals and day-to-day activities. Workload tracks perceptions of the amount of work people are required to perform. These findings underline the importance of line managers in helping organisations to optimise the output and performance of their workforce, since it is primarily down to these individuals to engage their staff and tap their discretionary effort and commitment.

The findings also illustrate the value of independent measurement when it comes to evaluating EWB. Left to the views and opinions of senior managers, some important gaps would have arisen. Additionally a clear understanding of issues, ranked by importance, would not have been possible. Having robust evidence of a workforce's EWB profile can inform decisions regarding strategy, priorities and budget allocation. By the same token, the absence of a clear evidence base could result in a strategy that is poorly aligned to the real needs of a population and that squanders important budget money and resources. The findings have been very well received within the PCT, and for the Workforce Team who lead on EWB this has been a valuable piece of work. This has helped in evaluating current policy and creating a strategy that is evidence-based and aligned with staff needs. Having evidence-based practice has been the key to securing the buy-in and commitment to EWB from the beginning within the PCT, and this further informs its work and the direction to be taken. The PCT approaches EWB on two levels – Well Staff who are Well Managed. This work has helped feed both branches of activity. The results themselves show where managers' roles can be developed and enhanced to better incorporate wellness, and indeed this will inform the work the PCT is undertaking on creating a Managers' Induction programme. Additionally the Leadership and Management Network events run by the PCT can use the results and the principles emerging from this work to inform good practice amongst this population. The findings were communicated with managers and employees in a number of ways. A paper detailing the project and the key findings was circulated to various groups, including to the Clinical Safety and Patient Safety Group (sub-board committee), the Workforce and Remuneration Committee as well as service level groups. It has been cascaded down to staff, in particular to those who took part in the research, via service managers. The paper stressed that the results were not to be an end in themselves but were to act as evidence and input for current work streams and action plans pertinent to the staff, such as those associated with the Annual Staff Survey results.

Revising the employee well-being policy

The results have directly informed a revision of the Wellness Policy within the PCT; where this had previously been configured around the six standards from the HSE with regard to Stress Management, the policy now captures the domains within this research to show the scope and breadth of wellness. The associated Wellness Strategy incorporates the need to have clear lines of communication and embedding of organisational values and objectives, to help give staff clarity of direction. The PCT is also pushing this angle with its corporate communications team and ensuring that, particularly at a time of change, this is delivered in as many formats and forums as possible. At the team level, the PCT has begun to incorporate wellness in discussions between HR and Service managers so that issues such as those raised in this research are picked up early. The PCT has also worked with particular areas to ensure that supervision and appraisal are being properly scheduled to give staff the support they need. The PCT plans to implement its strategy over the next five years, looking at how it can increase engagement with staff and increase the level of input, particularly with regard to supporting the psychological needs of the workforce. To this end, it aims to have discussions with in-house psychology services to look at how it could be advising staff in terms of self-management of stressors. Additionally the organisation will continue to work with public health on issues of physical well-being and communications around direction issues, and to monitor well-being and engagement across the PCT via staff survey, absence and turnover as well as local events (e.g. a Wellness Day) and questionnaires, from time to time.

Activities and discussion questions

1. Does your organisation have a wellness strategy? If so to what extent are the factors identified in the literature evident in this strategy? If you do not have a wellness strategy, examine the **ideas** behind the management of employee well-being and apply these to your organisation (or one with which you are familiar). To what extent are any of these ideas evident within the organisation?

2. You are a middle manager working for a medium-sized local authority (or for your organisation). Prepare a report for your executive team, making proposals to develop and implement an Employee well-being strategy. This should be a succinct report which details the aims and objectives of the strategy as well as the measurable outcomes and also includes a fully costed business plan. In addition you should prepare a presentation to sell this proposal to the decision-makers.

3. The case research examines the measurement of employee well-being, based on the employees' own self-assessment. Examine the case and comment on the statement that 'Although the PCT participates in the mandatory annual NHS staff survey, the results, to date, have failed to provide a comprehensive measure of employee well-being'. Does your organisation have a regular staff survey? If so what useful information does this provide on employee well-being and what actions are taken?

4. Many organisations offer wellness programmes, including smoking cessation, healthy eating, weight reduction, exercise regimes and gym membership among others. A difficulty with this is the lack of evidence

that any of these are relevant for any particular organisation. Identify the wellness programmes offered in your organisation and investigate how these are monitored and what measurements are made as to the effectiveness of this provision.

5. The case research identifies 10 domains, which it identifies as 'having been shown to impair employee well-being' and which are factors that the organisation can act upon. Comment on the appropriateness of these domains and identify possible actions that employers might take to decrease the scores in any of the domains.

Bibliography

Berry, L.L., Mirabito, A.M. and Baun, W.B. (2010). 'What's the hard return on employee wellness programs?' *Harvard Business Review*, 88(12): 104–12.

Bevan. S. (2010). *The Business Case for Employee Health and Well-Being*. Lancaster: The Work Foundation.

Bowden, D.E., Fry, L., Powell, D.R., Rosene, P.M. and Shewanown, M. (2010). 'Do wellness programs really work?' *Benefits and Compensation Digest*, 47(9): 20–24.

Business in the Community (BITC) (2011). *BITC Public Reporting Guidelines: Employee Wellness and Engagement*. London: BITC.

CIPD (2005). *Reflections on Employee Well-Being and the Psychological Contract*. London: CIPD

CIPD (2007a). 'What's happening with well-being at work?' *Change Agenda*. London: CIPD. (Electronic version) http://www.cipd.co.uk/subjects/health/general/_wllbngwrk.htm

CIPD (2007b). *Annual Survey Report: Absence Management*. London: CIPD.

CIPD (2010). *Annual Survey Report: Absence Management*. London: CIPD.

Cooper, C.L. (2011). *Are Managers Bad for Your Health?* (Electronic version), accessed on 11 August from http://www.hrmagazine.co. uk/hro/features/1019909/ are-managers-bad-health?utm_content=Are%20managers%20bad%20for%20your%20health%3F& utm_campaign=HR%20magazine%20news%209%20August&utm_source=HR%20Mag azine&utm_medium=adestra_email&utm_term

Faragher, E.B., Cooper, C.L. and Cartwright, S. (2004). 'A shortened stress evaluation tool of live and clinical trials', *CMAJ: Canadian Medical Association Journal* 134(8): 889–95.

Guyatt, G. H., Veldhuyzen Van Zanten, S. J., Feeny, D. H. and Patrick, D. L. (1989). 'Measuring quality of life in clinical trials: a taxonomy and review'. *CMAJ: Canadian Medical Association Journal* 140(12): 1441–8

Jack, R. (2004). 'How to implement a wellness strategy.' *People Management Guide to Wellness at Work*. October, CIPD.

Juniper, F., Guyatt, G. and Jaeschke, R. (1996). 'How to develop and validate a new health-related quality of life instrument', in B. Spilker, (ed.), *Quality of Life and Pharmacoeconomics in Clinical Trials*. Philadelphia: Lippincott-Raven Publishers, pp. 75–84.

Kraybill, K. (2003). *Creating and Maintaining a Healthy Environment: A Resource Guide for Staff Retreats*. Retrieved from http://www.nhchc.org/wp-content/uploads/2011/10/ ResourceGuideforStaffRetreats.pdf

Krizner, K. (2010). 'Employers not ready to give up on health and wellness programs'. *Managed Healthcare Executive*, 20(8): 29–31.

Mills, P.R. (2005). 'The development of a new corporate specific health risk measurement and its use in investigating the relationship between health and well-being and employee productivity'. *Environmental Health: A Global Access Science Source*, 4(1). Retrieved from http://www.ncbi.nlm.nih.gov/pmc/articles/PMC548523/?tool= pubmed

Smethurst, S. (2007). 'Health and wellbeing'. *People Management*, 25 January 2009: 24.

Sparks, K. Faragher, B. and Cooper, C.L. (2001). 'Well-being and occupational health in the 21st century workplace'. *Journal of Organizational and Occupational Psychology*, 74(4): 489–509.

Wainwright, D. and Heaver, E. (2009). 'Can the economic and social costs of sickness absence be reduced by improving the quality of working life'. *Employee Well-Being and Working Life: Towards an Evidence Based Policy Agenda. Proceedings from the Public Policy Seminar at HSE on 5 February 2009.*

World Economic Forum (2010). *The Wellness Imperative: Creating More Effective Organisations.* Geneva: WEF.

CHAPTER 20

Health and Safety at Work
Looking after hearts and minds

David Hall and Peter Cartwright

There is a strong business case for effective management of health and safety, particularly for those organisations who, by the very nature of their business, involve their employees in potentially dangerous work activities. Across all sectors, employee well-being has emerged as an important health and safety issue because of the significant costs associated with absence through stress-related illness and the implications this can have for organisational performance. This chapter looks at

- Approaches towards and models of health and safety management,
- The role of HRM in health and safety management,
- A case that illustrates 'business partnering' of HRM and line management at strategic level in managing a health and safety culture at a global chemicals manufacturer.

Health and safety in the workplace

In the UK 2.2 million people will claim to suffer from a work-related illness caused directly or indirectly by the job they do. The Chartered Institute of Personnel Management (CIPD) estimate the cost of sickness, on average, in the UK amounts to £601 per worker each year. Ill health is costly for business, particularly as sickness-related absence impacts on productivity and performance. The Health and Safety Executive (HSE) reports that the cost of workplace accidents and work-related ill health cost employers between £3.9 billion and £7.8 billion, and the UK economy between £13.1 billion and £22.2 billion, based on 2001–02 data (HSE, 2004). The *Annual Survey Report* on absence management by CIPD states that the median cost per employee per year to employers because of absence is £673, compared with £600 in 2010 (CIPD, 2011).

In 2009–10, 147 workers were killed at work in the UK, compared with 295 in 2000–01 (Health and Safety Statistics, 2000–01, 2009–10). The incidence of workers' fatalities has fallen considerably since the 1980s, largely due to a decline in employment in the relatively dangerous engineering and manufacturing sectors, and more workers being employed in the safer work environments of the service sector. This decline in fatalities is also due to the efforts of the

Health and Safety Executive (HSE), which is the independent regulatory body responsible for enforcing workplace health and safety standards in the UK.

The incidence of non-fatal workplace injuries has also been in decline since the 1980s for the same reasons. In 2009–10, there were 121,430 reported work-related non-fatal injuries in the UK, and a further 113,000 injuries that resulted in absence for over three days, compared with 161,629 workers in 2000–01 who suffered a work-related injury that warranted more than three days' absence from work.

Workplace stress and related psychological illnesses are a major hazard and are a significant cause of absence. In 2009–2010, ca. 10 million days were lost due to self-reported incidents of stress, depression or anxiety caused or made worse by work. This translates to 0.42 lost days per year per employee in the UK (HSE, 2010).

The *Annual Survey Report* on absence management by CIPD states that the median cost per employee per year to employers because of absence is £673, compared with £600 in 2010 (CIPD, 2011).

The business case for effectively managing health and safety management to reduce risk to employee health and to minimise absence because of work-related ill-health would appear to be a compelling one based on productivity, performance and reputational grounds alone. However there is also the 'human case' to consider, based on the human cost, to individuals, families and society, which makes health and safety a strategic people management issue for all stakeholders.

Approaches to health and safety

There are two main 'philosophies' or ways of thinking about health and safety in the workplace and, in practice, both influence the involvement of HRM in developing and promoting effective health and safety policy management.

The compliance perspective is based on the duty of employers to comply with their legal responsibility to maintain a healthy and safe workplace under the Health and Safety at Work Act (HASAWA) 1974 in the UK. The main purposes of this act are as follows:

- To secure the health, safety and welfare of people at work,
- To protect the public from risks arising from workplace activities,
- To control the use and storage of dangerous substances,
- To control potentially dangerous environmental emissions.

The consequences of injury and illness because of management neglect in this area can be serious. Litigation in the courts brought about by victims who have directly (or indirectly) suffered as a result of inadequate health and safety management, and actions by official bodies responsible for ensuring that employers comply with health and safety legislations, for example Health and Safety Executive (HSE) in the UK, can result in significant costs and reputational damage. This approach to health and safety is compliance-driven and minimises cost to employers by ensuring the minimum requirements are met.

The commitment perspective is founded on the fundamental belief that employees are an organisation's most valued assets and are essential to the delivery of high performance. This ethos drives health and safety management in a very different way, making it a strategic people management issue, having implications for managing performance and the role of HRM in health and safety. The case towards the end of this chapter illustrates how vision and values are used by a global leader in its sector to encourage desired employee behaviour that supports effective health and safety practice in the workplace. This strategic approach to health and safety connecting employee behaviour with performance can be seen in the way an increasing number of organisations view this management function.

Dow Corning, the company featured in the case in this chapter, is a good example of an organisation with a progressive approach towards health and safety founded on effective strategic leadership and management. Progressive thinking organisations like Dow Corning view their management systems in all areas of operations, including health and safety, as sources of competitive leverage, which, provides opportunities to differentiate themselves in highly competitive circumstances.

Models of health and safety management

The careless worker model is the traditional approach to health and safety in the workplace, based on the assumption of employers, courts and regulating bodies that most accidents result from an employee failing to take the necessary safety precautions to protect themselves. However this model does not address illness and injury caused by toxic substances, badly designed and hazardous work systems, and more. It also does not take into account stress, fatigue and poor working conditions. This approach did not identify many hazards in the workplace and it put the onus on employees to take the necessary measures in order to protect themselves. In the early 1970s, a major investigation into occupational health and safety in the UK led the investigators to argue 'for both humanitarian and economic reasons, no society can accept with complacency that such levels of death, injury, disease and waste must be regarded as the inevitable price of meeting its needs for good and services' (Robens, 1972: 1).

The shared responsibility model emerged as a consequence of this report, which was developed and promoted by HRM. It represented a new approach to health and safety. This approach assumes that the best way to improve health and safety in the workplace is to put the onus on employers *and* employees to cooperate in managing the risks that cause accidents and illness; an approach that is evident in health and safety management today.

The trade union approach was described in the late 1970s by the British Trade Union Congress (TUC) that highlighted the hazards and risks built into work processes and the workplace as the 'root cause' of accidents in the workplace. The trade union advocated that organisations and work systems should be redesigned to remove hazards and risks at source. This approach is an important feature of work and operational design today to minimise risk to employees and other stakeholders.

The employer responsibility model is based on a 'Duty of Care' (a legal requirement) to protect employees and other individuals whose health may be affected by what they (employees) do in terms of health, safety and welfare. By law, an employer is expected to do whatever is reasonably feasible to minimise and control all the risks that exist in the workplace to prevent them from causing harm or injury.

This approach requires proactive strategic management of health and safety for which Bratton and Gold (2004) propose the framework:

- Design safer systems of work,
- Exhibit commitment to health and safety,
- Inspect the workplace regularly,
- Establish procedures and controls,
- Develop training programmes that emphasise health and safety,
- Establish health and safety committees,
- Monitor health and safety policy,
- Draw up an action plan.

HRM's role in health and safety

Health and safety at work is particularly relevant to HRM because of its implications for the design and implementation of work activities, for example the potential risk to employee health, safety and well-being because of work processes. As mentioned earlier, there are significant costs associated with absence through work-related illness, and HRM has an important role to play in supporting managers and employees to reduce absence caused by work-related illness. At a strategic level, effective governance requires management to ensure compliance and manage performance. These are key areas where HRM can play a strategic partnership role in a business. Traditionally employee welfare has been the domain of personnel management.

HRM theory has contributed towards the debate in positioning HRM with respect to health and safety, with the Harvard model of HRM (Beer, Spector, Lawrence, Quinn Mills and Walton, 1984) identifying employee well-being and organisational effectiveness as long-term consequences of HRM policy choices, influenced by stakeholder interests and situational factors. Guest's theory of HRM (Guest, 1989) proposes that the outcomes of HR policy design and implementation include lower absence and higher performance. This connection is also made by Pilbeam and Corbridge (2006) who propose that the effective management of human resources may offer a link between employee well-being and business performance.

The causal relationship between HR policy deployment and employee performance is a complex one, proposing that fairness, trust and commitment (features of a positive 'psychological contract') are important factors in influencing employees to exercise discretionary behaviour to go beyond the contracted or legal minimum requirements (Purcell, Kinnie, Hutchinson, Rayton and Swart, 2003). How organisations manage health and safety is an important factor in forming positive psychological contracts with employees, as the workers expect and trust their employer to be responsible for their health and safety.

Effective management of human resources through effective policy and procedure implementation extends to all areas of health and safety, providing interventions to support the development of a strong health and safety culture. The case article describes how Dow Corning Corporation's health and safety culture is supported by policies that incorporate health and safety in managing performance and reward. The role of proactive, high-level leadership and training is also highlighted as being critical in the development of safe and productive operations.

Tensions in managing health and safety

The cost and performance outcomes of managing health, safety and well-being potentially sets up a tension for HRM and other managers in terms of how to reconcile delivery of good organisational performance with the need to at least comply with health and safety legislation. It also raises the important question of what is reasonable in terms of the legal requirements surrounding 'Duty of Care'. This tension is highlighted by Gilmore and Williams (2010: 195) when they pose the question: 'To what extent does the desirability of maintaining a healthy and safe working environment conflict with the pressure managers often come under to maximise productivity?'

The answer can be found by finding consensus among stakeholders, particularly between employers and employees to help ensure that a positive psychological contract can be developed and maintained. Legislation plays an important role as the legal requirements pertaining to health, safety and well-being can influence the relationship between employers and employees, and their abilities to form good 'contracts'.

Managing health, safety and well-being

Occupational health is defined by the ILO/WHO (1950, cited in Harrington, Gill, Aw and Gardiner, 1998) as 'the promotion and maintenance of the highest degree of physical, mental and social well-being of workers in all occupations by preventing departures from health, controlling risks and the adaptation of work to people, and people to their jobs'.

Typical occupational health interventions include risk assessments, education and training on various aspects of health, safety and training, medical assessments, health screening, counselling and sickness-absence monitoring. The *Black Review* of the health of Britain's working population (Black, 2008) presented a view of work as being beneficial for health and having the ability to reverse harmful effects of long-term unemployment and prolonged sickness absence. The practical implications of this perspective are far-reaching and would require a fundamentally different approach by employers and the health-care professionals in advising and administering health and well-being related to the workplace. This review has been instrumental in ending the culture of sickness certification, based on individuals' not being able to work, and in changing it to what individuals are deemed to be fit enough to do in work.

Organisational interventions aimed at supporting employee health and well-being typically fall into one of three categories: tertiary, secondary or primary.

The most common in practice tend to be tertiary and secondary, which focus on the individual. Tertiary interventions usually involve programmes designed to encourage and improve lifestyle, for example Employee Assistance Programmes (EAP), exercise and relaxation techniques. Secondary interventions usually focus on appropriate coping strategies and methods, for example stress management and cognitive strategies, while primary interventions involve the employer taking direct action to deal with well-being issues which have an organisation focus, for example management style, work activity and organisational structures.

This case below describes the role of HRM in health and safety management at Dow Corning Corporation, a global chemicals manufacturer, in leading and supporting managers and employees in the development of an 'advanced safety culture'. This is a good example of 'Business Partnering' (Ulrich and Brockbank, 2005), with HRM working alongside business and functional managers in a strategic partnership role to deliver policies that have long-term added-value outcomes for the business.

The role of effective human resources in Dow Corning's safety performance – a case study

Dow Corning Corporation

Dow Corning is a US multinational chemical company, employing more than 10,000 people and serving about 25,000 customers worldwide. More than half of Dow Corning's annual sales are outside the United States. Dow Corning's global operations adhere to the American Chemistry Council's Responsible Care initiative, a stringent set of standards designed to advance the safe and secure management of chemical products and processes.

Between 2005 and 2009, Dow Corning reduced the rate of injuries and manufacturing accidents by more than half. Recently Dow Corning designed, built and commissioned a large chemical facility near Shanghai, China, with an unparalleled safety record during construction involving more than 20 million hours of construction work without a single occurrence of time lost due to injury. Dow Corning recently won EHS Today's 'America's safest company award' and a Royal Society for the Prevention of Accidents gold award for its UK operation. One of the foundational elements allowing Dow Corning to achieve this is a strong HR management system underpinning improvement programmes.

Safety in a chemical company

Over the past 40 years, there have been several industrial and chemical events that have served to highlight the responsibility of companies undertaking high-risk operations to ensure safe operations. These catastrophic events, Seveso, Bhopal, Texas City, Piper Alpha, Buncefield or Longford, resulted in either multiple fatalities, significant property damage or both. A common message to senior managers is 'If you think safety is expensive, try having an accident' (anon.).

Maintaining and continuously improving safety performance in a large chemical company is a complicated and challenging task for which effective HR systems and processes are crucial.

There are many aspects of safety in such an operation which include:

- Dealing with hazardous chemicals which can corrode, catch fire or explode under certain conditions,

- Dealing with manufacturing operations which present significant hazards that have the potential to injure or kill workers – activities such as working at heights, in confined spaces with little oxygen, or machinery with potential to maim or amputate,

- Dealing with the general risks that are common to society, including manual activity such as lifting, twisting for shop-floor workers, driving for salespeople, keyboard ergonomics and walking up and down staircases for administrative employees.

Within the chemical industry, strong corporate values, an advanced safety culture, well-trained employees and the active involvement of executive leadership are all critical factors in maintaining safe operations and continuously improving performance. Appropriate Human Resource Management policies, processes and practices provide the foundations for or underpin the success of those factors.

Safety at Dow Corning

Dow Corning has had safety as one of its seven corporate values for many years, demonstrating its long-term commitment to employee health and safety. It divides safety into two areas, which have some common requirements but are very different in how they are managed:

- *Occupational Health and Safety* – which deals mainly with preventing injuries and illnesses for all employees and contractors working within our facilities.

- *Process safety* – which deals with the prevention of spills, emissions, fires and explosions at manufacturing sites.

Vision for safety – for each 'human resource' whether experienced or new, fitter or CEO

In 2006 Dow Corning developed a vision for safety, which aimed to refocus and apply safety as a part of every employee's activity and thought process. This vision and associated branding, which is simply titled 'Safe Work IS Our Job', is used in all communication materials internally.

Practical application – what good safety looks like

Before the launch of the vision, Dow Corning carried out two benchmarking exercises to develop a system which leaders and managers could use as a framework for practical application to improvement:

- A six-month process of analysing those elements that were a common part of Dow Corning's best performing sites – to determine what had worked within the company culture,

- Discussion with other leading companies seen to be safe – to identify further opportunities.

Dow Corning then communicated the four critical elements which each site, laboratory or office would be required to carry out excellently to produce the fifth element, which was a sustained long-term trend for the reduction of injuries or incidents – known as 'What Good Safety Looks Like!' See Table 20.1 below.

Table 20.1 What good safety looks like

Element	Examples
Demonstrated Leadership	– Leaders are communicating vision and spending time observing, praising, coaching, disciplining, as appropriate – There are safety plans based on the list of risks of the manufacturing location, sales team, office or laboratory
Clarity of Expectations	– People know exactly the procedures and practices they have to follow to ensure safety – Procedures are up to date and reflect reality
Operational Discipline	– People follow procedures 100% of the time – Housekeeping is always excellent and people wear necessary protective equipment 100% of the time
Learning from incidents and near-misses	– There is an open culture, which encourages accurate and timely incident and near-miss reporting – Incidents have investigations that identify the real root cause, which can be fixed long-term – Accidents with global application are openly shared, and improvements from these events are applied using a preventive action process
Sustainable long-term reduction in injuries and incidents	– The focus is primarily on leading and measuring the first four elements rather than on applying pressure on individuals to suppress information to improve safety statistics – There is a three-to-five-year downward trend in injury and incident rates

Human resources and its role in achieving success

Each of the five elements can provide some illustrative examples of where HR becomes a critical partner in safety improvement.

Demonstrated leadership – people management and senior leader active interest

This begins at the executive level and cascades through to all supervisors – the expectation is written in objectives as part of Dow Corning's performance management process.

'Balance of Consequences' is a programme used throughout the company for supervisors to fairly praise and reward employees showing excellent safety behaviour – following procedures, reporting near misses and incidents, spotting hazards and resolving issues before they lead to an accident. The balance is provided by coaching for those who are not and do not have an understanding of the expectations. In rare cases, this can lead to discipline or termination of employment for those wilfully not following standards or procedures. The company's aim is to have approximately a 9:1 ratio of praise/coaching or discipline. At the corporate level a portion of the annual bonus relies on a balance between training attendance and corporate safety results.

Active engagement is a critical role of executive and all senior management. In several instances of chemical industry events, incident investigations have revealed executives stating the importance of safety but not actively probing and welcoming information on where weaknesses or resources are needed. In a recessionary environment, mixed messaging is often a cause of reduced spending on critical safety infrastructure as outlined by Professor Andrew Hopkins (2008). Dow Corning's senior executive team receive training in safety from the VP of EHS and the Corporate Safety Director two to three times per year.

Clarity of expectations – involving training

This starts with a commitment from leadership to invest the appropriate resources to ensure that engineering standards, procedures and practices are clear, current and reflect the best way to do something safely. It is followed by an equal commitment to provide the time and methods to train all employees on exactly what they need to do to be as safe as possible in their roles and the consequences of doing it or not. This applies whether employees are running a hazardous manufacturing plant, taking a sample in a laboratory or driving safely. Dow Corning recently installed a driving simulator at its corporate headquarters site to allow hands-on driver training in a variety of high-risk driving scenarios.

As Dow Corning designed and built its newest large-scale facility in China, it made a considerable investment in supervisory training and high ratios of supervisors to local contractors. Coupled with the presence of a large number of skilled and committed expats, facilitated by excellent, flexible HR relocation assignments, this contributed to an extremely low injury rate for contractors (in the top 10 per cent performance for all such projects globally).

Operational discipline

Human nature often works against this element of being safe – whether this is obeying speed limits, or wearing safety helmets when riding a bicycle. In a large chemical company like Dow Corning, this is no different. For an innovative company with different cultures in many plants, laboratories and offices throughout the world, and a large influx of new people each year, educating and maintaining a consistent, safety culture remains a constant challenge. Training, communication, leadership inspections and the Balance of Consequences system forms the backbone of Dow Corning's commitment to ensuring a good environment for continual compliance.

The Balance of Consequence checklists used by all supervisors can provide leadership with 'dashboard data' to show where there are weaknesses. For example the site manager in the UK facility regularly does a safety walk-around, with the results of inspections allowing him to congratulate an area on their diligence in certain tasks yet focus on a couple of other areas that have seen some issues with compliance. Not only can he/she ask questions about whether procedures are appropriate or why there is no 100 per cent compliance, but the workforce also recognises the manager is engaged in displaying a specific focus on fixing what is wrong in their area, in addition to engaging in a general safety discussion.

Learning from incidents and near misses

Probably the most critical element is having a corporate culture that is open, fair and valued, and wants to find any defects in processes before larger accidents occur. One of the major reasons for large safety incidents is a culture where the final safety numbers are the basis for financial benefit and an implied pressure on workers and managers not to report small deviations (Hopkins, 2009.) The results of such hidden defects (which always occur in systems involving humans) can be that the 'process or behaviour-break' is only seen when the final consequence cannot be hidden, such as a serious injury, fatality or major catastrophe. Often the presence of a knee-jerk blame culture of blaming the front-line worker unfairly can result in suppression of reporting.

Dow Corning encourages and rewards near-miss reporting with Manufacturing and Research and Development laboratories having targets for openly recording 'close-calls', and using the data collected to drive future safety improvement plans.

Sustainable long-term reduction in injuries and incidents

The word 'sustainable' and phrase 'long-term' are critical to avoid a short-term focus on reducing incident rates and a pressure to hide incidents. In Dow Corning's experience an effective combination of the four 'leading elements' described in the five elements above will result in consistent improvement and a safer and more productive workplace. HR leadership practices, culture, policies and performance management processes have been shown to be essential contributors to this.

Activities and discussion questions

1. Identify the main risks to health, safety and well-being in the work/ learning environment you operate in, and then find out how these risks are managed to minimise the potential danger they present.

2. Discuss the damage that can be done as a consequence of ineffective risk management and health and safety management by considering who is affected and how. You may wish to look into the BP Gulf of Mexico drilling incident in 2010.

3. Identify the key components of Dow Corning's approach to managing health and safety as described in the case, and consider how these are linked and why.

4. Debate the use of performance management methods to support the development of a health and safety culture. Refer to the case of Dow Corning above and see Chapter 11 in this book.

Bibliography

Beer, M., Spector, B., Lawrence, P.R., Quinn Mills, D. and Walton, R.E. (1984). *Managing Human Assets*. New York: Free Press.

Black, C. (2008). *Working for a Healthier Tomorrow*. London: Stationary Office.

Economic Advisers Unit. (2004). *Cost to Britain of Workplace Accidents and Work-Related Ill Health*. Retrieved on 25 October 2011 from the Health and Safety Executives website: http://www.hse.gov.uk/search/results.htm?q=costs&sitesearch=&cx=015848178315289032903%3Akous-jano68&cof=FORID%3A11#998

CIPD (2011). *The Annual Survey Report: Absence Management*. London: CIPD.

Fuller, C. and Vassie, L. (2004). *Health and Safety Management: Principles and Best Practice*. Harlow: Financial Times/Prentice Hall.

Gilmore, S. and Williams, S. (2010). 'Health, safety and employee well-being in Human Resource Management', in S. Gimore and S. Williams (eds), *Human Resource Management*. Oxford: Oxford University Press.

Guest, D. (1989). 'Personnel and HRM: can you tell the differences?'. *Personnel Management*. January.

Harrington, J., Gill, F., Aw, T. and Gardiner, K. (1998). *Occupational Health* (4th edn.). Oxford: Blackwell Science.

HSE (2004). *RIDDOR – Reporting of Injuries, Diseases and Dangerous Occurrences Regulations*. Retrieved 25 October, 2011 from the Health and Safety Executive website: http://www.hse.gov.uk/statistics/tables/index.htm#riddor.

Hopkins, A. (2008). *Failure to Learn: The BP Texas City Refinery Disaster*. Australia: CCH.

Hopkins, A. (2009). *Learning from High Reliability Organizations*. Australia: CCH.

Hughes, P. and Ferret, E. (2011). *Introduction to Health and Safety at Work* (5th edn.). Oxford: Butterworth-Heinemann.

Pilbeam, S. and Corbridge, M. (2006). *People Resourcing: Contemporary HRM in Practice* (3rd edn.). Harlow: Financial Times/Prentice Hall.

Purcell, J., Kinnie, N., Hutchinson, S., Rayton, B. and Swart, J. (2003). *Understanding the People and Performance Link: Unlocking the Black Box*. London: CIPD.

Ridley, J. and Channing, J. (2008). *Safety at Work* (7th edn.). Oxford: Butterworth-Heinemann.

Robens, L. (1972). *Safety and Health at Work*. Cmnd 5034. London: HMSO.

Self-Reported Work-Related Illness (SWI) and Workplace Injuries: Results from the Labour Force Survey. (2010). Retrieved 25 October 2011 from the Health and Safety Executive website: http://www.hse.gov.uk/statistics/lfs/index.htm#stress

TUC (1979). *The Safety Rep and Union Organization*. London: TUC Education, 10.

Ulrich, D. and Brockbank, W. (2005). *The HR Value Proposition*. Boston, MA: Harvard Business School Press.

CHAPTER 21

HRM Adding Value

Managing and measuring HR's contribution

David Hall, Yves Emery and Mark Power

Understanding how people management practices influence performance and add value for organisations is an area of intense interest to academics and managers. Research in this area has played a major role in shaping the concept of HRM and its role in contributing to organisational performance. The design and application of metrics and management systems are a challenging area as organisations seek to determine the value of their 'human capital' and the contribution this makes to the business. This chapter looks at:

- Research that developed understanding and helped shape concepts of how HR influences employee and organisational performance,
- Management and measurement of HRM practices that add value to organisations,
- Two cases that examine how HRM can add value and an approach to manage HRM contribution by using metrics.

People assets

Driven by increasingly competitive markets and increasing pressure to deliver value for money, employers in all sectors are focused on improving productivity to create value. Employees are a significant cost to most businesses, so it is not surprising that employers look closely at the contribution employees make, particularly managers who are responsible for 'getting the best' from their people. There is another reason why employers should turn their attention to their people, based on a different perspective that considers employees as assets who have economic value and contribute value to an organisation; a concept known as 'human capital'. This theory proposes that employees create or 'add value' for their employers through the application of their knowledge and skills or, to put it another way, by using their expertise and experience. This resource-based view (Barney, 1995) proposes that organisations can gain competitive advantage by investing in and utilising the unique capabilities of their employees. The challenge is for managers, particularly HR managers, to manage this valuable human capital resource in such a way that it ensures business sustainability by meeting stakeholder requirements. A primary concern for HRM (and for most business leaders) is to demonstrate its capability to contribute to the value of organisations through effectively managing the people resources who work for them.

Positioning HRM and performance

The first HRM models began to appear in the 1980s, and many of these early models suggested that HR policy and practice influenced organisational outcomes, including performance. Performance is positioned at the centre of the first HRM models, including the Michigan model of HRM (Fombrun, Tichy and Devanna, 1984) which assumed that managing the activities of selection, appraisal and development HR activities influenced employee performance. The Harvard model of HRM (Beer, Lawrence, Quinn Mills and Walton, 1984) recognised the influence of stakeholder interests in informing HRM policy formulation, and how these policies produce outcomes that have long-term organisational consequences, including firm effectiveness. Guest's theory of HRM, with its four HR policy goals of strategic integration, commitment, flexibility and quality, provided a more detailed thesis on how HR policy implementation can lead to certain organisational outcomes, including job performance and other outcomes that improve organisation performance (Guest, 1989).

These models were helpful in identifying the content and processes involved in HRM, employee and organisational performance. They also had the common idea that HRM policies should be aligned with business strategy, that is policies should be designed and implemented to contribute towards producing strategic business outcomes; a concept that has become known as 'strategic HRM'. Boxall and Purcell (2003) capture the meaning of strategic HRM when they describe it as the ways in which HRM influences organisational performance. Strategic HRM is not any one particular HR strategy (or policy) but is a framework for shaping and delivering a number of people management strategies.

HR influence on performance

Several studies carried out in the US in the 1990s concluded that there is a positive association between the number of HR practices employed and firm performance, including increasing market value and productivity, and lower labour turnover (Huselid, 1995). Jeffery Pfeffer (1998) in his book *The Human Equation* claimed that people were at the heart of business success and that the management requirement could be reduced to a set of seven specific HR policy areas that could be adopted to facilitate business improvement:

■ Employment security,
■ Careful recruitment,
■ Teamwork and decentralisation,
■ High pay with incentive element,
■ Extensive training,

- Narrow status differential,
- Effective two-way communication.

This research influenced the development of the concept of 'best practice', that is specific HRM practices that can be adopted across sectors and countries to improve performance. The approach of 'best practice' to HRM has been criticised because it fails to take into account the specific environmental and business contexts of organisations, including location, sector and organisational and national cultures. Other researchers argue that each institutional setting requires its own unique HRM model (Brewster, 2004) and advocate a 'best fit' approach.

In the UK, Patterson, West, Lawthorn and Nickell (1997) carried out longitudinal studies and found an association between HRM and increases in productivity and financial performance. They found a 19 per cent increase in company profitability could be explained by HRM, claiming that people management was a better predictor of company performance than strategy, technology or research and development. Analysis of the 1998 Workplace Employee Relations Survey (WERS) based on over 2000 workplaces by Guest, Michie, Sheehan and Conway (2000a) confirmed the link between the use of more HR policies and practicesand a range of positive outcomes, including greater employee involvement, satisfaction and commitment, productivity and better financial performance. Although careful not to make claims about cause and effect, Guest, Michie, Sheehan, Conway and Metochi (2000b) suggested that the application of HR practices translate into better employee and organisational performance by facilitating a higher sense of commitment on the part of employees.

The People and Performance model

John Purcell and his team of researchers at the University of Bath describe in their 'People and Performance model' how employees' discretionary behaviour (how individuals choose to behave) positively influences performance and how these choices are influenced by people management policies (Purcell, Kinnie, Hutchinson, Rayton and Swart, 2003). At the heart of the People and Performance model is the fundamental proposition that performance is a function of ability (A), motivation (M) and opportunity (O), expressed as Performance $= f$ (A, M, O).

This thesis asserts that for people to perform beyond the minimum requirements, they must have the motivation to perform well, have the ability through their knowledge and skills to perform well and have the opportunity to use their skills in their specific roles and in a wider organisational context. This model describes how (strategic) HRM works in practice to influence positive performance outcomes, through the design and implementation of HR strategies as policies and practices. Purcell describes these practices as 'performance-related HR practices', also known as 'High-Performance Work Practices' (HPWPs). These HR strategies and practices are applied in combination as sets or 'bundles' of HPWPs, enabling an integrated approach within the specific context of the organisation and operations.

This research was based on 12 case study organisations, including Tesco, Jaguar, Nationwide Building Society, The Royal Mint and Siemens Medical.

High-performance work organisations

A study of HPWPs based on a case study of 10 organisations and a survey of 294 companies in the UK identified specific HPWPs being employed in a number of business sectors (Sung and Ashton, 2004). This study concluded that the degree of HPWP adoption is linked to organisational performance, and that 'High-Performance Work Organisations' (HPWOs) employ a higher level of HPWPs than other organisations. Specific examples of HR practices in use at some HPWOs include:

■ Continuous professional development,
■ 'Back-to-the-floor' managers (managers spending time with employees working in operations),
■ Profit-sharing,
■ Performance-related pay,
■ 360-degree appraisals for all,
■ Appraisal against attributes for all-round performance,
■ Recruit top candidates exclusively at entry level,
■ Continuous training for leadership.

Some HPWPs have been largely adopted in the UK, for example appraisals are used by 95 per cent of the organisations sampled in the survey. However other HPWPs such as share options for all employees have only been adopted by 16 per cent of the organisations in the survey. It is interesting to speculate why the uptake of HPWPs is not more extensive than it appears and what the barriers to adoption are.

HR adding value through partnership

As the basis of what became known as *HR business partnering*, Dave Ulrich (1997) proposed that HR needed to transform itself and suggested that HR professionals could add value to organisations in four ways, which helped align HR activity with strategic business outcomes:

■ Management of strategic human resources,
■ Management of firm infrastructure,
■ Management of employee contribution,
■ Management of transformation and change.

The HR 'Business Partner' model came to the fore as a result of this work in 1997 and was reviewed by Ulrich and Brockbank in 2005. The model is based on two main perspectives: strategic and operational, and identifies five areas where HRM can work together or 'partner' with the business (line management) to contribute towards achieving the organisational aims. These areas are:

- Strategic Partner,
- Human Capital Developers,
- Functional Expert,
- Employee Advocates,
- HR Leader (spanning the other four areas.)

The Business Partner model describes how HR managers can work in partnership with other managers to develop and implement performance strategies based on HR policies and practices to achieve common business goals. The main revision to the original concept, the addition of 'HR Leader', predominantly focuses on senior HR roles and also suggests the relevance of all HR professionals taking responsibility and demonstrating personal leadership in their work and interactions. Underpinning the 'business partnership' model is the key idea that HR professionals can contribute towards creating or adding value to their organisations by focusing on these areas of activity. Also if HR can *demonstrate* that it does deliver added value as a management function, it will help convince senior management of HR's contribution and help it gain credibility and respect. In this way HR can become more involved and influential in organisations.

Demonstrating HR's contribution

In the 1990s, as a response to inadequate methods of managing and measuring performance in organisations, the 'Balanced Scorecard' was developed and described by Kaplan and Norton (1996). The main feature of this performance measuring and management system (it was also described as a strategic management system) were the four 'generic' dimensions of organisational performance:

- *Financial* – financial viability and prosperity,
- *Customer* – the customer value proposition,
- *Business Processes* (operational) – the internal processes and systems,
- *Innovation and learning (people)* – the human contribution through knowledge and skills.

The main idea was that these dimensions considered a broad view of organisational performance while focusing on areas of the business where value was created, contributing to the future success of the organisation. Up until this point, most businesses had focused only on the financial results, which meant looking at past performance and not at business activities that influence future performance. The story of the Balanced Scorecard has been one of incredible success as it has been widely adopted across the globe in all organisational sectors. The effectiveness of the Balanced Scorecard depends on using relevant and reliable measures (metrics) of performance, which can be used to determine progress against objectives and even targets. Applied in this way, these measures are often referred to as Key Performance Indicators or 'KPIs'. The objectives are aligned with the strategic aims of the organisation and are cascaded and translated throughout the organisation, from board level to team and even individual performance. This gives a thoroughly aligned, integrated and coherent performance management framework.

The 'HR Scorecard' is based on the principles of the Balanced Scorecard as a systematic performance management and measurement framework. It is specifically designed to support a strategic HRM approach in determining the contribution of HR policy and practice towards creating shareholder value (Becker, Huselid and Ulrich, 2001). An HR Scorecard is a mechanism for describing and measuring how people and people management systems create value in organisations, as well as for communicating key organisational objectives to the workforce. This approach can be helpful to organisations interested in determining the 'human capital' value their employees bring with the help of appropriate metrics. However this is a challenging area as it is not always straightforward to relate particular expertise to economic value and the bottom line. The use of business-focused metrics in an HR scorecard enables strategic HR 'business partners' to converse in the language of business performance and provide a basis for defining:

- key measures associated with the workforce,
- trends in performance, over time, as metrics are tracked,
- measurable workforce outputs and areas of weakness or underperformance,
- feedback about measurement methods and the metrics to be tracked,
- appropriate interventions to address deteriorating or underachievement.

The first case at the end of this chapter looks at the pioneering work of Fitz-enz and other researchers in added-value HRM. A case study from Switzerland examines how the introduction of flexible working patterns contributed towards adding value, and highlights some of the metrics used in determining value added by HR. The second case looks at the development and implementation of a Workforce Scorecard at an NHS Primary Trust based on the principles of the Balanced and HR scorecards.

HRM on the road towards added value – a case study

When the HR department stops reporting feelings and begins to report efficiency and productivity data, it will be perceived as a mainstream function and not as a nice-to-do activity.

(Fitz-enz, 1984)

Almost 25 years ago, one of the pioneers of added-value HRM, Fitz-enz, highlighted the missing data that could demonstrate the genuine contribution of HRM to the business. Unfortunately many HR managers are still not able to deliver 'facts and figures', despite being under pressure from other members of the board. HRM suffers from a 'non-measurement tradition', which needs to be seriously questioned

(Phillips, 1996; Le Louarn and Wils, 2001). HR practitioners often argue that measuring HR is difficult, costly, focused on details and failing to capture the core business, or a useless activity because of many other factors that affect organisational performance (Fitz-enz, 1990). These arguments have to be taken seriously, but they are not *per se* sufficient to abandon the powerful idea of measuring added-value HR activity. This chapter will identify the main levels of HRM added value, and then illustrate the approach with a case study relating to the introduction of a flexible working model.

The HRM mutation towards concern with adding organisational value

In the past decade, in many public and private organisations, the HRM function has become more professional by empowering itself through the programmes of action in what are now well-known HRM activities, such as human resource planning and talent management, appraising and rewarding performance and training and development (Emery and Gonin, 2006). As these HRM activities are refined there is a danger that they are seen as the main purpose of HRM, but it is important that HRM is not evaluated by what it does, but by *how it contributes to the organisation's performance*. A radical change in outlook may therefore be a condition of HRM's survival in organisations in the twenty-first century. This need for an outlook change is evident in literature driven initially by Fitz-enz and Ulrich (Ulrich and Losey, 1997; Ulrich, 1998). The emphasis on added-value HR activity emanates from diverse, and sometimes contradictory, research stemming from either financial considerations, such as return on investment, characteristic of the works of Fitz-enz (1984), or other authors who refer to 'human capital' (Davidson, 1998; Mayo, 2001; Baron and Armstrong, 2007), social capital (the *social balance sheet* developed initially in France, see (Béland and Piché, 1998) or are geared towards strategic management (Kaplan and Norton, 1996; Leopold, Harris and Watson, 2005). This research can be summarised in a three-level value chain of HRM practices as shown in Figure 21.1 below.

Level 1	Level 2	Level 3
HRM activities and processes	Intermediary results	Impact on organisational performance
HR operational results	HR added value	External added value
Efficiency and quality of the processes and services delivered by the HR Department service centre	Performance, satisfaction and employability of employees Employer attractiveness and staff retention	Organisational performance-quality and attractiveness of the products, profitability and customer satisfaction

Figure 21.1   Value chain of HRM practices

Level 1 is mainly about implementing up-to-date HRM processes, which means a high level of 'professionalisation' for the HR department. The questions to be answered at this stage (Crow and Hartman, 1995) are: does HR deliver value for money and does it meet quality standards for internal customers – upper management, line managers, the staff and labour unions? Level 2 represents all the HR results produced by the HRM processes. Basically HRM needs to make employees more productive, more satisfied, more skilled and more committed to their jobs and to the objectives of the organisation. The main question is: To what extent do the HRM practices really contribute to a more effective and motivated workforce? Level 3 relates to evaluating the impact on organisational performance. The HR department therefore needs to ensure that data are generated at all three of the added-value levels, being fully responsible for the first level, and partially responsible, with line managers, for the second and third levels.

A study of the introduction of the flexitime system and the evaluation of the added value

The CIPD report (2005) on the implementation of flexible working highlights the potential positive effects of flexible working practices relating to employee retention, motivation and employer brand. According to the Emery model, these effects are examples of second-level added value. It is possible to demonstrate how such flexible working patterns can be evaluated at all three levels, having positive effects not only on the staff, but also on efficiency, productivity and quality of the products, as shown in the literature (Pilbeam and Corbridge, 2006).

The following case study from Switzerland is an illustration of a flexible working pattern combining annual hours and a compulsory reduction of the normal full-time hours from 40 to 32 hours per week, and a reduction in pay. It was introduced in a small public sector organisation dealing with social benefits.[1] Several objectives were associated with this project, and consequently evaluated; these included improving productivity and flexibility of the workforce, enhancing employee satisfaction by offering a better work–life balance and also creating new job opportunities. The characteristics of this flexible working model are shown in Table 21.1 below.

The model was piloted for a year and then, with the full agreement of employee representatives, extended to almost all units of the organisation.

Added-value analysis of the pilot project:

1. **At the first level:** The time management system, both hardware and software, was already in place prior to the introduction of this new model. There was little difference in terms of resources needed, apart from the fact that there are fewer exceptions and queries from staff to manage. There were some project development costs.

2. **At the second level:** The global employee satisfaction index increased by 8 per cent and satisfaction regarding tasks, responsibilities and functional flexibility rose for more than 75 per cent of respondents. A small number of employees felt more stressed, and in some units more isolated, but 96 per cent of employees

reported a neutral or positive influence on their social, family and leisure activities. Surprisingly 85 per cent of employees found that a pay decrease of 10 per cent, was not a problem, particularly in relation to an improved work–life balance.

3. **At the third level**: Employee productivity increased on average by 13 per cent and in some cases by up to 20 per cent.[2] Almost no overtime was needed, because of greater organisational flexibility to match variable work demands during the year. More than 50 per cent of randomly selected customers for a survey reported improved customer service, and more than 60 per cent perceived better quality of the services provided – principally due to the extended compulsory presence of employees and a more flexible workforce. In addition the organisation created three new full-time jobs, demonstrating responsible citizenship for the whole of society.

Table 21.1   Flexible working model

	Full-time hours per week	Full-time job percentage	Expected level of productivity (%)	Salary paid (%)	Comments
Old time system	40	100	100	100	Classical system
New time system	32	80 per cent	90	90	10% of salaries to create new jobs

1. The annual hours to be worked are 1,550 and the working pattern is to be from Monday to Saturday between 6.00 am and 11.00 pm, instead of Monday to Friday between 7.00 am and 7.00 pm.
2. A flexitime account defines the maximum accumulated hours.
3. A compulsory employee presence for internal and external customers is determined weekly, each employee having a two or three half-day presence each week. Otherwise there is no 'blocked time period'. The old time system had blocked time periods from 9.00 to 11.30 am and from 2.00 to 4:15 pm, but there is no compulsory presence requirement for customers.
4. Each employee is responsible for the effective management of their work-time in relation to the objectives to be achieved and the prevailing organisational priorities.

Introducing such a flexible working time system must be carefully planned and evaluated and managers and employees need to be well prepared to act in more entrepreneurial and innovative ways. Perhaps only a mature company can successfully introduce such a time system, which requires the improved coordination of all activities, but the process can generate genuine added value for all stakeholders.

Workforce Scorecard metrics for HR performance reporting – a case study

Most organisations are likely to rate their employees as being their most important resource, or 'asset'. For many organisations the largest financial investment is associated with the maintenance of a workforce that is appropriately sized, skilled and developed, and that is efficiently managed and deployed. Despite this many employers find difficulty in establishing a performance-reporting framework that includes those core measurements, or metrics, which clearly demonstrate the impact of employee activity and contribution to the bottom line. Portsmouth Hospitals NHS Trust (PHT) is a large acute trust with an annual turnover of £400 million, a multi-professional workforce of 7,000 employees and provides emergency, general and specialist health care to more than 250,000 people each year, across three geographically displaced sites. The requirement to consistently meet national access targets, whilst also striving to achieve Foundation Trust status (which will afford greater operating freedoms and financial autonomy) and to deliver recurrent financial surpluses, creates a significant challenge for the senior leadership team. For those charged with the effective utilisation of the Trust's diverse workforce, this challenge is manifest in the need to establish a business-focused HR performance reporting system. The aim of this system is to ensure there is a clear 'line of sight' between the Trust's HR interventions and the impact the workforce has on service reform, productivity improvement (and hence patient care) and overall organisational efficiency.

The case for developing HR reporting metrics

The case for developing and establishing robust HR reporting metrics is based on the adage 'we can't improve what we can't measure'. This applies as equally to the measurement of employee input, as it does to other organisational resources. A strong argument is made by the HR consulting organisation Watson Wyatt (2007) using a Human Capital Index, which seeks to demonstrate a correlation between high performance in the five key practices of *recruiting excellence, clear rewards and accountability, effective use of human resources, communications integrity and a collegial flexible workplace*, and a significant increase in organisational performance and profitability. The definition of these practices, not just their measurement, requires the effective capture of metrics. With respect to the provision of quantitative information, HR functions are often criticised for producing 'soft' and/or unintelligible data, which have little resonance with business decision-making and lack credibility.

Adopting a metrics reporting system that is more scientifically based, well presented and aligned with core business objectives helps to raise the profile of the HR function and increase its organisational impact. This is significant because corporate 'cost centres' are striving to transform themselves into strategic business partners. A persuasive argument for establishing business-focused metrics is that they enable HR practitioners to better converse in the language of business, by providing a basis for defining:

- key measures associated with the workforce,
- trends in performance, over time, as the metrics are tracked,

- measurable workforce outputs and areas of weakness or under performance,
- feedback about measurement methods and the metrics to be tracked and to determine appropriate interventions to address deteriorating achievement or underachievement.

Therefore the development of any reporting metrics needs to be based on the priorities of the strategic plan and objectives. These define the key business drivers and, in turn, provide the criteria for those metrics that managers most desire to monitor. Processes must also be designed to collate data relevant to the metrics and reduce them to numerical form for presentation and analysis. If the chosen reporting metrics are to be effective in informing and initiating improvements, action must follow analysis – there is little value in measuring and presenting performance data if this information is then not acted upon.

Adapting and applying the Balanced Scorecard concept

Key PHT business imperatives are the delivery of high-quality care to patients (the organisation's customers) and the achievement of financial surplus. The means by which the Trust has started to demonstrate the influence of good people management practices and robust workforce planning, in both these areas, is through the application of the 'Balanced Scorecard' concept. Concerned with both *measurement and* management, the Balanced Scorecard system enables organisations to clarify their vision and strategy and translate them into action. It provides feedback around both the internal business processes and external outcomes to continuously improve performance and results. Effectively deployed, the Balanced Scorecard is capable of transforming strategic planning from being a high-level academic exercise into the very fabric of any business enterprise (Kaplan and Norton, 1996). The Balanced Scorecard provides simple but effective answers to the questions: 'What must the organisation be doing to succeed?' and 'How can the organisation ensure every employee is working in the same direction, to achieve a common goal?' The generic Balanced Scorecard model recognises the importance of 'hard' financial measures of performance, but balances these by also defining the elements of performance that lead to those financial results, typically customer satisfaction, business processes and organisational capability. The rational link between these elements is that it is the organisation's workforce that designs, operates and continuously improves business processes to deliver customer services. This should ultimately result in positive, long-term financial performance. Hence, provided the 'inputs' are fully aligned with, and supporting the organisation's strategic aims, the 'outputs' (the business results) will be positive.

The application of the management concept associated with the Balanced Scorecard methodology to Human Resource Management supported the development of a 'Workforce Scorecard', the objectives of which were threefold, namely

- to align local workforce strategies and HR interventions with organisational goals,

- to measure the contribution of these strategies and interventions to improved organisational performance and patient and staff experience,

- to support efficiency improvements: increased productivity linked with financial improvement.

PHT metrics are associated with four key perspectives, or 'domains'. These domains are directly linked to the delivery of the Workforce Strategy and all directly influence the Trust's ability to achieve its business objectives, and all are interdependent. This interdependency, together with the strategic aims associated with measuring each of the four domains, is shown in Figure 21.2.

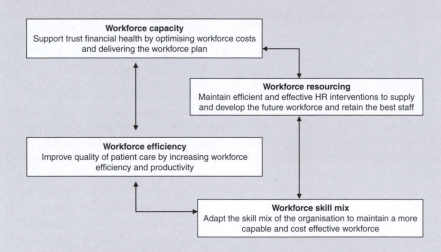

Figure 21.2   Workforce scorecard at Portsmouth NHS Trust

Determining the metrics

In determining the individual metrics to be included within each of the four domains, a systematic approach was taken. As an essential first step it was necessary to revisit the organisation's core business objectives, since these provide the anchor point for any reporting framework that aims to inform and support the process of continuous improvement. This analysis was conducted in parallel with a review of the Workforce Strategy, to ensure synergy between the two. Having established this alignment, the number and type of metrics to be reported on were carefully considered. Informed by the views of senior clinical staff and general managers, the collective advice at this stage was 'make it relevant and keep it simple'. This view supported the underpinning principle associated with scorecard methodology, which contends that data should be clearly presented and not overly complex. In other words the true value of the data lies in their relative simplicity and ability to focus on key measures that really matter. Therefore only those measures that could demonstrate the 'line of sight' with the achievement of the business objectives, and which could be presented in a straightforward manner and effectively benchmarked, were selected. Applying this testing process eventually reduced the number of key metrics to four within each domain. Broadly these are substantive workforce, temporary workforce, overtime, total workforce capacity, sickness absence, turnover, unit staff costs, workforce productivity, percentage of staff at particular bands/grades, by specialty (i.e. skill mix), percentage of professionally qualified clinical workforce, recruitment effectiveness, workforce stability, diversity profile and essential skills training.

While the organisation was accustomed to receiving data relating to those metrics within the scorecard that might be considered as 'routine' (e.g. sickness absence, turnover and workforce stability), other measures had not previously received attention. Hence, for the first time, a measure of the overall 'cost-effectiveness' of the workforce is being provided through both the unit staff costs and workforce productivity metrics. The latter is the product of the total monetary value of all health care delivered by the Trust, over the defined period, divided by the total workforce capacity for the same period and is defined as a monetary value. Supporting a much greater focus on improving workforce productivity through the redesign of services and traditional roles, the skill mix metrics provide an essential starting point for highlighting opportunities for redistributing/rebalancing skills across the organisation.

The real value of these new metrics will be realised as data are compiled and mapped, over time. Current data collation and analysis processes dictate that most metrics are historical, in that data are typically collated one month in arrears. This provides a good indication of overall organisational 'health', but has the disadvantage of potentially delaying timely intervention when problems arise. While likely to increase existing workloads, establishing additional processes to aid the provision and analysis of more real-time data remains a longer-term consideration.

Learning points

The success achieved, to date, is attributable to the preparatory work undertaken to ensure the scorecard reporting framework underpins the delivery of the core business objectives, and that those metrics associated with the four scorecard domains all directly impact on productivity and efficiency. One method of achieving this is to apply a rigorous testing process to each potential measure: this way the reporting metrics are likely to transform HR data into value-adding information that supports business improvement.

Activities and discussion questions

1. What employee activities in the organisation you work in or attend to study would contribute to the strategic purpose of that organisation and how could HR maximise these efforts to add value?

2. In the first Case, based on a Swiss organisation, identify how added value was achieved by the introduction of a flexitime system. What indicators

and measures were used to demonstrate that value had been added as a result of this HR intervention?

3. For the activities identified in (1) above, what measures/indicators could be employed to enable HR determine employee contribution towards organisational goals, that is added value?

4. Is the 'Workforce Scorecard' from a large UK public sector organisation described in the second Case a Balanced Scorecard or an HR Scorecard? Explain.

Notes

1. Caisse de compensation du Canton du Jura. www.caisseavsjura.ch.
2. A set of productivity indicators was available (quantity and complexity of the cases handled).

Bibliography

Baron, A. and Armstrong, M. (2007). *Human Capital Management: Achieving Added Value through People*. London: Koogan Page.

Barney, J. (1995). 'Looking inside for competitive advantage'. *Academy of Management Executive*, 9(4), 49–61.

Becker, B., Huselid, M. and Ulrich, D. (2001). *The HR Scorecard: Linking People, Strategy and Performance*. Boston, MA: Harvard Business School Press.

Beer, M., Spector, Lawrence, P.R., Quinn Mills, D., Walton, R.E. (1984). *Managing Human Assets*. New York: The Free Press.

Béland, P. and Piché, J. (1998). *Faites le bilan social de votre entreprise*. Montréal: Les Editions Transcontinental Inc et les Ed. de l'entrepreneurship.

Boxall, P. and Purcell, J. (2003). *Strategy and Human Resource Management*. Basingstoke: Palgrave Macmillan.

Brewster, C. (2004). 'European perspectives on Human Resource Management'. *Human Resource Management Review*, 14, 365–82.

Brockbank, W. and Ulrich, D. (2005). *The HR Value Proposition*. Boston, MA: Harvard Business School Press.

CIPD (2005). *Flexible Working: Impact and Implementation – An Employer Survey*. London: CIPD.

Crow, S. and Hartman, S. (1995). 'A constituency theory perspective of human resources effectiveness'. *Employee Relations*, 17(1), 38–50.

Davidson, L. (1998). 'Measure what you bring to the bottom line'. *Workforce*, 77(9), 34–40.

Emery, Y. (2003). *Renouveler la gestion des ressources humaines*. Lausanne: Presses polytechniques et universitaires romandes.

Emery, Y. and Gonin, F. (2006). *Dynamiser la gestion des ressources humaines*. Lausanne: Presses polytechniques et universitaires romandes.

Fitz-enz, J. (1984). *How to Measure HRM*. New York: McGraw Hill.

Fitz-enz, J. (1990). *Human Value Management*. San Francisco: Jossey-Bass Pub.

Fombrun, C.J., Tichy, N.M. and Devanna, M.A. (1984). *Strategic Human Resource Management*. New York: Wiley.

Guest, D., (1989). 'Personnel and HRM: can you tell the difference?'. *Personnel Management*, January, 49.

Guest, D., Michie, J., Sheehan, M., and Conway, N. (2000a). *Employment Relations, HRM and Business Performance: An Analysis of the 1998 Workplace Employee Relations Survey.* London: IPD.

Guest, D., Michie, J., Sheehan, M., Conway, N. and Metochi, M. (2000b). *Effective People Management.* London: CIPD.

Holbeche, L. (2008). *Aligning Human Resources and Business* (2nd edn.). Oxford: Butterworth-Heinemann.

Huselid, M. (1995). 'The impact of human resource management practices on turnover, productivity and corporate financial performance'. *Academy of Management Journal*, 38, 635–70.

Kaplan, R.S. and Norton, D.P. (1996). *The Balanced Scorecard.* Boston, MA: Harvard Business School Press.

Le Louarn, P. and Wils, T. (2001). *L'évaluation de la gestion des ressources humaines.* Paris: Editions Liaisons.

Leopold, J., Harris, L. and Watson, T. (2005). *The Strategic Managing of Human Resources.* London: Prentice Hall.

Mayo, A. (2001). *The Human Value of the Enterprise: Valuing People as Assets – Monitoring, Measuring, Managing.* London: Nicholas Brealey Publishing.

Patterson, M., West, M., Lawthorn, R. and Nickell, S. (1997). *Impact of People Management Practices on Business Performance.* London: Institute of Personnel Management.

Pfeffer, J. (1998). *The Human Equation.* Boston, MA: Harvard Business School Press.

Phillips, J. (1996). *Accountability in HRM.* Houston, TX: Gulf Publishing Company.

Pilbeam, S. and Corbridge, M. (2006). *People Resourcing: Contemporary HRM in Practice.* Harlow: Prentice Hall FT.

Purcell, J., Kinnie, N., Hutchinson, S., Rayton, B., and Swart, J. (2003). *Understanding the People and Performance Link: Unlocking the Black Box.* London: Chartered Institute of Personnel and Development.

Sung, J. and Ashton, D. (2004). *High Performance Work Practices: Linking Strategy and Skills to Performance Outcomes.* London: Department of Trade and Industry/Chartered Institute of Personnel and Development.

Ulrich, D. (1997). *Human Resource Champions: The Next Agenda for Adding Value and Delivering Results.* Boston, MA: Harvard Business School Press.

Ulrich, D. (Ed.) (1998). *Delivering Results.* Boston, MA: Harvard Business Review Book.

Ulrich, D. and Brockbank, W. (2005). *The HR Value Proposition.* Boston, MA: Harvard Business School Press.

Ulrich, D. and Losey, M. (1997). *Tomorrow's HR Management.* New York: Wiley.

Watson Wyatt Data Services. www.watsonwyatt.com (accessed 9 October 2007).

CHAPTER 22

Managing Change and the Role of HRM

David Hall, Amanda Harcus, Donna Bohnet and Gary Rees

Change continues to dominate the management landscape as organisations across all sectors respond to external and internal forces to deliver stakeholder expectations. The post-2007 banking crisis and the financial meltdown that followed have resulted in a period of accelerated change as organisations and governments attempt to respond to forces on a global scale. This chapter examines:

- Forces or 'drivers' of change and types of change,
- Management intervention in change and the role played by HRM,
- Two cases on HR involvement in managing change in public and service sector organisations.

The business of managing change

All organisations are in the business of managing change, regardless of the purpose, products and services they are involved in because managing organisations is the 'business' of managing change. In other words organisations are managing change continually as they react to the changing business environment. It is interesting to consider why 'change management' has been the subject of thousands of books, research papers and college management courses over the past 20 years when it is, fundamentally, about managing business. How well organisations manage change is a key determinant (and differentiator) in the sustainability and success of organisations, that is it is a source of competitive advantage or 'leverage' that determines outcomes. But it is important to recognise that change management is not a distinct discipline but is an integral part of managing organisations. However there will be situations where it is appropriate to make the issue of change more overt or explicit within an organisation, which we shall return to later.

Managing change is defined as 'a form of management control through the application of systematic management interventions that involve people to achieve a desired future state with defined performance outcomes in-line with the organisational strategy' (Hall and Rees, 2010: 99).

This definition highlights the inextricable links between change, strategy and performance. This definition also emphasises the involvement of people at all levels in organisational change, focusing attention on the role of HRM and line managers in facilitating change. It is useful for managers and academics to understand the characteristics of change in order to be able to develop and implement effective change management interventions. A good place to start is to consider the forces that drive change in the business environment.

Drivers of change

Drivers or forces of change are wide ranging and have a variety of sources. Drivers of change can be considered from an external environment perspective, and Aguilar (1967) presented 'ETPS' as a mnemonic to represent the four sectors: economic, technical, political and social. Variations of this include 'PEST' and 'PESTLE', which later added the legal and environmental dimensions. An example of such a taxonomy is shown in Table 22.1 below.

Table 22.1 Taxonomy of external change factors

Change driver	Typically considerations
Political	▪ Taxation and other policies ▪ Current and future political support ▪ Funding, grants and initiatives ▪ Trade organisations ▪ Internal and international relationships
Economic	▪ Economic situation ▪ Consumer spending ▪ Levels of government spending ▪ Interest rates, inflation and unemployment ▪ Exchange rates
Social	▪ Demographics and social mobility ▪ Lifestyle patterns and changes ▪ Peoples' attitudes and actions ▪ Media perception and influence ▪ Ethnic and religious differences
Technological	▪ Research, technology and innovation funding ▪ Consumer behaviour and processes ▪ Intellectual property ▪ Global communication technological advances ▪ Social networks
Legal	▪ Legislation in employment, governance, competition and health and safety ▪ Trading policies ▪ Regulatory bodies ▪ International protocols
Environmental	▪ Clean technologies and processes ▪ Waste management and recycling ▪ Attitudes of government, media and consumers ▪ Environmental legislation ▪ Global warming and emission protocols

The case based on change at Hampshire County Council later in this chapter identifies political and economic factors as the main driving forces of change affecting this organisation. It is not always external factors that trigger change; internal forces can also come into play, including:

- New leadership
- New strategy
- Restructuring
- Organisation growth
- Redesign of jobs
- Redesign of business processes
- Outsourcing
- Change of location
- Installation of new technology and systems
- Being acquired or merged with another organisation.

Although many of these factors can be linked with external forces, they can also influence internal management decisions that drive organisational change.

Types of change

It is helpful to be able to describe different 'types' of change because understanding this helps managers to make better decisions about the choice of interventions they might use. One typology of change is to consider the magnitude or scope of change and the timescale for achieving change. Hall and Rees (2010: 102) describe this as 'change momentum' and their model is presented in Figure 22.1 below:

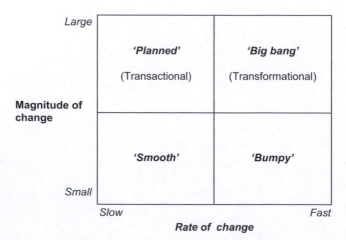

Figure 22.1   Change momentum

Change momentum is not always predictable but if it can be anticipated or defined, for example, by the scope of a change management programme, appropriate interventions may be considered from a range of options. 'Smooth' and 'Bumpy' change are both characterised by relatively small (and less complex) change but differing in speed (rate) of implementation, with 'Smooth' being slower to implement. Smooth change tends to occur in small steps and is often described as being 'incremental', allowing it to be managed as part of the day-to-day (operational) business of an organisation, for example, minor changes to policies and procedures would be examples of this type of change. This type of change is typically driven by internal factors.

'Bumpy' change is more noticeable as the speed of change is fast and requires a quicker response time by managers and employees to deal with it. This type of change is typically driven by external factors, which require faster response times. Examples of this would include organisations responding to crisis situations where significant investment or changes in policies and practices are required, for example, health, safety and the environment, regulatory reform or legal proceedings. Private sector companies involved in fast-moving markets frequently manage this type of change in response to changing consumer opinion and buying tastes. How quickly an organisation can respond in this type of business environment can be a source of distinct competitive advantage.

Grundy (1993) describes three types of change related to speed of change. The first is 'smooth incremental' change that evolves slowly in a systematic and predictable way. He also describes 'bumpy incremental' change as periods of relative calm punctuated by short bursts of fast change. The third type is 'discontinuous' change, which he describes as 'change which is marked by rapid shifts in strategy, structure or culture, or in all three' (Grundy, 1993: 26). This would equate closely with a 'Big Bang' change in terms of change momentum.

Grundy's 'discontinuous' change and 'Big Bang' change have many of the characteristics of what is often described as transformational change, that is an evolving process of change that requires changes in perception, attitudes and behaviours of the people that will ultimately influence the culture and direction of an organisation (see Organisational Development below). This type of complex change focuses on the commitment and engagement of employees with an emphasis on their contribution towards performance outcomes. Leadership that emphasises these employee attributes in managing change is described as 'transformational leadership' (Bass, 1985).

Hard and soft changes

The Open University (1985) describes two types of problems as *difficulties* and *messes*. Paton and McCalman (2000) used the terms 'hard' and 'soft' respectively to describe these same sets of problems, and they devised the 'TROPICS' test as a guide to help determine the nature of change in terms of a continuum from hard to soft (see Figure 22.2).

Many change programmes will have elements of hard and soft changes, and it is important to recognise that the TROPICS test is a continuum that includes both types of change. With knowledge and understanding of the issues involved when faced with change scenarios, managers are in a better position to respond by choosing appropriate interventions to control the change process.

'Hard'	'Soft'
Timescales clearly defined/ short-to-medium term	Timescales ill-defined/ medium-to-long-term.
Resources needed identified	Resources uncertain.
Objectives specified and quantified ('bounded')	Objectives subjective and ambiguous ('unbounded')
Perceptions of the problem shared by all	No consensus of problem
Interest in problem limited and defined	Interest in problem is wide-spread and ill-defined.
Control within managing group	Control is shared with people outside of managing group.
Source of the problem within organisation	Source of the problem is from outside the organisation.

Figure 22.2   The TROPICS test

Management interventions

There are a range of interventions available to organisations faced with managing change and the decisions about which to use are key to effective change management. Change management is contextual and situational, requiring a flexible approach, and it is also a dynamic and continuous process, which advocates a holistic and integrated approach. An example of this would be a relatively fast and well-defined 'bumpy' change occurring within a much slower 'big bang' or transformational change process, for example, a project or event occurring within a programme or long-term process. Therefore many organisations choose to employ a range of interventions that are integrated and complement each other, enabling managers to effectively manage different types of change, often at the same time, as part of the continuous management process.

Clearly such an approach requires a strategic perspective, which is why it becomes more difficult and, perhaps, less relevant for distinguishing between strategic management and change management when taking a long-term view. Strategic management and change management become easier to distinguish when considering change that is well-defined and shorter-term, which 'hard' types of change often are. Harder types of change are more suited to what many organisations describe as 'change programmes', which tend to be planned and systematic interventions. Such programmes comprise well-defined sequential steps driven forward in a project management style. This approach to change management has been criticised for being too linear and 'one dimensional', not taking into account the wider organisational factors. John Kotter's eight-stage change model for managing change is a well-known example of such an approach and has been used extensively to manage large change programmes (Kotter, 1996):

1. Establish a sense of urgency – *the need to change.*
2. Create a guiding coalition – *with authority and credibility.*

3. Develop a vision and strategy – *a clear aim and way forward.*
4. Communicate the change vision – *promote understanding and commitment.*
5. Empower broad-based action – *enable people to act and overcome barriers.*
6. Generate short-term wins – *to motivate and ensure further support.*
7. Consolidate gains and produce more change – *maintain change momentum.*
8. Anchor new approaches in the culture – *new values, attitudes and behaviours.*

There are several other change process models similar to Kotter's (e.g. Kanter, 1985) in which many of the stages are effectively the same in terms of the outcomes. This prescribed approach to managing change reflects an overriding unitarist paradigm, which assumes that managers and employees are aligned with the objectives of the organisations and offer minimal resistance, if any at all.

Organisational development

Another approach to managing change and improving performance is organisational development (OD), which is particularly appropriate for dealing with the 'softer' aspects of change. However it is important to remember that when managing change, organisations will apply a range of interventions, which can include planned programmes and OD. The following definition by French and Bell (1999: 25–26) highlights the holistic nature of OD and the emphasis on learning and team problem-solving, supported by a collaborative management approach to organisational culture:

> a long-term effort, led and supported by top management to improve an organisation's visioning, empowerment, learning and problem-solving processes, through an on-going, collaborative management of organization culture – with a special emphasis on the culture of intact work-teams and other team configurations, using consultant-facilitator role and the theory and technology of applied behavioural science, including action research.

OD is a process-based, multifaceted strategic intervention that focuses on the culture of an organisation to influence employee attitudes, values and behaviours which pervade all activities and interactions, that is the way things are done within an organisation. With an emphasis on learning and improvement at individual, group and organisational levels, using techniques such as action learning, it develops and sustains organisational change and performance capability through investment in people, that is the human capital of an organisation. This prepares organisations for dealing with continuous change by developing an enduring state of 'readiness' to deal with change rather than 'manage' it as a separate phenomenon.

Organisations that make OD part of their approach tend to have an ethos that encourages embracing change as a 'normal' way of doing business. These organisations tend to rely less on planned-change programmes but approach change as a normal part of everyday business. In the UK, the NHS has taken this approach, having undergone radical change and a multitude of 'change programmes' since the inception of the modernisation programme. The OD approach implies that normal business is about change and, dealing with change is implicit in what organisations and their people do. In other words, managing change is just 'business as usual'.

HRM's role in change

How employees, at all levels, respond to change is one of the most important factors in organisation sustainability and success. Organisations that manage change effectively add value in doing so, not just in terms of the tangible 'bottom line' but also of their intangible human capital asset, that is the capability of employees to contribute to the objectives of their organisations. HRM have a crucial role to play as 'strategic partners' and as change agents. The Business Partner concept (Ulrich and Brockbank, 2005) proposed that HR professionals *deliver value* to their organisations by fulfilling five roles: HR leader, strategic partner, human capital developers, functional experts and employee advocates. While there is much debate about to the extent to which HR professionals can effectively perform in all these roles, it is clear that these roles are important in leading and contributing towards managing change. The Business Partner model, with its multifaceted roles, has been questioned as a concept (Francis and Keegan, 2006) because of perceived compromises that the different roles imply. The Strategic Partner role is specifically about bringing HR expertise to their partnership with line managers to manage strategy and change.

Trust and fairness are important factors in managing change, particularly when dealing with resistance to change, and they feature at the heart of the 'psychological contract' (Rousseau, 1990): the tacit, unwritten understanding between managers and employees based on a set of mutual expectations. HR polices, including 'high-performance work practices' are described by Guest (2001) as being antecedent to an organisational culture that supports 'healthy' psychological contracts based on trust, fairness and delivery of 'the deal'.

The role of HRM in managing change is a significant and wide-ranging one encompassing strategic and operational activities. The Business Partner concept is helpful in framing these activities in terms of managing processes and people. The psychological contract is a useful concept for considering the dynamics involved when a change of expectations occurs and how this relates to individual organisational outcomes. The theories and models of change and of HRM help to inform organisations and managers to make good decisions about their choice of interventions so that the best outcomes will be achieved for all stakeholders. The first case below looks at research into the role of HR in managing change in several service sector organisations. The second case considers change in a large public sector organisation and the role played by HR in supporting managers and employees.

Influence of HR within change management in the service sector – case study research

The process of change is a multifaceted subject. Pettigrew (1988), cited by Buchanan, Fitzgerald, Ketley, Gollop, Jones, Lamont and Burnes (2009: 199), provides the following description of change:

> A complex and untidy cocktail of rational decisions, mixed with competing perceptions, stimulated by visionary leadership, spiced with power plays and attempts to recruit support and build coalitions behind ideas.

Change is endemic to organisations across public, private and not-for-profit sectors. This chapter focuses on change within the service sector. The UK's Office of National Statistics (2004: 4) reported: 'Service industries now dominate the UK economy. . . . Private sector services alone account for over 50 per cent of gross domestic product.' These figures are based on all businesses across the service sector, including the vendor/service provider companies.

The role of HR during change

The role of HR has changed over time; historically HR has 'reacted to perceived needs and pressures from stakeholder groups, both internally and externally to the organisation' (Ogilvie and Stork, 2003: 254). Ogilvie and Stork cite Ulrich's (1997) more up-to-date depiction of HR's involvement in change management as 'champions of change' and Caldwell's (2001) description of HR as 'transformative change agents'.

More recently the role and responsibility of HR during change programmes have shifted to a more 'strategic' position, a notion supported by Ogilvie and Stork (2003: 264–265), who discuss 'vertical linkage' between HR strategy and 'the business strategy', resulting in HR being 'directly aligned with managers' interests'. They identify that HR needs to either 'represent the interests of senior management, or "sell" the change by convincing senior managers that the change reflects their interests'. Furthermore they suggest that HR has been infused with 'two newer views of organisational change'. First adapting to external circumstances, the degree of fit between external and internal factors, and second, Human Resource Planning is anticipating or being proactive with respect to changing external events.

Similar parallels are drawn with the work produced by Ulrich and Brockbank (2005), who consider that the HR function needs to demonstrate its value through the following factors:

- Knowing external business realities,
- Serving external and internal stakeholders,
- Crafting HR practices,
- Building HR pesources,

The research and findings

Eight service sector companies were chosen at random from the London Telephone Directory. In-depth semi-structured interviews were conducted with all eight Company Directors. The Companies surveyed ranged from 105 to 3,700 employees, with a mean average of 760 employees. The research objectives were to analyse how these service sector companies approach change and the extent to which HR functions are involved in major change initiatives. The research design included a combination of in-depth semi-structured interviews, together with a focus group (comprising a range of managers and staff from one of the organisations represented).

Interestingly the Company Founder was still working in all the Companies surveyed, and played a major role in decision-making. All the founders maintained control and took responsibility for leading corporate strategies, reviewing costs and budgets, and acting as the main contact for senior clients. Just over a third of founders were responsible for staffing, with the founders of the three largest companies delegating responsibility for staffing. The nature of business for all eight companies related to meeting contractual agreements and managing client relationships, all through their employees' actions and behaviours.

Three categories of HR function emerged from the research:

1. *Internal HR:* half of the companies exemplified this, with half of these considering the HR function to be administrative/office support.

2. *External HR service:* 50 per cent used HR consultants for help and guidance for employment law/legal reasons and to avoid Employment Tribunals.

3. *No HR support.*

The need for organisational change was explored, with 62 per cent of companies quoting business survival, half quoting business growth and a quarter citing client-driven reasons. In terms of what actual *changes* took place, the following areas were identified:

- restructuring and HRM,
- business expansion,
- changes to policies,
- technological changes.

In preparing for change, all eight companies identified change agents and costs, and considered timescales. All but one of the companies identified materials needed for change and made consideration for the stakeholders. Half of the organisations surveyed considered possible resistance to change. Unsurprisingly there was a high correlation between organisations carrying out pre-change preparations and reported improvements or success as a result of the change process.

Throughout the change process, none of the Company Directors questioned stated that employees were a major consideration in change. However 87 per cent of companies were concerned with keeping contracts and winning new business. Interestingly companies that sustained substantial improvements incorporated team decisions and involved front-line managers in implementing the change(s). Where the Company Director was the sole driver of change, two-thirds of these companies achieved minor or no improvements.

Although HR was viewed primarily more as a support role rather than a strategic function within the service sector, where HR was involved in the change process the companies achieved 'substantial' or 'some' improvements; those not utilising HR only achieved minor improvements. With respect to the impact of the change intervention on the companies' employees, where the risk to employees was 'substantial', there was reported high resistance to change, and where risks were minimal the impact on the change planner was minor.

When considering factors that affected change plans, the following results emerged. First 83 per cent of companies expanded their communication strategies because resistance was brought on by employees not understanding the proposed changes. Second 75 per cent of companies that changed estimated timescales did so because of the resistance to the changes due to 'confusion', and recruitment problems. Third 25 per cent of companies' change plans were influenced by inadequate planning. Generally the companies that experienced resistance (deviations from their change plans) failed to assess the power/influence of their stakeholders in order to plan how to overcome any potential resistance.

The majority of the companies adopted a systems /unilateral approach to implementing change with 62 per cent ultimately attempting to force change through. All companies incorporated the following elements of the unilateral approach to change:

- changing behaviour to change attitudes,
- top-down,
- task/resource allocation focused.

The research identified that elements utilised from the systems approach had a more significant (positive) impact on the change outcomes, which is probably due to the 'type of changes' that the companies made. All companies made 'technical–structural' changes (mainly 'structural') and only one company also made 'behavioural–social' changes; interestingly that company had the most comparables to the participative approach to change.

In sustaining change, only 25 per cent of companies utilised positive reinforcement (i.e. financial incentives), out of which 50 per cent achieved substantial improvements and 50 per cent achieved minor improvements. Conversely 62 per cent of companies used negative reinforcement (i.e. threat of dismissal, disciplinary action and forced change), 80 per cent of which obtained substantial or some improvements.

Conclusions

1. Change is more effective when pre-change preparation has been completed. Stakeholder analysis, consideration of resistance to change and evaluation of change strategies are important to success.

2. Having a change plan in place is important, but of equal importance is the flexibility of planning in order to deal with contingencies.

3. Supervisors and line managers are important change agents within the service sector and need to be appropriately briefed, trained and skilled.

4. The importance of communication cannot be underestimated and is an essential tool in maintaining effective change. Fear and mistrust need to be tackled appropriately.

5. Despite the reliance on employee participation and commitment, employees accept that they are not the major consideration in change, and 'allow' this.

6. Punishment is predominantly utilised over rewards.

7. The reputation of HR within the service sector suffers credibility and is viewed as supportive rather than strategic.

8. During change interventions, HR's strengths lie in devising and supporting change rather than leading it.

The overarching conclusion is that HR needs to both be present and take an active (proactive) role at strategic, tactical and operational levels of change and demonstrate how they add value to business within the context of change.

Change management and HR in Hampshire County Council – a case study

For the past seven years the Government has awarded Hampshire County Council (HCC) a top rating for performance and quality of services. At the same time the Council has the lowest precept of county council tax in South East England. HCC seeks to become an 'employer of choice' and strives to provide 'value for money' for all residents across the county as shown in Figure 22.3 below. It employs circa 42,000 staff

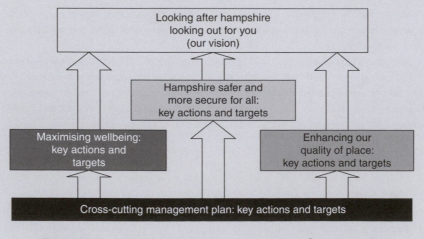

Figure 22.3   HCC strategic aims – corporate performance plan

(27,644 in schools) and is led by a non-elected Chief Executive and seven Directors of Services (Adult Services; Children Services; Culture, Community and Rural Affairs; Environment; Chief Executives, including HR; County Treasurers; and Property, Business, Regulatory and IT services). Services need to respond quickly and flexibly to change to ensure HCC achieves its long-term aims.

HCC adopted the Ulrich (1996) model of HR and established dedicated HR Business Partners (BPs) across the organisation to match each of the seven directorates. The role provides governance, guidance and strategic support to each departmental management team (DMT); in some cases the role is an integral part of the DMT. The role is critical to leading and managing people and organisational change requirements in relation to HR. Change in HCC is influenced by internal and external demands placed on services and also set by each DMT in response to modernising and changing service requirements.

HR has a five-year vision and people strategy with four associated key aims to enable HCC to achieve its corporate outcomes, as shown in Figure 22.4 below. In parallel HR developed KUDOS,[1] which establishes how HR teams should operate with each other, and their customers and staff, to deliver outstanding services. The Coalition Government requires significant financial and austerity measures of Local Authorities. HCC faces unprecedented changes due to skills shortages and the changing workforce profile, together with decreasing grant funding for service delivery, set against ever-increasing demands by residents.

Figure 22.4   Hampshire County Council's HR vision 2007–2012

This requires a workforce that is responsive, agile and flexible to change. In parallel HCC is committed to continually improving performance, providing greater efficiency and doing more with less, whilst modernising how it operates.

The HR issue

In recognition of the changing agenda and focus, HR introduced and utilised Business Partners and specialist centres. There are a total of 287 HR staff members to support the whole organisation, which is an approximate ratio of 1:132 HR to employees. This represents good value for money against benchmarked services.[2] HCC's HR Department is structured into the following functional sections:

- Employment Practice Centre: providing employee relations services (excluding schools), employment policies, procedures and guidance and trade union consultations;
- Resourcing Centre, providing all recruitment activities and support for HCC;
- Pay and Contract Support Services;
- Workforce Planning, Projects and Remuneration, providing performance data and analysis, setting and agreeing to national pay arrangements on behalf of HCC;
- Education Personnel Services providing end-to-end HR services for schools;
- Hampshire Learning Centre, providing consultancy, strategic direction for management leadership and corporate courses, including e-learning.

Initially HR was reactive to transactional HR demands from the organisation. To move towards a proactive approach, HR realigned and became more credible, through building its reputation, embedding improved delivery standards and focusing approaches in departments through both operational and strategic support, utilising a consultancy approach via its Business Partners and Heads of Centres. This has enabled HR to become pivotal in supporting the organisation to deliver its transformation and change agendas. Whilst the Ulrich model enabled better business understanding and higher levels of influence and strategic input at local and corporate levels, it has also created specialist centres with some limits in flexibility.

Over the past 12 months, significant changes have taken place. These include structural reviews to realign and review the full-time equivalent headcount, whilst introducing more flexible and smarter ways of working, requiring improved space utilisation such as 'hot desks', 'drop in stations' and, in addition, changing working practices. This is set against a context and organisation culture of being predominantly paternalistic, and generally risk-averse, within a traditional and hierarchical setting. Over the past two years HR has provided challenge and critical support to key senior managers to help shift and change some of the traditional elements that existed.

Three new challenges have emerged for HR during the past 18 months. First is HR's ability to support the scale of change required over the next two to three years within the current model of operation. Second is the organisational ability to manage and enable cultural change. Third is how to support the development of HR staff to ensure a consistent approach in how change is led, managed and coordinated. An example of how HR supports HCC to drive change and deliver efficiency has been a realignment of key HR policies to support a more modern way of doing business, enabling managers to make expedient decisions. HR has identified associated key saving areas thereby influencing the senior management team by making the business case for change. For example, a review of reimbursements, rationalisation of role profiles and pay grades and provision of high-level advice on organisation design have all demonstrated tangible financial savings.

The way forward

The strategic value HR provides in implementing strategies and transformation has contributed to the growing demand for strategic and operational HR requirements, and support for managers implementing change to meet local challenges. This is a continual challenge in a climate where HR is already lean and perceived to be delivering good value for money. HR reviewed its processes and ways of supporting across all sections and considered how it needed to support current and future change. In particular the need to be responsive and flexible and continue to successfully deliver HR services meant the model required further refinement. The Business Partners recognised that large-scale changes would impact on capacity, and the Employment Practice Centre (EPC) area needed to meet increasing demand for the delivery of strategic projects. EPC implemented a revised structure creating two hubs, one to focus on 'operational' activity and the other, a 'core' team, encompassing project, policy and business development functions. The new model enables EPC to maximise the flexible deployment of resources to meet the priority needs of customers and increases the effectiveness and responsiveness of the HR service to the business.

HR continuously reviews, develops and supports change programmes, thereby influencing the strategic and operational agenda and providing support at an organisational and a departmental level. Balanced against this, HR is striving for a climate in which HR staff are encouraged and supported in developing change skills and where strategic level planning is led by HR Business Partners and Heads of Centres. A change framework linking major change, improved workforce planning and the development of a manager's 'change toolkit' is a further example of what HR has developed. This has led to HR staff approaching organisational change issues and service reviews in a more consistent way. HR is a key influence within the Corporate Management Team and is involved in change at early stages to provide support, advice and robust challenge.

The HR learning points and next steps

There is a need to continually learn and develop from the changes, and the HR management team has identified some internal HR challenges that need to be addressed, namely

- An emerging gap between the level of operational HR staff understanding and the ability to link to wider HCC requirements; in part caused by the Ulrich model focusing on specialised centres and in part due to the need to 'join things up' for staff much more.
- The limited capacity of transactional and operational HR staff to take on more of a 'consultant' role, whilst providing advice and being able to initiate insightful questions.
- Balancing the 'policing' and compliance tendency of HR, through its legal and governance role, against enabling HR to translate activity into practical actions.
- Facilitating the flexible and appropriate deployment of HR resources across the business, utilising skills and knowledge of staff, and aligning them to activities.

HR is working hard to involve its staff through seeking engagement and commitment on key projects and utilising the change toolkits to aid collaborative approaches. The establishment of the HR Collaborative Working Group, the focus of which is 'to champion and drive the provision of a seamless service' and 'one' HR through sharing customer intelligence and aiding collaborative working, is supporting more effective sharing of information across HR staff, whilst also ensuring consistent practice. Opportunities need to be developed to enable HR staff to move across different sections of the business in order to broaden experience, skills and knowledge, and to provide stimulation and motivation for HR staff. HCC will seek to develop staff knowledge through improving commercial focus, embedding value-for-money strategies and continuing to develop a continuous improvement and sociable climate and culture aligned to the Corporate Strategy and HR vision.

Activities and discussion questions

1. What specific factors or forces have caused an organisation you have worked for, or your place of learning, to change aspects of its business? Have the origins of these forces been external or internal? *(Hint: see Table 22.1 Taxonomy of external change factors)*.

2. The world is constantly changing – discuss the key external drivers that are likely to influence organisational change in the private and public sectors over the next five to ten years.

3. Summarise the research findings discussed in Case 1, looking at HR in the service sector, focusing on the 'people' aspects of change and the role played by HR.

4. After reading Case 2 of this chapter, identify the challenges HR faced and the way in which HR changed to support Hampshire County Council.

5. Compare the role of HRM in managing change in Case 1 and Case 2. What conclusions can you draw based on this comparison, and what recommendations would you make regarding the role of HR in managing change?

Notes

1. HR Staff charter, Knowledge and Understanding to Deliver Outstanding Services, containing six keys to drive internal HR development, outline expectations of HR managers, staff and senior managers which will deliver the six keys.
2. Tested 2009 as part of Corporate Service Reviews.

Bibliography

Aguilar, F.J. (1967). *Scanning the Business Environment*. New York: Macmillan.
Bass, B.M. (1985). *Leadership and Performance beyond Expectations*. New York: The Free Press.

Buchanan, D., Fitzgerald, L., Ketley, D., Gollop, R., Jones, J.L., Lamont, S.S. and Burnes, B. (2009). *Managing Change* (5th edn.). Harlow: Financial Times/ Prentice Hall.

Caldwell, R. (2001). 'Champions, adapters, consultants and synergists: the new change agents in HRM'. *Human Resource Management Journal*, Special Issue, 11(3), 39–53.

Francis, H. and Keegan, A. (2006). 'The changing face of HR: in search of balance'. *Human Resource Management Journal*, 16(3), 231–249.

French, W.L. and Bell, C.H. (1999). *Organizational Development: Behavioural Science Interventions for Organizational Improvement* (6th edn.). Upper Saddle River, NJ: Prentice-Hall.

Grundy, T. (1993). *Managing Strategic Change*. London: Kogan Page.

Guest, D. (2001). 'International relations and human resource management', in Storey, J. (ed.), *Human Resource Management: A Critical Text* (2nd edn.). London: Thomson Learning, p. 107.

Hall, D. and Rees, G. (2010). 'Managing change', in Rees, G. and French, R. (eds), *Leading, Managing and Developing People*. London: CIPD, 97–124.

Hayes, J. (2010). *The Theory and Practice of Change Management* (3rd edn.). Basingstoke: Palgrave Macmillan.

Kanter, R.M. (1985). *The Change Masters: Corporate Entrepreneurs at Work*. London: International Thomson Business Press.

Kotter, J.P. (1996). *Leading Change*. Boston, MA: Harvard Business School Press.

Neath, A. and Whitby, E. (2005). 'No going back: A review of the literature on sustaining organizational change'. *International Journal of Management Reviews*, 7(3), 189–205.

Office of National Statistics (2004). *The UK Service Sector*. London: ONS.

Ogilvie, R.J. and Stork, D. (2003). 'Starting the HR and change conversation with history'. *Journal of Organisational Change Management*, 16(3), 254–271.

Paton, R.A. and McCalman, J. (2000). *Change Management: Guide to Effective Implementation* (2nd edn.). London: Sage.

Pettigrew, A.M. (1998). *The Management of Strategic Change*. Oxford: Blackwell.

Pettigrew, A. and Whipp, R. (1993). 'Understanding the environment', in Mabey, C. and Mayon-White, B. (eds), *Managing Change* (2nd edn.). London: Paul Chapman Publishing, pp. 5–19.

Purcell, J., Kinnie, N., Hutchinson, S., Rayton, B. and Stuart, J. (2003). *People and Performance: How People Management Impacts on Organizational Performance*. London: Chartered Institute of Personnel and Development.

Rousseau, D.M. (1990). *Psychological Contracts in Organizations: Understanding Written and Unwritten Agreements*. London: Sage Publications.

Senior, B. and Swailes, S. (2010). *Organizational Change* (4th edn.). Harlow: Financial Times/Prentice Hall.

Ulrich, D. (1996). *Human Resource Champions: The Next Agenda for Adding Value and Delivering Results*. Boston, MA: Harvard Business School Press.

Ulrich, D. (1997). *Human Resource Champions: The Next Agenda for Adding Value and Delivering Results*. Boston, MA: Havard Business Press.

Ulrich, D. and Brockbank, W. (2005). *The HR Value Proposition*. Boston, MA: Harvard Business School Press.

CHAPTER 23

More Effective Implementation of Strategic Change

Managing the change process

Marjorie Corbridge, Mark Power and Rebecca Kopecek

There are many important strategic development tools such as SWOT – TOWS, PESTLE, Porter's five forces analysis, the STEP model and Scenario planning, which have stood the test of time and have provided alternative ways of approaching the job of strategic planning, and these will not be rehearsed here. However according to Jackson

> Good strategies don't create value; it's implementing good strategies which creates value. But ... getting new business strategies successfully implemented can be really tough. ... You might think that implementing strategy in the corporate setting should be easy. The [leaders] in the corner offices simply lay down the plan, and the rest of the organisation gets into line, right? Actually, it doesn't work like that.
>
> (2011: 61)

Sterling (2003: 27) also contends that '... effective implementation of an average strategy beats mediocre implementation of a great strategy every time. ... Yet companies nonetheless often fail to operationalize their strategies in ways that improve the likelihood that they will be implemented effectively'. The common factor is not the development of the strategy that determines its success but rather the implementation of strategy and the need to manage the change effectively that are the key success factors. The common message from this is that whilst developing strategic business plans is important in ensuring the viability of an organisation it is from the execution of those plans that the real business benefits are derived.

Implementing strategic policy change

Effective implementation of strategic change involves a structured and well-managed approach to ensure that the right things are done at the right time. Raps (2005) identifies 10 critical points to address the difficulties that can emerge in implementation. First it is important to have the commitment of senior managers; one might expect that this is a given but experience shows that this is not always the case. As Raps says (2005: 141), 'senior executives must abandon the notion that lower level managers have the same perceptions of the strategy and its implementation, of its underlying rationale, and its urgency. Instead they should believe the exact opposite. They must not spare any effort to persuade the employees of their ideas'. All too often the managers charged with implementation at the local level are expected to take this on without the necessary knowledge and skills to do this effectively and also possibly without the commitment to the strategy to deal positively with issues raised by staff. The second point follows on from this, stressing the importance of involving the middle manager's valuable knowledge. Raps states (Raps, 2005: 141) that 'strategy implementation is not a top-down approach. The success of any implementation effort depends on the level of involvement of middle managers', and by involving them in the formulation of strategic policy by using their extensive knowledge of the organisation it is also possible to capture this and to use it as a catalyst for change in the implementation process. Third is the recognition that 'communication is what it is all about', and while studies indicate that this is a critical success factor in strategy implementation communication often happens too late in the process, and this failure may compromise the success of the implementation. It is also important to acknowledge that communication is a two-way process, and just informing people is not an alternative to giving employees the option to ask questions and to offer feedback. The fourth factor is defined by Raps as '[taking] an integrative view' which seeks to reflect that by focusing solely on the single strategic policy implementation without taking into account aspects such as organisational structure, and soft issues such as organisational culture and people issues, the success of the activity may be jeopardised. Fifth is the importance of assigning clear responsibilities. Any large-scale policy change is likely to mean that many people in many departments and functions become involved in implementation. Without clear assignment of responsibilities there is the potential for power struggles to take place in terms of the detail of implementation and to avoid this, a clear implementation plan must be drawn up, which identifies who is responsible for the detailed implementation activities. The sixth critical point is the importance of taking 'preventative measures against change barriers'. Barriers to change need to be identified and actions developed to address and remove the barriers if the implementation is to be effective. This will be discussed in more detail later in the chapter. Seventh is the emphasis on the importance of teamwork and of bringing together the most appropriate people in effective teams to maximise the positive impact on the implementation. To ensure that the most effective teams are built, many organisations use a typology such as the Myers–Briggs Type Indicator to ensure that the team gets the benefit of a range of personality types appropriate to the task in hand. As Raps points out (Raps, 2005: 143), citing Noble (1999),

'More than any other field of activity, implementation is the area that benefits most from a trained and personality sensitive management team'. The eighth point is to 'respect the individuals' characters'. Research shows (Lorange, 1998) that the employees in an organisation are critical to the success of implementing changes in policy and strategy and that they are also a key factor in failures of implementation. Employees reflect different personalities and exhibit different behaviours; they will respond in different ways to different management styles. This needs to be reflected in bringing together the key players in the team and in seeking ways to maximise the involvement and engagement of the staff. Nine is to 'take advantage of implementation tools' to support the processes that are put in place to manage the implementation. For example the balanced scorecard is a useful tool that allows a range of measures to be incorporated into the planning and implementation process. Making effective use of tools and techniques facilitates the monitoring process, making sure that the implementation stays on track and that key aspects of the implementation do not get missed. Finally it is important to factor in 'buffer time' or a contingency to allow for the unexpected. A planned implementation with an unachievable deadline puts everyone under pressure and increases the likelihood of failing to complete on time. It is good practice in any project to build in contingency and the implementation of strategic policy change is not an exception to this rule. While this may seem like a long list of considerations needed in planning implementation, it goes without saying that the implementation of a key strategy or strategic policy change needs to be managed carefully if it is to achieve its goals.

Strategic policy changes are normally initiated at Board level with the driver being the need to make the policy change to achieve a strategic objective. Brauer and Schmidt (2008: 655) examine the role of the Board in policy determination and implementation, and their findings are interesting, indicating that strategy 'unfolds continuously rather than being implemented in a single event... the time it took to realign its resource allocation with its announced strategy varied across the period'. This finding is worthy of further consideration as it seems intuitive that the implementation of a strategic policy change should consider any potential resource dislocation if it is to be successful. This resource mis-alignment should encompass the range of resources, including physical, financial and people resources. The resources that are in place to support a current policy may be at odds with what is required in the new situation, and therefore any implementation plan should examine the current resource allocation and mix and assess these against what will be needed to support the changed approach.

Managing organisational change

Implementing strategic policy changes is often a significant change management initiative within an organisation and therefore encompasses some of the techniques used in any change management activity. There are many tools and models to assist in the change management process, such as appreciative inquiry, the 7S matrix and critical path analysis; and it is inappropriate to review all of these here. However one of the most appropriate to use in strategy implementation is force field analysis. Thomas (1985) indicated that it was a tool that could provide new insights into the implementation and evaluation of corporate strategies. It is a simple practical tool that can be used in many different change situations and which, with regular use, can develop change management skills in the user. Force field analysis grew out of the work done by Lewin (1951), who suggests that organisations are not normally in a stationary state but may be moving at a pace in the same general direction for a period of time which he terms a 'stable quasi-stationary equilibrium' and that the organisation is held in that state by a balance of forces acting for or against change. Ford and Ford (1995: 2), cited in Hayes (2010: 43), explore this further and contend that 'the intentional management of change occurs when a change agent deliberately and consciously sets out to establish conditions that are different from what they are now'. Putting Lewin's model into practice, implementing a planned change requires that the behaviours creating the force field that is holding the organisation in the 'stable quasi-stationary equilibrium' should be changed either by adding to the forces acting for change or by reducing the resistant forces. Either of these actions can bring about change, but Heyes argues that

> where change is brought about by increasing the forces for change, this will result in increased tension [which] . . . may be accompanied by high aggressiveness, high [emotions] and low levels of constructive behaviour'. On the other hand, where change is brought about by diminishing the . . . [resistant] forces, the secondary effect will be a state of relatively low tension.
>
> (2010: 43)

This seems to indicate that in order to enhance the chance of a successful planned change programme, attention needs to be given to the forces acting against the planned change.

How to use the force field analysis change management tool

The force field analysis tool is best seen as an eight-stage process. The process takes the user through the steps in a helpful and constructive way, facilitating a structured approach and developing user skills and understanding. The process includes the following steps:

1. *Describe the change you want to make*: For example this can be articulating a new goal or a vision, examining a service you want to improve or implementing an agreed strategy at a local level. Whatever it is, be very clear about the reason behind the change and why it is needed.

2. *Describe the current situation*: this needs a careful analysis of the situation as it exists before the change and needs to include what works well in the current situation and what does not work well. This will help one to understand the forces at work in the '*stable quasi-stationary equilibrium*'.

3. *Describe the situation as you see it after the change (the desired state)*: this requires the change manager or team to build on the description in the first

stage of the process. This description should be as detailed as possible at this stage to provide a framework for communication to the stakeholders.

4. *Mind-map or list the driving forces for the change*: this means all of the forces that will impact positively on the change initiative. This can be a very extensive list and consideration needs to be given to the reason for the change and the resources available for the change, including financial, physical and people resources. It will be practically impossible to have a successful change programme if there is no budget, no location or no people with the required knowledge and skills to deliver the desired state. Record these on a template (see Figure 23.1 as an example).

5. *Mind-map or list the restraining forces for the change*: this requires all of the forces that will impact negatively on the change initiative. As above this means a thorough review of all aspects of the workplace that might inhibit change. Record these on the template.

6. *Evaluate the driving and restraining forces*: to do this rate each force out of five, with one being a weak force and five being a strong force. This requires objective consideration of each force and it needs to be done either by a person with detailed knowledge of the organisation or perhaps more effectively by a small team drawn from different parts of the business to help to get a more balanced assessment. Total the scores for in one column and those against in the other column.

7. *Review the outcome of the scores*: identify where there are opportunities to act on the forces to increase the likelihood of success. It is worth recalling here that research shows that acting to increase the scores of the positive forces may get a better outcome than acting on restraining forces. This means that this is probably where to start.

8. *Develop the strategy for implementation*: This requires a detailed examination of each force and an action agreed to have the desired impact on the force. There are many options for action, including communication, training and development, employee engagement initiatives, mentoring, resource planning, systems of work and process planning, technology, etc. Important at this stage is to be open and honest about the changes and to engage those affected with the decision-making.

The case studies

The following two case studies provide a valuable framework for looking at the issues associated with implementation of a strategic policy change, including how the change is managed and how the implementation process is handled to ensure a successful and effective outcome is achieved. These are practical actual initiatives that were implemented not just in the Portsmouth Hospitals Trust but across the NHS as a whole. They demonstrate the importance for the managers within organisations of using their knowledge and developing their skills to enable them to handle strategy implementation. The first study looks at the Agenda for Change initiative, which was a pay harmonisation process bringing

Figure 23.1 provides the following template:

Template for force field analysis of strategic policy implementation

Describe the change you want to make, including the reasons for change:

Describe the situation before the change:

Describe the situation after the change:

Situation before the implementation	Driving forces →	Score	Score	←Restraining forces	Situation after the implementation
		Total		Total	

Figure 23.1   Template for force field analysis of strategic policy implementation

together onto a single pay spine many of the workers in the NHS (it excluded doctors, dentists and some senior managers). Agenda for Change replaced the previous system of Whitley Councils, which covered the pay and terms and conditions of much of the NHS workforce. It was a strategic policy change on a vast scale requiring that the NHS Trusts and other NHS employing bodies implement the change. This is a major change, which required agreement across a range of professional bodies and trade unions. This in itself was a challenge but at a local level its success is measured by the perceptions of those affected by the change and the outcome on a personal level. The second study considers the introduction of the Electronic Staff Record (ESR) across all NHS organisations, which was completed successfully in 2008. This initiative was one of the world's largest IT implementations, and it was completed on time and on budget and seen as a major success story for the NHS. While each of these studies deals with a strategic policy change, which was devised outside the local NHS employing organisation, they were implemented at a local level and therefore required careful local implementation planning, with systems and processes devised to ensure success.

Managing the change process: NHS Agenda for Change and implementation of pay reform – a case study

Portsmouth Hospitals Trust (PHT)

PHT is one of the largest acute trusts in the country, providing emergency, general and specialist care to more than 250,000 people each year. With over 7000 staff, a turnover of £360 million and a track record in achieving national access targets and financial balance, PHT has maintained its position within the top 40 performing hospitals for the past five years and has been invited to apply to become a Foundation Trust (FT) from April 2007. PHT's 10-year HR Strategy received Trust Board approval in late 2002 and has established a challenging work programme that is firmly aligned to the Trust's overall corporate objectives, and has recognised that establishing excellent people management interventions is vital to the organisation's continued success. Consistent with the broader tenets of the HR in the NHS Plan, the key themes associated with the Trust's local HR strategy all support the aim of establishing PHT as a recognised model employer, with respect to the attraction, recruitment, development, retention and reward of its multi-professional staff.

The NHS Pay Reform Agenda – radical change required

In 1999 NHS pay modernisation proposals highlighted the need to, first, remove artificial barriers between professional/occupational groups; second, address equal pay; and third, improve low pay. Following national negotiations involving the four UK Health Departments, the NHS Confederation (representing NHS employers) and over 20 trade union and representative bodies, the new 'Agenda for Change' terms and conditions were agreed to in 2002. The new pay structure consists of only nine national pay bands to reward staff for the work they actually undertake and the skills and knowledge required for their particular role. Career enhancement and associated pay progression within the bands are to be linked to the NHS Knowledge and Skills Framework (KSF), managed through regular appraisal and personal development planning. Piloting of the new system in 12 'early implementer' sites preceded national rollout, which commenced in late 2004. Since then NHS HR professionals have been leading a radical change management initiative to modernise the biggest pay system in Europe, affecting over one million employees. Agenda for Change delivers the most comprehensive overhaul of pay and terms and conditions for all directly employed staff (with the exception of doctors, dentists and the most senior managers at the board level) since the inception of the NHS, nearly 60 years ago. Pre-existing pay and grading structures were outdated, inflexible and failing in terms of awarding equal pay for work of equal value. These structures had evolved under Whitley Council Agreements and local trust contracts.

Agenda for Change is one of three distinct pay reform programmes that also included new rewards and incentives for hospital consultants and for general practitioners. These programmes underpin service modernisation and represent a key element of the NHS human resources strategies. The 'HR in the NHS Plan' establishes the overarching workforce objectives as increasing capacity, quality and productivity across all areas of the Health Service and is built on four main pillars:

- Establishing the NHS as a model employer,
- Ensuring the NHS provides a model career, through offering a Skills Escalator – essentially transferring skills down through the organisation,
- Improving staff morale,
- Building people management skills.

Agenda for Change supports these pillars by promoting the main principles of pay reform as:

- Simplification – a single pay system,
- Fairness – pay transparency and harmonisation of terms and conditions, including hours, leave and overtime,
- Rewards – directly linked to skills and knowledge.

Essential foundation activities for managing the change

Local implementation of Agenda for Change represented the biggest single project to be undertaken in PHT's recent history. From the outset, the Trust recognised a unique opportunity to improve patient care by introducing a different way of approaching staff career planning and progression and of managing the employment relationship. Therefore it was vital the initial task of implementation was conducted in a planned, structured, affordable and transparent way that would secure the confidence of staff and provide the cornerstone for realising future benefits, both for employees and for patients. Although predominantly HR-led, the process of implementation needed to include the active engagement of key stakeholders and, prior to any detailed work being undertaken, five essential foundation activities were completed:

Project scoping: Initial scoping of the project demonstrated the complexity of the work involved, with the need for changing the terms and conditions of 6,500 staff within a demanding time frame (nine months) and concurrent with the requirement to achieve other national targets. Clearly in order to satisfy all demands, a well-defined project structure and dedicated project team were required. Furthermore work through collaborative partnership, both with PHT staff representatives and with partner primary care trusts (PCTs), was an essential success criterion.

Collaboration: Early collaboration with local PCT HR colleagues included the submission to the Strategic Health Authority (SHA) of a detailed joint business plan and project initiation document. This partnership approach continued throughout implementation, in the form of a monthly pan-organisation project leads' forum that supported consistency of application and knowledge sharing within the local HR network.

Project planning and steering groups: The project plan identified the various work streams associated with implementation and established the membership of the Project Board, which included the HR Director, Deputy Finance Director, project leader and key staff and trade union representatives. The remit of the Project Board was to monitor progress against key milestones, assess risks and appraise the Trust Board. Steering groups were established to oversee the main work streams, including partnership work and communication, job description collation, job evaluation, terms and conditions harmonisation and administration.

Communications strategy: A comprehensive communications strategy was initiated early in the preparatory phase. Line managers were a key group in which to raise awareness of the job evaluation process, and of the need to validate and submit accurate job descriptions. The project team used every available means to communicate with line managers and staff groups, including a programme of 'road show' events, invitations to regular team meetings and one-to-one briefings. Each member of staff was issued a concise briefing booklet, which, combined with regular update bulletins and the establishment of a dedicated intranet site, including frequently asked questions and a help desk, provided an effective method of communication. Essentially the project team aimed to demystify the implementation process, to tackle any misconceptions and to allay suspicions.

Job evaluator expertise: one manager and one trade union representative were trained as nationally accredited Agenda for Change job evaluators. Having undertaken this training, both were seconded to the SHA to conduct roll-out training across the region, including within PHT. The funded secondment arrangement ensured the newly acquired skills of the two evaluators were further developed. Volunteers were sought within PHT to undertake 'second generation' training and almost 100 members of staff became locally accredited job evaluators.

Key success factors

Time invested in these foundation activities was fundamental to ensuring the project was adequately resourced and supported, and that the Trust was able to effectively move staff on to the new pay system. The robust structures, processes and clear objectives established at the forefront of the project secured the engagement and involvement of key members of staff, who continued to work effectively in partnership throughout implementation. These partnerships also ensured that efficient and pragmatic handling strategies were in place to deal with unforeseen issues that inevitably arose during the main project phase, without recourse to more formal procedures. In this sense although this challenging project was HR-led, the task was very much 'owned' by a wider community within the organisation. Undoubtedly this aided the overall success of the project locally. When implementing radical pay reform the advice is to consider the five foundation activities of *project scoping, collaboration, project planning and steering groups, communications strategy* and *job evaluator expertise*.

Modernising and integrating payroll and HR systems: benefits and impact at Portsmouth Hospitals NHS Trust – a case study

The local health economy

Portsmouth Hospitals Trust (PHT) is one of the largest acute trusts in the country, providing emergency, general and specialist care to more than 250,000 people each year. With over 7000 staff, a turnover of £360 million and a track record in achieving national access targets and financial balance, PHT has maintained its position within the top 40 performing hospitals for the past five years and has been invited to apply to become a Foundation Trust (FT) from April 2007. Primary Care Trusts (PCTs) have been undergoing significant changes, and within the local area there are three – Portsmouth City Teaching Primary Care Trust, East Hampshire Primary Care Trust and Fareham and Gosport Primary Care Trust. The 'patch' is completed by the Isle of Wight NHS Trust and its associated PCT. Combined, this local health economy has a payroll of 20,000, which is provided by Hampshire Shared Business Services.

The Electronic Staff Record (ESR) and why it was needed

The Electronic Staff Record is the 'world class', national, integrated HR and Payroll system currently being introduced in all 600 plus NHS organisations throughout England and Wales. One of the largest ICT implementations ever, ESR was developed and is being delivered by a consortium of companies. A Central Team, responsible for design and implementation, comprises both consortium and NHS staff. ESR will replace the 29 Payroll and at least 38 HR Resource systems currently used in the NHS and will pay approximately 1.2 million employees (7 per cent of the working population in England and Wales) when fully established. Extensively piloted across 39 NHS trusts, covering 108,000 employees, complete national 'roll out' is being managed in 12 waves of about 50 Trusts every 2 months. While supporting Payroll and HR functions with traditional accountabilities, ESR also enables devolved HR, employee self-service and manager access, whilst permitting management reporting at local, supra- and national levels. Prior to ESR most existing systems required double-entry transactions, which was labour-intensive and time-consuming. Development of the ESR system presented an opportunity to reduce inefficiencies, streamline the HR administration/payroll interface and provide the timely and accurate information that is necessary to inform strategic decision-making. From a national perspective, the range of different and incompatible administrative systems that existed across NHS organisations sustained high levels of licensing and maintenance costs and hindered central reporting and benchmarking of data. PHT also recognised the opportunity presented by ESR (the introduction of which immediately followed the implementation of a new staff pay and reward system) to encourage greater devolution of routine HR transactional activity to line managers and even individual employees. These considerations demanded that the ESR programme was viewed as a key component of the Trust's plans to improve overall service delivery and workforce productivity.

Essential foundation activities for managing the change

Local implementation of ESR represented the biggest single change management project to be undertaken by the Portsmouth patch. Therefore it was vital for the task to be conducted in a planned, structured and transparent way in order to deliver the new system on time and within budget. Securing the confidence of staff was equally important to ensure ESR provided the cornerstone for realising future benefits for all the partnership organisations. Although predominantly HR led, it was essential that the process of implementation included the full engagement of other key stakeholders, particularly the finance and ICT teams. Four key areas of work were:

Project planning and profile: Drawing on the experiences of several early pilot sites, the project plan identified the various work streams associated with implementation and established the Project Board. Chaired by an HR Director, the Board's membership included Director-level representation from each of the other patch organisations and from the Strategic Health Authority (SHA), which manages the performance of local trusts. The remit of the Project Board was to monitor progress against agreed key milestones, assess risks and regularly appraise the various organisations' Executive Boards. This signalled the importance of the project and ensured it received sufficient senior-level attention. An implementation group was established to oversee the project detail and manage the associated work streams.

Technicalities and initial training: The NHS Central Team provided the patch with a Project Manager to oversee the technicalities of switching to a fully integrated HR/payroll system. A key activity involved data cleansing, prior to partial and then full migration. An iterative process, this demanded the painstaking checking and updating of staff records, which continued throughout the life of the project, until confidence levels were sufficiently high to support data transfer. Concurrently with this activity, an equally important task involved the training of sufficient numbers of users to ensure the new system was sustainable from the outset. The 'trained trainer' concept was deployed within the core HR administration, payroll and finance teams.

Collaboration: Strong and effective collaboration amongst the patch organisations underpinned the successful delivery of the project and began with the submission to the SHA of a detailed joint business plan and project initiation document. This early work was essential in providing top-level assurance that the scope of the project was sufficiently well understood and the associated work streams adequately resourced. Regular meetings of the implementation group ensured problems were identified and addressed early, and provided an effective vehicle for knowledge sharing.

Communications strategy: A comprehensive communications strategy was initiated early in the preparatory phase. The project team used every available means to communicate with line managers and staff groups, including a programme of 'road show' events, a staff information letter, regular updates in organisations' newsletters and frequent briefings for staff representatives. The provision of a dedicated help desk proved a successful method by which to answer particular individual queries.

Benefits and impact of ESR

Besides the advantages and economies associated with a national integrated HR Payroll system, ESR implementation should deliver real benefits for staff management at the local operational level. Already the immediate benefits of full HR/payroll integration, with single entry and the automation of many previously manual transactions, are apparent. As the system becomes more embedded and staff better skilled in its use, other business performance benefits will include:

- improved workforce planning, through the provision and presentation of more accurate and timely data;

- better local management of staffing issues, as all operational areas will have direct access to essential employee information, such as work rosters, attendance records and skills profiles (in time ESR anticipates also incorporating occupational health and risk management modules);

- more effective career management, through the provision of an electronic staff appraisal and personal development planning tool and better recording of competence information;

- improved staff training and development, derived from streamlined administration, accurate recording of training and development activities, self-service booking of training courses and integration with e-learning programmes.

Perhaps one of the most significant benefits will be derived from greater devolution of administrative HR activities to line managers and, where appropriate, to individuals – 'self service HR'. This will release the operational HR resource to better concentrate on organisational development activities that support the realisation of local business objectives. With increased devolution of HR inputs comes challenge, principally in the form of the raised expectations for managers to compile and maintain accurate staff records, to derive reports and act on the data provided. Consequently some traditional roles will need to be redefined and managers adequately trained and empowered to assume greater responsibility and accountability for the staff they directly manage. The impact of these changes should not be underestimated and must be managed both effectively and sympathetically, and fully supported by HR teams. Without such support, change is unlikely to be either effective or sustainable as, ultimately, additional routine HR activity will be 'devolved upwards' by concerned and/or confused line managers. On a national scale, the benefits derived from ESR will be even greater as, for the first time in its history, the NHS is supported by the integration of data and processes across all its organisations. Any administrative data will need to be entered just once, but can thereafter be accessed and used as part of any of the processes, subject to security and privacy safeguards. The resultant reduction in the duplication of effort will realise significant time savings and make the management and reporting of NHS staff information far more consistent.

Conclusion and learning points

As in all major change management initiatives, time invested in the foundation activities was fundamental to ensuring the project was adequately resourced and supported, and that HR, payroll and finance partners were able to effectively introduce a new integrated system on time and within budget. However the important message is that in order to achieve real benefits from the implementation of new technology, the impact on its users must be fully appreciated and the associated implications effectively managed. To gain the most from the ESR system implementation, the key local challenge is to ensure it supports new ways of working and thereby helps improve organisational performance and workforce productivity.

Activities and discussion questions

1. Identify a strategic change that has taken place within your organisation in the past year. Use the 10 critical implementation points discussed in the chapter to review the effectiveness of the implementation and highlight the strengths and weaknesses of your implementation. Present your findings to your group or to your management team and use these to consider how you might do things differently next time.

2. Select one of the case studies and examine the key activities that were considered essential by the Portsmouth Hospitals Trust before the process of implementation was finalised. In a small group examine these 'foundation activities', identify the key features of each and comment on why it was considered that it was essential that these activities be completed prior to any detailed implementation work was done.

   Discuss these within the group and be prepared to feed back your findings to other groups.

3. Identify a change that is taking place at your place of work. Use the Force Field Analysis template (Figure 23.1) to:

   - describe the situation before the change;
   - describe the change you want to make;
   - describe the situation after the change;
   - identify and score the forces acting against the change;
   - identify and score the forces acting to support the change;
   - describe **in detail** the actions you will take to minimise the forces against change and also the actions you will take to maximise the forces for change.

Report back on the issues experienced in using the tool. What did you find difficult? What did you find easy to do? To what extent do you understand why some aspects were easier than others and what can you do to enhance your knowledge and understanding of planned change management?

Bibliography

Alban, B. and Bunker, B.B. (2009). 'Let your people take you higher'. *People Management* February: 22–5.

Allen, J., Jimmieson, N.L., Bordia, P. and Irmer, B.E. (2007). 'Uncertainty during organizational change: managing perceptions through communication'. *Journal of Change Management* 7(2): 187–210.

Allio, M.K. (2005). 'A short, practical guide to implementing strategy'. *Journal of Business Strategy* 26(4): 12–21.

Brauer, M. and Schmidt, S.L. (2008). 'Defining the strategic role of boards and measuring boards' effectiveness in strategy implementation'. *Corporate Governance* 8(5): 649–60.

Burnes, B. (2004). 'Kurt Lewin and the planned approach to change: a reappraisal'. *Journal of Management Studies* 41(6): 977–1002.

Burnes, B. (2009). *Managing Change*. Harlow: FT Prentice Hall.

CIPD (2006). 'HR and technology: beyond delivery'. *Change Agenda Report*. June.

Ford, D.J. and Ford, L.W. (1995). 'The role of conversation in producing intentional change in organisations'. *Academy of Management Review* 20(3): 571–600.

Getz, G., Jones, C. and Loewe, P. (2009). 'Migration management: an approach for improving strategy implementation'. *Strategy and Leadership* 37(6): 18–24.

Hayes, J. (2010). *The Theory and Practice of Change Management*. Basingstoke: Palgrave Macmillan.

Jackson, S.E. (2011). 'Reaching for value: making strategies stick'. *Journal of Business Strategy* 32(1): 61–3.

Kaplan, R.S. and Norton, D.P. (2001). *The Strategy Focused Organisation: How Balanced Scorecard Companies Have Thrived in the New Business Environment*. Boston: Harvard Business School Press.

Lewin, K. (1951). *Field Theory in Social Science*. New York: Harper and Row.

Lorange, P. (1998). 'Strategy implementation: the new realities'. *Long Range Planning* 31(1): 18–29.

Noble, C.H. (1999). 'Building the strategy implementation network'. *Business Horizons* 42(6): 19–28.

Pascale, R.T. and Sterin, J. (2005). 'Your company's secret change agents'. *Harvard Business Review* 83(5): 72–81.

Raps, A. (2005). 'Strategy implementation – an insurmountable obstacle?' *Handbook of Business Strategy* 6(1): 141–6.

Schein, E.H. (1996). 'Kurt Lewin's change theory in the field and in the classroom: notes towards a model of management learning'. *Systems Practice* 9(1): 27–47.

Speculand, R. (2009). *Beyond Strategy: The Leader's Role in Successful Implementation*. San Francisco: Jossey Bass.

Sterling, J. (2003). 'Translating strategy into effective implementation: dispelling the myths and highlighting what works'. *Strategy and Leadership* 31(3): 27–34.

Thomas J. (1985). 'Force field analysis: a new way to evaluate your strategy'. *Long Range Planning* 18(6): 54–5.

www.dh.gov.uk/PolicyAndGuidance/HumanResourcesAndTraining/ModernisingPay/AgendaForChange/

CHAPTER 24

Strategic People Management in an International Context

The challenges of managing international assignments

Stephen Pilbeam and Liza Howe-Walsh

International assignments

International assignments are a high-cost method of resourcing staff in overseas locations, with the cost to the organisation often exceeding £250,000 per annum per assignment (Black and Gregersen, 2007). However the need for global mobility of employees continues to receive significant focus in multinational organisations, with not one of the 53 organisations surveyed anticipated reducing the number of expatriates during 2010 (RES Forum Survey, 2010a). It is apparent that, irrespective of the prevailing financial climate, organisations cannot postpone the requirement to become ever-more global. The selection and management of employees for international assignments plays an important role in enabling international organisations to compete effectively in an international arena. This chapter explores the strategic people management challenges for organisations involved with assigning and managing overseas expatriate employees.

Organisations that operate in an international arena may need to consider an international assignment to resource an overseas vacancy, and strategic people management activity is crucial to achieving successful outcomes. Three key reasons for utilising international assignments are to fill a vacant position, to develop global competences in the management team and to acquire and transfer knowledge within a foreign subsidiary (Dowling and Welch, 2004; Tarique and Caligiuri, 2004; Vance, 2005). Whilst resourcing a vacant position is a primary aim, the assignment provides opportunities for the individual to develop their knowledge and skills, to gain international experience and to develop a global mindset. The assignee may perceive the assignment as an opportunity for career advancement or may be motivated by the financial incentives. Managing successful international assignments requires giving thought to the challenges faced by both the assignee and the organisation, and a clear international assignment policy will promote a transparent and consistent approach.

The overseas assignment lifecycle includes different types of assignments:

- *Full international assignments*: normally over a year in duration, where typically the assignee is accompanied by a partner, increasing the housing and living allowance costs.
- *Short-term assignments*: which are generally less than a year in duration and are often unaccompanied, thus reducing the costs.
- *Virtual assignments*: where the employee manages a global team, involving extensive travel and reliance on information technology.
- *Business travellers*: frequent flier/commuter assignments undertaken by employees who frequently travel for business.

Whilst all types of assignment have their own challenges, the focus here is primarily on full international assignments.

Selecting assignees

According to Harris and Brewster (1999) selection often takes place informally during discussions based on opportunistic office conversations, such as 'we need to find a systems person to replace the current assignee in Chicago...have you heard about the person on the second floor, she is a whiz with systems?' Selecting an assignee requires more care and attention when compared with the organisation's domestic selection procedures, because the selection of expatriate workers is a more complex task. This is because predicting performance in a foreign environment adds an additional layer of uncertainty. The questions to be answered are:

1. How can the organisation be sure that, in addition to the technical competencies required for the overseas assignment, the employee has the right behavioural competencies such as adaptability, flexibility, conflict resolution skills, questioning and listening skills, cross-cultural awareness, communicative ability, influencing skills, emotional maturity, self-motivation and resilience?

2. What are the key drivers for accepting the international assignment and the potential barriers, and how receptive will the employee be to an assignment?

Clearly the organisation needs to define and assess both the job-specific and the behavioural competences required for a particular international assignment and then select against the identified criteria. The CIPD (*International Resourcing and Recruitment*, 2011) notes the increasing use of psychometric assessment and assessment centres in the selection of employees for international assignments to improve the predictive validity of the process.

A significant assignee concern, and a potential barrier to undertaking an expatriate assignment, is the effect it will have on their family, with up to half of all assignments being refused for this reason. Providing partner assistance and continuity of schooling are crucial and supporting the partner in terms of job hunting, work permit assistance, training and development as well as additional allowances are all important features that can enhance the chances of a successful assignment.

Assignee failure

The complexity of expatriate selection and predicting future performance of employees are particularly challenging, and the key questions are – What can be done to facilitate expatriate adjustment and what can be done to avoid the high cost of expatriate failure? The costs of failure are both direct in terms of pay, training, travel and relocation, and indirect in terms of poor job performance, premature return, damaged customer relations, impact on market share and impaired reputation. Reasons for assignee failure include:

- Poor assignee selection,
- Inability of the assignee, or partner, to adjust,
- Other family-related issues – childcare, schooling, health care provision,
- Assignee's lack of motivation, competence, cultural awareness, language proficiency *inter alia*,
- The expatriate's 'quality-of-life' experience,
- Lack of organisational support for the assignee,
- Insufficient training,
- Inadequate pay and rewards – extrinsic and intrinsic,
- Lack of repatriation guarantees – position, rewards, timing, support, re-integration programme and involvement in decisions.

In addition to the technical expertise and the behavioural competencies identified above, the assignee needs to be flexible, to tolerate ambiguity, to be sociable, to be empathetic and to have good communication skills, as well as be open to new experiences – it all sounds a tough call!

Assignee support and adjustment

Whilst sophisticated selection processes enhance the potential for international assignment success, the support provided to employees is critical. Many support mechanisms can be utilised for the assignee and their family. The organisation can provide home and host links for the assignee before the assignment begins, and pre-assignment trips to properties, schools and local amenities are important in establishing initial support. Local relocation agent expertise during a pre-assignment trip includes pre-selecting houses and schools and assisting with local registration documents, such as health and social security. Furthermore the relocating agent provides continuity on arrival for the assignee, supporting settling into the new home and dealing with local queries. Other supporting activities include cultural briefings and language lessons, and assistance with pay and financial arrangements. Cultural briefings help to focus on the key cultural differences faced by the assignee. Assignments often perceived to be relatively close in culture, such as the UK to the US, still require a cultural briefing. Providing advice on coping strategies can lessen or shorten the effects of culture shock. Stahl and Caliguri (2005: 611) suggest that coping strategies are influenced by factors such as host country, position and time on assignment. Important decisions need to be made in terms of the reward structure, particularly – will it be based on that in the home country or the host country? Many factors influence the appropriateness of the pay and rewards, and these include the cost of living, housing, health care, education of children, local taxation and currency fluctuations. An International Assignments Manager can support the host line manager to provide a clear focus for tasks and to support social integration and cultural adjustment. Sometimes neglected whilst on an international assignment is the link to the home organisation, and in addition to the International Assignments Manager it can be valuable to appoint a person of senior standing to the role of sponsor. The sponsor would be involved in the determination of the terms of the assignment, have an interest in the assignee's career development during the assignment and be crucially involved in the repatriation to a suitable position on the assignee's return, particularly because the first year after repatriation is the most likely time that an assignee will leave the organisation (Gribben, 2006).

Some or all of the elements of selecting and managing an assignment can be outsourced. Outsourcing provides particular specialist services that may not be readily available within the organisation, for example securing work permits, tax advice and assignment costings, assignee selection and repatriation services. An external provider can design international policies and processes to be managed within the organisation. There are cost implications to outsourcing and invariably it will depend on the volume of assignments, but organisations new to international assignments may well benefit from some outsourcing advice. The cost of not managing the assignment in terms of assignee selection during the assignment and in the repatriation phase can result in the loss of a valuable employee whose knowledge and experience developed on an international assignment. Managing international assignments is therefore an important dimension of talent management (see Chapter 10).

The International Assignment Manager

Managing the overseas experiences of staff and increasing their retention form part of the challenge for International Assignment Managers. RES Forum

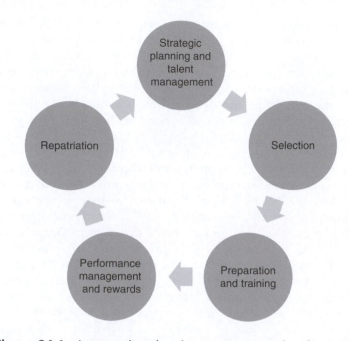

Figure 24.1   International assignments – a cycle of strategic
people management activity

research (2010b) highlights the major challenges of balancing transactional
and transformational management activities, and an International Assignments
Manager can handle the entire life cycle of an assignment from assignee selection to repatriation (see Figure 24.1 – above). The International Assignments
Manager role encompasses:

- Managing relocation – coordinating the transfer from the home to the host
  country, including pre-screening, internal approvals, briefing the assignee
  and their family, immigration clearance, calculation and payment of assignment allowances and expenses, organising home-finding, school search,
  shipment and settling-in arrangements, spousal support and international
  payroll arrangements;
- Reviewing assignment calculations to assess cost of the assignment;
- Tax calculations, to highlight tax equalisation costs;
- Management reporting, including cost analysis and recharges to the different
  businesses;
- Stakeholder management and training, including line managers, local HR,
  payroll and finance;
- Procurement activities, such as engaging global and local service providers
  for immigration processes;
- Local legal compliance, shipping, housing and education search, cultural and
  language training;

- Managing outsourcing providers;
- International assignment policy design and review;
- Talent management/succession planning.

The International Assignments Manager is often located within the HR department, effectively creating an international-HR (i-HR) function. There is considerable debate surrounding the role of the HR professional in an international context, but the role and responsibility of the line manager as a mediator of delivery of HRM is also much debated (Brewster and Sparrow, 2007). Management of the international assignee includes transacting with not only internal stakeholders, such as line managers, sponsors, HR, training department, payroll and finance, but also with external stakeholders for relocation processes and compliance service provision. The International Assignments Manager becomes the central communication point for the assignee and has to balance time spent liaising with the assignee with the requirement to coordinate with all the stakeholders. It is important to note that the organisational responsibilities for the international assignments may become less distinct for the international assignee because there is duplication in organisational relationships in the home and host countries. In addition there may be regional and global reporting lines that may not have existed in the pre-assignment location.

The RES Forum works with organisations on any aspect of their global mobility or international HR strategy, as well as on developing policies, practices and procedures, and their research (2009, 2010a, 2010b), conducted via a survey of organisations from a variety of sectors, including banking and finance, hi-tech and FMCG, sought to develop a greater understanding of the role of International Assignments Managers and identify key trends in managing international assignments. A key finding was that the transformational roles performed by International Assignment Managers included advising the business in international assignment matters, talent management, producing assignment costs, meeting with and briefing assignees, cultural training, supplier management and international assignment policy development, whilst significant transactional management activity, in the compliance areas of taxation, immigration and health and social security, tended to be outsourced.

Assignee retention on repatriation

Global mobility is important in the development of global managers and future leaders, and there is a direct cost associated with high attrition rates of such key employees on repatriation from an international assignment. The indirect costs, such as loss of knowledge, loss of an employee to a competitor, the violation of the psychological contract when promises are not kept and damage to the self-esteem of the individual, can impact negatively on the organisation. It makes financial and human capital management sense to harness the return on investment in the international assignee.

The rate of change in organisations makes it difficult for employers to offer cast-iron repatriation guarantees, and the potential problems from the repatriate perspective include concerns about loss of status, loss of autonomy, loss of career direction and feeling that the international experience is undervalued. Therefore a critical issue in repatriation is the management of assignee expectations in relation to job position, pay and rewards, employment security and opportunities to use skills gained on assignment. The interest of the sponsor, the line manager and the International Assignments Manager in facilitating the reintegration into the home organisation is critical. The facilitation of assignee reintegration and the retention of talent require a proactive focus on succession planning, pre-return career discussions, re-entry counselling, a family repatriation programme, assignee debriefings and training needs analysis for the home position.

A cycle of strategic people management activity

In conclusion, and to increase the potential for success in international assignments, it is necessary for organisations to engage in a cycle of strategic people management activity, and the elements are exposed in Figure 24.1.

The case study research that follows is located in the Cayman Islands, where expatriates form 50 per cent of the working population. The case explores 'self-initiated expatriation' and the benefits this can bring to the employee and to employers.

Alternatives to international assignments: female self-initiated expatriation in the Cayman Islands – case study research

The Cayman Islands

The Cayman Islands, consisting of the three islands of Grand Cayman, Cayman Brac and Little Cayman, is a relatively young country that was discovered by Columbus in 1503; settlement commenced in the seventeenth century, and Cayman was recognised as a British possession by the Treaty of Madrid in 1670. As a British Overseas Territory, the Cayman Islands has a Governor (the Queen's representative), its own Constitution and a Legislative Assembly, which performs many of the functions of the British Parliament. The latest population estimate is about 55,000, representing a mix of more than 100 nationalities. Out of that number, about half are of Caymanian descent. The vast majority of the population resides on Grand Cayman. Cayman is one of the world's leading offshore financial services centres. The Cayman Islands financial services industry encompasses banking, mutual funds, captive insurance, vessel and aircraft registration, companies and partnerships incorporation, trusts, structured finance and the Cayman Islands Stock Exchange. Over 70,000 companies are incorporated on the Cayman Islands, including 430 banks and trust companies, 720 captive insurance firms and more than 7,000 funds. With about half of the jobs filled by expatriate workers, international assignments are a significant feature of the Cayman labour market.

International assignments and self-initiated expatriates

Self-initiated expatriates are becoming more common, and as yet there is little research associated with this category of employees. Within this case, we discuss the role of self-initiated expatriates, providing a summary of research undertaken as part of a Master's dissertation by Ceili Fitzgerald (Fitzgerald, 2008). The research explored the self-initiated expatriation experiences of female managers. The aim was to gain insights into the career issues of women who have chosen to work in another country. Since the reasons for using expatriates may change, so too may the types of assignments change. This will influence the prevalence of self-initiated expatriation as an alternative to an expatriate assignment. Self-initiated expatriates are international workers who, of their own volition, move overseas to take up a position of employment, rather than being sent to a foreign location by their employer. Existing research indicates that women constitute a higher proportion of self-initiated expatriates, compared with the conventional company-initiated approach. For the purposes of this study an expatriate was taken to mean 'someone who left their homeland to live or work in another country, usually for a long period of time' (Vance, 2005: 375). Much of the existing literature on expatriation focuses on the organisational perspective, for example the reasons why multinational companies use expatriates and how the expatriation and repatriation processes should be managed. However there is an increasing interest in the experiences of expatriate staff, particularly women, who are under-represented in international assignments. Therefore this study sought to contribute to the existing knowledge about self-initiated expatriates, and in particular about the motivations and experiences of female workers.

The research and the findings

The research was conducted via 10 face-to-face semi-structured interviews of female self-initiated expatriates working in the Cayman Islands. The interviews generated rich and meaningful data, with the data analysed on a case-by-case basis by using an interpretative philosophy. The findings indicated that, with respect to the decision to embark upon international work experience, a number of factors were evident. Career development was the principal reason why the women opted to undertake self-initiated expatriation and to work in an international context. It is a common perception that undertaking international work experience will both enhance career progression on return and provide opportunities in the host country for advanced promotion and additional responsibility. The location was a further contributory factor, with the lure of working in a warm and sunny climate being a draw for many Europeans. Furthermore the Cayman destination was familiar to some and was not their first international work experience. Additionally the desirability of initiating a lifestyle change was a major draw, combined with lifestyle timing – many of the women were independent and able to act on opportunistic positions. The desire to opt out of the 'rat race' and benefit from an easier commute to work was identified as reason enough to pursue an international experience in a desirable location.

There were a number of other contributory factors stemming from proactive behaviours. The most common behaviours included professional networking, seeking job opportunities and visiting the location prior to moving. In some cases a combined holiday and job search led to securing a position, resulting in a relatively short lead time between informal and exploratory discussions regarding a position and starting the job. Undoubtedly another contributory factor was the desire to pursue outside leisure interests, such as scuba diving and other water sports, available in abundance on the Islands. Some of the respondents had initially searched for positions online using 'careers in the sun' as key search words. However they did face some challenges once they had taken up their positions. Difficulty in adapting to the prevailing work culture and environment was the most significant problem, since their high work ethic was often identified as different from that of their local work colleagues, and this created tensions. Other challenging factors within the work environment included ambiguous job descriptions and the challenges associated with working with a multitude of nationalities.

Outside of work, for the most part, the self-initiated expatriates coped by forming and participating in social networks, generally with other expatriates, demonstrating proactive attitudes towards seeking activities and clubs. The very high cost of living surprised the expatriates and this limited the value of the financial rewards received. Female expatriates reported little evidence of gender discrimination, with discriminatory treatment being linked to their identity as expatriates rather than as women. Efforts by the Cayman Islands government to ensure that Caymanian workers are not excluded from the labour force, including the operation of a work permit system which limits most foreigners to a maximum period of seven years' residency, generated feelings of anxiety among the self-initiated expatriate women. Respondents reported feeling 'scared to say anything', for fear that their work permit would be withdrawn, thus terminating their employment, and were therefore 'living with some kind of threat over their heads' (Fitzgerald and Howe-Walsh, 2008: 167). Overall, however, the negative features of their experience as self-initiated expatriates were significantly outweighed by the positive benefits that accrued from working in an international environment, not least the high potential for career development. Overall the women viewed their international experience positively, and thought 'it would benefit their career prospects and employability' (Fitzgerald and Howe-Walsh, 2008: 169).

Organisational interventions in self-initiated expatriation

The organisation can support the self-initiated expatriates' own efforts to adapt to their new workplace and country, ultimately leading to successful adjustment. Thus consideration of interventions aimed at aiding such an adjustment, such as providing opportunities for training and mentoring, and support in non-work issues can promote self-initiated expatriates' effectiveness within a shorter period. A recruitment strategy that acknowledges the advantages of self-initiated expatriates can provide the organisation with a strategic advantage, in enabling it to attract quality candidates globally, thereby contributing to meeting the growing challenge of managing talent. Self-initiated expatriates are therefore an attractive alternative to more expensive expatriate assignments. A defining feature of this research sample was that the participants demonstrated highly desirable competencies across many levels of global leadership. This provides some useful insights for the recruitment and selection process, because the female self-initiated expatriates offer 'ready-made' candidates for multinational organisations (Fitzgerald and Howe-Walsh, 2008: 169). The fact that the respondents had a positive attitude towards international work experience, as well as the receptivity to working overseas, forms part of the core competencies for a successful expatriation, and therefore enhances employability in the future. Furthermore all of the participants expressed how they had grown, professionally and personally, as well as how they had gained technical and organisational skills, which would enhance future career prospects.

Activities and discussion questions

1. In relation to international assignments what advice would you give to an organisation wishing to ensure that an individual has the behavioural competencies needed to be successful as an international assignee? These competencies include adaptability, flexibility, conflict resolution skills, questioning and listening skills, cross-cultural awareness, communicative ability, influencing skills, emotional maturity, self-motivation and resilience.

2. What processes are necessary to identify the key drivers and the potential barriers to an employee accepting an international assignment? What support should be provided to international assignees and their partners/families?

3. The issue of retention of international assignees following repatriation is key because up to 50 per cent of repatriates leave the organisation within two years of return from assignment. What can the organisation do to reduce rates of attrition for returning international assignees?

4. Prepare a generic job description and a person specification for an International Assignments Manager.

5. Using 'Figure 24.1 International assignments – a cycle of strategic people management activity', identify the activities that need to take place at each stage in the cycle and prepare a PowerPoint presentation with a slide of introduction, a slide for each of the five components of the cycle and a conclusion slide in which you identify the critical success factors for effective international assignments. Then deliver your presentation and take questions.

6. In relation to the case study research in the Cayman Islands relating to 'self-initiated expatriation:
   - What are the potential benefits to the employer of such an approach to international assignments?
   - What are the upsides and the downsides of undertaking an international assignment in the Cayman Islands for the assignee? Discuss the extent to which these upsides and downsides are common to all international assignments.

Bibliography

Black, J. S. and Gregersen, H. B. (2007). 'The right way to manage expats', in Mendenhall, M. E., Oddou, G. R. and Stahl, G. R. (ed.), *Readings and Cases in International Human Resource Management*, 119–28. New York: Routledge.

Brewster, C. and Sparrow, P. R. (2007). 'Globalising HR: Roles and challenges for the International HRM function'. *Lancaster University Management School Centre for Performance-led HR*, Working Paper, 2007–04.

Caligiuri, P. M. and Colakoglu, S. (2007). 'A strategic contingency approach to expatriate assignment management'. *Human Resource Management Journal*, 17(4), 393–410.

Caligiuri, P., Tarique, I. and Jacobs, R. (2009). 'Selection for international assignments'. *Human Resource Management Review*, 19(3), 251–62. September.

Carp, J. (2009). *Drafting Employment Documents for Expatriates*. Bristol: Jordans.

Clouse, M. A. and Watkins, M. D. (2009). 'Three keys to getting an overseas assignment right'. *Harvard Business Review*, 87(10), 115–9. October.

Dowling, P. and Welch, D. (2004). *International Human Resource Management: Managing People in a Multinational Context*. London: Thomson Learning.

Fitzgerald, C. (2008). 'Alternatives to international assignments: female self-initiated expatriation in the Cayman Islands'. University of Portsmouth MSc HRM Dissertation.

Fitzgerald, C. and Howe-Walsh, L. (2008). 'Self-initiated expatriates: an interpretative phenomenological analysis of professional female expatriates'. *International Journal of Business and Management*, 3(10), 156–75.

Gillis, L. (2009/2010). 'When employees cross borders'. *Employers' Law*, December/January, 20–1.

Gribben, R. (2006). 'Rising stars who jump ship on re-entry'. *The Daily Telegraph*, 26 November.

Harris, H. and Brewster, C. (1999). 'The coffee-machine system: how international selection really works'. *The International Journal of Human Resource and Management*, 10(3), 488–500.

Harzing, A. W. K. and Christensen, C. (2004). 'Expatriate failure: time to abandon the concept?'. *Career Development International*, 9(7), 616–26.

Hippler, T. (2010). 'A comparative study of domestic, European and international job-related relocation'. *International Journal of Human Resource Management*, 21(10–12), 1837–62.

International Mobility (2011). CIPD Factsheet. London: CIPD.

International Resourcing and Recruitment (2011). CIPD Factsheet. London: CIPD.

Koumans, J. and Powers, R. (2010). 'Mapping moves in a changing world: how mobility practices have evolved'. *Workspan*, 53(8), 22–8. August.

Matthewman, J. (2009). 'Global mobility'. *Benefits and Compensation International*, 39(1), 21–6. July/August.

Pricewaterhousecoopers (2010a). 'Global mobility map: three eras of international assignments 1970–1990'. (Electronic version), www.pwc.com/gx/en/managing-tomorrows-people/future-of-work/global-mobility-map.jhtml

Pricewaterhousecoopers (2010b). 'Managing tomorrow's people: talent mobility 2020: the next generation of international assignments'. (Electronic version), www.pwc.com/gx/en/managing-tomorrows-people/future-of-work/index.jhtml

RES Forum Survey (2009). 'The role of the International Assignment Manager', April. (Electronic version), www.theresforum.com

RES Forum Survey (2010a). 'Objectives Roadmap, March'. (Electronic version), www.theresforum.com

RES Forum Survey (2010b). 'International Talent Management', August. (Electronic version), www.theresforum.com

Reuvid, J. (2009). *Working Abroad: The Complete Guide to Overseas Employment*. London: Kogan Page.

Robertson, J. (2010). 'Employee mobility'. London: Incomes Data Services – *HR Studies Series*. http://www.cipd.co.uk/search/results/bookrow.asp?ID=210293

Sparrow, P., Brewster, C. and Harris, H. (2004). *Globalizing Human Resource Management*. London: Routledge.

Stahl, G. K. and Caliguri, P. (2005). 'The effectiveness of expatriate coping strategies: the moderating role of cultural distance, position level, and time on international assignment'. *Journal of Applied Psychology*, 90(4), 603–15.

Tarique, I. and Caligiuri, P. (2004). *International Human Resource Management*. London: Sage.

Vance, C. M. (2005). 'The personal quest for building global competence: A taxonomy of self-initiating career path strategies for gaining business experience aboard'. *Journal of World Business*, 40, 374–85.

Yeargan, A. M. (2008). 'A globally mobile workforce: HR's role'. *WorldatWork Journal*, 17(3), 55–64, third quarter.

Glossary

360-degree feedback: a form of appraisal where the learner receives feedback from all around them – managers, peers and subordinates, and maybe even customers or clients. The person being '360 degreed' retains sovereignty over the acceptance or rejection of the feedback, but embraces it as a potential development opportunity.

Action learning: a learning process where learners in small groups, called learning sets, reflect on their actions and experience to improve individual and group performance, and plan further learning.

Actors: individuals or groups who act and interact to influence the outcomes of organisations.

Added value: the contribution of an individual or group towards providing products and services, which are in demand by customers/users. In marketing terms, added value is the difference between a product's selling price and the cost of the total input in making that particular product.

Agency: the action of an individual or group to influence organisational outcomes on behalf of an interested individual or group.

Agents: individuals or groups who represent the interests of stakeholders.

Aligning: to bring into line or to point in the same direction.

Applied: to put into practical use or to make use of by practice.

Assessment centres: An assessment centre is a process rather than a place. Assessment centres seek to improve validity and reliability in selection decisions through the integration of multiple selection techniques and are founded on the identification and assessment of competencies which are judged to be necessary for performance of a particular job. They exhibit certain characteristics: a variety of assessment methods that form a total assessment system, the bringing together of a number of candidates and multidimensional evaluation of candidate competencies and motivation.

Assignee: an assignee is an employee assigned to work at an overseas location by his/her employer, and thereby becomes an expatriate worker.

Balanced scorecard: a scorecard was developed as a strategic management system by Kaplan and Norton in the 1990s but it is now largely used as a performance management system. The rationale for its development was to reflect a more 'balanced range of measures rather than have an over-reliance on financial measures'. The four perspectives are financial measures, customer-related measures, business process measures, and innovation and learning.

Behavioural predisposition: the strength and probability that a personality characteristic or trait will result in a particular behaviour.

Best fit: the application of specific HRM practices based on the particular situational circumstances where they will be used.

Best practice: the application of specific HRM practices that are known to have been adopted across sectors and countries to improve performance.

Blended learning: a mixture of learning and teaching interventions that can be accessed and delivered to learners, for example 'academic' study based on books and typically delivered in the classroom, work-based learning, action learning, online learning, coaching and mentoring, project work and so on.

Boundary workers: workers in contact with external clients and stakeholders are boundary workers. Any worker who operates at the boundary between the organisation and its customers and other stakeholders should have as an aspect of their role the scope to act as a boundary worker. Those who deliver goods and services need to bring into the organisation information for sharing and feeding into the processes. This includes sales staff, technicians, van drivers as well as senior members of the organisation as they are sources of information about what clients and others want/feel.

BRIC countries: The BRIC countries, Brazil, Russia, India and China identified by Wilson and Purushothaman (2003) as the *powerhouse economies* that are expected to outperform major Western economies. These can be seen as representative of those economies which are having, or will have a significant impact on the global economy in the next decade.

Civil Society: Civil society is a public space between the state, the market and the ordinary household, in which people can debate and tackle action. It can also be described as where people come together to make a positive difference to their lives and the lives of others for mutual support, to pursue shared interests, to further a cause they care about or simply for fun and friendship. It is where me becomes we.

Civil Society Organisations (CSOs): CSO is a convenient label to encompass the variety of bodies that inhabit civil society, those that are not part of the state or the market. CSOs include charities, faith groups, voluntary associations, advocacy bodies, social movement organisations, campaigning groups, community bodies and other non-governmental organisations (NGOs).

Cloud computing: a model for enabling anywhere, anytime, on-demand network access to a shared pool of configurable computing resources such as networks, servers, storage applications and services that can be rapidly populated with information and released with minimal management effort or service provider interaction (adapted from the US National Institute of Standards and Technology).

Coach: can be internal to the organisation, either separate from or integrated within the line management role, or the role may be better performed by an external coach. The role of the coach is 'to enable the learner to learn, rather than to teach the employee'.

Coachee: A coachee is the learner who is being coached and it is necessary for the coachee to have organisational awareness, self-awareness and accept responsibility for unlocking potential within, together with the personal responsibilities for thoughts and actions.

Coaching: the 'unlocking of an employee's potential in order to maximise not only their performance but also that of the team and the organisation', and the role of the coach is 'to enable the learner to learn, rather than teaching or training the employee'.

Competence-based recruitment and selection: competencies are identified prior to the recruitment and selection process and selection activities are designed to assess candidates' abilities against these competencies, rather than basing selection on qualities and experience.

Competencies and competences: these can be 'behavioural competencies' and 'outcome-based competences', with the difference being that competencies are about the people who do the work and their input abilities, while competences are about the work and its outcomes.

Competency-based interviewing (CBI): CBI deploys job competencies in order to develop questions and assess responses in relation to job applicants, with the aim of improving predictive validity in recruitment and selection of talent.

Competency frameworks: originally consisted mainly of behavioural elements, an expression of the softer skills involved in effective performance, and it is common for these to be expressed within a single organisational framework termed a competency map. They now include a mix of behaviours and technical skills.

Compliance: actions to ensure a state of being in accordance with regulations.

Construct of personality: a construct is a dimensional construction of personality, enabling measurement to take place. Examples of construct dimensions include introversion and extraversion.

Construct validity: the extent to which a selection technique or instrument has a sound and valid underpinning theory or, in the case of personality assessment, a sound and valid construction of personality dimensions.

Corporate governance: the system by which (private sector) companies are directed or controlled to create value.

Corporate Social Responsibility (CSR): conceptions of CSR differ according to national social and economic priorities, which are themselves influenced by historical and cultural factors, but CSR consists of a balanced approach by organisations towards economic, social and environmental issues that aims to benefit individuals, communities and society.

Discretionary behaviour: a course of behaviour chosen through free will.

Dysfunctional behaviour: unintended or undesirable behaviour which has negative implications for organisational and employee performance.

Emergent strategy: business strategy which is not 'deliberate', which emerges incrementally in response to internal and external factors to enable organisations to be responsive in dynamic environments.

Emotional intelligence: the influence of an individual's emotions on their cognitive and behavioural abilities to act and relate to others to achieve certain outcomes.

Employee well-being strategy: this strategy describes the organisation's articulated approach to well-being with clear aims and objectives and identified measurable outcomes. These outcomes should be reviewed and the impact of the strategy assessed on a regular basis.

Employee wellness programmes: these programmes do not constitute a strategy but are health initiatives, such as smoking cessation, healthy eating campaigns and fitness provision, which could form elements of the employee well-being strategy.

Employer brand: an employer brand is the perceptions of employees and potential employees of how it is or what it will be like to work for that organisation. It includes aspects that differentiate one organisation from another, and promises a particular employment experience with distinctive rewards and benefits. To build a successful employer brand there needs to be a close link with the organisational strategy.

Employment relationship: the workplace relationship that exists between employers and employees based on a 'wage for work bargain'. The employer attempts to harness the hearts and minds of employees through employee engagement; it requires an understanding of the complex psychological contracting involved.

Employment (or employee) value proposition: the employment (sometimes called the employee) value proposition is the worth that employees and potential employees place on working for an organisation. That worth is described as the 'appeal' of working for a particular organisation and it includes the work experience itself, the success of the organisation, financial and non-financial rewards and opportunities for personal development. While the employment value proposition is seen as having some worth for the employee and potential employee, it fulfils its function in recruitment and retention.

Environmental scanning: the managerial activity of learning about events and trends in the organisation's environments; it is the first step in the ongoing chain of perceptions and actions leading to an organisation's adaptation to its environment.

Epistemology: branch of philosophy concerned with theories of knowledge; particularly regarding methods to acquire knowledge.

Expatriate: an expatriate is a person temporarily residing in a country and a culture other than their legal residence. In the case of international assignments the person is an expatriate worker.

Experiential learning: learning through making the link between the theory and action (practice) by planning, acting out, reflecting and relating it back to the theory.

Explicit knowledge: knowledge that has been captured and expressed.

Extrinsic reward: usually tangible rewards that satisfy the lower-level psychological needs, for example pay, working conditions and fringe benefits.

Face Validity: the extent to which a selection technique or instrument appears to the candidate to bear a resemblance to the job for which they have applied. A word processing test for a secretary has high face validity, whilst making a bridge out of barrels and planks to cross imaginary crocodile-infested water for a retail management position will have low face validity. Face validity and predictive validity are not necessarily correlated, and low face validity is not necessarily a bad thing.

Front-Line Manager: a supervisor or team leader in the lower layers of the management hierarchy, where the employees who report to them do not themselves have any managerial or supervisory responsibility – they are in the management front line and critical to organisational performance.

Globalisation: globalisation is the process of interaction and integration across international boundaries. It is driven by information technology, trade and the flow of investment. It impacts on organisations, working arrangements and culture as well as on prosperity around the world.

Governance: the system by which organisations are controlled or directed to deliver certain outcomes.

Holistic: all encompassing; taking the whole entity into account.

HR scorecard: a performance management system based on metrics that determines the contribution of the HR activity in an organisation.

Human Capital: value that people contribute towards organisations, using their expertise and experience.

Information technology: information technology refers to the use of telecommunications, computers and software to manage data and information. It also includes the storage, protection processing and transmission of information as well as the retrieval of information as necessary.

Intangible value: value that cannot be easily expressed in such a way to be able to manage and account for.

Intellectual capital: knowledge that individuals and groups have which is of value to organisations.

International Assignment: an international assignment describes a period of work in an overseas location by an employee to fulfil a task for the employer. There are different types of International Assignment depending on the length and frequency of the stay.

International Assignments Manager: this is a person appointed by the organisation to manage international assignments. This management of international assignments is often located within an HR function, but there is a shared responsibility with the assignees' line manager and sponsor.

Interruptive technologies: communications applications and technologies (e-mail, Smartphones, laptops, social networking sites, instant messaging) which distract individuals from the job they are employed to do. The interruptions may be work-related but they may also be because of personal communication unrelated to work.

Intervention: planned action that modifies and changes employee behaviour to influence outcomes, for example policies, selection and coaching.

Intrinsic reward: usually intangible rewards that satisfy the higher levels of a person's psychological needs, for example recognition, appreciation and challenging work that develops an individual.

Job analysis: job analysis is the systematic process of collecting information about the tasks, responsibilities, competencies and contexts of a job. The outputs of the job analysis process are job descriptions and person specifications.

Job description: a job description specifies the purpose, the task and the scope of the job – the job description is the 'what' (has to be done).

Knowledge-intensive organisations: organisations that heavily depend on knowledge to create value.

Knowledge transfer: knowledge transfer is the process by which knowledge that is available with departments, sections and individuals within an organisation is captured, stored and made available to the rest of the organisation. It is not to be confused with information as it includes not just information but also the development of the skills and abilities of individuals to use the information for the benefit of the organisation.

Knowledge workers: employees who focus on using and acquiring knowledge as a main feature of their work.

Learning contract: a formal record of the learning objectives of a WBL project, the learner's reflection on the skills and knowledge which the learner has already developed, the assessment of the resources needed to complete the project, the reflection on the skills and knowledge needed to complete the project successfully, the agreed assessment criteria which will be used to judge the evidence presented.

Learning organisation: an organisation that systematically manages knowledge and learning for the benefit of employees and the organisation as a whole, where the rate of learning is at least equal to the rate of change in the organisation.

Learning professional: an individual with expertise and experience of designing and implementing learning solutions.

Learning set: a small group of individuals engaged in a planned learning activity or event, such as a work-based project. A learning intervention that provides opportunities for social learning (learning from others) and progression, through feedback and reflection.

Macro-environment: the outer-environmental layer; consists of the general political, economic, socio-cultural and technological (PEST) domains.

Management Development: identification of those competencies necessary to be an effective manager followed by the design of formal and informal learning interventions, both pre- and post-appointment, in order to develop management competencies to enhance individual and organisational performance.

Mentor: an experienced individual who can provide career and personal development guidance to employees, typically a senior manager who is not a line manager to those he/she advises.

Metrics: measures and indicators.

Micro-environment: is the inner layer and consists of customers, competitors, suppliers, employees and other stakeholders.

Moderating variables: factors that influence the strength of the causal relationship between behavioural predispositions and enacted behaviours. In the workplace these will include factors such as the relationships, the power balance, the contract of employment, the degree of engagement, the growth-need strength of the individual, job understanding and acquisition of the competencies needed for the job and much, much more.

Myers–Briggs type indicator (MBTI): is an instrument developed by Isabel Briggs-Myers and Katherine Briggs, which enables individuals to categorise their personality types. It asserts that people get the most satisfaction when doing work that enables them to express their psychological type preferences. It is a tool that is widely used in management and leadership development as well as in team building as it enables people of complementary types to be brought together for the benefit of the team.

Occupational standards: specified standards of performance expectations based on defined competencies within a competency framework, for example National Occupational Standards for management and leadership by the Management Standards Centre and the NHS Leadership Standards.

Organisational culture: the underlying values, beliefs and attitudes that govern how things are done within the organisation and the way in which members of the organisation relate to and respect one another.

Organisational development: a strategic, systematic and social approach towards developing an organisational culture that facilitates capability through learning and problem-solving.

Organisational learning: organisations are recognising the increasing importance of continuous learning as a driver of strategic decisions and actions in order to adapt to and engineer changes in today's rapidly changing environment. The cognitive perspective of organisational learning takes the view that collective individual learning results in organisational learning, whereas the behavioural perspective proposes that learning manifests itself through behavioural outcomes. The technical perspective sees organisational learning as the processing and interpretation of information from internal and external sources, and the social perspective contends that learning emerges from social interaction and engagement in the work environment.

Outcomes: consequences of actions which may be tangible and easy to measure, for example financial quantities, or intangible, which are difficult to measure, for example customer or employee satisfaction.

Performance: a combination of effectiveness and efficiency in the effort of achieving outputs and outcomes.

Performance management: is a process of maximising employee performance by managers and consisting of a cycle of setting objectives and clarifying performance standards, monitoring and supporting performance, appraisal of performance, financial and non-financial reward allocation and the identification of future development needs. It is a holistic process.

Performance management system: a strategic and systematic approach to measuring and managing the performance of individuals and groups in organisations.

Person specification: the person specification profiles the people characteristics and competencies required to do the job effectively – the person specification is the 'who' (does it).

Personality traits: individual characteristics and tendencies to show consistent patterns of thoughts, feelings and actions.

PESTLE: A mnemonic for Political, Economic, Social, Technological, Legal and Environmental influences which are external to the organisation, providing a business tool that enables an analysis to be made of external factors and their impact on the context within which the organisation operates.

Podcast: the term podcast (or webcast) describes a collection of files (audio or video) that are released by an organisation on a regular basis for downloading by those interested, when it is convenient for them to listen or watch.

Practitioners: employees who apply or 'practice' their knowledge and skills in the workplace.

Predictive validity: the extent to which a selection technique or instrument is valid in predicting performance in a job.

Private cloud: a resource accessible by a single organisation, which gives more control to the organisation and maximum data security. This may be an in-house data centre or a specialist provider's facility.

Provisions: stipulations that prepare for future situations.

Psychological contract: the perceptions of both parties to the employment relationship (the organisation and individual) of the reciprocal promises and obligations implied in that relationship. A healthy psychological contract can be a measure of a healthy employment relationship.

Psychometric assessment: a collective term for 'measurement of the mind' and includes attainment, general intelligence, cognitive ability, trainability and personality assessment. It generates information, which can be used in the selection and development of employees.

Public cloud: a shared resource enabling organisations to get maximum cost efficiency.

Repatriation: repatriation is a term for the return and settlement process for the assignee, following an international assignment.

Return on (training) investment: a quantitative and qualitative assessment of the costs and resources required for a training and development process in relation to the beneficial impact of the process on individual and organisational performance.

Rewards: rewards consist of a portfolio of financial and non-financial elements that can be flexibly deployed by managers to extract performance, compliance and loyalty to the organisation from employees. Financial rewards are extrinsic and consist of pay and employment benefits, whilst non-financial rewards tend to be intrinsic, such as work–life balance, development opportunities and interesting work.

Scenario planning: also known as scenario thinking or scenario analysis, it is a way of strategic planning used in organisations, which facilitates the development of a flexible approach to planning by seeking to examine different models of the future. It is a group process where a group within the business generates alternative visions of the future, often using models such as PESTLE as a framework. The underlying driver is a starting point that the world will be a very different place to that in which they operate now. Once the alternative futures are generated, then the group looks at the generating responses to each of these futures with the outcome being that they should be prepared for all eventualities.

Span of control: refers to the number of employees reporting directly to a supervisor or a manager. Downsizing and delayering can lead to a flatter organisation, with fewer levels of supervisors or managers. This leads to managers having an increased span of control and more employees reporting directly to them.

Stable quasi-stationary equilibrium: it is a term coined by Lewin (1951) which refers to the state that exists inside an organisation when the forces for and against change are more or less in balance. It does not mean that the organisation is stationary and not changing, but it does imply that the changes that are occurring are incremental and largely unplanned and could inhibit the required process of adaptation leading to a need for planned change. Lewin argued that in order to achieve a planned change that lasts, a three-stage action process is required: *unfreezing*, which means destabilising the balance of the forces – this may be done by creating a different vision which motivates people to question their current ways of doing things and be prepared to do things differently; *movement*, which is where the balance of the forces is changed to move to a new equilibrium – this can be achieved by changing attitudes and beliefs or changing processes or systems of work; and *refreezing* means taking action to reinforce the attitudes and beliefs, perhaps through incentives that reward the new behaviours.

Strategic HRM: how HRM influences organisational performance through aligning HR policy and practice with business aims.

Strategic people management: the coordinated planning and activity of people resources in an organisation to achieve longer-term performance outcomes.

Tacit knowledge: knowledge we have that we are not aware of, that is 'what we do not know we know'.

Talent management: talent management is about attracting and retaining high performing employees. It requires robust systems for recruiting, developing and the retention of all key employees, not only the 'high fliers' but also those employees who are in a position to add value or have the potential to add value in the future.

Talent management pipeline: this pipeline is the collection of processes that enable the talent management strategy to be implemented. These processes include attraction, retention, engagement, performance management, reward, development, deployment and exit.

Talent pool: the term talent pool is used to describe a collection of talented employees. Individual members are selected for membership, based on performance review, assessment centre 360-degree appraisal or line manager nomination. Talent pools are not static, with membership changing in line with business needs and talent supply. Organisations with an exclusive approach to talent management may have just one talent pool while those with an inclusive approach will have more than one – it will have a number of different talent pools to reflect its need for talented employees across its grades and levels.

Tangible value: value that can be expressed in such a way that it can be managed and accounted for.

Tayloristic: relates to Frederick Taylor's scientific management philosophy that there is 'the one best way' of doing something and, in the case of personality assessment, that there is the 'one best personality' for a job.

The balanced scorecard: developed as a strategic management system by Kaplan and Norton in the 1990s but it is now largely used as a performance management system.

Theory X: a management perspective which assumes that most people dislike work, are lazy and have to be coerced and controlled to fulfil their responsibilities. Motivation occurs at lower-level needs.

Theory Y: a management perspective which assumes that most people generally enjoy work, have initiative and are self-directing, and want to accept responsibility. Motivation occurs at higher- as well as lower-level needs.

Virtual learning environment: is a set of learning and development tools designed to enhance the learning experience of the participant by including computers and the Internet in the learning process. This will normally include some of the following elements: online learning material, multimedia links, online chat rooms for learner-to-learner communication, online tutorials, assessment and feedback channels.

War for talent: a term first used by McKinsey in 1997 to describe the intense competition to attract and retain high-performing employees.

Webinar: the term webinar is short for Web-based Seminar – a presentation, lecture, workshop or seminar that is transmitted over the Web. The service allows information to be shared simultaneously, across locations in nearly real time, with participants having the facility to ask questions and participate in the discussion.

Wellness management: means dealing with the health of an employee in a holistic way and working with employees to promote their health and well-being so that they are physically and mentally well and able to make a positive contribution to organisational performance.

Work-based learning: directed and supported learning that takes place in or is related to the workplace.

Work simulation: it takes an element of the real job as the basis for a design for a simulated assessment task for candidates for employment. A car mechanic could be asked to diagnose an engine fault, a quality manager could be asked to assess the quality of service provided, an HR practitioner could be asked to conduct a training session, a leader could be asked to lead a team in a job-related activity and so on.

Workforce scorecard: a performance management system based on metrics that determines the contribution of the workforce in an organisation.

Workforce strategy/HR strategy: a coordinated plan and activities that focus on people management interventions to deliver organisational performance outcomes.

Work–life balance: the extent to which an employee perceives that their work life and personal life are in balance, so that they can pursue personal as well as work objectives.

Author Index

Subject Index